'A revealing and thorough analysis of the man
and his style'   *Observer*

'An intelligent book . . . Lovejoy is one of the
most astute and well-informed journalists
 round'   *Time Out*

     definitive biography of Sven'
                                  Daily Telegraph

'Throws up plenty of treats'   *Boys Toys*

'A good story . . . and a great read' *Fitness First*

'A perceptive biography'   *Sunday Times*

'Plenty of detail on Sven'   *FourFourTwo*

'Lovejoy has set the standard for Eriksson
biographies'   *When Saturday Comes*

'A fascinating story'   *The Bookseller*

Joe Lovejoy has been Football Correspondent of *The Sunday Times* since 1994. He was previously the chief football writer at the *Independent* and has also worked for the *Mail on Sunday*.

SVEN
THE FINAL RECKONING

Joe Lovejoy

CollinsWillow
An Imprint of HarperCollinsPublishers

First published in hardback 2002 by
CollinsWillow
an imprint of HarperCollins*Publishers*
London

First published in paperback, and revised and updated 2004

9 8 7 6 5 4 3 2 1

A CIP catalogue record for this book
is available from the British Library

ISBN 0 00 714069 X

Set in Linotype Palatino by
Rowland Phototypesetting Ltd, Bury St Edmunds, Suffolk

Printed and bound in Great Britain by Clays Ltd, St Ives plc

The HarperCollins website address is www.harpercollins.co.uk

Photographic acknowledgements
ACTION IMAGES: pp 6 (top and bottom), 7 (top), 9 (centre),
15 (centre)
BICPICTURESPHOTO.COM: pp 1 (all except top left),
2 (top left and right), 4 (centre and bottom), 12 (both)
CAMERA PRESS/Scanpix: pp 2 (bottom right), 3
COLORSPORT: pp 5 (top right), 15 (bottom)
EMPICS: pp 4 (top), 6 (centre), 8 (both), 13 (both), 14 (bottom left)
GETTY IMAGES: pp 5 (top left and bottom), 9 (bottom), 14 (top),
16 (top, centre and bottom left)
MIRRORPIX/POPPERFOTO/SCOPE FEATURES: p 9 (top)
NEWS OF THE WORLD/NI SYNDICATION: p 16 (bottom right)
REX FEATURES: pp 7 (bottom), 10 (both), 11 (both),
14 (centre and bottom right), 15 (top).

CONTENTS

WHAT'S LOVE GOT TO DO WITH IT?

'My advice to Sven is to quit his job, too. Those bastards at the FA want to destroy him. The knives are out.'

FARIA ALAM, after resigning as personal assistant to the Football Association's executive director, David Davies, August 2004

It was all a far cry from the heady days of November 2000, when Sven-Goran Eriksson was warmly greeted as England's saviour on taking up the management at a time when Kevin Keegan's abrupt departure had left the national team rock bottom, not just in their World Cup qualifying group, but mentally as well. Now, nearly four years on, the FA wanted him out, and were happy for it to be known that the best paid coach in the world was on borrowed time. If his employers were dissatisfied with Eriksson, the feeling was certainly mutual. He had been 'hung out to dry', as he put it, over the 'Fariagate' sex scandal that had threatened to bring down the hierarchy of English football's governing body, and briefly considered sueing for constructive dismissal before opting to soldier on until the next attractive job offer came along.

How had it come to this? It is a story that makes 'Footballers' Wives' look tame, a tale of unbridled lust, greed, intrigue and xenophobia, laced with a lot of football – some good, some bad. When all is said and done, the final verdict has to be that England's first foreign coach proved to be an expensive disappointment. He deserves credit for reviving the dispirited and disorganized team he inherited from Keegan, but having raised morale, performance and public expectation, he achieved no more than quarter-final places at the 2002 World Cup and 2004 European Championship when, with a more adventurous approach, England might have done much better.

In football terms, history will judge Eriksson to have been too defensively orientated, too inflexible in his team selection and tactics, and too indulgent of his players. In the big matches, England paid the ultimate price for timidly circling the wagons and defending slender leads instead of trying to improve them; they had no Plan B when bog standard 4–4–2 went awry; and, even for those patently out of form, it seemed harder to get out of the team than it was to get in it in the first place. This was most glaringly apparent in the case of David Beckham who, on his own admission, was not as fit as he should have been at Euro 2004, yet was invariably allowed to play the full 90 minutes, or even extra-time, when he should have been substituted.

One of England's most experienced defenders

propounds an interesting theory here. Remarking on a quote from Nancy Dell'Olio, Eriksson's former partner, who told a TV chat show that he disliked one-on-one conflict, the player suggested this was evident both in the coach's personal and professional lives. The coach had remained with Ms Dell'Olio for at least a year after the relationship had run its course because breaking up would have been too confrontational, and he was reluctant to substitute senior players for the same reason.

Be that as it may, Eriksson often seemed to be in his captain's thrall – so much so that when the squad went to Sardinia in May 2004, for pre-tournament preparations, the coach and Nancy moved out of the best suite at the Forte Village, which they had been routinely allocated by the hotel management, to allow Beckham and his wife, Victoria, to move in. This sent out all the wrong signals, fuelling resentment within the squad of the special treatment, and unprecedented influence Beckham enjoyed.

Eriksson has always asked to be judged on results alone, in which case he was clearly overpaid on £4 million a year compared to the £1.1 million earned by Luis Felipe Scolari, who won the 2002 World Cup with Brazil and took Portugal to the final of Euro 2004. Given that disparity, it is unrealistic for the England coach to expect the media to focus entirely on football matters and ignore his private life. The intrusion Eriksson often complains about comes with the pay packet. As the *Sunday Times* put it, if he wants to be free to romance whoever and behave however he chooses, without it getting into the papers, let him go and manage Austria or Switzerland for £250,000 a year.

Initially, there was no shortage of sympathy when the stormy nature of Eriksson's relationship with Ms Dell'Olio was made public, but gradually it dawned on people that for a man who craved anonymity he chose some strange partners, and strange venues at which to parade them. Not many women seek publicity as avidly as Ulrika Jonsson, and it surprised nobody but poor old Sven when she made a small fortune out of her kiss-and-tell tittle-tattle about their affair. Similarly, if you want to stay out of the newspapers, the celebrity haunt that is London's San Lorenzo restaurant is hardly the best place to do your courting.

It was a close run thing at the time, but Eriksson got away with the Ulrika business. It was when others followed that public sympathy swung away from him, towards the much-put-upon Nancy, his live-in partner, who continually declared her love for him, and behaved accordingly, only to be repeatedly reduced to tears and tantrums by his serial unfaithfulness before they finally broke up, towards the end of July 2004.

Eriksson seems to enjoy risky, and risque, behaviour, and thought nothing of entering into a liaison dangereux with Faria Alam, a 38-year-old ex-model of Bangladeshi extraction who was employed on secretarial duties by his friend and most supportive ally at the FA, David Davies. Ms Alam had already had an affair with the FA's chief executive, Mark Palios, and when the newspapers got wind of what was going on, the inevitable furore became known as 'Fariagate'.

Eriksson's stock was already at an all-time low after England's disappointing performance at Euro 2004, and at first it seemed he was behaving wisely straight after their elimination, when he retreated to his native Sweden and kept his head down. In fact he was seeking solace in the ample charms of his latest conquest, who had joined him at his palatial villa in Sunne, not far from his parent's home. He had been seeing Ms Alam since January, and telephoned her every day during the championship in Portugal. Now they had another of their clandestine trysts, but this time the secret was out. The *News of the World* were on to them, and what followed was, according to one senior FA source, '. . . a glaring, startling nightmare that caused everybody to lose faith in the whole organization.'

The crisis was provoked not so much by the affair as by Eriksson's ambivalent reply when questioned about it by Davies – that and the fact that Palios had also been involved with Ms Alam. Eriksson told Davies in a telephone conversation deemed by the coach to be personal and private that it was all 'nonsense'. He was therefore both surprised and incensed when this brief chat with a friend led to a formal, public denial by the FA, which subsequently had to be retracted, causing great embarrassment to all concerned. The key word 'nonsense' had referred to the fact that Eriksson's love life was under scrutiny again; it was not a 'categorical denial' that the relationship had taken place.

It was when Palios was implicated as another of Ms Alam's lovers that an awkward situation became a full-blown scandal. The FA's chief executive had been a man on a mission, the mission being 'to clean up the game', and *News of the World* exposés of his own behaviour would not do at all. Through his head of communications, Colin Gibson, he offered the paper a deal. They would be given full details of Eriksson's affair, the *quid pro quo* being that they left Palios' name out of the story. For a few days Palios and Gibson thought they had pulled it off, but then the *News of the World* decided that the attempted cover-up was the best story of all, and printed a transcript of their taped telephone conversations with Gibson, during which he said: 'What I'm proposing is that I give you chapter and verse on her and Sven. And that the pay-off, obviously, is that we leave MP [Palios] out of it. I've got the details, I've got the places, I've got the phone calls. I've got everything.'

When news of their machinations came out, Palios and Gibson were both forced to resign, and for a time it seemed that Eriksson would have to follow suit. The chairman of the FA, Geoff Thompson, instigated an investigation into the coach's conduct, hiring an independent lawyer to interview all those involved and prepare a report to be considered by an emergency meeting of the FA's twelve-man board. The feeling was that Eriksson could be sacked, without the £10 million or so compensation entailed in paying up his contract, if he was found to have committed 'gross misconduct' by misleading his bosses when he told Davies the original *News of the World* story was 'nonsense'.

There was a great deal of off-the-record briefing and 'spinning' against Eriksson by members of the board, reflected in an article in the *Daily Express* on 31 July, when Harry Harris wrote: 'Sven-Goran Eriksson will be sacked next week. The FA board is split 11–1, overwhelmingly in favour of ending his reign as England coach.' Steve McClaren, of Middlesbrough, was to take over.

Two days later, on returning from holiday in Spain, Davies misjudged his employer's mood, and gave Eriksson a handsome testimonial which effectively put him, too, on trial. The executive director said: 'Sven is very popular and respected by the players. He has a consistent track record everywhere he has worked. He is one of the outstanding coaches in the world, that is why many clubs seek his services.' The board were furious. Unwittingly, Davies had guaranteed his friend a handsome pay-off in the event of his dismissal. One board member, wearing a cloak of anonymity, thundered: 'Davies had no business making those statements. It was taken as a vote of confidence in Eriksson when Davies is in no position to do it. It is for the board to decide whether Eriksson goes or not. Davies should have been told to keep his mouth shut.'

It was against this bloodthirsty background that the board met on 5 August. By this stage, the FA were so paranoid about leaks and adverse publicity that they booked three suites at different hotels and didn't tell members where they were going until they were on their way. The real venue was the Leonard Hotel in Marylebone, where there was one absentee, Mike Rawding, from the East Riding FA, who was in hospital.

Blood on the walls? Hardly. After so much hype and hullabaloo, the meeting was the soggiest of damp squibs. The independent lawyer, Peter Norbury, had found no evidence that Eriksson had deliberately misled the FA over his affair with Ms Alam, concluding that the key conversation between Davies and the coach has been a personal one, and was therefore inadmissible. The meeting therefore broke up without a vote being taken on Eriksson's position, and it was announced that he had 'no case to answer'. There was criticism of Davies, for failing to phrase his question more precisely, and on a formal basis, and also for his fulsome praise of the subject of the inquiry in advance of its outcome, but a slap on the wrist and a reminder to restrict his comments to his area of jurisdiction was deemed sufficient action.

What did Eriksson make of it all? He laughed dismissively over dinner with his assistant, Tord Grip, but would have been far from amused had he heard what was said before the meeting, when there was broad support for one of his most trenchant critics who declaimed: 'It's time we were looking for a new coach as well as a chief executive. We need honourable, straightforward leadership.'

On a strictly non-attributable basis, senior football correspondents were told that Eriksson would be on trial in England's first two World Cup qualifying games, away to Austria and Poland in September. Failure to win either of these would provide an excuse to sack him for footballing reasons. Ms Alam, who had been privy to the FA's thought processes from 'pillow talk' when Palios was her lover, said they thought Eriksson was 'more trouble than he was worth'. They believed his 'sexual shenanigans detracted from his job'. Her advice was to get out before they got him.

Predictably, the England team leapt to the support of their beleaguered coach, but history tells us that players are motivated mostly by self-interest, and always rush to speak up for the man who picks them. They backed Bobby Robson, Terry Venables and, to a lesser extent, Kevin Keegan until they left, when it quickly became a case of: 'The king is dead, long live the king.' Claudio Ranieri, at Chelsea, was another good example.

The reserves, who rarely get a game, even when Beckham and company are playing poorly, are nowhere near as supportive, and one former England captain, who played throughout Euro 2004, told me, on the understanding that he was not identified: 'We could qualify for tournaments with my dad as manager. Sven is paid all that money to win the big games – Brazil, France and Portugal – not the qualifiers, and the fact is we haven't done that.'

Elsewhere in this book there is glowing testimony to Eriksson's ability and success at club level. Unfortunately for England, in two major tournaments he has failed to live up to his reputation in the very different world of international management, and he seems unlikely to have another chance. The mystique that served him well in the early stages of his management has been stripped away by the passage of time and, in the places that matter, increasing familiarity was bringing with it something dangerously close to contempt.

CHAPTER ONE

'PERDENTE DI SUCCESSO' (THE SUCCESSFUL LOSER)

The epithet the Italian media accorded Sven-Goran Eriksson during the 13 years he plied his trade in their country sprang to mind after England's second successive elimination from a major tournament at the quarter-final stage. When the Football Association recruited him in November 2000, at unprecedented expense, they expected sustained progress. Getting no further than the last eight of a European Championship won by Greece was definitely not what had been envisaged.

The administrators at Soho Square discussed England's disappointing performance at Euro 2004 upon their return, and there was criticism of Eriksson's management. It had not gone unnoticed that while the FA had the best-paid coach in the world, it clearly did not have the best coach. It was the cause of some embarrassment when a league table of remuneration revealed that Luis Felipe Scolari, who had won the World Cup with Brazil before taking Portugal to the European final, earned £1.1m a year to Eriksson's £4m. Worse still, Otto Rehhagel, who was appointed at roughly the same time as Eriksson, had brought Greece from nowhere to European pre-eminence on just £490,000 per annum.

The FA considered the fact that France, Italy, Germany, Holland, Spain and Sweden, among others, had all changed their coach, for one reason or another, after the tournament. While privately rueful about getting railroaded into handing their man an extended, enhanced contract before Euro 2004, when he threatened to decamp to Chelsea, they were not, pre-'Fariagate', seriously tempted to follow the trend.

The chief executive who had pushed Eriksson's appointment through, Adam Crozier, had long gone, and his successor, Mark Palios, was nowhere near as enamoured with him, yet the equable Swede survived for a number of reasons, which may be enumerated as follows:

1. Arsenal's David Dein, the most influential of all the FA mandarins, remained staunch. Dein had effectively blocked moves to replace Kevin Keegan with Arsene Wenger, who initially had been the choice of the head-hunting sub-committee, and had gone to Rome with Crozier to secure Eriksson's early release from Lazio. He was standing by his man.

2. The respect Eriksson had from the players and his popularity with them impressed his employers. Despite the shortcomings of some of their football, the England team felt they were unlucky to go out to Portugal in the quarter-final in the light of Sol Campbell's dubiously disallowed goal

and the early loss to injury of Wayne Rooney. It was easy for the FA to concur.

3. England's players were overplayed at club level. The excuse was tediously familiar, but a valid one nevertheless. It was not only David Beckham and Steven Gerrard who looked tired after a demanding season, none of Real Madrid's 'galacticos' did themselves justice at the tournament, and it was surely no coincidence that the winners, Greece, had not been burdened by lengthy Champions' League commitments.

4. Sacking, and paying up Eriksson, who had a new contract with another four years to run, would be ruinously expensive, and there was no obvious replacement to hand. Wenger had said he intended to stay with Arsenal for another season at least, and although Steve McClaren (Middlesbrough), Alan Curbishley (Charlton) and Sam Allardyce (Bolton) had their advocates, it was generally believed that there was no English candidate ready for the job. Fanciful suggestions that Scolari or Rehhagel might be engaged were no more than that. Not only were they committed to Portugal and Greece respectively, neither spoke any English.

From Eriksson's point of view, although he has made no secret of his preference for the day-to-day involvement of club football, the jobs he coveted most, at Chelsea, Manchester United, Real Madrid and Juventus, were no longer available. In the circumstances, coach and employers were both content to soldier on. That said, there was an acknowledgement that England had under-achieved in Portugal. They had travelled with high hopes, only for the country's best crop of good young players for a generation to return with tails lodged firmly between their legs, using a side door to avoid supporters who had turned out to meet them at Luton airport.

Gary Lineker, no Eriksson fan, was not alone in laying the blame squarely at the well-heeled size nines of the coach and David Beckham. The former England captain said: 'England looked jaded. We couldn't keep the ball and defended too deep, but the most disturbing thing was how we proved that we have no Plan B. Plan A was to allow Wayne Rooney to play opponents virtually on his own, filling up all the space between the forwards and midfield, as well as scoring most of the goals. When Rooney went off, we didn't know what to do. We lost all shape and there was no link man to the forwards. The whole back four just stood practically on David James' toes, where any sort of contact on the ball from the attacker is likely to end in a goal.

'England made that mistake throughout the tournament, and I kept waiting for them to get it right. It's just basic stuff, and you have to raise a question mark against the coach when such things are continually allowed to happen. England also suffered from having David Beckham clearly not fit. He had a very poor tournament, and that was down to a lack of conditioning. To put it bluntly, he was off the pace, and a shadow of the player I saw in his first six months at Real Madrid.'

The FA's response came from their executive director, David Davies, who said: 'We are lucky to have Sven – and we're proud of "Becks". People very quickly forget, in the disappointment of going out of a tournament, that Sven is a manager many teams around the world covet. He is licking his wounds at the moment, but he has told us he is already looking forward to the next World Cup. Everybody knows David Beckham has had a difficult time recently, but he is immensely proud to be captain of England, and we are immensely proud to have him.'

The party line was unconvincing. It was true that Eriksson had been coveted, and clandestinely sounded out, by Manchester United, Chelsea, Real Madrid, Barcelona and Internazionale in the 18 months leading up to Euro 2004, but no one was chasing him after the tournament. Beckham meanwhile had given England no reason for pride – on the contrary, his condition in Portugal was little short of a disgrace. It was one thing for the captain to be hampered by injury at the World Cup, quite another for a lack of fitness, due to laxity in training, to render him a passenger in the closing stages of big matches at the European Championship. His excuse, that conditioning work at Real Madrid was not as rigorous as it had been at Manchester United, was a poor one, instantly refuted by Carlos Queiroz, Real's coach for 2003/04, who said: 'During the last three weeks of the season, Luis Figo was at every training session, giving 100 per cent, but David missed some for various reasons, or sometimes for no reason at all. Figo didn't go skiing in April when the team were still playing in the Champions' League. That's where the difference lay. In the final analysis, one player keeps performing to the end and the other doesn't.'

Beckham's exhaustion was plain for all to see in the latter stages of the quarter-final against Portugal, and it was the captain who should have been substituted, not Steven Gerrard. Twice signals went out from the bench, suggesting Beckham came off, but on both occasions he waved his hands dismissively, clearly gesturing his unwillingness. Eriksson's failure to insist on his removal from the action was rooted partly in loyalty to a player who had become a trusted lieutenant, but also in a character flaw. As his partner, Nancy Dell'Olio, said a few weeks after the tournament, in another context: 'Sven tries to avoid confrontation.' It was an observation that explained a lot – those ridiculous wholesale changes in friendly internationals at the behest of the club managers for one thing, the continued presence in the squad of Emile Heskey for another. The really successful managers have no such qualms about difficult decisions that are likely to cause conflict.

Support for Eriksson, albeit qualified, came from one of his predecessors, Sir Bobby Robson, who thought he had been 'too negative' at times, but said: 'When I took England to the 1990 World Cup, I was a far better coach and manager than I had been at Mexico '86 or the '88 European Championship, and it will be the same for Sven. There is nothing like having two major tournaments under your belt to help you deal with different situations when they arise. My view is that a couple of the changes Sven made against Portugal were a bit negative, but I support his right to have the chance to show what he has learned in 2006.

'In one sense, he was very unlucky against Portugal. Had Sol Campbell's legitimate goal stood, we would have been in the semi-finals. Having said that, Portugal were the better side on the night, and if Sven has learned anything, it is probably to be a bit more positive, particularly with substitutions. The decision to send on Phil Neville in central midfield was a negative move, and handed the initiative to Portugal. He is essentially a full-back, and doesn't have the energy to get up and down in international football.

'The tournament proved that it is becoming harder to sit back and defend a 1–0 lead. It is not just England who were caught out, Italy defended very deep against Sweden and conceded an equalizer late on, as did Germany against Holland. The game has changed in the last ten years, and every country seems to have a supply of quick, talented attacking players. These days, the best way to keep a lead is to try to score the second goal, rather than lock the back door as we tried to do against France and Portugal.

'I was so disappointed when we came back from Euro '88 having lost all three matches, but two years later we reached the World Cup semi-finals, with a lot of the same players hitting top form whereas in

'88 they couldn't get going. The message is that to rip up and start again now would be self-defeating. The best solution is to give Sven and his men another chance to show that, with a little more devil may care and confidence in their own technical ability, England can compete with the best.'

The players' view was articulated by Gary Neville, England's longest-serving international, who had a good tournament, on and off the field. Whenever the team needed real leadership, such as after the defeat by France, it was usually Neville who provided it, with the uplifting dressing-room oratory that was so conspicuously lacking in others. 'Gutted' by the outcome in Portugal, the Manchester United defender said: 'We were totally sincere when we told everybody we could win it, and I do believe that we were only just the wrong side of a thin dividing line. But at the end of the day, we weren't quite good enough. Just for once, it would be nice to get those close calls that can decide a big game, like the goal Sol had disallowed, but the fact is that we didn't have that extra edge to get us through.

'There will be a big debate now about whether we are good enough, whether we were fooling ourselves when we said we could win the competition. Portugal did keep the ball well, and put us under amazing pressure, but I don't think we should beat ourselves up about our passing after every tournament. I watched Portugal dominate Spain in just the same way.

'This team has passed the ball as decisively and confidently as any of the England teams I have been involved in. We always seem to have to find a scapegoat when we go out of any tournament, but nobody deserves to be nailed. We just need to keep taking more of the strides forward that we have already made under Sven, who is the best England manager I have known.'

CHAPTER TWO

SVEN'S VERDICT

Sven-Goran Eriksson rejected criticisms of his 'negativity', but as significant as Rio Ferdinand's suspension from Euro 2004, or the injury sustained by Wayne Rooney in the quarter-finals, was the absence of Eriksson's assistant, Brian Kidd, who was recovering from prostate cancer. Kidd was a positive influence, an attack-minded coach, whose reaction to adversity was to throw another man forward. Terry Venables said of their time together at Leeds: 'Whenever we were in trouble in a game, Brian would always say: "Let's go 4–3–3."' When Kidd was not fit enough to travel to Portugal, he was replaced by Steve McClaren, who is much more defence-orientated. His inclination was to concentrate on organizing the back four, where he had mixed success. Three of England's defenders – Gary Neville, Ashley Cole and Sol Campbell – shone throughout, but as a unit the defence operated much too deep, and proved alarmingly fallible at set pieces. That Kidd was missed is beyond question.

Eriksson felt England had been unlucky, and said

the difference between success and failure was infinitesimal. A debriefing went as follows:

Question: What more do England need to win a major tournament?

Eriksson: Very little really. A little bit of luck would be nice. I still think we can win the next World Cup.

Q: Will you be around to try in 2006?

Eriksson: If it is the wish of the English people, or the FA, I will leave, but I don't think that is the case. When I called the players together for a meeting the day after we lost to Portugal, I talked about 2006, and said I was committed to taking them to Germany.

Q: Were mistakes made in selection?

Eriksson: Absolutely not. The 11 players I picked were the best available, and the team will not change much before 2006.

Q: Are new players needed to take the team forward?

Eriksson: No, definitely not. This generation is still young, and can play at the 2006 World Cup for sure, and most of them in 2008. How old is David Beckham? Twenty-nine. At 31 he should be even better. Steven Gerrard is still only 24. It's too early to talk about a new generation. Some new players will come in, but not many. Jermain Defoe will get a chance. He's quick and a goalscorer. And we'll have a look at Chris Kirkland in goal – if he stays fit for once.

Q: Before the tournament, England's midfield was regarded as a strong suit. What went wrong?

Eriksson: I don't agree that it did go wrong. All of them could have played a bit better, but their discipline was good, and they will be in the squad – the team probably – for years to come. In the quarter-final their legs went because we were chasing the ball so much. Steven Gerrard had cramp, and couldn't do the running any more, so we had to put another player on.

Q: Beckham had looked more tired than Gerrard. Was his condition a disappointment?

Eriksson: When we went to Sardinia to prepare, we found that four or five players needed to work on their fitness. He was one of them. He worked hard at it, but maybe it was a bit too late. We have seen Beckham better, there's no doubt about that.

Q: Why did you not bring him off?

Eriksson: If I could have changed one more player in the quarter-final it would have been Beckham, but they were all tired, and I'd made my three substitutions. Remember, Portugal had two more days to recover between games, and at some stage we were always going to pay for that.

Q: Why did England sit back and invite pressure?

Eriksson: Why didn't we attack? It was the same as the Brazil game in Shizuoka. I wanted us to attack, but to do it you have to have the ball. If you don't have it, you have to defend, it's as simple as that. I like to defend high up the pitch, not on our 18-yard line, but if you come up against a team who are gambling a bit, you have to defend deeper. Also, if you are tired, as we were, you make more mistakes and keep the ball less, and it becomes very difficult.

Playing defensively was not a tactic, not something we set out to do.

Q: So it was not all down to bad luck, England needed to retain possession more?

Eriksson: We work on that every time we have a practice session. We concentrate on ball retention in the warm-up, and also as part of the main session. I think we are improving at it, but Portugal, technically, are the best team in Europe, just like two years ago, when Brazil were technically the best team in the world when we played them. When I use the word technically, I mean they are best at keeping the ball.

Q: Why was there such a gap between the midfield and the strikers?

Eriksson: There's a dilemma there. You want to play the ball forward as early as possible, but to keep the team together as a unit you need to play three, four or five passes and then get it forward. That gives time for the defenders and midfield to move up. If you just kick the ball long, then the strikers make their runs and the rest of the team is not there with them, and when they lose possession, there is that gap there. That happened too often, and it's something we'll have to work on.

Q: You seemed to be more emotionally affected than you had been at the World Cup.

Eriksson: When we went to the World Cup, we weren't sure that we could win it, but during the tournament we started to believe that it was possible. At Euro 2004 I was always convinced that we were one of the teams capable of winning it. We didn't and I'm sorry. I've lost many football games in my career, but to go out like that, on penalties, was awful. The difference between winning and losing was like this (he held up a thumb and fore-finger, half an inch apart). We are so nearly there.

Q: What are the positives to be taken from the tournament?

Eriksson: Sol Campbell was a rock. Incredible. He could have been the match winner against Portugal – should have been. Ashley Cole also had an extremely good tournament. And then there was Wayne Rooney. We knew about him in England beforehand, but he proved to be even better than we thought, and he is a big name now, not just in Europe, but around the world. I think he will be a star of the World Cup in 2006, the European Championship in 2008, and way beyond that. If you are that good at 18, then by the time you're 22 or 24 you could be phenomenal. Wayne is already one of our jewels, and he will get better and better. It is not just about his goals, it's about how he plays football and the thought behind it. He's always a thought process ahead in the positions he takes up, and the way he links up our game is just fantastic from one so young. With him in the side, it's so much easier for us to play out with the ball. You can target him and he'll keep it or get fouled, in which case he has got us a free-kick. I'd expected him to play well, but not at that level.

Q: What would be your abiding memory of Euro 2004?

Eriksson: The last three minutes against France I

guess (when England went from winning 1–0 to losing 2–1). That or the last penalty against Portugal. No, definitely the last three minutes against France. That was awful – complete madness.

True enough – it was 'madness' reminiscent of the circumstances in which he got the job in the first place . . .

CHAPTER THREE

THE VACANCY

In hindsight it is clear that Kevin Keegan should have gone straight after Euro 2000, when the 'Three Lions' returned from the Low Countries with their tails lodged firmly between their legs. Tactical naïvety has become a clichéd criticism, trotted out ad nauseam on every radio phone-in, but Keegan was its personification. Against Portugal in Eindhoven, with England leading 2–0, he opted not to shut up shop and man-mark Luis Figo, arguably the best player in the world, with the result that England let slip what should have been a winning position and lost 3–2. Their hopes were resurrected with a 1–0 victory over the worst German team in living memory, but then a deserved 3–2 defeat against Romania, in Charleroi, where some of his choices were exposed as inadequate at international level, brought Keegan and company home before the competition proper had started.

After Glenn Hoddle had psycho-babbled himself out of the job, Keegan was portrayed as 'the people's choice' by the Football Association. He wasn't. That the label stuck was something of a triumph for the spin doctors at the FA, for in the opinion polls it was not Keegan but Terry Venables who had emerged as the clear favourite, both with the fans and with the professionals in the game. In the aftermath of Euro 2000, it was apparent that 'King Kevin' had feet of clay. The players liked him, but despaired at his lack of tactical nous, the public could see through his crass, British bulldog tub-thumping, and his employers were beginning to have their doubts.

The change should, and probably would, have been made before the start of the World Cup qualifying campaign, but for the absence of a suitable candidate who was available and, crucially, on whom the FA mandarins could agree. Venables, who had proved his worth in taking England to the semi-finals of Euro 96, would have had a second crack at the job but for the intransigence of Noel White, the influential chairman of the FA's international committee. So Keegan was allowed to continue – a decision the FA was to rue.

By one of the quirks of fate that abound in football, the first game in World Cup qualifying saw England at home to Germany, the old enemy providing the opposition for the last international to be played under Wembley's twin towers. The game would be followed by a second qualifier, away to Finland, four days later. Traditionally, the Germans were something of a bête noire, but there were no Beckenbauers, Netzers or Mullers in their millennium class, and England, who had just beaten them 1–0 in Euro 2000, should have had nothing to fear.

But that was reckoning without Keegan's

selectorial waywardness. For some unfathomable reason, he played Gareth Southgate, a central defender, in midfield, where this most willing and diligent of professionals was a four-square peg in a circular hole. England were depressingly poor, but Germany were not much better, and the only goal of a low-quality game was more the product of defensive deficiency than Teutonic inspiration. There should have been no more than token danger when Liverpool's Dietmar Hamann stepped up to take a free-kick fully 30 yards out, but England neglected to form the customary defensive wall, with the result that Hamann was able to beat David Seaman's slow-mo dive, low to his right.

England were booed off the pitch and Keegan was verbally abused by his erstwhile admirers as he made the long, disconsolate trudge around the perimeter, during which the extent of his inadequacy finally hit home. By the time he reached the sanctuary of the dressing room, he had made a fateful decision. It was time to quit. Disarmingly honest, he told the players and his employers, and then the nation, via television, that he was not good enough for the job. Somebody else should have a go.

In the dressing room, there was emotion and confusion in equal measure. Some of the senior players, such as Tony Adams and Graeme Le Saux, urged the manager to 'sleep on it' before finally making up his mind, but he was adamant. Adam Crozier, the FA's Chief Executive at the time, and did most to try to persuade Keegan to reconsider.

Recalling one of his worst days in the job, he told me: 'Losing to Germany was an incredibly disappointing way to start the World Cup qualifying series. It set us right back on our heels. To lose your first game at home to your main rivals would be a major setback for anybody, but it was the way we lost it. The way we played that afternoon, we seemed to have gone backwards again.

'From my conversations with him, I know Kevin could see that there were good young players coming through, who were going to improve the team over the next couple of years, and he wasn't sure that he was the right man to get the best out of them. Kevin is a great patriot, and he had always had a great rapport with the fans. Not everybody will agree with this, but I felt it was a very brave thing for him to say: "I don't think I'm up to the job." The thing I didn't agree with him over, and I told him so, was his timing. My view was that if that was the way he felt, the time to go was after the game against Finland, four days later. Quitting after Germany left us completely rudderless for the trip to Helsinki. Another false start in the second game, which was what we had, was always going to make the task of qualifying even more difficult for whoever took over permanently. So I felt Kevin should have stayed on for that one, and I certainly tried very hard to persuade him, as did a number of the players and Noel White, Chairman of the International Committee.

'In the dressing room straight after the game we all tried – Tony Adams particularly – to get him to reconsider. Don't forget, he was very popular with the players, and even after that game there was still a lot of love for Kevin and a great deal of support. They wanted him to stay, but there was no persuading him. Anybody who knows Kevin will tell you that one of his characteristics is that once he has made up his mind about something, that's it. He won't budge.

'Crucial to his decision, I think, was the reaction of the fans as he came away from the pitch. He had always had that fantastic relationship with them; now they were booing and insulting him. In the dressing room, his mindset was complete. He wasn't emotional, not at all. People imagine that he was, but he wasn't. He came to a very clear-headed decision, and I think he made it with the best of intentions. He felt it was the right thing for his country. Even for the game on the Wednesday, his point of view was that the team would do better under someone else. He said to me: "I don't think I can lift them [the players] because I don't feel up there myself."'

For Crozier and White, the urgent task that chaotic Saturday night was to find a stand-in to take the squad to Helsinki, less than 48 hours later. Crozier explained: 'It wasn't just that we'd lost, or that it was the last game at Wembley, but the England coach had resigned, so there was a huge furore about what had happened and where we went from here. In terms of the Wednesday match, there was only one sensible solution, and that was to get our technical director, Howard Wilkinson, to do it. Given the timescale [the England squad flew out to Helsinki on the Monday morning], it had to be somebody from within, and Howard had the knowledge, both of our players and of international football. So on the Saturday night, by about 7.30pm, we'd agreed that he would be in charge for Finland. I spoke to Noel White about it, and checked with the FA chairman [Geoff Thompson] to make sure that he was comfortable with it. But in the final analysis, our options were so limited that it had to be Howard. To have put someone in from scratch would have been asking the impossible.'

One of the more fanciful tabloid newspapers reported that Crozier had left the dressing room and telephoned Eriksson's agent, Athole Still, to enquire about his availability. (An interesting, cosmopolitan character, who trained as an opera singer in Italy and worked as a swimming coach, TV commentator and journalist, Still got to know Eriksson in the mid-1980s when they met during abortive negotiations to take Still's first football client, John Barnes, from Watford to Roma, who were then coached by Eriksson. A friendship was forged over the next few years and, when Eriksson's first agent, the Swede Borg Lanz, died in 1993, Still replaced him.) 'That was rubbish,' Crozier said, laughing. What did happen was that before England left for Finland, Crozier formed a sub-committee whose brief was to draw up a list of candidates. As is his wont, he wanted to be seen to be proactive. The new manager would be his man.

The assumption was always that Wilkinson was a

non-runner. As a manager of the old school, at Leeds, he had been good enough to win the last First Division title before the advent of the Premier League, and in those days he had confided that his driving ambition was to manage England. He had done it once before in a caretaker's capacity, after Hoddle's abrupt departure, but a comprehensive 2–0 defeat by France at Wembley did nothing for his credentials, and England's goalless bore with Finland on 11 October 2000 merely confirmed the impression that the game had moved on and passed him by. The occasion was more remarkable for what happened before, and afterwards, than for anything that happened in the 90 minutes. The final training session before the match was witnessed by a group of English football correspondents and by two members of the FA's international committee, all of whom were distinctly unimpressed. The journalists noticed that England's game plan seemed to revolve around hitting long balls, right to left, for Emile Heskey to knock down. The FA kingmakers noted that Wilkinson's man-management methods left as much to be desired as his tactics. Watching him bark out orders via a microphone headset, one said to the other: 'We've no chance of winning here, he's lecturing international footballers like school-boys.' As if to reinforce the point, two of the senior professionals present, Stuart Pearce and Teddy Sheringham, exchanged horrified looks behind Wilkinson's back.

The poverty of England's performance in the Olympic stadium, and a table which showed them bottom, with one point and Germany top with six, moved one reporter to enquire whether it might be better to forget about qualifying for Japan and Korea, and use the remaining matches to bring on younger players with Euro 2004 and the 2006 World Cup in mind. Instead of the expected 'each game is there to be won' response, Wilkinson replied: 'The possibility you've raised obviously has to be considered. In the interests of the long term, we could go into it [the rest of the qualifying series] picking a team that's going to be there in four years' time.'

But would the public stand for the jam tomorrow approach? 'If it's the right thing to do in the opinion of the professionals, they've got to. What's the alternative? To keep doing what we're doing at the moment, riding the rollercoaster? Quite frankly, I'm fed up with that. I don't even enjoy the highs particularly, because every time we're up there I think: "Here we go again, hold on to the bar because we'll be going down any moment." No, the real alternative is to go in with realistic expectations and to outline clearly to the players what is expected of them. We've got to make sure that their expectations are realistic, and that they don't fall into the trap of trying to achieve what you lot [the media] set out in your agenda.'

Any slender chance Wilkinson might have had of getting the job on a permanent basis disappeared in this puff of pomposity. Abandon the World Cup, and a lucrative ride on the gravy train? This was heresy at the FA. Crozier says: 'I'm not sure Howard wanted it, and the general feeling among the sub-committee was that he was never going to get it.' There is conflicting testimony as to what happened next. Crozier would have it that he was immediately intent upon crossing the Channel, and the Rubicon, by appointing from abroad. Always the mover and shaker, he made all the running. 'In the period between the games against Germany and Finland, I compiled what I thought was the right short list. Then I got the sub-committee together, and spoke to them about why I'd done what I had, and said: "These are the people who should be in the frame. For a job of such magnitude, I thought there were only five who could rise to the challenge."'

Apart from Crozier, the head-hunting sub-committee comprised: Geoff Thompson (the FA chairman), Noel White (chairman of the international committee), David Richards (vice-chairman of the international committee and chairman of the Premier League), David Dein of Arsenal and Peter Ridsdale of Leeds United (both of whom represented the Premier League on the FA board) and Wilkinson (FA technical director). It was to these men, Crozier says, that he took his five potential candidates. He told me: 'We talked a lot about the criteria for the job, and the most important one for me, right at the very top of the list, was a sustained record of success. At the time I said success internationally, which was misunderstood. I didn't mean a record of success in international football, but success wherever the person had coached, across the world. Our man had to be successful, not just as a one-season wonder, but somebody who had really achieved, wherever he had been. We wanted it all – international credibility, tactical nous, man-management expertise and the ability to handle the media. We were looking for respect within the game and the right personality and cultural profile for international football, where the highs are incredibly high, the lows really low, and there's a lot of time between games to fret over a bad result or get over-excited by a good one. We needed somebody who could cope with both extremes in a very level-headed way. An emotional person over-reacts, and it becomes a rollercoaster existence. A calm personality is essential for international management.

'I started with a long list, then broke it down and said to the committee: "There is a maximum of five who could meet our criteria and do the job." At first I had people on the list who seemed to be good candidates, but then we thought: "Hang on, have they genuinely got all this?" The truth was that not many had.' While others scratched their heads and dithered, Crozier drove the process forward. 'I said: "Right, this is the short list. Before we go any further, does anyone disagree? No? Right, leave it with me, I will go away and look at this lot and find out everything I need to know about them."'

Ridsdale remembers the sequence of events rather differently. According to him, he proposed Bobby Robson, who became the sub-committee's first choice, ahead of Eriksson. The former Leeds chairman told me: 'After the Germany game, on the Monday, Adam asked me, and the others, if we would form the sub-committee. We flew out to Finland and all the members of the sub-committee were there, apart from David Dein, and we thought it was a good opportunity to have our first meeting. We got together in the team's hotel, and Adam produced a flip chart with a clean sheet of paper – nobody's name was on it. He divided the board into four sections: English managers, non-English managers working in England, foreign managers and I think the fourth category was up and coming. On the English side, we had Bobby Robson, Terry Venables, Roy Hodgson and Howard Wilkinson, with a question mark against him. Of those working in England but non-English, we had Alex Ferguson, Arsene Wenger and Gerard Houllier, the foreigners were Eriksson, Johann Cruyff, Marcello Lippi and Hector Cuper, and in the up-and-coming category were Martin O'Neill, David O'Leary, Peter Taylor and Bryan Robson. These names were solicited by Adam and written on the board by him. He said: "These are the categories, do we agree? Can anyone think of anybody else? No? Right." So we went through the names, and everybody agreed that the ideal was an Englishman with another young Englishman backing him up. We had Bobby Robson and Peter Taylor as manager and heir apparent. There was a long debate about whether Terry [Venables] should be considered, and everybody agreed that if "New England" was to represent what the FA wanted it to stand for, we couldn't discount Terry's non-footballing reputation, whatever its rights and wrongs. The view was that, given what we were trying to achieve at the FA, we had to have a new beginning, and therefore Terry was not appropriate. That was unanimous. Whether it was fair to him or not, the baggage that came with him counted against him, and he was out of it.

'Having debated all the rights and wrongs, we came out of it with two names: Bobby Robson and Sven. The agreement was that Adam would go away and seek permission from Newcastle to talk to Robson, to see if he was an option. We weren't just talking about having him for one or two games, as was widely reported at the time, we wanted him on a permanent basis. There was, though, a suggestion that if Bobby would only agree to do it for the rest of the season, that would buy us time.'

Ridsdale, now Chairman at Barnsley, adds that Crozier was told: 'If you go to Newcastle and get permission to speak to him, and Bobby says: "I'm not interested, but I'm prepared to help you out as a stopgap," that would be better than nothing. Adam was sent away from the meeting with two alternatives to explore: Bobby Robson with a young English coach, or if not, Sven. After that first meeting, Bobby was in front of Sven. Everybody's perception was: "Ideally, we appoint an Englishman. If not, we'll go overseas." Bobby only ceased to be the front runner when Newcastle were approached and said they wouldn't release him.'

Crozier denies much of this and, in fairness, it is his version of events that ties in with that of Noel White. During the course of his research, Crozier said, he relied heavily on the advice of Sir Alex Ferguson, who had ruled himself out of the running for the job, but was willing to assist the FA in their quest.

'I spent a lot of time with Alex, who was tremendously helpful. The night Manchester United played PSV Eindhoven in the Champions' League (18 October 2000, seven days after the Finland game) he gave me a couple of hours at Old Trafford. When I went to see him I actually had a dual purpose, although nobody knew it at the time. I went to pick Alex's brain about getting the right manager, but also to get his agreement to let us have Steve McClaren, his assistant, as part of our new coaching team. I wanted continuity, a long-term strategy, and I'd got the sub-committee to agree that we'd have three or four coaches under the manager, none of whom would be "The Chosen One", as Bryan Robson was under Terry Venables, but any one of whom might emerge as the heir apparent over a period of time. For me, you see, there were two searches going on at the same time. Everyone thought I was looking for an England manager, but I was looking for a manager and his back-up. As it turned out, I ended up getting the support team first: Steve from United and Peter Taylor from Leicester, plus Sammy Lee, from Liverpool, for the Under-21s.'

When it came to the top job, Ferguson helped to point Crozier in Eriksson's direction. 'Having found out as much as I could about potential targets, and having listened to what expert witnesses like Alex had to say, I became absolutely convinced that Sven was our man after that first week. Alex was very helpful. We also talked about his players' feelings about the England set-up. When they went back to Manchester United after international duty with us, what were they saying about us? From what they had told him, and from what he had seen, what did Alex think about our way of doing things? Where were we going wrong? That helped us to identify the sort of person we needed to fix it.'

Where Crozier and Ridsdale agree is that after the first week, Eriksson topped the wanted list. Crozier says the peripatetic Hodgson (ex-Malmo, Switzerland, Grasshoppers, Internazionale, Blackburn, Udinese etc) fell at the first hurdle, failing the 'sustained success' test, and Ferguson and Houllier were discounted on grounds of unavailability. So, too, was Wenger. Arsenal were naturally keen to keep the manager who led them to the Double in 1998, and the presence of Dein, their vice-chairman, on the sub-committee inevitably led to suggestions of a conflict of interests. The smooth poise for which Dein is renowned was disturbed momentarily when Wenger went on Sky TV and said he could not understand why England had not asked about him.

Before cottoning on to Eriksson, the media had made the Arsenal man the favourite for the job. So was he considered or not? Dein havered, saying: 'He [Wenger] had gone public many, many times with the fact that he was going to respect his contract with Arsenal, and this was all about the art of the possible. Who could we get? There was no point wasting our energies on somebody we couldn't get.'

When the sub-committee met for the second and last time, Eriksson was 'a clear front runner', Crozier says. The fans' favourite, Venables, had disappeared off the radar. 'If you measure his record against all our criteria, he didn't stack up as well as Sven. It's a subjective thing, and I'm sure there are people who still disagree, but if you are a leader, you have to back your judgement. The only time I got upset during the whole process was when some journalist friends of Terry's wrote that we'd chosen integrity as one of our criteria specifically to rule him out, as if he didn't have any. I found that upsetting for him because: (a) I wouldn't want a friend to write that about me, and (b) it wasn't true, so it was very unfair. We were looking for a broad spectrum of qualities, and my hunch was that Sven had them all – or at least more so than anybody else we were considering.'

Eriksson had been Crozier's choice from day one. 'That wasn't the case with everyone on the sub-committee,' he acknowledged. 'Peter [Ridsdale] was always for Bobby, and initially other people had other views. At our first meeting some said we should go for Alex Ferguson, others Arsene Wenger, and there was a lot of discussion about Johann Cruyff. But at that second meeting, it became unanimous for Sven. I have to say I did corral everyone in, admittedly with David Dein's assistance. It was a case of: "OK, is everyone now 100 per cent up for this?" They were.'

Ridsdale begs to differ again. 'For Adam to say he forced the issue is wrong. We followed a very methodical process. And if David feels he initiated it, that is disingenuous, because he wasn't at the first meeting. With the benefit of hindsight, Adam might say: "I always had this solution in mind, I led them there," but I don't think that's true because we started with a blank sheet of paper, worked through all the possibilities, and everybody had their particular suggestions written down.

'I don't remember who first mentioned Eriksson – it might have been Adam, to be fair. I said Bobby Robson. I was saying that whatever we did, we should have the next man in place, so we wouldn't have to go through the whole process again from scratch. The young bucks, maybe two or three coaches, should work alongside the main man, so that a ready-made successor could come from Peter Taylor, Steve McClaren or Bryan Robson, whose names all came up.'

Had Dein blocked any move in Wenger's direction? Ridsdale was adamant that he did not. 'People said because I was on the sub-committee, David [O'Leary] couldn't be picked, which was a joke. He was on the list, but what had he done? He was never seriously considered for that reason. The same people said Wenger couldn't get the job because of David [Dein], but it was at that first meeting that Sven emerged as our preferred foreign candidate, and David wasn't even there. Wenger was considered, as was Alex Ferguson, but Sven was the number one non-English choice.'

Dein, away on Arsenal business, could have been contacted by mobile phone, but was not consulted either before or during that first meeting. Had he had any input? 'No,' Ridsdale said, emphatically.

'Well, I know he didn't speak to me, or to Dave Richards, Noel White or Howard Wilkinson. To Crozier . . . who knows? But Crozier never said: "I've spoken to Dein and we wouldn't get Arsene Wenger."'

For the second meeting, it was Ridsdale's turn to be absent, on club business. Everybody else was present, Dein included. Ridsdale says: 'All I know about what happened was from a briefing I had straight afterwards by phone, and that was to say that the second meeting had confirmed the conclusions of the first, and that thereafter Adam had the authority to go and try to get Sven.'

CHAPTER FOUR

THE MOVE

Having agreed on the man they wanted, the Football Association's problem was that Eriksson was under contract to Lazio, the Italian champions, who were still in the Champions' League and intent on winning the European Cup. Naturally they wanted to keep the coach who had brought them the coveted scudetto. Adam Crozier, however, was not about to be deterred, and within two days of his first approach to the Roman club he had his man. He recalled: 'My attitude was: "If you're going to go for someone, do it properly. Make your move quickly, equipped with everything you need to get the business done. Get it done there and then, on the spot." So I prepared everything I'd need to have with me when I got to speak to Sven about the job. I had analysis of matches, profiles of the players – not just the senior squad but the Under-21s and those coming through the youth scheme, right down to the Under-15s. I had videos of all the key games, statistics, everything. That enabled me to say to him: "Look, this is where we are, this is where we're going, this is what we want to try to do."

'The other key thing when I made the move was to be able to offer our man a long-term contract. I'd got the people here [the FA] to agree to five years. If our objective was to win a major tournament by 2006, the contract should last until then. We needed stability, and five years provided the opportunity to train up people with the potential to take over.'

Crozier and David Dein, who has emerged in recent years as the most dynamic member of the FA board, flew to Rome by private jet on Sunday 29 October 2000, and prepared overnight for their meeting with Lazio and their coach the following day. Crozier said: 'We met Sergio Cragnotti [the Lazio president], his son, Massimo, Dino Zoff [Lazio vice-president and former coach] and one or two others at the club's training ground, at Formello. Sven was present for some of the time. Cragnotti senior was an absolute gentleman. Top class. We explained why we wanted to speak to Sven, and Mr Cragnotti said he was caught in two minds. Lazio had just enjoyed their most successful season ever, and were on a high, but he and Sven had become very close. A bond had been built up between them over a momentous season, and he didn't want to stand between his friend and what he wanted. From our point of view, that was a great attitude – one not many would have taken.

'At this stage Mr Cragnotti asked Sven to join us, and said: "Do you want to talk to them?" Sven said: "Yes, I would very much like to. This is the sort of job I've dreamed about, it's something I've always wanted to try." The second stage was for us to talk to him, and we did that there and then. Everything was agreed between us within 24 hours.' Money was never a problem, Crozier insisted, and nor should it have been, with £2.5m a year, plus bonuses, on the table. In comparison, just four years earlier Terry Venables was on £125,000 a year when he took England to the semi-finals at Euro 96, and Kevin Keegan had been getting £800,000 annually. At Lazio, Eriksson earned £1.75m a year, tax free. 'The third stage,' Crozier said, 'was agreeing with Mr Cragnotti the timing of the changeover. Initially, Lazio were unhappy about Sven leaving them before the end of the season because they were still in the Champions' League, but eventually we managed to persuade them to meet us halfway. Sven would join us part-time from February, in time for our game against Spain at Villa Park. Sven wanted to finish on a high with Lazio, to repay Mr Cragnotti. He didn't want to leave them in the lurch. There was that closeness between the two of them.'

Reluctantly, Crozier and Dein accepted that there was going to be an interregnum. Fortunately, they thought, they had just the right man to plug the gap. 'We had a friendly coming up against Italy,' Crozier explained, 'and our initial objective was to get Bobby Robson as caretaker for that one game, with Steve McClaren and Peter Taylor backing him up. We were a bit surprised when Newcastle said no to that, and poor old Bobby was devastated. He really wanted to do it, and I don't really see why he couldn't have done so. After all, it was never the intention to have Bobby for more than that one game. What we said to Newcastle was: "Look, we don't want your manager full-time because it's not the future for us, but depending on who we go for [we didn't want to give away who we were after], could we have him part-time?" Once we couldn't get him, we made the decision to promote Peter and Steve. The reason for that was that Bobby was unique. He'd done the job before, and everybody would know that he wasn't going to be our future because of his age. There was no point drafting somebody else in for one game, better to go with youth.'

Eriksson's decision had been quickly made. He said: 'My intention had been to stay another year with Lazio, but when the offer from the FA came, I immediately felt: "This is exactly what I want to do." Such an offer comes only once in a lifetime. I never analysed the risks involved. I never thought: "I might not succeed." On the contrary, I thought: "If I don't accept, I won't be able to sleep at night, wondering what I could have done with the job." My intuition told me what to do, as it has done every time a new offer has come up. Of course it was a big change to take on England, but it was a bigger step, and an even greater risk, to move from the little village of Torsby and the coaching job with Degerfors to a club the size of Gothenburg. The step from Rome to London didn't feel as big.'

He had not given much thought to being a foreigner. 'Sweden had an English coach [George Raynor] in 1958, when they went to the World Cup finals. Why, then, shouldn't a Swede take England?

I read the book *The Second Most Important Job In The Country*, which is all about the England managers from 1949 through to Kevin Keegan. It showed that all of them were declared idiots at some time, even Sir Alf Ramsey, so I knew what to expect.'

It was as well that he was prepared. The FA's decision to appoint their first non-English manager in 128 years of international football immediately polarized public opinion. John Barnwell of the League Managers' Association and Gordon Taylor of the PFA objected strongly, on the grounds that the job should always go to an Englishman. Barnwell described it an 'an insult' to his members, and Taylor accused the Football Association of 'betraying their heritage'. Their comments were widely reported, and, as tends to be the way of it, the newspapers split roughly on tabloid–broadsheet lines, with the likes of *The Times* and the *Daily Telegraph* open-minded while others were anything but. The *Sun* was at its most xenophobic, declaring: 'The nation which gave the game of football to the world has been forced to put a foreign coach in charge of its national team for the first time in its history. What a climbdown. What a humiliation. What a terrible, pathetic, self-inflicted indictment. What an awful mess.' Jeff Powell, in the *Daily Mail*, was outraged, fulminating: 'England's humiliation knows no end. In their trendy eagerness to appoint a designer manager, did the FA pause for so long as a moment to consider the depth of this insult to our national pride? We sell our birthright down the fjord to a nation of seven million skiers and hammer throwers who spend half their year living in total darkness.' The speed with which these opinions changed, once Eriksson's England started winning, will be seen later.

The new manager was presented to the English media at the ungodly hour of 8am on 2 November 2000. The venue chosen was the Sopwell House Hotel, St Albans, which is convenient for Luton airport, and the time unusually early to enable Eriksson to get back to Rome (by private plane, of course) in time to take Lazio's training that afternoon. His arrival at the hotel, which used to be Arsenal's training base, was akin to a presidential procession. Surrounded by FA flunkies, who resembled an FBI close protection squad, his every step through the corridors was tracked by television camera crews, whose lights had him transfixed, like a startled rabbit caught in the headlamps of an oncoming car. The tabloid rottweilers were out in force, scrutinizing his every move and nuance. Much was made of the fact that he wore a poppy, with Remembrance Day in the offing. The *Daily Express* sarcastically (but accurately) observed that, coming from a nation of pacifists, he must have had it pinned on him by one of the FA's spin doctors.

Once television and radio had finished playing 'how-do-you-feel?' softball, the press let fly with a few bumpers. Eriksson had little experience of English football, how was his knowledge? Could he name, say, the Leicester City goalkeeper, or the Sunderland left-back? He failed on both counts, and there were those (the author among them) who took delight in pointing out that the two players in question, Ian Walker and Michael Gray, should both be in contention for places in the next England squad. What about David Beckham? Was his best position on the right of midfield or in the centre? 'Please don't ask me that today,' Eriksson said. 'For sure he's a great player, but I think I need at least a couple of practices with him before I decide that.'

What did he have to do to turn the England team into winners? 'The most important thing, as always, is to create a good ambience within the group. If you don't have that feeling, you will never get good results.' Tactically, he was not prepared to disclose whether he would be playing 4–4–2 or 4–3–3. 'But the players' attitude to the game is much more important, and much more difficult to get right, than finding a formation.' He was not going to discuss individual players before he started working with them. What he would say was that there was no question of abandoning the 2002 World Cup and concentrating on building beyond it. 'I think you can do both. Of course you should plan for the future, but to give up on qualifying for the World Cup would be very stupid. As long as there is the slightest possibility still there, you should go for it. I think it is possible to win the group. Even second place in qualifying could get you a gold medal in the end. Give up at this stage? I don't know those words. I never give up.'

Eriksson met every googly with a bat of Boycottesque straightness, hiding behind his un-familiarity with the language when it suited his purpose, to the frustration of his inquisitors. Rob Shepherd, then of the *Daily Express*, whose no-nonsense directness has been the bane of many a manager's life, turned to me afterwards and said: 'Christ, to think it's going to be like that for the next five years.'

It was announced at the press conference, almost by way of afterthought, that Eriksson's number two at Lazio, Tord Grip, would be coming with him to England, as David Dein put it: 'as his eyes and ears'. In fact Grip, unlike his boss, was released immediately by his Italian employers, and was scouting in England for three months before Eriksson finally arrived to join him. It was Grip, for example, who spotted, and recommended, Chris Powell, the 30-something Charlton Athletic full-back, who was the first rabbit to be pulled from the new managerial hat.

England's next game, however, was the friendly fixture against Italy in Turin, where Eriksson and Grip were no more than observers. It was left to Peter Taylor to start the overdue process of rejuvenation with a young, forward-looking squad, and a team led by David Beckham for the first time. England lost 1–0, but gave a good account of themselves and Eriksson, who attended the match, was encouraged by the likes of Gareth Barry, Rio Ferdinand, Jamie Carragher and Kieron Dyer. His tenure was brief, but Taylor served England well by giving younger players the opportunity to catch the eye. The public liked what they saw, and Eriksson had a fair wind.

Meanwhile, events had taken a turn for the

worse at Lazio. The revelation that their coach was keen to leave them for pastures new did nothing for the players' motivation, and after the England announcement, on 2 November, Lazio's form disintegrated. They won only six of 14 games, dropping to fifth in Serie A, and Eriksson saw his Champions' League dream turn to ashes with defeats by Leeds and Anderlecht. By the turn of the year it was apparent that one manager could not properly serve two masters, and on 9 January 2001 Eriksson resigned at Lazio to devote his full attention to England.

The quick-break decision had been made in a petrol station, during the drive to training. It was then that he realized he was running on empty. 'I just knew I couldn't go on.' Minutes later, he drove through the gates of Formello and told his players he was on his way. There were tears, and later an emotional meeting with Cragnotti. At a highly charged press conference, Cragnotti said the man who took Lazio to the title would always find a home back in Rome. 'I want to see you back here, celebrating a long list of victories with England.' To which Eriksson leaned across and told him: 'Yes, and with the World Cup.'

Breaking his contract had cost Eriksson £1.3m, but money was the last thing on his mind. 'I didn't like what I did, but it was best for the club. Results in football are everything, and the results had been bad. It was better for Lazio to have somebody else come in and administer the shock that was needed.'

The Lazio fans had been resentful when the news

broke of his imminent defection, but that same night he was given a standing ovation when he took his seat for a match against the Chinese national team, which was part of Lazio's centenary celebrations. The warmth of the reception melted 'The Ice Man', reducing him to tears. 'And believe me, I am not a man who cries easily.' Cragnotti led the Roman salute, with the words: 'It is only right that Lazio applauds the man who gave us so much.'

A delighted Crozier was relieved that the waiting was over. He remembered it thus: 'Lazio found that once it was announced that Sven was going to be the England manager, the public profile that goes with that job made it impossible for him to continue in Rome. There were English journalists camped outside the training ground every day and, as a lot of managers have found, once the players know you are going, discipline and motivation is eroded. It was a difficult situation all round, and just before Christmas we all agreed that, even with the best intentions, the halfway house arrangement just wasn't going to work. Events were conspiring to make it in the interests of all parties to say: "That's it. Let's move on."'

CHAPTER FIVE

THE MAN AND HIS METHODS

'Its mystery is its life. We must not let in daylight upon magic.'

WALTER BAGEHOT, Social scientist 1826–1877.

It ill behoves a newspaperman to say it, but the most perspicacious comment I have heard, or read, about Sven-Goran Eriksson's public persona came from the BBC's Head of Sport, Peter Salmon. Contrasting Eriksson's detached, almost introverted manner with the rentaquote familiarity of his predecessors, Salmon said: 'The interesting thing about the England managers that I've seen is that the closer we've got to them, the more difficult the relationship becomes. You're no longer as impressed as you were in the days when they were still remote figures. The better we know them, the less we respect them. Eriksson has brought the authority back to his position. He's rather mysterious, hard to get a handle on. We feel there must be a lot going on up there. We might not know what it is, but it has obviously got results.' It was only when we got to know the man that he lost a lot of our respect.

Salmon's theme was echoed by Gareth Southgate, the most erudite and articulate of all England players, who says: 'The fact that we didn't really know him is a tremendous strength for a manager to have. That distance brought him more respect. Because we didn't know too much about him, and vice-versa, he was able to detach himself when he made decisions. He took those decisions purely on the basis of the players he saw and the form they were in. One of his strengths has been concentrating on performance. Because he's from another country, the nationalistic pride of playing for England hasn't been at the forefront of his thinking. We're all very proud to play for England, that goes without saying, but that's also true of every other country. Every team we face is going to be passionate about playing for their country, so you have to produce the quality to be better than them. He has been able to distinguish between the two elements, and I think these players are more comfortable with that than people were in the past.'

Eriksson was neither a ranter and raver, nor a John Bull patriot. 'At half-time,' Southgate says, 'he won't talk for maybe five minutes, until everybody has calmed down and got their thoughts together. As a manager, you need to get your message across in a short space of time, and flying off the handle isn't constructive. He never shouted at us, but then I don't think there's been a performance where he's needed to. He has a calming, relaxing influence that helps. If you get a manager who is agitated and not totally in control, I'm sure it transmits itself to the players.'

People who have played for, or worked with, him are among the best equipped to define Eriksson's *je ne sais quoi*. David Platt, recruited by Eriksson to manage the England Under-21 team, comes into both categories. He told me: 'In my two years at Sampdoria, playing for him, I knew I enjoyed his training, I knew I enjoyed working for him and I had massive respect for him, but when people asked me why, I could never put my finger on it. Now that he's over here, and I'm working for him again, I think about it a lot, but I still can't hang my hat on what it is that he's got. I could eulogize, and come out with all sorts of things, but then you'd go to him and he'd probably say: "No, I'm not like that at all." I don't think he has ever consciously decided: "Right, this is the way I'm going to be." It's just the way he has evolved.

'I think he gets his respect from his ruthlessness. He doesn't come across that way, and nobody is ever frightened of him, but he does command total respect. Everybody understands that if you don't do whatever he wants, or if you fall below his standards, he'll have you out and lose no sleep over it. There are no favourites, no concessions made. He loved Roberto Mancini, but he left him out at Lazio, and doing it didn't bother him at all. Sven is controlled, and in control, whatever he does. At Sampdoria, he never came into the dressing room at half-time angry. He was always calm, and if he did have a go at us he was always totally in control of his emotions.

'Mancini came out with a good statement the

other day, to the effect that things don't annoy Sven. He's an enigma in that respect. I really don't know if it's a conscious effort on his part, telling himself: "I'm not going to let this get to me." It's probably a characteristic he's developed over his career. You can imagine the politicking that goes on within the FA, and sometimes it gets me stirred up. I find myself thinking: "What on earth is going on here?", and it must be so much worse for Sven. There are obstacles put in his way that would make a saint swear, but his attitude is always: "Fair enough, I'll come at this a different way." Nothing seems to annoy him, or knock him out of his stride. He follows his own path, and won't veer off it, come what may.'

The furore over whether Lee Bowyer and Jonathan Woodgate of Leeds United should be chosen for England after the Sarfraz Nejeib court case provided a good example of Eriksson's single-minded approach. He wanted to pick both players, despite FA disapproval. Platt, who was party to the discussions on the subject, explained: 'I warned Sven that if he picked them, there would be a media circus, and other people at the FA spelled that out to him, but his reaction was: "Well, I'll deal with it." Not "Bloody hell, perhaps I'd better avoid all that." You can imagine other people, myself included, thinking: "Hang on, let's work out the pros and cons here – where could this all lead?" For Sven, the court had administered justice, and now it was 100 per cent about football and nothing to do with what the reaction might be. If you present him with a major problem, he has the ability to absorb it and deal with it. There's no panic, no "How are we going to get out of this one?" He's very good like that. I think the politics he had to handle in Italy equipped him for just about anything.'

On the training pitch, Eriksson worked by the power of suggestion. 'A good phrase, that,' Platt said. 'He would stand there while we were playing a practice match, and he might walk over to me, and then Attilio Lombardo, and say "Why don't you switch?" It wouldn't be a case of stopping everything and saying: "Right, now I want you to do this." He'd just sidle over every now and then and suggest something. Players would do it, and if it worked it would become ingrained in their subconscious. With good players, that's what happens – you don't have to keep telling them over and over again. That way it becomes too robotic. '

A man of egalitarian principles, Eriksson does not hold with the concept of favourites, but Mancini came close to it, as did Jonas Thern, the multi-talented Swedish midfielder who played for him at Benfica. Thern, recently manager at Halmstad, followed the same path, from part-time football in Sweden to the high-pressure environment of one of the most famous clubs in the world. In an interview for this book, he told me: 'In Portugal, the country was different, the people were different and especially the football was different. It was more technical, and we trained much harder, as full-time professionals. In Sweden at that time, you had to have a job, as well as football, to make a good living, and I had been working for my father's printing company in Malmo. In Portugal I went full-time, and found it hard work at first. Often we trained morning and afternoon.'

Thern's mentor had been Roy Hodgson, who had signed him for Malmo. He says: 'Roy and Bob Houghton, when they came to Sweden in the late seventies, made Swedish football what it is today. They brought English organisation to our game and a new way of playing. Instead of standing off and counter-attacking they pressed when the opposition had the ball. They introduced all the things I'd seen as a kid every Saturday when I watched English football on television. There was conflict in Sweden before that style was accepted, but after a few years even the most conservative Swedish trainers changed over to the new, English approach. Nowadays, Swedish trainers are brought up on the methods and style of play that Roy and Bob brought over. 'Svennis' [as Eriksson is known to friends and family] made minor changes to suit Swedish players better, and when those changes took full effect, he won the UEFA Cup with Gothenburg.

'When we were at Benfica, they weren't a really rich club, but they had enough money to sign good players, and they also had their famous name to trade on. It was quite something to pull on the shirt of Benfica, with all their history. I think we had a squad of 24, and every one of them was an international of some sort. You expected to win things with players like that around you. Svennis was good at bringing the best out of everyone and finding their best roles. He's very clever at moulding players so that they fit together to form the best possible team. Stefan Schwarz [another Swede] was a good example. He got the best out of him, to the benefit of the team, at left-back, left-wing and centre midfield.'

Thern admitted that he was basing his own managerial style on Eriksson's. 'I learned a lot from Svennis, sometimes without knowing it at the time. The way to treat people, for one thing. Whatever the circumstances, whether they criticise or support him, he always tries to treat everyone the same. Also, he has an aura of calmness around him that he brings to his teams. He is a person you like to listen to because when he says something it is always interesting, always constructive and beneficial. As a player, he makes you feel confident. If you are worried about your form, and you go to him for advice, he'll always be reassuring. He'll say: "No problem. Everybody has their ups and downs, trainers as well as players. Just keep on working on what you are good at. I know that when you are in good shape, you're one of the best." After you'd been talking to him, you felt: "He thinks I'm one of the best players in Europe and he's a top trainer, so he can't be wrong." In a couple of minutes he'd have restored your self-confidence. He's very good at building that up, for his players and his teams.'

In common with every other player who has spoken on the subject, Thern had never seen Eriksson lose that famous self-control. 'I never heard him even raise his voice in the three years I played for him at Benfica. But as soon as he came into the dressing room at half-time, you knew if he was not satisfied. It was a case of: "Oh oh, best to be quiet here and just listen." He wouldn't shout. He just stared at you and immediately you knew you had to play much better in the second half, otherwise you'd be off and dropped from the team. He didn't have to say anything. That look of his said it all.'

Thern explained: 'Sometimes we'd start a game and wouldn't be playing well and the opposition would be in command. He'd spot it from the bench and change things very quickly. He'd swap players around or change formation, from four in midfield to five. He was particularly good at knowing what the opposition's strengths and weaknesses were. I remember when we were playing Porto once he said: "They're a bit lacking here, on the left", so we knew exactly where to concentrate our attacks. It sounds obvious and easy, but you'd be surprised how many trainers don't brief their teams like that. I had a lot of big-name trainers after Svennis. Some of them were good coaches during games, some of them good only at giving instruction during the week. Sven is spot on at both. Overall, he's the best I've played for.'

There had been no favouritism shown towards, and certainly no socialising with, the Swedish triumvirate (Thern, Schwarz and leading scorer Mats Magnusson) at Benfica. Thern had heard that Eriksson had been closer to his players at Gothenburg, but said: 'I think the relationship has to be different in the professional world. For example, sometimes the Swedish players at Benfica would ask for an extra day when we went home for Christmas.

He'd say: "I know you'll behave if you have another day away from the club, but I can't be seen to be favouring you because you are Swedish." He always made a point of treating all his players equally.

'Yes, he kept his distance, and I think that's very important for a trainer in the professional game. You have to have a good relationship with your players, but you mustn't get too close. Everybody has to know who's boss.'

Peter Taylor was England's caretaker before Eriksson took charge, and continued as part of the new coaching set-up until his work at Leicester City precluded further involvement. He says: 'All of a sudden, I got the opportunity to be caretaker manager for a non-qualifying game, and decided that I had enough good, young players who could do well. I'm not sure Italy tried that hard against us, but we did do well. Sven looked at that game and saw decent performances without players like Campbell, Scholes, Owen and Gerrard, and thought: "We're not bad at all." We had a new, foreign manager, fresh to the players, who were starting to feel more together. We played *Who Wants To Be A Millionaire?* in Italy, and everybody seemed to want to join in. For Sven's first game, against Spain, we had a golf competition at the hotel, and again everybody wanted to do it. The team spirit started to look very good. Players changed from being low on confidence to being on a high, and they're good enough to take some stopping when they're like that.'

Of Eriksson's personality, Taylor added: 'They [the players] love his calmness. They like the fact that he lets people get on with their work. They like his sense of humour. They know he's got a fantastic background. With a CV like his, he'd cracked it before he walked through the door. And they enjoy listening to him talk. It's not complicated stuff, it just makes loads of sense to the players. The last time I was fully involved was Greece away [6 June 2001] and I've never seen such a confident group. We could have beaten anybody.'

Ruud Gullit played for Eriksson for two season at Sampdoria, and holds the man, and his methods, in the highest esteem. In an interview for this book, the 1987 World Footballer of the Year told me: 'Milan wouldn't play me regularly, they said I had knees of glass, so I went to Sampdoria in 1993 and played nearly every game. We came third in Serie A and won the Italian Cup. Nobody thought we had it in us, but the key was how Eriksson handled everything. I was really charmed by him. He's a real gentleman. If you didn't do what he wanted, or just did your own thing, his character meant that it would only affect you. He was so nice, such a good man in the way he treated people that it seemed rude, as well as silly, not to do what he asked. Because of the regard we all had for him, he never had to raise his voice to anyone. He would talk to you, one-on-one, in a very civilised way. He was genuinely interested in you, personally – not just what you were doing on the pitch.'

Juan-Sebastian Veron was first brought to Europe by Eriksson, who signed him for Sampdoria from Boca Juniors of Argentina. Veron, who won

Serie A with Eriksson at Lazio, said the Swede was a more straightforward personality than Sir Alex Ferguson. 'Eriksson is the same person inside the dressing room as outside. Ferguson will challenge the team with strong words, which is not Eriksson's way. For me, the best coach is the one who is best at building a relationship with his players, so that they feel at ease, feel supported. When, sitting on the bench, there is more than just a coach but a friend too, you perform to the best of your ability. There aren't many like that, but it is the mark of Eriksson.'

John Barnwell, of the League Managers' Association, and Gordon Taylor, of the Professional Footballers' Association, had both objected strongly to England's appointment of a foreigner. Barnwell described it an 'an insult' to his members, and Taylor accused the Football Association of 'betraying their heritage'. Within a year, they were completely won over. Barnwell now says: 'His [Eriksson's] achievements have been quite stunning. He has created an atmosphere of trust with the managers of the top league clubs and he has used common-sense to handle fragile relationships. As a result, not one manager in the country would say anything detrimental about his approach or his attitude. There's a confidence and an understanding and a great optimism for the future.'

Taylor said: 'One thing he has brought with him is an aura of stillness, which is particularly useful in moments of crisis. He deals sensibly with problems and instils confidence in the players. His philosophy is that you're never as bad as they say, and probably never as good either. You just need to know what you're aiming for. He's got a good understanding of footballers, and he treats them with respect. There's an element of Alf Ramsey in him, and that kind of loyalty to players can make the difference when it comes to the crunch. In those respects, he has been a very good influence.'

David Beckham, the England captain, says: 'Mr Eriksson has a lot of experience, and the players realize that. He trusts all of us to do our job, and every one of the players has got massive respect for him. That's a vital thing for any manager.'

Glenn Hysen, a championship winner with Liverpool, played for Eriksson at Gothenburg and Fiorentina. He says: 'When we first saw him, at Gothenburg, he seemed such a small guy that we didn't think much of him. But when you've listened to what he has to say, you have to respect him. And you really do listen to him. He goes around the players, talks to them, jokes with them. He always used to get changed in the players' dressing room. I don't know if he still does that [he does]. He's such a smart person. He knows a little about everything, not just football. I don't think you could find anyone to say anything against him.

'As a coach, he's not a magician. His coaching is nothing unusual: blackboard, paper, charts, diagrams of free-kicks for and against. But he's good at seeing what's going wrong during a match.

Eriksson had the 'karma' of a latter-day Gandhi. 'He always keeps a level head, especially in a crisis,' Hysen added. 'And he knows that even when he's happy, and things are going well, it can all be different the next day. That knowledge helps to keep him calm at all times.'

Eriksson was Glenn Stromberg's mentor with Gothenburg, in the Swedish Under-21 team and at Benfica. Stromberg says: 'He was always very calm – and for the full 90 minutes. Many managers will panic after 80 minutes if things aren't going their way. Not Sven. He knows it is as easy for his team to score at the end as it is at the beginning. He is a very hard-headed man, he goes his own way and whatever he thinks is right, he will do it to the very end. He never panics, and players like that. I think England benefited from that when they played Greece in the last of their World Cup qualifiers. When I played for him, there were many games like that, when we got important goals very late, or held out when it seemed impossible. At Gothenburg, and again at Benfica, the players came to think of him as a lucky manager, and themselves as a lucky team.'

At Benfica, Stromberg says, Eriksson was the voice of reason in the dressing room, rather than Mr Big. 'He didn't behave like some sort of genius who wanted everybody to know how many things he'd won. Some coaches are like that, but he certainly wasn't. Each week, he just told the team how he wanted them to play. By personal example, he was good at creating the kind of hushed, thoughtful atmosphere you need in the dressing room before important games. When Sven left Benfica in 1983, I left as well. I knew it wouldn't be as good there without him. He is the best coach I ever had, in a long career.

'I've seen so many coaches who have thought one thing at the beginning of the season, then panicked and changed when results didn't immediately go their way. They change players, change tactics, change their style of play, and how often does it pay off? Sven is always calm, and always sticks to his method. His strength of character is his biggest attribute.'

Stefan Schwarz, the Swedish international midfielder, won the Portuguese league and cup, and was a European Cup Finalist during Eriksson's second spell at Benfica. Schwarz told me: 'He's also a very good psychologist, clever at getting into his players' minds. At Benfica in those days he had Brazilians and Russians, as well as Portuguese and Swedes to deal with, and because his ability overall was so impressive, he commanded the respect of them all. He never raises his voice, and I think that's because he doesn't need to. You can see when he's upset from the look on his face, and if you don't respond the way he wants you to, you'll be the one who suffers.'

England's goalkeeper, David James, is also a fan, his comments clearly including a thinly veiled criticism of Eriksson's predecessor, Kevin Keegan, whose relentless mateyness could be wearing. He said: 'Mr Eriksson is one of the quieter managers I have worked with, but he is no less effective for that. You don't necessarily want the boss plonking himself next to you every time you sit down for a bowl of soup. As a tactician, I would say that he puts the team together like a jigsaw. Different players are treated as individual pieces as he pulls them aside for a quiet chat, telling Michael Owen, for example, to run from deep. That conversation will be in isolation, but when the team comes together, all the pieces drop into place. The training is certainly more serious than under the last regime, with most of the work related to real match scenarios. Mr Eriksson, though, is very careful not to make it obvious from day one who is in his starting eleven, in case the other players switch off.'

The man himself borders on the esoteric when discussing his man-management catechism. 'The ability to make the right decision, and then dare to do the right things in all situations, is decisive at the top of the modern game,' he says. 'If one player isn't up for it mentally, the whole team can collapse. When we have to give a performance – a competition, a match, some task at work – there are two forces inside us, pulling in different directions. One is ambition, and this is a positive force. Our ambition wants us to improve, to succeed, to attain the goals we have set ourselves. The other force is performance anxiety. This is a negative force. It produces a fear of failing, of making mistakes, of disgracing ourselves and, as a result, of not being accepted by others. These "others" might be our trainer, our teammates, the media, the supporters and, in everyday life, friends, neighbours and workmates.'

Eriksson works on accentuating the positive and

eliminating this fear of failure, in the belief that mental strength is ultimately decisive. He reasons: 'If you look at the top footballers, playing ability among many of them is very even. We can't train more than we do, we're already at the maximum that players can take nowadays, so it is mental differences which will decide who the real winners are.'

From day one at Lazio, and again with England, he had set out to break down the mental barriers that prevented players from going beyond the limit of what they believed was possible. 'We often find it difficult, both intellectually and emotionally, to accept a sufficiently high level for our performance,' he says. 'We dare not pass our upper limit and reach our maximum. We have an inner mental barrier that stops us from succeeding, and have to break through the barriers we mentally erect that prevent us from using all our resources. For a long time, it was considered impossible to run a mile under four minutes, but then Roger Bannister did so, and it was not long before a number of other runners managed it. Bannister showed that it was permitted to run that quickly. Any breaking through such barriers has to be done first in the mind. The mind must prepare the way for the body.'

He invited the England players to try a mental exercise. They were to think about the phrases 'I must', 'I should', and 'I've got to'. Then think of 'I want to', 'I'll have a go', and 'I can'. He explained: 'It is fairly natural that we will not perform as well if we are forced to do something, rather than being free to do the same thing. It is also true that many sportsmen feel an unexpressed compulsion from their environment to reach certain goals. A typical example of the wrong type of thinking is the thought: "I mustn't miss." Close your eyes, relax and imagine you are in a match that is coming up. You see yourself on the pitch and you think: "Must, should, got to". How do you feel? Don't you feel that your personality withers and your mood sinks? After a moment or two, repeat the exercise, but think instead: "I want to", "I'll have a go", "I can". You immediately feel better, you're practically raring to go.'

On less esoteric lines, Eriksson articulates his managerial style as follows: 'First of all, the leader must be a complete master of what he is going to teach others, and he must also dare to be himself. Don't try to be somebody else, or you will be found out very quickly. I would feel extremely stupid if I were to stand at the bench screaming and whistling at the players and the referee.

'There must always be a target, or goal, and clear lines: "This is the way I want you to play football." As a leader, you must be clear in what you say and explain everything to the group so that they really understand what you have in mind. When you have come that far, only one thing remains, and that may well be the most difficult one: having everybody in the team accept it. The important thing is having everyone understand that this is an agreement. Everybody must be moving in the same direction.

'You have to be generous with praise, but in sport

the big reward is the event itself. That's where sport is simple and straightforward – win or lose, reward or punishment. You must set your goals high, but they must be realistic ones. You cannot go around promising titles if the material at your disposal is not good enough to do it. There is also the matter of fingertip feeling and intuition, which I think all good bosses have. When, as a coach, you have a team which is a goal or two down at half-time, you have to do something about it. Often it comes down to changing one or two players. It is a decision which seldom has a logical basis, but something has to be done. It does not always change the outcome of a game, but if it works, you will be called a genius.'

So is he a genius? He smiled at the suggestion. 'A bit of modesty does not hurt. During the success of the past few years, more than once I have had to pinch myself. Then I say: "Hey there, Sven, you were born in Torsby." By remembering your origins you get the proportions right in life.'

CHAPTER SIX

AN ENFIELD TOWN FULL-BACK

Sven-Goran Eriksson spends nearly every Christmas at the parental home in Torsby, and if you saw the place you wouldn't blame him. To visit this sleepy, snowy Swedish village in winter is to be put in mind of Bing Crosby's *White Christmas* idyll, and to wonder how anybody could ever leave.

Sven-Goran was born on 5 February 1948, while the rest of the world was preoccupied with Gandhi's assassination and the gathering crisis in Berlin. He was the first child for Sven senior, a 19-year-old bus conductor, and Ulla, who supplemented the family income with a variety of jobs, which took her behind the counter at the village newsagent and later to the local hospital, as an auxiliary.

Torsby these days is 'New England' in more ways than one, a postcard-pretty collection of clapboard houses surrounded by frozen forest and lakes. Originally a centre for iron production, drawing on power from the Klaralven, or Clear river, there is no industry to speak of now. There is a high-tech, state-of-the-art sawmill, owned by the Finns, and a small electronics plant, but the main employer is the hospital. With a population of 5,000, the village is the municipality for the northern part of the mostly wooded picturesque province of Varmland, which measures some 200 km in length. The region prospers on two tourist seasons, catering for all the usual winter sports and summer activities like canoeing and rafting. Lake Vanern, the largest in Scandinavia, is a magnet for anglers, while for wildlife enthusiasts there are elk and wolves in abundance. The wolf is Varmland's official emblem.

It is against this bucolic background that young Sven, or 'Svennis' as he was quickly to become known, was raised. He grew up in a small, working-class home – so small that a lounge-diner-kitchenette was the main living room. A neighbour recalled: 'They weren't poor, but they had hard times. There were not many luxuries.' It was a close family, in every sense, and the England coach still talks to his parents on the telephone every day.

Ski jumping, with a club called SK Bore, was his passion more than football when he was very young. He told me: 'I learned from the age of five, and became quite good at it. With the club, I travelled all over Varmland, and into Norway, for competitions. It is a sport you have to start when you are very young, and have no fear. You'd never dare to have a go when you were older. The trouble was, when I was little they didn't have skis for kids, we had to use adult ones. To get mine to the top of the slope, ready to push off, I had to carry them up one at a time. They were very heavy for a little boy, much too heavy to take two.' In common with all the other children making their first jump, the diminutive Svennis started at 15 ft, before eventually working his way up to 65. 'I loved it,' he says, 'but by the age of 15 I had to choose between ski jumping and football, and football won.'

The extremes in Swedish society made him a young socialist of the old school. 'When I was young, I was far out on the left politically. I thought everything was unfair then. I was never politically active, but I was radical in my opinion.' A friend from his teenage days said: 'One of his dreams, when he was 19 or 20, was to move to South America, buy a plantation there and be nice to the workers, paying them well. He wanted to be a philanthropist.'

Charity had its limits, however. Sven's brother Lars, eight years his junior, recalls how Sven always had to beat him at everything, irrespective of the age difference. 'He was very competitive, even when I was little.'

Eriksson is a typical product of his environment, according to Mats Olsson, of the Torsby Tourist Bureau, who has worked with him in promoting the area. Olsson told me: 'If you meet his parents, you will see where he got his calmness and laid-back character from. He's a typical guy from around here. We have a saying that goes: "Let ordnar sig alltid, och om det inte gor det, sa kvittar det." Roughly translated, it means: "Everything will fix itself, and if it doesn't it won't be so bad."' Eriksson knows the adage well, but while he accepts the translation, he prefers his own interpretation. 'I like to think it means: "Don't worry about things you have no control over," which is a good way to live your life.' He accepts that the pace of life is very different in Varmland, which is backwoods in more ways than one. 'Their attitude is: "Never do today what can be put off until tomorrow." It must be nice to be able to live that way, stress-free.'

Discussing old times with Eriksson's parents is no longer easy. My predecessor at *The Sunday Times*, Brian Glanville, tells a story about two groups of journalists, tabloid and broadsheet, journeying together through the desert. Stumbling upon an oasis, the broadsheet boys fall to their knees to drink, only to spot the tabloid hacks relieving themselves upstream. The waters around Torsby have been well and truly poisoned by the redtops, whose foot-in-the-door intrusions in search of dirt at the time of Eriksson's appointment have left the locals wary, and sometimes downright hostile, to English visitors. His friends are very, very protective, and in the case of Sven and Ulla Eriksson, reporters from their son's adopted country are no longer welcome. 'They have had a bad rap from your people, who came pestering them, knocking on their door uninvited and misquoting them to make their stories more dramatic,' Olsson explained. 'The English reporters made them almost reclusive.'

Sven-Goran told me: 'If you go to see them now, they will welcome you, and give you coffee, but they won't tell you much I'm afraid. They learned to be like that the hard way. It started as soon as the FA offered me the job. In the next few days they [the tabloid press] interviewed my mother, my brother in Portugal, my son in America, my ex-wife, who I hadn't seen for six years, my ex-mother-in-law and my old maths teacher in Torsby. I want to be friendly, but I must try to defend my privacy and my family, especially when lies are written.'

Understandable this may be, but it is also a great pity, not least because the Erikssons have an interesting story to tell. In an interview conducted through a third party, Ulla said: 'His [Sven-Goran's] foundations are still very much in the Torsby values we have here. We care deeply about home, family, community, hard work and respect. I think he has carried those values with him all his life, and he takes them with him in his work. He tries to instil these values in his football teams. When he was young, it was always sport, sport and more sport. In the summer months we only ever saw him at mealtimes. He would go out in the morning and only return to the house to eat. Then he would be out again, always to the athletics track or football pitch. It was the same during the winter. Then it would be skiing, skating and hockey. He was best at ski jumping. He was never afraid of how dangerous it might be. Sometimes he would fall, but he was never seriously injured.

'Sport always came first in his life, but he was good at school as well. He loved to read books – anything from children's adventure stories to Hemingway. I had to join a book club just to keep up with his hunger for reading. His school grades were good, but he always did best at sport. With most children, if you throw a ball to them, they will try to catch it and throw it back to you. Sven didn't. He always wanted to kick it. If there was no ball, he would make do with anything, usually stones in the street. I remember dressing him up in his best clothes and a new pair of shoes for a day out, and while he was waiting he went outside and had a kick around. His shoes were almost ruined. When I told him off, he said: "You won't be saying that when I'm a football star."'

Sven senior says of his pride and joy: 'Even when he was young, he had the sort of mind which wanted to analyse everything he did. He kept a notebook to record all his performances and chart his progress at every sport. He was a well-behaved boy. He kept himself too busy to get into any trouble. But we never pushed him into anything. We just wanted him to grow up a good person and to fulfil himself.'

Sven remembers watching English football on television every Saturday. 'From when I was about 14, I sat down with my father every Saturday afternoon and didn't move. It was the highlight of the week. When I was younger, I supported Liverpool.' And now? 'Today I support England, no club team.'

A visit to the young Svennis's secondary school, Frykenskolan, found his old maths teacher, Mats Jonsson, happy to reminisce about his most celebrated former pupil, who lived just across the road, 50 metres from the schoolhouse. Jonsson, 65 but still teaching part-time, also coached Torsby when Eriksson started playing, and told me: 'I had him in my maths class from 13 to 16. He was a clever boy. Very quiet and calm. He did everything I hoped he would do. He was always a pleasant pupil. I had a class of just over 30, and he was always in the upper half at maths.

'He played football every day, it was always his passion. I was the coach at Torsby FC at the time, and when he was 16 he came to play there. He was in the first team at 17, but while he was always regarded as a good footballer at school, at club level he was never more than second rate. He wasn't top class, never a remarkable player. But in football, as at school, he worked very hard and made the best of himself. At that time, we played with two markers and three players just in front of them, and he played on the right of those three. Today, you would probably call it right wing-back. It was a role for which he had to be very fit. It was a hard job – I know, I've tried it myself – always up and back, up and back. Sven was always a hard worker, so it suited him. When he went on to play for better teams, it was as an out-and-out defender. Eventually, he was right-back in a 4–4–2 formation.

'We had a good team when he was here. We were in the Third Division for three years, then we got relegated. I have to say we had better players in that Torsby team, but he was always a very nice person to work with. When I told him to do something, he did it. You could always rely on him. As a coach, you have to say to a player: "You do that, and don't worry about anything else." If I taught him anything, it was that. The team worked in zones.

We divided the pitch into zones, and in your zone, you were the boss. You might be needed to help out elsewhere, but first and foremost you had to be in control of your own area. It's the same today, and I like to think I gave Svennis a little bit of grounding there.' Eriksson smiled at the notion. 'Mats was a nice man, but he knew nothing about football,' he told me. 'When he was in charge, we did a lot of running. That's all I remember.'

Academically, the young Eriksson was a diligent, above-average rather than brilliant scholar. The school records are kept on file at the municipal offices in Torsby where, obliging to a startling degree for a Brit accustomed to bureaucratic bloody-mindedness, they searched the vaults and came up with Svennis's exam papers. In his last year at Frykenskolan, aged 16, he gained very respectable grades in all subjects, doing best in maths, where he was marked AB. In Swedish language, an essay entitled 'A Summer Place' brought him a BA, and he gained the same grade in English, where a paper notable for its meticulous, painstaking writing included the translation of such portentous phrases as 'He looked at me with pain-filled eyes,' and 'They're going to X-ray him soon.' The marker's corrective red ink was in evidence only once, where Eriksson had written: 'I finely [sic] knew my husband would bee [sic] alive.' It will do his reputation with England fans no harm at all that his worst subject was German, where he got a straight B, one delicious howler seeing his word 'Chou' [sic,] corrected to 'Auf Wiedersehen'.

'My English wasn't up to much, but I was good at writing when I was at school,' Eriksson says. 'I wrote a lot about Ernest Hemingway and his life. He was my favourite author. I also read a lot about the Greek philosophers. For a time, I wanted to be a writer – a sports reporter – and I thought about going to a sports journalism college.'

At Torsby FC – the ground is called 'Bjornevi', or 'Bear Meadow' – there is Eriksson memorabilia everywhere. There are bigger, better stadia to be found in non-league football in England, but the importance of this one to the local community extends way beyond its raison d'etre, and on my various visits there were Mothers' Union meetings, IT for Beginners classes, and sundry similar extra-curricular activities making use of the clubhouse facilities. On entering, the first thing you notice, immediately to the left, is an impressive trophy cabinet with more than 50 exhibits, central to which is a framed portrait of Eriksson in England garb. Closer examination reveals an autographed picture of the England squad, next to the Junior Football Shield 1999 and the Svennis Cup for Boys and Girls (10–13 age group). There are pennants from every club Eriksson has managed, a framed picture of Sampdoria, 1992/93 vintage (Des Walker to the fore) and, tucked away above a waste bin bearing the legend 'Knickers', Torsby team groups from 1966 and 1967, featuring a youthful Svennis, complete with luxuriant blond thatch.

When I called, nobody at the club spoke English, but the two old stalwarts present could not have been more helpful. By sign language, a man who appeared to be the caretaker indicated that I should follow him, and took me on a five-minute drive to meet one of Eriksson's former teammates and best friends, Morgan Oldenmark (formerly known as Karlsson) who, together with his brother, runs the family printing business. Morgan (he changed to his wife's surname because Karlsson is so common in Sweden), played in the same Torsby team as Eriksson before the latter left in 1971. Oldenmark, né Karlsson, was a striker, Eriksson played right-back. 'Sven did nothing special, he just did his job,' his friend recalled. 'He was a good player for a coach to have. He did what he was told. He never lost his composure, or his temper, never shouted. He was a fine person. He was quiet, but he did have a sense of humour. He liked to laugh, and when we all went out together he'd enjoy himself and behave just like everyone else. He wasn't always, how do you English say it? A goody-goody.

'When a few of us went to Austria, skiing, we shared a room and he enjoyed himself all right. He was quite a good ski jumper, and when we were alpine skiing he'd never make any of the turns I made to slow down. He was fearless, never afraid of the speed of the downhill. Another time, when he was playing for Sifhalla, Torsby went on a trip to Gran Canaria – no more than a holiday, really – and Sven came with us.' To emphasize Eriksson's sociability, Morgan produced snaps of the players on sun loungers by the swimming pool, the England manager-to-be clearly having a laddish good time.

'Sven has always been a bit reserved, but when he knows the company he does like a laugh.'

The man himself tells a slightly different story. 'Being in the limelight has never appealed to me. At Christmas [2001] I was invited to a concert, and a dinner for 70 afterwards. I arrived at the concert after it had started, and then said "no" to the dinner. I don't like the celebrity thing. If I go to a party, I prefer to sneak in and stand in the corner. I don't want to appear to be better than anyone else because I don't consider myself special. My parents were ordinary working-class people, and that has definitely influenced me.'

Torsby Football Club have had their days in the sun, too, and were in the top division in Sweden as recently as 1997. In Eriksson's time, however, they were never better than Division Three. His first 'trophy', in the year England were winning the World Cup, was a tin of coffee presented to each of the Torsby players promoted to that level. Oldenmark spoke nostalgically of the era when 3,000 would turn out for the local derby against Rannberg. 'Nowadays, it's 150.'

When the teacher, Mats Jonsson, stopped coaching the club, the local baker, Sven-Ake Olsson, known as 'Asen', took over, using flour on a baking tray, in place of the conventional blackboard, to school Eriksson and company in tactics. His old protegé remembers him well – and not just for football. 'I used to work in Asen's bakery to make some money,' Eriksson says. 'He was good at his job – and he knew his football, too.'

Now in his mid-seventies, Olsson remembers his doughboy-cum-right-back for his activities off the field, rather than anything he did on it. 'Sven never drank much, unlike the others, but he had plenty of female attention.' Eriksson's first serious relationship was with Nina Thornholm, a beauty pageant contestant he met on his 18th birthday. After dancing the foxtrot at the local hop, he escorted her home. 'Nothing more.' They dated for nearly a year ('he was always well-mannered, very proper', Nina, who is now in her fifties, insisted), eventually moving into a flat together. Earning next to nothing from what was virtually amateur football, Eriksson supported them by working in the social security office, dealing with sickness benefits, where his colleagues included Mats Jonsson's wife. It was not the life he wanted, however, and the relationship foundered on his sporting ambitions.

At 19 he did his National Service, spending 12 months in the Swedish Army. It was not a regime he enjoyed. 'It was compulsory, so I had to do it, but it was not my sort of life,' he told me. 'You knew when you woke up in the morning what you'd be doing every minute of the day until you went to bed at night, and that's extremely boring. I'm not one who likes having everything regimented and programmed for him like that.'

It was with great relief that on demob he resumed his studies at Gymnasium Amal, a college 160 km from Torsby, and then at Orebro, where he took a university course in sports science. It was at teacher-training college, at Amal, that he met

Ann-Christin Pettersson ['Anki' to her friends], the daughter of the principal. They started dating in 1970 and married on 9 July 1977. Intellectually well-matched, and both keen to better themselves, they seemed ideally suited. Their first child, Johan, was born on 27 May 1979.

Ann-Christin says: 'His determination to achieve what he wanted in life was the first thing that appealed to me, so you could say football brought us together. He never gives in. He knows what he wants and goes for it. I should know. I was his wife for 23 years.'

While studying at Orebro, Eriksson joined Karlskoga, where Tord Grip was player-coach. It was a bigger club, with a modern stadium, but it would be wrong to draw the conclusion that Eriksson's playing career was taking off. Sten Johansson, a midfielder, played in the same Karlskoga team and told me: 'In those days, we were always mid-table in the Second Division. Sven was not much of a player, and never our first choice right-back. He came here, from Sifhalla, when he was studying at Orebro. It was his choice to come – the club didn't go out to sign him, or anything like that. He asked to join because we were nearer to his studies. The club paid him almost nothing. I remember him as a good team man, nice to have around. He left when Tord took him to Degerfors, as assistant coach. That was the end of his playing career.'

He was not greatly missed. Bryan King, the former Millwall goalkeeper, has been living and working in Scandinavia since the 1970s as coach, manager, scout and players' agent. He has known Eriksson since his playing days, and remembers him as ordinary, at best. 'In English terms, I'd say he was an Enfield Town sort of full-back.' The man himself feigns offence at that. 'I wasn't much of a player, but as far as I know, Bryan King never saw me play.'

Before he quit, Eriksson learned a valuable lesson. Playing for Karlskoga in a 3–0 defeat against Helsingborg in 1975 taught him, the hard way, to what extent full-backs were dependent upon protection. In his customary right-back station, he was given a never-to-be-forgotten run around by a fast winger by the name of Tom Johansson. 'It was like a circus,' Eriksson admitted. 'It didn't matter what I tried, he just disappeared away from me. I said: "Damn, I need support," but at that time full-backs were not given support. They were good times for attackers, because there was so much space behind us. That game at Helsingborg changed my mind about defensive tactics, and made me think about pressing the opposition.'

Johansson, now a plumber in Helsingborg, said: 'I don't remember much about the game, but I do know that I was faster than him, and got past him three or four times.' Another Helsingborg player that day, Thomas Sternberg, is now the club's director of sport. He said: 'Sven wasn't a player you would notice. He did nothing to stand out. He wasn't playing at the top level, so nobody had heard of Sven-Goran Eriksson at that time. In that game, Tom went past him a few times.

'I'd say there is no great connection between

being a good footballer and a good manager. Often it is just the opposite, and the players who are medium-grade have more to offer as coaches. Sven was not a great player, but he is a fantastic coach. The strong mentality all his teams have is unbeliev- able. We are very proud of him. He has been away a long time, and we are waiting for him to come home. I hope it will be as Sweden's manager.'

CHAPTER SEVEN

ON BOARD WITH TORD

'Tord Grip is my eyes, and one of the best coaches in the world. Nobody has the feeling for football in his blood like he has.'

SVEN-GORAN ERIKSSON.

Tord Grip is Eriksson's assistant and long-time confidante. They have a relationship that dates back over 30 years, during which time their roles have reversed. When they first worked together, in 1970, Grip was the manager and Eriksson the worst player in his run-of-the-mill team of Swedish part-timers. Later, Grip ran Sweden's Under-21s, with Eriksson his assistant.

Tord Grip was born in 1938, one of four children fathered by a woodcutter in the tiny village of Ytterhogdal. There was no professional football in Sweden when he left school, so he went to work in the local bakery. By the time he was 18, his father had branched out into haulage, graduating from a horse to a tractor to a truck, and he invited young Tord to join the business but the offer was rejected. 'It was heavy work, and I wasn't built for that,' Grip says. 'The bakery was perfect. I started work at six in the morning and finished at two, so I had plenty of time for football.' All the training paid off. At 18 he moved from the village team to Degerfors, in the top division of the Swedish league. 'For the first year there I carried on in the bakery, after that I went to work in a steel mill. There was no money for playing football, not even proper expenses. My father would drive me 450 km from where we lived to Degerfors, for which the club gave him £5.' Grip, unlike Eriksson, was a top player, an old-fashioned inside-right who was to play for more than a decade in the Swedish Premier League, and win three international caps. He played for Degerfors from 1953 until 1966, during which time he had trials with Aston Villa, then under the management of Joe Mercer. 'I came over and played three games for the reserves, but nothing came of it,' he told me. Instead, he transferred to AIK Stockholm for a couple of seasons before becoming player-manager of Karlskoga, then in Division Two. He takes up the story of his fateful conjunction with Eriksson as follows:

'We were promoted to the First Division, and then one afternoon in 1970/71 Sven came and asked me if he could train with us. He was studying to be a PE teacher at Orebro, just as I had done. He wasn't specializing in football, as some have said. He wanted to be a PE teacher. We had a good team at that time, very close to getting in the Premier League, and I thought he'd struggle to get a game, but eventually he did get in the side. His technique wasn't very good, but he worked at it on his own. He was the right full-back, playing immediately behind me, so he had to learn to defend, because I couldn't. He always reminds me: "You told us that when we lost possession everyone should drop back and defend. Everyone except you, that is. You never did it."

'I was five years at Karlskoga. In 1974/75 I quit playing and became manager of Orebro, in the Premier League. Sven stayed and played on for Karlskoga, but then he got badly injured and didn't play for a year. From Orebro I went back to Degerfors. I went back to work in the steel factory there, in their rehabilitation department, and also to manage my old club, who were now in the Second Division. I knew about Sven's ambition, so I asked him to join me. He would have been 28.'

The manager immediately had the awkward task of telling his new recruit that he had no future as a player, and that he should concentrate on coaching. 'Tord telling me that I would be better off if I stopped playing was not very nice,' Eriksson says. 'For a long time I regretted not fulfilling my ambition to play in Italy, but I'm over that now.'

Grip takes up the story: 'He became my assistant, and we worked together like that in 1975. Then I got an offer from the Swedish FA, to run the Under-16 team and be assistant to the Sweden manager, Georg Ericsson. We qualified for the 1978 World Cup, in Argentina. Anyway, in 1976 Sven took over at Degerfors. He was in charge for three years.' Two decades passed before master and pupil were to be reunited.

Degerfors, two hours' drive from Torsby, is a frost-bitten town of 10,000 inhabitants, with a local football club not unlike Charlton Athletic. Runners-up in the top division twice, most recently in 1963, they have led a yo-yo existence since, but have forged strong links with the community, and consequently enjoy more support than they might otherwise expect. The clubhouse is full of merchandise – fleeces, T-shirts, mugs, schnapps glasses, hats, scarves etc – but noticeably short on Eriksson memorabilia, although there is an England 2006 calendar in the corridor, a relic of the failed bid to stage the next World Cup.

Degerfors have punched above their weight in producing 23 players for the national team, all of whom have their pictures in a make-shift gallery in the equivalent of the Liverpool 'Boot Room', where the kit man, Karsten Kurkkio, holds court. Kurkkio, 56, has worked for the club for longer than he can remember, in a voluntary capacity before he was put in charge of the kit. His room, he says proudly, is used by the coaches when they draw up their training schedules over coffee. Dashing hither and thither, he points to the snapshots of distinguished former players on the walls, where Olof Mellberg, of Aston Villa, was the latest addition. Pride of place, however, went to the legendary Gunnar Nordahl, possibly Sweden's most famous player of all time. Born in 1921, Gunnar was one of five brothers, all of whom played at top level. A goalscoring phenomenon, the best of the brood began his career with Degerfors, before moving on to Norrkoping, whom he shot to four successive championships, with 93 goals in 92 appearances. Gunnar Nordahl won a gold medal for football at the London Olympics, in 1948, forming with Gunnar Gren and Nils Liedholm the celebrated Gre-No-Li trio. All three played professionally in Italy, where they made a huge impact, Nordahl joining Milan, and scoring a record 210 goals, collecting Serie A titles in 1951 and 1955. After a brief spell with Roma, he returned home to coach Norrkoping. He died in 1995. 'He was our best,' Kurkkio said, reverentially. 'Sven-Goran Eriksson was not a good player. Tord Grip, on the other hand . . . Now he was good. He ran and ran.'

Kurkkio remembered Eriksson best for the innovation which saw Degerfors use a sports psychologist for the first time. The engagement of Dr Willi Railo started a collaboration which endured for 25 years. The guided tour of his dark domain complete, the kit man passed me on to Degerfors's latest manager who, with ice on the pitch, had taken his charges inside for midweek training in a hall that doubles as a basketball arena. Dave Mosson is the sort of gnarled Scot you stumble across coaching in remote outposts all over the world. Going into 2002, he was in his third stint at Degerfors, having initially replaced Eriksson in 1979. Originally from Glasgow, he was apprenticed to Nottingham Forest, under Johnny Carey. By way of residential qualification, he played for the England youth team, but realizing early that he might not be good enough to make a decent career out of playing the game, he attended Loughborough College as a PE student, and made the move to Sweden after his fiancée's father, who was on the board at Karlstad FC, invited him over for a trial. 'I did quite well, and I've been here ever since.' He has coached five different clubs in the Swedish First Division.

Mosson first met Eriksson as a player. 'I played for Karlstad and Sven for Karlskoga, the neighbouring town, so we came up against one another quite a few times. He was a very ordinary right-back. You would never have noticed him in a game. He never kicked his winger or overlapped much. He just did his job as best he could. I don't think anybody in those days admired how he played football, but he was very passionate. The game has always been a passion for him.'

The expatriate Scot was later in charge of the coaching course which set Eriksson on the path to greater glory. Was the England coach-to-be a natural? 'Yes, I'd say he was. Some are, some aren't. He was not the dynamic sort. Some use a lot of vocals and gesticular [sic] action, and are generally dynamic in the way they work. He was never like that. He did things methodically, talking a lot. He was always a good communicator. When he talks now, of course, people are more inclined to listen.'

When Mosson took over from Eriksson at Deger-fors they had just missed out on promotion from the First Division. 'Under the Swedish system,' he explained, 'it wasn't enough to win your division, you also had to get through a play-off system to get up. Under Sven, they were in the play-offs twice, and were promoted once. I took them up straight away.' At this stage, it became apparent that Mosson was holding something back. There was an ambivalence behind the praise. When I mentioned this, there was a pregnant pause before he decided not to reveal all. 'I won't tell you what Sven was really like, because I don't think it would do anybody any good. Let's just say that he's very good at maintaining a front.' No amount of prompting and pressing would persuade him to elucidate. Steering a determined course away from the dangerous waters he had ventured into, he went on: 'Sven has learned to keep his cool, to stay inside his shell. Swedes do that. They are very polite and reserved. They don't like to be associated with any diversionary activity. He lived his life here no differently to anybody else. He was a family man fairly early, marrying a girl from Amal, which is between Karlstad and Gothenburg, and quickly having a couple of children [Johann and Lina]. When he came on to the coaching scene, there was never any scandal. He just got on with life.'

Mosson was the first of many to hint that Eriksson had always been something of a ladies' man. As a coach, Eriksson had always been an anglophile. 'Right from his early days, Sven was heavily influenced by the English style of play, zonal defence and 4–4–2,' Mosson said. 'When he did his final coaching course over here, he had to submit a written paper, which I read, and that's what he did it on – his adaptation of the English game.' Bobby Robson was something of a mentor in the late 1970s, Eriksson journeying to Portman Road to study the methods and pick the brains of the manager who was rivalling mighty Liverpool's pre-eminence in England with unfashionable Ipswich. Eriksson recalls: 'I went to Ipswich on a Friday and watched the team train. I asked Bobby Robson if I could put some questions to him after training, and we ended up sitting in his office for two or three hours, talking about football. Fantastic. He didn't know me, and I was no one. He asked if I was coming to see the game the next day, and if I had a ticket. I said I was going to buy one. "Well," he said, "do you want to sit on the bench with me?" Can you imagine? I was sitting next to him and the game was being shown live in Sweden. Beautiful. He is a very special man.'

Mosson's predecessor as manager at Degerfors, Kenneth Norolling, has also known Eriksson for many years, and says: 'Tord Grip and Svennis were the first coaches in Sweden to take ideas from England. That's where they got the 4–4–2 system and the flat back four. They took ideas from Bob Houghton [the Englishman who took Malmo to the 1979 European Cup Final] and Roy Hodgson, at Halmstad. There was a lot of discussion in Sweden around that time about how we should play, who we should follow. Tord was the first Swede to copy the English system, followed by Sven.'

Hodgson told me: 'From 1974 to 1980, of the six Swedish championships available, Bob won three and I won two. Then Bob and I left Sweden [to go to Bristol City together] and there was a period of Gothenburg domination until 1985, when Malmo took over. All credit to Tord and Sven who were the first to hitch on to our bandwagon. To be honest, there's nothing really new in the game. All of us, somewhere along the line, have looked at somebody who has done something and been successful and thought: "Yeah, that's me, that's what I want to do as well." For me and Bob it was Don Howe and Dave Sexton. With Sven, it was probably more Bob than me, because he was the first.

'Fair play to them, Tord and Sven had to fight a lot of battles because Bob and I weren't popular in Sweden in those days. Not only had we anglicized their game, but we had locked out the Swedish coaches when it came to winning things, and they didn't like it. We engendered great loyalty among our players, and it became a bit of a war between the Halmstad–Malmo faction and the rest of Sweden, including the football federation and the media. Tord and Sven aligned themselves with us, the group that was under fire, which can't have been easy. But then, when they did it our way and gained their own success, our methods became popular everywhere because it was no longer the English who were doing it. In 1979, though, there were only three clubs playing with a back four, zonally, and pressurizing: Bob's, mine and Sven's. All the others were still playing the German way, man for man.

'The national coach was a guy called Lars Arnesen, and he was one of the bastions of anti-British feeling. "This is not the right way to play," he said. "It stifles initiative and turns players into robots." All the old claptrap. But the national team had a strong contingent of Sven's Gothenburg players, and they went to Arnesen and told him: "We've had enough of this system of yours. The way Gothenburg play is the way we should, too."

'I got to know Sven and Tord in 1979 and 1980, and felt an affinity with them because they'd had the courage to go with us. Other Swedish coaches were distancing themselves from us, but Sven and Tord said: "No, this is good football, this is the way football should be played. It's how we're going to play." Tord took over the national Under-21 team, with Sven as his assistant, and they played the English way while the seniors were still sticking to their guns. I know they came under all sorts of pressure, but they stood up to the criticism, and I think the experience probably did Sven good. Taking on a fight like that prepared him for what happened later at Benfica, and in Italy.'

Grip told me: 'When Sven started to work for me at Degerfors, I was the one with the experience in coaching and management. I was ahead of him in that respect, so I suppose I helped him to learn how to organize a team. At that time, a lot of coaches in Sweden were learning new ways. It was a period when we were starting to update our methods. It was an exciting time – a time of constant improvement. We took a lot, including our playing style, from England. The physical requirements we had already. There is not much else to think about in Sweden during the winter! Our strength was always our strength. It was when the other countries caught up with our fitness levels that we had to improve our organization. In Sweden, we've never been great technically, so we had to organize our teams cleverly and work hard to compensate. We did that.'

After Grip had left, Eriksson took Degerfors to the Third Division championship in his first season in management. The play-off system, involving four regional winners, was known as the Kval. At the end of 1976, Degerfors lost all three games, and were not promoted. In 1977, they did marginally better when, having won the league again, they took only two points from three matches in the Kval. In 1978 they made it third time lucky, winning the Third Division, by five points from Karlskoga, and all three games in the play-offs to go up to Division Two (North).

Eriksson attributed the decisive improvement to the work of Willi Railo. He says: 'My team always played well in the Kval, but when it came to the play-off, we'd mess up. At my invitation, Willi came and worked with us for one whole day. He made a cassette for individual players to listen to so that they could practise mental training on their own. We even stopped the bus on the way to the match so that they could use their cassettes to prepare mentally. We won the play-off and went up.'

People were starting to take notice.

CHAPTER EIGHT

INTO THE BIG TIME

Gothenburg is where Swedish football began, and is the city that is most passionate about the game. The oldest club in existence today, Orgryte IS, formed there in 1887, as did the first governing body, in 1895. IFK Gothenburg, founder members of the league in 1904, have long been Sweden's most successful and best-supported club, having won more championships than any other. When Sven-Goran Eriksson, of little Degerfors, heard they wanted to speak to him in 1979, he assumed that if there was a job on offer it would be with the youth team. He was wrong. At 34, Svennis had arrived in the big time.

Sven Carlsson was the finance director on the Gothenburg board at the time of the appointment. How had they identified Eriksson in the obscurity of the lower divisions? 'It was well known that we were looking for a trainer, and Sven-Goran was recommended to us as one who was particularly good at youth development,' Carlsson told me. 'So the club president, Bertil Westblad, called him and he came to speak to us. We liked him straight away, and he agreed to take the job.'

It could have been one of the shortest appointments on record. After losing each of his first three games in charge, Eriksson called a team meeting and told the players, who had scorned the arrival of this 'nobody' from the backwoods, that if they wanted him out, he would go. It was a winning gamble, a turning point. He had confronted them and they admired him for it. So what if he was not the big name they had expected? They liked his style. One of the club's best players was Glenn Hysen, the cultured central defender who was to win 70 international caps in a distinguished career which took him to PSV Eindhoven, Fiorentina (with Eriksson again) and Liverpool. Now retired, and back in Gothenburg, where he works as a commentator with Swedish television, Hysen says: 'When Sven was appointed, he was a complete nobody. He walked into the dressing room, and all the players thought: "Who are you?" Here was this really shy man, who had been the manager of a little team called Degerfors, and now he was suddenly in charge of the biggest club in the country. We had never heard of him, as a player or as a coach, and it took us a while to get used to him and respect him. We made a terrible start, losing our first three matches that season, which was almost unheard of at Gothenburg.

'In the third game we lost to a side newly promoted, and afterwards Sven asked the whole team if we wanted him to quit. He said he would walk away if we wanted him to. We all agreed that it was too early for him to resign, and decided we would give it time to see how things worked out. The rest is history. Sven won the UEFA Cup with Gothenburg, who became the first Swedish club ever to win a European trophy.

'Now I hear he's incredibly popular in England, but if that Gothenburg side had told him to go, his career might never have recovered. I don't think he would have ended up working in a Volvo factory, but nor do I think he would have gone on to become a top manager if he had walked out of his first big job after three games.'

In 1978, Gothenburg finished third in the league, a distant seven points behind the champions, Osters Vaxjo. In Eriksson's first season they were runners-up, just one point behind Halmstad, and they won the Swedish Cup, thrashing Atvidabergs 6–1 in the final. The championship had its most dramatic denouement for many years, boiling down to a last-day finish between Gothenburg and Halmstad, who were coached by Roy Hodgson. Halmstad were at home to relegation-bound AIK Stockholm, Gothenburg away to mid-table Hammarby. At half-time in the two games, when it was 0–0 in Halmstad and Gothenburg were leading (they won 3–2), it looked like Eriksson's title, but Hodgson's team scored twice in the second half to clinch it.

Hodgson remembers it well: 'I'd been at Halmstad since 1976. In 1979 we led the league from start to finish, but we were lucky when we played Gothenburg at home in the autumn. We were top but they were having a good spell, winning games while we were drawing, and therefore closing the gap. When we played them, we were very fortunate. We won because the referee disallowed them what was a perfectly good goal. Our defence had pushed out, one of their strikers stayed in, and when the ball came to him he looked 20 yards offside. But what the referee and linesman hadn't picked up was that it was a backpass from one of our defenders. That goal, had it stood, would have put them 1–0 up, and made it a very different game. Instead, we went on to win 2–1. We continued on our way, staying top but faltering a bit because we weren't winning every game and Gothenburg were, and we came to the last day with only one point in it. We were at home to AIK, who were a poor team, and all we had to do was get the same result as Gothenburg. But if we drew and they won, they'd take the title on goal difference. They had a difficult away game, against Hammarby, in Stockholm.

'We had a full house. The capacity at Halmstad was only 16,000, but fans were packed into our little stadium, waiting to celebrate a championship which we'd been on course for, really, from the first day. In 26 rounds of matches, we'd been top for 23. It was a big day for a small club – Halmstad had a population of barely 40,000 – and the players were nervous. We played very poorly in the first half, and should have been 2–0 down at half-time, but they missed a couple of gilt-edged chances, and we came in at 0–0. In the second half we scored a wonder goal after five minutes, and that settled the players down. We went on to win quite comfortably, 2–0, but I shall never forget that first half, when they could have put us away. Gothenburg had won as well, so we were champions by a single point.'

Runners-up and cup winners, it had hardly been a bad season for IFK, but not everybody was happy. Frank Sjoman, a respected journalist, wrote: 'Eriksson has been at variance with the ideals of the fans since, like most managers, he wants results before anything. Before long, he had introduced more tactical awareness, workrate and had tightened the old cavalier style. The result has been that while Gothenburg are harder to beat, they are also harder to watch, and though they were challenging for the title, the average gate dropped by 3,000 to 13,320 – still the best in the country.'

Eriksson was changing from the traditional sweeper-controlled, man-for-man marking defence, to what became known as 'Swenglish' 4–4–2. He had taken the ferry across the North Sea to study Bobby Robson's methods at Ipswich, and also journeyed to Liverpool's Melwood training ground to learn from Bob Paisley, the most successful English manager of all time. Bobby Ferguson, then Robson's assistant, said: 'He [Eriksson] would stand by the side of the training pitch and note down everything. He never took his eyes off Bobby, and how he was organizing things.'

Glenn Schiller, a defensive midfielder who had come up through the youth team, recalled that it was almost a case of playing by numbers at first. 'I remember it as if it was yesterday,' he told me. 'We worked all the time on pressing the opposition and running in support of the man on the ball. Svennis would place us like chess pieces on the training pitch. "You stand here, you go there," and so on. It was hard work. The biggest problem was fitting all the pieces together and getting them all to move in harmony. The defensive part was the key to it all. When we were attacking, there was a fair amount of freedom to express ourselves, but we had to defend from strict, zonal starting positions.'

The new 'Swenglish' was deeply unpopular at first, but in fairness, the Gothenburg team that won the cup (needing extra-time and penalties to see off Orebro on the way) scored 29 goals in seven games in the process, which suggests 'the old cavalier style' was not entirely a thing of the past. Apart from the 20-year-old Hysen, notable members of that side included Torbjorn Nilsson, the most accomplished player in Sweden, who could scheme as well as score, 19-year-old Glenn Stromberg, an attacking midfielder who played in 24 of the 26 matches in his breakthrough season, and Olle Nordin, the team captain and engine room artificer.

Eriksson says of that first season: 'During my first year, IFK were regarded as a rebellious bunch, and we suffered disciplinary problems, with too many bookings and sendings-off. But we overcame that by hard work, and in the end our behaviour was impeccable, on and off the field. We travelled a lot in the cup, and we used the trips to build a winning culture. Nobody moaned about waiting times, depressing airports or grotty hotel rooms.'

A rebellious bunch? Schiller, now a football agent, wouldn't go quite that far, but admits: 'We came to be looked upon like rock stars, and after games we would all go out for a few drinks. I have to say we did have fun on all our trips.' The downside of this good-time culture saw Schiller spend a month in prison for a drink-driving conviction, when he took his car in search of further refreshment after a party at home. 'It was a long time ago, and I learned my lesson,' he says. Eriksson said his piece at the time, but after that was steadfastly supportive, and welcomed the prodigal son back to the club immediately upon his release. 'He is a very understanding man, and it was not a problem after that,' Schiller told me.

That first season, Stromberg had been the major find. He told me: 'Because I was only young, and already 6 ft 5 in, I'd had a lot of back trouble the previous season, when I was 18. But when Sven took over, he promoted me straight away to the first-team squad, and after a couple of months he put me in the team, in the centre of midfield. I couldn't believe it, because I'd had so many problems with injuries and it took a lot of courage for him to do it. Straight away he left out some of the older players and gave the younger ones their chance.'

Of Eriksson's early difficulties, Stromberg says: 'When he arrived, he was unknown, which was one problem. Another was that he made us play in the English style – long balls and pressing the opposition all over the pitch. In Sweden, the national team and the bigger clubs were used to the short passing game, the continental way, and for a long time there was much criticism of Sven's way of playing.'

The following season, Gothenburg dropped back to third in the league again, behind Osters Vaxjo and Malmo, while their performance in the European Cup Winners' Cup was no better than ordinary. After making hard work of beating Ireland's Waterford and Panionios of Greece, both on a 2–1 aggregate, they fell apart against Terry Neill's Arsenal, and were trounced 5–1 at Highbury in the first leg, in March 1980. The North Bank was shocked into silence when Torbjorn Nilsson opened the scoring on the half-hour, but Alan Sunderland equalized within a minute, and after 35 minutes Arsenal were ahead, through David Price. Sunderland again, Liam Brady and Willie Young were also on target to make it a deflating night for Eriksson and his team. The return, in Sweden, was goalless, and remarkable only for a nasty scare for Neill and his players when their plane's landing gear malfunctioned, causing their first approach to Gothenburg airport to be aborted.

It had not been a good season, and criticism was mounting. 'Sven's second season was more of a problem than his first,' Stromberg says. 'There was a big debate about our long-ball game, but we kept playing our way, and the national team stuck to theirs. Sven is very hard-headed, he will always keep to his way. By this time, the team and the whole club were behind him, but there was a lot of criticism from the fans and the press. Eventually, of course, everybody in Sweden went over to the English style. It all started just before Sven. Bob Houghton was at Malmo and Roy Hodgson at Halmstad, and they first brought that way of playing to Sweden. It became Sven's way, too, and it brought good results for Gothenburg for the next ten years.'

For 1981, Eriksson strengthened his backroom staff with the recruitment of a new assistant, Gunder Bengtsson, and the team by signing three internationals. Sweden's goalkeeper, Thomas Wernersson, joined from Atvidaberg, and Stig Fredriksson and Hakan Sandberg, defender and striker respectively, arrived from Vasteras and Orebro. Finance director Carlsson says: 'When Sven joined us we already had quite a few good young players, so it was quite a good situation for a new trainer, but after a year or so he came to us with his proposals for improving the team. We backed his judgement as far as we could, depending on the finance involved. We were very impressed with the way he handled himself there. He would say to us: "This is a player I want to sign, but if we haven't got enough money, I'll accept that."'

The consequent improvement was not quite enough, Gothenburg finishing second in the league again, four points behind Osters Vaxjo, and so far, Eriksson had done not much more than satisfy minimum expectations. Managerial take-off came with the *annus mirablis* that was 1982. That year, Gothenburg did the league and cup double and triumphed against all odds in the UEFA Cup, becoming the first Swedish club to win a European trophy. By this stage the erstwhile 'Mr Who?' had full and enthusiastic backing in the dressing room. Hysen says: 'Even for a Swede, Sven was amazingly calm. In all the time I played for him, he never once raised his voice, and I can't say that about any other manager. I used to imagine that he had a secret darkened room somewhere, and that he would go there on his own and shout, scream and kick the walls and trash the place. I know Swedes are supposed to be relaxed about things, but I thought it was impossible for a man to be that calm all the time.

'On the other hand, Sven is also the best motivator I ever played for, and that is what you'd call a typical English quality. He treated everyone like adults, and they respected him for his honesty. If a player was dropped, Sven would take him to one side and explain his reasons. That approach made you even more determined to do well for the guy. He was an expert at man-management.'

Bengtsson, two years Eriksson's senior, was manager of Molde, in Norway, when we spoke in April 2002. He told me: 'We've known each other since 1975, when some mutual friends introduced us. I was player-coach at Torsby, Sven's home town, before he took me to Gothenburg as his number two. We had a few problems at first, with results not going so well, but we had good players and eventually it all came right. Gothenburg had always been a team who played attacking football, but until Sven took charge they weren't well organized, and so they hadn't been winning anything. Implementing any new style takes time, all the more so when it is as unpopular as Sven's was at first, but when results picked up, everything we were doing was accepted.'

Stromberg by now had developed into a key player, for club and country; indeed Gothenburg as a unit had matured nicely and were approaching their collective peak. They were still part-timers (Hysen was an electrician, Tord Holmgren a plumber), and were patronized by the European elite, but everybody was about to sit up and take notice. The first round of the UEFA Cup brought a routine demolition of Finland's Haka Valkeakosi, and there was no hint of the glory nights to come when Sturm Graz, of Austria, pushed the Swedes all the way before going out on an aggregate of 5–4. By the third round, however, Gothenburg were into their stride, beating Dinamo Bucharest at home (3–1) and away (1–0), and when they eliminated Valencia in the quarter-final it was clear that they were a force to be reckoned with. Stromberg remembers the trip to Spain with much amusement. He says: 'You have to remember that the club didn't really have the money to compete at this level. When we played Valencia away, we didn't have any directors with us. The club had severe financial problems at the time, and the four directors were all standing down. For nearly a month we had no administration, and when we went to Valencia there were no directors, just the Swedish journalists with us.

'There was a formal dinner the night before the match, and we had nobody to sit at the table with the Valencia directors, so we took the club doctor, a radio reporter and the kit man. It was unbelievable, to see these guys eating with the people who owned one of the biggest clubs in Spain.'

The financial situation had improved by the time the semi-final brought Gothenburg up against Germany's Kaiserslautern, who had just inflicted the heaviest-ever European defeat (5–0) on Real Madrid, and were therefore hot favourites. 'We were getting 50,000 gates for the European games, and Valencia had eased the cashflow problem,' Stromberg explained. 'Everything really started to come together that month. We were saved, as a big club, by our European run.' Again Eriksson's game plan worked to perfection. The draw and away goal he wanted from the first leg in Germany shifted the odds in Gothenburg's favour for the return, and a 2–1 win at home completed the upset. 'At that time,' Stromberg says, 'I think we could have taken on almost any team in the world. We were very confident, we had a lot of good players and we had a method we all believed in. Everybody believed in the things we were doing, the way we were playing. In Europe, the teams we played were having a lot of trouble with Sven's pressing game. They were used to being allowed to build up their passing from their own half, without pressure, but we started challenging for the ball very high up the field, and worked very hard at it. It also helped, of course, that there was a lot of quality in that side.'

The final was against another Bundesliga team, Hamburg, who were stronger than Kaiserslautern, and confident of winning with something to spare. Only once before had a Swedish club reached a European final, and the poverty of Malmo's performance in losing 1–0 to Nottingham Forest in the

1979 European Cup Final was not about to strike fear into Franz Beckenbauer and company. Bengtsson says: 'To be honest, getting to the final was a surprise, even for us, but there was a good feeling, a good spirit about that team – the best I've ever known. We also had an advantage. When a team like Gothenburg are coming up from nowhere, nobody really believes they are going to go all the way, and obviously it helps if you have a good team and nobody really takes you seriously. In the quarter-finals, nobody had said much or thought much about us, so Valencia expected to win. You could tell that. It was the same in the semi-finals, and particularly in the final. Nobody thought we could play as well as we did. We took them by surprise.'

Gothenburg were ten games unbeaten coming into the final, with their twin strikers, Torbjorn Nilsson and Dan Corneliusson, in prolific form. The first leg, in the Ullevi stadium, left the tie intriguingly balanced. Tord Holmgren's only goal of the match, in the 87th minute, gave the underdogs a lead to defend, but Hamburg thought they could easily overcome such a slender deficit at home. 'Nobody gave us a chance over there,' Eriksson recalled. 'Hamburg had flags printed with "Hamburg SV – winners of the UEFA Cup '82" all over them. You could buy them before the game. I still have one at home.'

His own players certainly regarded themselves as rank outsiders, albeit in a two-horse race. Stromberg says: 'An hour and a half before the game, Sven told us: "You know, we have a good chance here." We all looked at him thinking "Yeah, yeah. A good chance. How?" He said: "We're a team who score a lot of goals, and we're always likely to get one. Then, if we get one, they'll have to get three." Sven reminded us that nobody had scored three times against us all season, and that got us thinking. We turned to one another with looks that said: "Yeah, he's right, we do have a chance here."'

Teutonic speculation focused on whether Beckenbauer would play and pick up the one trophy that had eluded him. Two weeks away from retirement 'The Kaiser' had only just recovered from a bruised kidney, and had been among the substitutes a few days earlier, for the 5–0 drubbing of Werder Bremen. Ernst Happel, Hamburg's Austrian coach, said: 'There is a possibility Beckenbauer will play, but there is often a hitch between theory and practice.' Too true; the great man never appeared. Nevertheless, Happel still had three formidable German internationals – Manni Kaltz, Felix Magath and Horst Hrubesch – at his command. Victory would be a formality.

The trip had inauspicious beginnings for Glenn Schiller. 'I'd forgotten my boots, left them in Sweden,' he says. 'Sven wasn't pleased. He said: "The only thing you have to bring with you is your boots, and you can't be relied on to do that." He made me buy new ones.' Keen to get out of the manager's way, Schiller was sitting in the toilet as the final preparations were made. 'I was starting on the bench, so I was in no great hurry, and I was sat in there reading the match programme, with all the adverts for Hamburg cup-winning souvenirs. You could see that they had taken too much for granted, and definitely underestimated us.

'When I came out, I could hear the crowd yelling and the dressing room was empty. I was locked in. I was banging on the door, trying to get out, but nobody came, and in the end I had to climb over the door. I was probably in there on my own for ten minutes. Just as I got out, Glenn Hysen was injured, and Svennis was asking everybody on the bench "Where's Schiller?" They looked around and told him: "He's coming." I was running around the track and was sent straight on, so you could say I did my warm-up in the toilet! I didn't get to sit on the bench, I sat on the throne instead.'

Hamburg started urgently, seeking the early goal which would square the tie and give them the initiative but, against all expectations, it was Gothenburg who played the better football. The Germans were too hurried, making mistakes which were ruthlessly exploited. After 26 minutes Eriksson's underdogs were ahead, Tommy Holmgren, the younger brother of Tord, breaking down the left and crossing for Corneliusson to score with a powerful shot. Hamburg's morale nosedived, Gothenburg's soared, and the issue was put beyond doubt after 61 minutes, when Nilsson, who was outstanding throughout, outran Magath over 40 yards before making it 2–0 on the night. The Swedes were now 3–0 up on aggregate with away goals in their favour. Hamburg needed four goals in half an hour, but were a broken team, and disappointed fans were streaming out of the Volksparkstadion when Nilsson was fouled inside the penalty area and Stig Fredriksson scored from the spot.

Stromberg says: 'It was one of those nights when everything is just perfect. Torbjorn Nilsson, our centre-forward, was probably the best striker in Europe for two or three years around that time, but I don't think it was down to him, or the midfield, or the defence. Everything, everybody, was just perfect. I remember Hrubesch turning to me during the game and saying: "You know, we could play you ten times and never win." On our form that night, he was right. We were that good. Every player knew what to do, where to be at any given time. Throughout the 90 minutes, I don't remember any player being caught out of position once. Sven had prepared us that well.'

After 4,000 exultant Swedes had acclaimed their heroes on a lap of honour, Eriksson said: 'I'm the happiest man alive. I thought we might sneak it 1–0, but never in my wildest dreams did I imagine that we could come to Hamburg and score three.' Happel offered no excuses. The first goal had been crucial, fracturing his team's morale, he said. 'In the end, they could have scored four or five.'

For winning the UEFA Cup, the Gothenburg players received £50,000 a man on top of their basic salaries of £1,500 per month. Schiller immediately put a big hole in his bonus by buying a Porsche. 'Glenn Stromberg bought one too,' he said, chuckling at the memory. 'We were the two single guys in the team, you understand.'

Eriksson was also in the outside lane. Suddenly all Europe had heard of 'Sven Who?', and Gothenburg couldn't hope to keep him. But he had built a young team good enough to dominate Swedish football for the next five years under Bengtsson, who succeeded him, and to win the UEFA again in 1987.

CHAPTER NINE

LISBON CALLING

At the end of the 1981/82 season, Benfica were looking for a coach to replace the veteran Hungarian, Lajos Baroti. The world-renowned Lisbon 'Eagles' had done the league and cup double in his first season, 1980/81, but second place in 1982 was not good enough for a club with stratospheric standards (winners of 30 championships since 1935, they had never finished below fourth), and he had to go. Gothenburg may be Sweden's biggest club, but Benfica operate on a higher plane entirely. They have always been number one in Portugal, and were, for a time, pre-eminent in Europe, making five appearances in the European Cup Final in the 1960s. When they want a coach, they usually get their man, and so it was in 1982 when, impressed by Eriksson's triumph with Gothenburg in the UEFA Cup, they sent a private jet to fetch him and offer him the job.

His first task was to change the players' mentality. Eriksson explained: 'This was a team who played well at home, with a lot of courage, but as soon as they had an away game it was a different story. It seemed that in the Portuguese league they had learned that by winning at home and drawing away they could win the championship. Their away matches in Europe were particularly disappointing. They didn't want to run and challenge the opposition and kept falling back. In the first round of the UEFA Cup, against Real Betis, I lost my temper. We were losing 1–0, but the players were happy. Losing 1–0 there was OK because we would beat them at home. At half-time I was furious. "What are you trying to do?" I said. "Are you here to play football or not?" One of the players spoke up. "Sure," he said, "this is how we play away from home." So I said: "The pitch is no bigger here than it is at home, the grass is the same. If you can play football at home, you must be able to play football here."

'We turned the match around and won 2–1. I was able to change their attitude to away matches. They played with spirit away, too. The team's self-confidence improved dramatically. From then on, Benfica always played attacking football, always played to win, home or away.' Even by their standards, Eriksson's start was extraordinary. After his first 11 league matches, he had a 100 per cent record, a maximum 22 points banked and just four goals conceded. Going into 1983, Benfica were still unbeaten and a new club record had been set – played 28, won 26, drawn 2, lost none, goals for 85, goals against 15 – when they eventually slipped up for the first time, losing 1–0 away to their arch rivals, Sporting Lisbon. Even that took a dodgy penalty, and Eriksson was characteristically sanguine in defeat. 'The run had to end some time,' he said with a shrug. 'It's no great catastrophe.' Indeed it wasn't, as Benfica had a comfortable four-point lead over Porto, who had the league's leading scorer, Fernlando Gomes, in harness with Micky Walsh, formerly of Blackpool, Everton and Queens Park Rangers in attack. Eriksson's strikers were Nene, an experienced Portuguese international, and Zoran Filipovic, a big, bustling Yugoslav. The other key elements in the team were Manuel Bento, Portugal's veteran goalkeeper, Humberto Coelho, the captain and accomplished right-back who was to become the country's most capped player, Diamantino, a goalscoring winger and the only ever-present that season, and Fernando Chalana, an attacking midfielder who six years earlier, at 17, had become Portugal's youngest-ever international.

The fans, dubious at first about the appointment of a 34-year-old Swede, were eating out of Eriksson's hand after his first 16 league and cup games had all been won. From 'Who is this young upstart?' it had become 'So what if he is the same age as his goalkeeper?' The first sign of a problem came towards the end of February 1983, when a club versus country row blew up before Portugal's match at home to West Germany. The national team had played another friendly, against France, a week earlier, and Benfica and Sporting Lisbon, both of whom were involved in European club quarter-finals, strongly objected to their best players being asked to play six games in 17 days. Negotiations failed to resolve the situation, and on the eve of the international, the clubs declared that enough was enough, and withdrew their players' labour. Of a total of 36 named by the manager, Otto Gloria, in his senior and Under-21 squads, 11 pulled out, including six from Benfica. Gloria, a Brazilian, who had managed the Portuguese team at the 1966 World Cup and Benfica when they lost the European Cup Final to Manchester United in 1968, now resigned, refusing to nominate replacements. 'How can I work in this madhouse?' he asked, rhetorically. But he did. The old boy was persuaded to change his mind, and sod's law dictated that Portugal, who had been beaten 3–0 by France when at full strength, defeated the mighty West Germans 1–0 a week later with their reserves.

Midway through that first season, Eriksson made his first signing, going back to his old club, Gothenburg, for Glenn Stromberg, now 23. Stromberg told me: 'I finished the season in Sweden and then joined Benfica. What Sven was doing took a lot of courage – from both of us. When I got there, he said: "Now Glenn, you're going to take the place of the fans' favourite player, Joao Alves." He was a clever wide midfielder, a real crowd-pleaser, whose trademark was always to wear black gloves. There were a lot of people who didn't believe their eyes the first time I played and Alves didn't. At first, it was very difficult there. When Sven spoke to me in Swedish, all the other players would look at us and wonder what we were up to. So after a short time he said: "Let's just try to talk only in Portuguese, even though we don't know very much, first so that everybody can see that we're one of them and

second, so they'll know what we're talking about."
I think it was more of a mixing-in exercise than
anything. He would have played me, whatever anybody thought. Sven was never one to be swayed by
anyone else's opinion. He thought me playing was
the best way for Benfica to get results, and we had
great results for the next 18 months. Alves still
played for Portugal while I was playing in his place
for Benfica.'

Stromberg had to wait what seemed like an
eternity before joining the action. 'I couldn't play for
a month or so when I first arrived', he explained.
'The clubs in Portugal were going to be allowed to
play two foreign players at the same time, instead of
just one, but the rule wasn't changed immediately,
as everybody had expected. They continued to
permit only one, and there was a Yugoslav striker
at Benfica, Filipovic, who was scoring a lot of goals
and couldn't be dropped because he was the only
forward we had who was West European in style.
He was tall, a very good header of the ball, and
because of his tactics, Eriksson needed a guy like
that up front. It was a frustrating time for me. In all,
I was there for three months without playing. Then
the rule change went through, we could play with
two foreigners, and I played for the last three
months of the season.'

Eriksson was tantalizingly close to winning
the UEFA Cup with different clubs in successive
years, Benfica losing their first European final since
1968 by the narrowest of margins. The competition was strong, with four English teams – Arsenal,

Manchester United, Ipswich and Southampton – all going out in the first round, but Eriksson's canny, cat-and-mouse tactics brought them past Real Betis, Lokeren and FC Zurich before they came up against Roma in the quarter-finals. The Italians, top of Serie A, and boasting international superstars in Falcao and Bruno Conti, had been good enough to put out Bobby Robson's Ipswich, and were clear favourites. Benfica, however, won 2–1 in Rome, Filipovic scoring both their goals, then made it 3–2 on aggregate in the Stadium of Light, with Filipovic again on target. Falcao's 86th minute consolation strike at least gave Roma the face-saver of an away draw. Benfica were through to the last four, where they needed the away-goals rule to over-come Romania's first-ever European semi-finalists, Universitatea Craiova.

Eriksson approached the final, against Ander-lecht, undefeated in 22 UEFA Cup matches, but that record went in the first leg against the Belgians, in Brussels on 5 May 1983. In their semi-final victory over Bohemians of Prague, two of Anderlecht's goals were scored by Edwin Vandenbergh, their centre-forward, who was one of five Belgian World Cup players in a team coached by one-time record cap holder Paul Van Himst. Anderlecht's strength was in midfield, where in Ludo Coeck, Frankie Vercauteren and Juan Lozano they had a unit that was the envy of most top clubs in Europe, but they were also well served up front, by Vandenbergh and Kenneth Brylle, the latter an energetic, incisive Dane.

For the first leg of the final, Benfica were well below strength. Nene was not fit enough to start, and had to be content with a place on the bench, Stromberg was suspended and Alves absent injured. The only goal in the first leg was an action replay of Anderlecht's winner in the semi-final, Coeck turning cleverly to beat two defenders in the corner and finding Vercauteren, whose left-footed cross was buried by Brylle's well-directed header. Any hope Benfica had of restoring the balance disappeared after 75 minutes, when midfielder Jose Luis Silva was sent off, for hacking down Brylle while the ball was out of play. Both managers professed themselves satisfied with the outcome. Van Himst said: 'I'm not disappointed in the least with 1–0. Benfica are very awkward to play against. They work carefully and methodically to break up their opponents' rhythm.' Eriksson thought the final was nicely balanced. 'We're far from out of it,' he said. 'Before the game, I told people that a narrow defeat wouldn't be a problem, and I haven't changed my mind. Anderlecht are a good team, but so are we, and it's still 50–50.'

For the decisive second leg, two weeks later, Nene and Stromberg were back, but now Filipovic was injured, and only on the bench. With just the one goal in it, there was everything to play for, and the match drew a crowd of 80,000 to the Estadio da Luz. Benfica were marginal favourites, but had an early scare when the Dutch referee, Charles Corver, disallowed a Vandenbergh 'goal' for offside. Humberto Coelho, taking every opportunity to venture upfield, volleyed a Diamantino cross into the side netting, and Benfica's positive approach paid off in the 36th minute, when Chalana's cross from the left was diverted to Han Sheu, who drove the ball high into the net. Overall equality had been restored – but not for long. Benfica relaxed, fatally, and three minutes later Anderlecht broke out of defence and a cross from Vercauteren was headed past Bento by Lozano, a Spanish-born midfielder who was seeking Belgian nationality. Premature celebration gave way to hushed foreboding in the packed stadium. Benfica were left needing to score twice to lift the trophy, and now Anderlecht's decision to go in with an extra defender, Hugo Broos, and use Luka Peruzovic as a sweeper, paid dividends. Stromberg's direct running from midfield, which had been a significant feature in the first half, was to no avail as his front men became enmeshed in the Belgians' defensive web. Nene had a header saved from Carlos Manuel's cross, and the introduction of the half-fit Filipovic was to no avail. He did manage to get the ball in the net, but from an offside position, and after successive European Cup wins in 1961 and 1962, Benfica had now lost their last four European finals.

At least domestic compensation was at hand. They won the league, by four points from Porto, and completed the double by beating the same opposition 1–0 in the Portuguese Cup Final. Two trophies and a European final in his first season – even directors who prided themselves in being the hardest of task masters were suitably impressed.

There was no runaway start to the 1983/84 season. Eriksson sold Alves, to Boavista, and signed Antonio Oliveira, a centre-half from Maritimo, to fill in for Humberto Coelho, who would need lengthy convalescence after a serious knee injury. This time Porto, spearheaded by the endlessly prolific Fernando Gomes, who had won the Golden Boot as the top scorer in Europe the previous season, with 36 goals, matched Benfica stride for stride. After their first seven league games, just two points covered the top three, with Benfica on 13, Porto 12 and Sporting Lisbon 11. After 13 matches, Sporting had dropped off the pace, but although Benfica had won 12 and drawn the other, Porto were still hanging in there, only two points behind. There would be no clean sweep of the honours board this time. Benfica were knocked out of the Portuguese Cup by Sporting and lost to Porto in the Super Cup.

Eriksson and his team had their eyes on a bigger prize – the European Cup. In the first two rounds, they made short work of Northern Ireland's Linfield and Olympiakos of Greece. Then, on the eve of the quarter-final draw, Eriksson was asked who he would like to get, and who he wanted to avoid. 'Ideally, I'd like Rapid Vienna,' he said, 'but I'd settle for anyone apart from Liverpool.' Almost inevitably after that, Benfica drew Liverpool. 'The worst possible opposition we could have got,' was Eriksson's reaction. 'I rate them the best team in Europe, as they have been for the past decade. But we have to play them, there's no escape, so play them we will, and we aren't going to be afraid of their reputation

or their ability. If we play well, there's no reason
why we shouldn't beat anyone, even Liverpool.
Other teams have done so. They lost last season to
a Polish team, Widzew Lodz, and I know we are
better than Lodz.'

Talking up the opposition was probably a mistake. The last thing the Benfica players needed was
to be reminded of Liverpool's strength. Stromberg
explained: 'It was a very difficult draw – all the
more so because the Portuguese players had so
much respect for English teams. They would rather
have played Real Madrid or Barcelona – any of the
south European sides – than a team from England
or Germany. They were afraid of their physical football. Against Spanish opposition, the Portuguese
always thought they could win, but not against the
English or the Germans. That was a big problem in
their heads.'

Nevertheless, Eriksson's well-organized team
defended assiduously at Anfield, where it was 0–0 at
half-time, with Liverpool labouring to break them
down. It took a substitution to do it, Joe Fagan
replacing Craig Johnston with Kenny Dalglish, who
had been out for eight weeks, and had played only
two reserve games since fracturing a cheekbone.
The class of 'King Kenny' was the vital difference
in the second half, when Ian Rush headed home the
only goal of the game from an Alan Kennedy cross.
Fagan said: 'It was a calculated risk playing Kenny at
all, but it paid off. He gave us a little more skill and
turned the game our way.' Eriksson said: 'Dalglish
was brilliant. He is the same player, even after being

away for two months. The away goal in Europe is very important, and I am disappointed we did not get one. It will not be easy for us in Lisbon now. Many teams play better at home than away, but not Liverpool.'

Prophetic stuff. Between the two legs, Liverpool signed John Wark from Ipswich, and the new arrival brought the best out of his rivals for a place, notably Ronnie Whelan and Craig Johnston. At the second time of asking, Liverpool were magnificent, although they were helped on their way by a maladroit piece of goalkeeping by Bento who, with nine minutes gone, allowed a header from Whelan to slip through his hands and then his legs. 'We'd played well at Anfield, and really thought we had a chance at home,' Stromberg said. 'But then our goalkeeper made that bad mistake early on which meant we had to score three, and that was too much for us.'

After 34 minutes Liverpool made it 3–0 on aggregate, putting the tie well beyond Benfica's recovery, when Dalglish exchanged passes with Rush and played in Johnston, who scored from the 18-yard line. Benfica had no option but to attack, and Eriksson sent on two attacking substitutes, Filipovic and Sheu. It was Nene, however, scorer in both legs against Liverpool in the same competition six years earlier, who reduced the deficit after 75 minutes, only for Rush to head in his 35th goal of the season and Whelan to make it 5–1 on aggregate in the dying seconds.

At least there was no hangover for Benfica.

Instead they took out their disappointment on little Penafiel, who were thrashed 8–0 in the next league game. That weekend, it was announced that Eriksson had agreed a new two-year contract with the club.

Nene's four goals against Penafiel was his third hat-trick in a month after scoring three against Braga (7–0) and another three at the expense of Farense (7–2). The 34 year old was to finish joint top scorer in the league with 21 goals, overshadowing his partner Filipovic, who was no longer a fixture in the side. A young Danish newcomer, Michael Manniche, was often preferred, and the Yugoslav didn't like it. The situation came to a head before the league match at home to next-to-bottom Estoril, when Filipovic hoped to net a hatful, only to get word that Manniche was in again. Sounding off in the local press, Filipovic insisted he was the better player. 'I have greater experience and technically I'm stronger,' he said. 'Also, his timing is often wrong when he challenges for the ball in the air. I understand that Glenn Stromberg has to play in midfield, and that it is between Manniche and myself for the other foreigner's place, but I have scored six goals in six matches for us this season, and four of those have been the winner. So why does he play instead of me? I don't understand it.

'The coach wants us to play a much more modern style of football than Benfica are used to. Eriksson wants us to run off the ball, when in the past, in the Portuguese style, we tended to do all our running on the ball. Eriksson must think Manniche is better suited to this game, but to be honest, although we have been winning, we haven't always been playing very well. I did well enough for Eriksson last season, scoring plenty of goals. He should give me a chance again.'

Eriksson's reaction to this outburst was surprising. He played Filipovic against Estoril. What followed was just one of many instances that fuelled his reputation as a lucky manager. Benfica took the lead midway through the second half, with a Diamantino header, but Estoril equalized after 75 minutes. Then, with eight minutes left, Filipovic and the Estoril goalkeeper, Manuel Abrantes, went for a loose ball, Filipovic made his challenge fractionally late and was booked. No problem there, but he launched into a tirade against the referee, Antonio Ferreira, who sent him off. Eriksson had no more trouble from his erstwhile critic, who admitted he had blown his last chance. 'It was my fault,' he said, 'but there was plenty of bad language from others out there, and I don't see why he had to pick on me. For a comeback game, things couldn't have gone worse.'

Benfica went on to win the league, for the 26th time, by four points from Sporting. The issue was decided on the penultimate day, when Chalana's goal, in a 1–1 draw with Sporting, rendered the last set of results of arithmetical interest only.

Eriksson had verbally agreed a new contract, committing himself to the club for another two years, but the European Cup Final, between Liverpool and Roma, on 30 May found him in Rome. Nils Liedholm had indicated that he would be leaving Roma, and when Eriksson flew in for the match, the suspicions of the Italian media were aroused. He told an impromptu press conference: 'I have a new, two-year contract with Benfica. That isn't easily broken, you know. In fact, I haven't even got a ticket for the game. Benfica applied for me, but we haven't received a reply.' Later, it transpired that Ann-Christin had been touring Rome, being shown luxury apartments, while her husband watched the final.

Eriksson now had had a change of heart, and told the Benfica president, a builder and property magnate named Fernando Martins, that he would be leaving, after all, for Roma. According to Eriksson, the president had agreed to sell Ricardo to Paris St Germain behind his back, which rendered their agreement null and void. 'If you are going to sell my players without telling me, then I'll go too,' he said. Martins, furious, followed him to Italy to demand compensation from his new employers. Stromberg was surprised, 'but only a little bit', by his mentor's decision to leave after all. 'He had told me, one month before, that he was going to stay, but I could understand what he did. Benfica are a great club, they won the league every year, so they were always in the European Cup, but for a coach like Sven, Italy meant a lot more. Football in Portugal is very big, but there are only three clubs of any real size – Benfica, Sporting and Porto. The rest don't mean much. Going to Italy, to train a team like Roma, was a dream for Sven. When I heard he was going, I went, too. To Atalanta.'

CHAPTER TEN

ALL ROADS LEAD TO ROME

Sven-Goran Eriksson could have come to England nearly 20 years earlier. In May 1984, Tottenham Hotspur were looking for a manager to replace Keith Burkinshaw, and the chairman, Irving Scholar, approached two candidates, one of whom was Eriksson. Scholar told me: 'Sven was just about to leave Benfica. He said he'd had a meeting with the people at Roma, and that basically he'd shaken hands on a deal, although nothing had been completely finalized. His agent at the time was a nice chap called Borge Lantz, who lived in Portugal, at Cascaes. I approached him because Sven had come to my attention as being a young, bright European coach with a future. He'd been successful at Gothenburg, winning the UEFA Cup, and he'd done well at Benfica. I'd heard a whisper that he was ready to move on, and so I checked him out.

'I'd just been let down by Alex Ferguson, and I do mean let down. We'd had a few meetings and a lot of conversations, and I'd said to him: "Look, when everything is sorted we'll shake hands, and that's it." He said: "Oh yeah, I'm that type of bloke as well," so that was fine. Or so I thought. Anyway, we had our last meeting in Paris. We'd agreed the contract, everything. All the "t"s were crossed, all the "i"s dotted, so I said: "Are you ready?" He said he was. We'd both made great play of this thing about the handshake. I put my hand out, we shook hands, and he said, "Right then, that's it." I thought "great", but five or six weeks later I started to get the impression that he was going to let me down. It was when he did that I spoke to Lantz about Eriksson. He said: "Go ahead, have a word with him, here's his number." So I called Sven and he made it clear that he had given his word to Roma, but that if the move fell through he would be very interested in coming to England. He went to Roma, and the rest is history. It was a shame. It would have been interesting to have a foreign coach all that time ago. It has become the fashion now, but it would have been ground-breaking then. Nobody in England had heard of him in 1984. It was "Sven-Goran Eriksson, who's he?" When I bumped into him in England just after his appointment, I reminded him of the Tottenham thing, and his face lit up. If only, eh?'

Having missed out on Eriksson and Ferguson, who stayed at Aberdeen for another two years before joining Manchester United, Spurs gave the job to Burkinshaw's number two, Peter Shreeves, and it was another three years before Terry Venables became the European-orientated coach Scholar wanted. In March 2002, in reflective mood, he said: 'My first two choices weren't bad ones, were they – Alex Ferguson and Sven-Goran Eriksson. I wanted

Ferguson because, like Eriksson, he'd been successful in Europe. He'd won the Cup-Winners' Cup and blazed a trail in Europe with Aberdeen.'

On 8 May 1984, three weeks before the European Cup Final, the president of Roma, Dino Viola, agreed with Eriksson that he would replace his fellow Swede, Nils Liedholm, as coach. He was not the first choice for the job, getting it only after Giovanni Trapattoni, then at Juventus, had spurned Viola's overtures, but however the chance came, this really was the big time. Italy's Serie A was undoubtedly the strongest, most glamorous league in the world at the time, and Roma had won the coveted scudetto in 1983. In 1983/84 they won the Italian Cup, beating Verona in the final, and were runners-up in Serie A, two points behind Juventus, as well as losing only on penalties to Liverpool in the European Cup. Eriksson, then, inherited a fine team, which had two world-class Brazilians, Falcao and Cerezo, at its fulcrum, with the 'golden boy' of Italian football, Bruno Conti, who had just made his international debut, wide on the right. Other significant individuals included the goalkeeper, Franco Tancredi, who had played twice for Italy, left-back Aldo Maldera, who had 10 caps, midfielders Carlo Ancelotti and Giuseppe Giannini, both of whom were to have substantial international careers, and strikers Maurizio Iorio, Roberto Pruzzo and Francesco Graziani. Iorio, 25, had been the leading scorer in Serie A the previous season, while on loan to Verona, and was naturally recalled, while Pruzzo, 29, had been the league's top scorer in 1980, and had scored a brilliant equalizer against Liverpool in the European Cup Final. He had six caps. The most celebrated of the front men was Graziani, 32, whose 64 appearances for Italy took in the 1978 and 1982 World Cups. Despite the talent in the team, however, Eriksson's first season was thoroughly disappointing. Defensively orientated to a tedious degree, Roma averaged less than a goal a game (33 in 34) in finishing a poor seventh in the league, and got no further than the last eight of the Cup-Winners' Cup, where they were eliminated by Bayern Munich, for whom Lothar Matthaus was at his peerless best.

In mitigation, Eriksson's entry into the Machiavellian world of Italian football was by no means straightforward. For a start, he was handicapped by the rule prohibiting foreigners from managing at club level (Liedholm had taken out dual citizenship to overcome this). Roma sought to get around it by naming a coach, Roberto Clagluna, as their official 'trainer', with Eriksson taking the title of director of football, but this use of a 'stooge' created more problems than it solved.

On taking over, Eriksson immediately asserted his authority by banning smoking, amending the bonus system to stop the players being rewarded for drawing games and ending 'retiro', the practice whereby the team 'retired' to weekend training camps. This latter decision, he now admits, was a mistake. He explained: 'I tried to put an end to the custom of meeting at a hotel before our Sunday matches. When we finished training one Saturday, I told the players: "See you at lunch tomorrow." This caused astonishment, and in the end I had to reinstate the meetings. Ritual and habit can provide security.'

In August, Roma won a pre-season tournament in Coruna, Spain, where top-class opposition was provided by Manchester United, Athletic Bilbao and Vasco da Gama, of Brazil, and the week before the Serie A programme started, they defeated Lazio 2–0 in the Italian Cup. After that it was a surprise, as well as a disappointment, when they were ominously slow out of the traps, with four successive draws in the league and a run of eight games without a win. A month into the season, the Italian Football Federation rejected the coaching association's complaint against the employment of Eriksson, in defiance of the ban on foreign coaches, and scrapped the prohibition altogether. Freed of all impediments, real or imaginary, he was able to immerse himself in his work, and Roma picked up nicely after their first victory, 2–1 at home to Fiorentina. That was the launching pad for an unbeaten ten-match sequence, yet it was to be a stop-start sort of season, and after 11 games in Serie A their modest return of 12 points had them only in fifth place, six behind the surprise leaders, Verona. They had their moments, thumping Cremonese 5–0 away, Di Carlo getting a hat-trick, but generally flattered only to deceive. Fairly typical was the struggle they had to overcome little Wrexham in the second round of the Cup-Winners' Cup in November. A single goal, scored by Francesco Graziani in the home leg, was enough to see off

Steaua Bucharest in the first round, after which
Welsh opposition, from the Football League's Fourth
Division, was expected to provide easy pickings.
Roma won 2–0 at home in the first leg, with goals
from Pruzzo and Cerezo, in a match notable for the
return of Carlo Ancelotti, the powerful Italian international midfield player, who had been out injured
for 11 months. The aggregate margin, 3–0, was comfortable enough, but *The Times* reported the decisive
second leg as follows: 'Only disgraceful refereeing
in the first leg, and a rush of blood to the head at
the wrong moment in the second stood between
Wrexham and an extraordinary overall victory.
Cushioned as they were by two highly debatable
goals in the first leg, it would be easy to say that
Roma, runners-up in the European Cup only six
months ago, did just enough to dispose of England's
[sic] 89th best team. But the truth is that they might
easily have trooped from the field here a beaten
team, had it not been for some hasty finishing
and the magnificence of Falcao, the Brazilian, who
covered an amazing amount of ground for someone
supposedly unfit.'

Falcao had joined Roma from the Brazilian club
Internacional for £950,000 in 1980, and was widely
acclaimed as the best midfield player at the 1982
World Cup. Twice Brazil's Footballer of the Year, he
came third in the World Footballer of the Year poll,
behind Paolo Rossi and Karl-Heinz Rummenigge,
in 1982. Extravagantly gifted and immensely experienced, the 30 year old was expected to be the
cornerstone of Eriksson's team, but he injured his

knee in a goalless draw with Verona on 21 October and then the president, Viola, complained bitterly about his failure to play against Juventus in Turin the following week. Falcao was carrying two stitches in his knee, but Viola felt he was fit enough to play, and a war of words ensued. Viola said that Cerezo, not Falcao, was Roma's key player, Falcao took umbrage and Eriksson was caught in the middle, very much the loser. Falcao suffered more knee trouble in a 0–0 stalemate, against Lazio, on 11 November, and the Brazilian's continuing fitness problems undermined the team that season. A superstar, on a two-year contract worth £1.5m, and a living legend among the club's supporters after his colossal contribution to the 1983 title win, he dated Ursula Andress while still living with his mum in a sumptuous villa in the fashionable Monte Mario part of the city, and was ferried to and from training (and everywhere else) in a chauffeur-driven BMW. Unfortunately for all concerned, he spent most of the 1984/85 season on various treatment tables, eventually undergoing surgery on his troublesome knee in the United States before a lengthy convalescence at home in Brazil.

His last game for Roma was away to Maradona's Napoli on 16 December 1984. Typically, he marked his farewell with a goal, but after celebrating with his usual jump, he returned to earth awkwardly, and the smile froze on his lips. Five days later, he was on the operating table for more surgery on his knee. The whole team had been dependent upon Falcao to an unhealthy degree, Eriksson felt. 'Due to his knee problem, he had only four matches with us during my time at the club, but in the games he played, Roma were a completely different team. He went around the pitch pointing and co-ordinating. When he wasn't able to play, the others would come to me and say: "We can't play without Falcao." That season we came seventh in the league. The following year, with just about the same team, we came second and won the cup. But it took me a whole year to get the players to understand that we could play without Falcao. Without him, the players had a mental block. Falcao's presence, or absence, was decisive in determining how the players felt, and this in turn determined how well they played.'

Searching for a contemporary comparison, Eriksson told me: 'If he was playing today, Falcao would be another Patrick Vieira.' When Falcao was unavailable, the Roma midfield was staffed by Cerezo, Ancelotti, Conti and Giannini, an elegant stalwart who was to make 318 appearances for the club between 1981 and 1996. For goals, Roma relied largely upon Pruzzo, the most prolific striker in the club's history, who weighed in with a modest eight in 21 league games. That Giannini, with four, was the second-highest scorer says it all about Roma's football that season. Graziani, a World Cup-winning striker with Italy two years earlier, managed only two in 19 matches.

By January they were moving up the table, after successive 1–0 wins against Torino and Avellino, but the crowd, and the critics, were not happy. The newspapers complained that Roma were playing in

an unsophisticated 'English' style. Quite right too,
after their defeat by Liverpool, countered Viola.
He'd had enough of Liedholm's 'lateral football'.

The cup competitions provided little by way of
relief. After knocking out Genoa 3–0 and Lazio 2–0,
Roma came unstuck in the quarter-finals of the
Italian Cup, where they lost on the away-goal rule
to Parma, who were then near the bottom of Serie
B. In the Cup-Winners' Cup, they reached the last
eight, where they came up against Bayern Munich.
It was billed as the tie of the round, but the first leg,
in Bavaria on 6 March, was something of a damp
squib. Bayern were without Michael Rummenigge,
who was ill, and rushed Soren Lerby back to bolster
their midfield when he was still suffering from the
after-effects of 'flu, but they were still too strong
for Roma, running out comfortable 2–0 winners.
Reinhold Mathy missed two easy chances, Matthaus
fired over when unmarked and Dieter Hoeness
headed negligently the wrong side of a post before
skipper Klaus Augenthaler finally gave Bayern
the lead, just before half-time, with a rasping shot
from distance. Pruzzo might have equalized after
72 minutes. Instead, Hoeness got the Germans'
second five minutes later, and Roma had it all to do
in the return.

By the time it came around, on 20 March,
Eriksson's team were a disappointing seventh in the
league, with 23 points from 20 games. Effectively,
the tie was all over by the 33rd minute, when
Tancredi fouled Mathy to enable Matthaus to make
it 3–0 on aggregate from the penalty spot. Sebas-

tiano Nela pulled one back after 80 minutes, but it was much too late, and anyway Bayern scored again within a minute, to win 2–1 on the night and 4–1 overall.

Finishing seventh in the league was nowhere near good enough for a club who had been runners-up and European Cup Finalists the previous year, and Eriksson needed something much better for the 1985/86 season if he was to keep his job. Poland's Zbigniew Bonick, from Juventus, was chosen to replace Falcao, who made his last appearance in a friendly against Ajax in May, then went home to Brazil. He was still under contract to Roma, but when he was summoned back to Rome for medical checks, he ignored the call, with the result that Viola applied to the Italian federation for permission to cancel his contract and, to considerable surprise, won the case. 'He'd had a couple of very bad injuries, and was never the same afterwards,' Eriksson explained. Furious, Falcao entered into abortive negotiations with Fiorentina, before joining Sao Paulo. Five major corporations raised the money the Brazilian club needed, which was £1m for one season. Some £600,000 of this went to Roma, with Falcao pocketing the rest.

Red tape meant it was 10 August before Roma's lawyers succeeded in getting his contract declared null and void, and at one stage, because of the limitation on foreign players, it seemed that they would have to 'park' Cerezo on loan somewhere to make room in the team for Boniek. 'Zibi', as he was known, had first come to the fore as a 22 year old, when he was one of the stars of the 1978 World Cup, in Argentina. Four years later, in Spain, he scored a hat-trick against Belgium, playing as a striker, and his all-round excellence was such that he finished his career in Serie A playing as a sweeper. When he arrived from Turin, it was said that he was Viola's choice, not Eriksson's, but the coach will not have that. He told me: 'It was a decision made jointly between us. Nobody was ever signed by a club president without my complete agreement.' Nevertheless, Eriksson had more arguments with Boniek than any other player, and was soon admonishing him for his passion for gambling (he bought a racehorse), suggesting he concentrate on his other off-the-field interests, chess and bridge. He was, however, a player worth indulging. 'He was a different type to Falcao, not so authoritative, but top-class technically,' Eriksson says. With Boniek at the hub of the team, Roma's improvement was startling. Such was Eriksson's success in convincing his players that they could win without Falcao that they challenged for the championship all season and won the Italian Cup. They started as they meant to go on, with successive victories away to Atalanta, 2–1, and at home to Udinese, 1–0. Pruzzo was quickly off the mark, scoring Roma's first goal of the season. Revelling in the improved lines of supply engineered by Boniek, the young striker rattled in 19 goals in 24 appearances, including all five in the 5–1 trouncing of Avellino. 'Pruzzo was extraordinary in the penalty area,' Boniek told me. 'He was a very good header of the ball, and lethal in front of goal. He scored so often because he was a natural finisher.' Boniek himself weighed in with seven in 29 games, five of them coming in a mid-season purple patch which brought five in five, and with Graziani also contributing five (in 14 matches), the team's total was up from 33 to 51.

After the first 11 games, Roma were only sixth in the table, six points behind the leaders, Juventus, but after 21 they had closed the gap to just three points, and lay second. They had won more matches – 14 to Juve's 13 – and had scored more goals (34 to their rivals' 31). Then, with six rounds of the championship left, Roma beat Juventus 3–0, with goals from Graziani, Pruzzo and Cerezo signalling the start of a charge.

From being 12 points behind Juve at one stage, they came within touching distance of the scudetto. Going into the penultimate round of fixtures there was just one point between Juve, who were playing Milan, and Roma, who were at home to Lecce. The momentum was with Eriksson's team, who were widely regarded as favourites for the title, when disaster struck. Roma, unaccountably, lost 3–2 to Lecce, who were bottom of the table and already condemned to relegation, thereby blowing their title chances. Everything seemed to be going to plan when Graziani scored after only seven minutes, but then Di Chiara equalized and a Berbas penalty gave Lecce the lead. Eight minutes into the second half, Berbas scored again, and Juve were home and dry. A goal from Pruzzo, after 82 minutes, was no sort of consolation. 'Still today I think about that match with a lot of anger,' Boniek says. 'That defeat against Lecce put an end to our dreams. It was a game we had to win and should have won. It can happen sometimes, that the top team loses to the bottom, but I still find that result hard to accept.'

Giannini, offering an interesting insight into the Italian footballer's mentality, says: 'We arrived at that game exhausted, and at the interval we made another mistake. We thought we could make a meal of Lecce, without ever trying to get them on to our side. It is probably not completely ethical what I say, but perhaps it would have been better to try to reason with our opponents, asking them openly not to overdo their efforts.'

Looking back, Eriksson says: 'If I could do it all over again, I would take the team away from Rome – away from the interference of club directors, the president, then fans and the media. Then, perhaps, things might have gone differently.'

Thoroughly deflated, Roma went on to lose their last match, 1–0 away to Como, and trailed four points behind Juventus. It was a colossal anticlimax, still bitterly remembered to this day, the pain in no way alleviated by the winning of the Italian Cup, where they put out Bari, Atalanta, Internazionale and Fiorentina before beating Sampdoria 3–2 on aggregate in the final.

At the end of April, Cerezo signed a pre-contract agreement with Milan, but a change of heart saw his old boss, Liedholm, decide to keep Ray Wilkins, and Cerezo moved to Sampdoria instead. Conti's disappointment was such that he, too, was on the verge of leaving, for Napoli, after what was described at the time as a 'heated discussion', with Viola. All was resolved the following day, however, when hours before Conti left with the Italian squad for the 1986 World Cup, he was handed a new contract for his perusal while he was away.

He signed on his return, but Boniek says Conti and Eriksson did not get on well. 'The relationship between them was not one of the best. I think the coach saw Bruno as an individualist, more like a South American than a European player. He always wanted him to play more as a team man. I remember Conti liked to wear the number seven shirt, and at one stage Eriksson gave him number six. They had a disagreement about that. I know that whenever Bruno was out, injured, he found it difficult to get back in.'

Conti confirmed to me that he had a 'disagreement' with Eriksson, as a result of which the number seven shirt in which he had spent his whole career [he was 29 at the time, with two World Cups behind him] was given to the young and relatively unknown Stefano Impallomeni. There had, however, been a rapprochment since. Conti finished his playing career in 1991, when 83,000 admirers packed the Olympic Stadium to make it an emotional farewell. To the surprise of many, Eriksson was among them, having made a special trip from Portugal, where he was coaching Benfica. 'It was a wonderful gesture, much appreciated,' Conti told me. 'He came from Lisbon to Rome just to celebrate my final game. He demonstrated then that he was a real gentleman.

That's why I was happy for him when he won the scudetto with Lazio, and that's why I wanted him to do well with England at the World Cup.' In the circumstances, Conti was not prepared to stir up problems that were in the past. Of their falling out, he would say only: 'He was the coach and I was the player, and he preferred to play first Impallomeni and then the Dane, Klaus Berggreen, on the wing. It was his decision. I was prepared to do anything to play, and so I took number six and played more in midfield. I had to accept it, but it was tough to see my shirt on someone else.'

Conti was at least in the Roma team that started the 1986/87 season with a low-key goalless draw at home to Como, notable only for the debuts of four players. Marco Baroni made his first appearance at centre-half, as did Impallomeni in midfield, Berggreen on the wing and 'The Condor', as Massimo Agostini was to become known, at centreforward.

With Viola's enthusiastic backing, Eriksson tried to sign Ian Rush from Liverpool, only to lose out again to Juventus. Reinforcements of international renown were needed to lift the club but none were forthcoming, and after a summer spent drowning their sorrows, Roma staggered into the 1986/87 season nursing a metaphorical hangover. After that 0–0 at home to Como, Ancelotti's goal was enough for a 1–0 win at Atalanta, but their second home game was another barren stalemate, with Verona, after which they were soundly beaten, 4–1, away to Internazionale. Four points from four games was hardly the flyer Eriksson wanted. It was to be a poor season, back to square one, with goals desperately hard to come by. Berggreen and Stefano Desideri were joint leading scorers with five apiece, the previously prolific Pruzzo managing just four in 19 appearances. Inconsistent throughout, Roma recovered from their beating by Inter to record successive victories over Brescia and Torino, but then lost 1–0 at home to Napoli. In fairness, Maradona's team were to be champions, but the win-some-lose-some pattern was to be repeated time and again.

Europe was again a disappointment. In the first round of the Cup-Winners' Cup, Eriksson was happy with a 2–0 win at home to Spain's Real Zaragoza in the first leg. Roma were confident that they could successfully defend their advantage in the return, but after starting well, they lost their composure when Gerolin was hit by a missile thrown from the crowd, and the indiscipline that followed saw Ubaldo Righetti elbow an opponent off the ball just before half-time and the English referee, George Courtney, award a penalty which Juan Senor duly tucked away. Imbued with fresh hope, Zaragoza seized the initiative, and Gerolin's foul on Michel Pineda gave Senor a second chance to show his expertise from the spot. Now 2–2 on aggregate, it stayed that way all through extra-time, necessitating a penalty shoot-out, in which Andoni Cedrun saved successive kicks from Boniek and Ancelotti to put Roma out.

The new year brought a new addition to the Eriksson family. Sven's daughter, Lina, was born on

2 January 1987. The birth didn't bring a lot of luck –
Boniek promptly broke a toe in a goalless draw with
Como. In urgent need of a reliable goalscorer, Roma
turned their attentions to Germany's Rudi Voeller,
and in February Dino Viola's son, Ettore, flew to
Germany to meet Voeller's lawyer and table terms
destined to transfer him from Werder Bremen at the
end of the season. The following month, Pope John
II received the Roma team at the Vatican. Conti took
his two children, and Boniek exchanged a few
words in Polish with the pontiff, leading to rumours
of divine intervention when Roma beat Torino 1–0
to move up to joint second place, five points behind
the leaders, Napoli. When they held Maradona's
Napoli to a goalless draw in their own San Paolo
stadium on 15 March , then beat Empoli 2–1 the following week, all things seemed possible – especially
after defeating the Argentinian national team 2–1
in Rome, with a couple of goals from Boniek, in a
match to celebrate the club's 60th anniversary.
Napoli's 1–0 defeat at Internazionale on 22 March
cut their lead over Roma to three points, but then it
all went horribly wrong for Eriksson and his team.

On 29 March, Roma threw away all their good
work by losing 2–1 to bottom-of-the-table Udinese.
Napoli, meanwhile, were beating Juventus by the
same score, and that was that for another year.
The following week, Roma could only draw 1–1 at
home to Fiorentina, and Inter took over in second
place. The dreaded vote of confidence from Viola on
11 April hardly helped, and on the next day a suddenly deflated team gently subsided to a 2–0 defeat

away to Juventus. The following week, Eriksson offered to quit after the fans staged a demonstration in protest at his team's poor performance in a 1–1 draw at home to Ascoli. Viola rejected his resignation letter, but Roma were now in freefall. They failed to win any of their last seven league games, and Eriksson resigned again, with no objection this time, after a 4–1 defeat away to Milan on 4 May. There were two Serie A fixtures still to fulfill, and after Eriksson's loyal assistant, Giancarlo De Sisti, had refused to take on the job, a Brazilian-born former Italian international, Angelo Sormani, was put in charge in a caretaker's capacity, pending Liedholm's return. Under Sormani, Roma lost their last two matches, 3–0 at home to Sampdoria and 2–1 at Avellino, to limp in seventh. Voeller signed for Roma on 27 May and Liedholm was officially reappointed on 2 June. Eriksson, still resentful about the behind-the-scenes machinations that undermined him, says: 'I learned many things from that experience, starting with the fact that in Italy, football is played not just on the field. A coach like me could never have imagined that the real championship – the most difficult one – is played outside the stadium.'

Disillusioned or not, he was quickly back in the saddle, in Florence, replacing Eugenio Bersellini at Fiorentina for 1987/88. Eriksson's first signing was Glenn Hysen, a pillar of his old Gothenburg defence, for whom he paid a Swedish record fee of £800,000. Hysen, 29, was being pursued by Manchester United at the time. Playing in the second leg of the 1987

UEFA Cup Final, against Dundee United, he arrived at Glasgow airport, with Gothenburg coach Gunder Bengtsson (Eriksson's old assistant), to be met by Alex Ferguson, but for once United did not get their man. Gothenburg won the UEFA Cup and Hysen decamped to Italy. He explained: 'I signed for Fiorentina on a two-year contract, worth £130,000 annually. Their financial terms were better than United's, and the money, combined with the opportunity to work with Eriksson again, made the decision easy. Apart from my dad, he is the one who taught me most about football.' Against Hysen's arrival had to be weighed the loss of Giancarlo Antognoni, club stalwart and fans' favourite, who indicated that he would stay, then changed his mind and left for Lausanne.

Eriksson's start at Fiorentina was disappointing, a goalless draw at home to Verona, but the fans took him to their hearts the following Sunday, when Milan were beaten 2–0 in the San Siro, the goals coming from Ruben Diaz and Roberto Baggio. After two games they could at least claim a decent defence, as the only team in Serie A not to have conceded a goal. Unfortunately for the new coach, an unbeaten sequence of five games (two wins and three draws) was misleading, and having been sixth after the first eight matches, the season deteriorated disappointingly. Nicola Berti, the team's rising star in midfield, burnished his burgeoning reputation by scoring a hat-trick in the space of six minutes for the Italy Under-21 team against Portugal in December, but by then Fiorentina were down to tenth place in

Serie A, having lost more games than they had won. Celebration of a 3–2 win against the league leaders, Napoli, in the second round of the Italian Cup was a case of crowing too soon. Napoli won the corresponding league fixture 4–0 four days later, then beat Fiorentina 3–1 in the return leg of the cup tie to go through 5–4 on aggregate.

Eriksson remembers the sequence well. He says: 'In the first cup game, one Wednesday, Maradona mostly loafed about for 90 minutes. After the match, he came up to me and said: "Congratulations on the win, Mister, but it will be different on Sunday." We played Napoli again four days later, this time in the league, and we weren't given a chance. Napoli won 4–0 and Maradona was brilliant throughout. Our left-back came to the bench and asked: "What should I do about Maradona?" I told him: "It beats me." That just shows what motivation can do. Maradona was incredibly motivated for the league match, but not in the cup.'

After 19 league matches, Fiorentina had won only four and were down in 11th place, with 15 points. Berti, however, was not the only highly promising young player of whom Eriksson had great hopes. His goalkeeper, Marco Landucci, was one of four newcomers picked by Azeglio Vicini for Italy's friendly international against the Soviet Union in February. The season, nevertheless, degenerated into a relegation dogfight, with Serie A status only secured in the last two matches, which brought two notable scalps. On 8 May, Fiorentina beat Maradona's Napoli, the defending champions, 3–2, with

Ramon Diaz (two) and Alberto Di Chiara scoring, and the following week they defeated Juventus 2–1 in Turin, with Baggio and Di Chiara getting the goals. Between those two games, Fiorentina and Roma discussed swapping strikers. Diaz had fallen out with the Pontello family, who owned Fiorentina, and an exchange was proposed which would have seen Voeller follow Eriksson's path, from Rome to Florence. In the end, it didn't happen because the German's interest was barely lukewarm.

Fiorentina finished a very ordinary eighth, with nine wins and 11 defeats and a meagre 29 goals scored in 30 league games. They lost only once at home in Serie A, but managed just nine goals in 15 away matches. For Florentine fans, it was an un-remarkable season, notable chiefly for the death of the club president, Piercesaro Baretti, who was killed when his Cessna plane crashed into a hill near Turin.

There had to be an improvement in the 1988/89 season, or Eriksson would be in trouble. During the summer, while his old mate, Tord Grip, was leaving Norway as national team manager to take over Young Boys of Berne, Eriksson lost two of his top three players, with Berti and Ramon Diaz both sold to Internazionale. By way of replacement, Fiorentina acquired a high-class Brazilian, Dunga, from Pisa, to strengthen the midfield and the 24-year-old Como striker, Stefano Borgonovo. It hardly augured well when the 'Viola', as Fiorentina are known, succumbed 4–0 to Milan, and a Pietro Virdis hat-trick, in the San Siro on opening day,

but it was a better season for a team built around
Hysen, Dunga in midfield, Borgonovo and the ever-
improving Baggio. 'The Divine Ponytail', as the
world was to know him, was coming on in leaps and
bounds, and this was to be his breakthrough season.
Signed in the summer of 1985, Baggio tore knee ligaments in his last game for Vicenza, delaying his
Serie A debut until 21 September 1986. In 1987/88,
at the age of 20, he had managed a promising seven
goals in 26 starts, and now that promise was to have
rich fulfilment. In September 1988 he produced
what he still considers to be one of his best-ever
goals, in a rollercoaster 4–3 victory away to Internazionale (for whom Lothar Matthaus scored
twice), in the third round of the Italian Cup. 'It was
extraordinary,' he says, 'one of those goals you
imagine scoring as a child, when you are playing
in the corridor at home. Under Eriksson, I felt good.
He put his faith in me, and that really was the
season I came of age.'

The uncapped Baggio was included in Italy's
squad for the friendly against Norway in Pescara
in October, and after their first half-dozen league
games Fiorentina were doing well enough, three
wins and only one defeat putting them in fifth
place, three points behind top-of-the-table Inter.
In November Barcelona offered £3.5m for Baggio,
which had the effect of temporarily turning the
player's head. His attitude became a problem for
Eriksson for a time, but the president stayed strong
before giving Italy's most coveted young player a
contract extension until 1991, on £250,000-a-year.

Results, however, were only a marginal improvement on the previous season's, and by January the pressure was mounting, and Eriksson was grateful for the 3–0 victory over Lazio that eased it.

On 15 January Fiorentina beat Juventus 2–1 with a last-minute winner, but they were still losing almost as many as they won, and a 1–0 setback against Bologna kept them anchored in mid-table. They had their moments, however, and on 12 February they inflicted Internazionale's first defeat of the season in a minor classic. Inter, who had previously conceded a parsimonious five goals in 16 league games, had their locks picked time and again by Baggio and Borgonovo, and were beaten 4–3. Matthaus set the rollercoaster ride in motion with a 14th minute penalty, equalized after 33 by Baggio. Roberto Cucchi shot Fiorentina into a 2–1 lead with 52 minutes played, only for Aldo Serena to score twice to put Inter 3–2 up. Borgonovo then beat Walter Zenga twice in the last 18 minutes to bring Fiorentina the points. Five days later Borgonovo was rewarded with a call into the Italy squad for the friendly against Denmark.

For his club, it was one step forward, another step back. On 19 February Marco Van Basten scored both goals, and was then sent off, as Milan won 2–0 in Florence, and nine days later Eriksson announced that he was thinking of returning to Benfica. He had a decision to make, and would be making it 'within a few weeks', he said. In fact, it took him less than one. On 6 March he confirmed that he would definitely be going back. 'I haven't signed the contract yet, but the president and I have a verbal agreement,' he said. Liedholm, at Roma, was installed as the favourite for the Fiorentina job.

The timing was all to do with presidential elections at Benfica, where the incumbent, Joao Santos, had received 81 per cent of the vote on a 'dream ticket' of which Eriksson was part. Fiorentina were compliant at first, but then did a U-turn when they were unable to prise away either of the coaches they wanted – Bologna's Luigi Maifredi or Emiliano Mondonico of Atalanta. Suddenly, Eriksson had to stay. Benfica announced that they expected the pre-contract agreement to be honoured, but ran into problems when it was revealed that it had been signed by Eriksson's agent, not by him.

Meanwhile, the season at Fiorentina still had two months to run, and in March they tried to sign Gary Lineker from Barcelona, and Lubos Kubik, from Slavia Prague. Lineker was dubious, but Kubik joined on 31 March, for £900,000. On 1 June, the Fiorentina secretary, Nardino Previdi, flew to Barcelona to open negotiations for Lineker. Two weeks later, when the England striker said he would rather join Tottenham, Fiorentina turned their attentions to a Brazilian, Walter Casagrande, at Ascoli.

In the final table they were seventh, which meant a play-off with Roma, who were eighth, for Italy's last place in the UEFA Cup. A goal from Roberto Pruzzo, who had been recruited from Roma after Voeller's arrival, enabled Eriksson's new team to beat his old one, who had sacked Nils Liedholm, earlier the same month. The occasion was marred by crowd trouble, which was a recurring theme in Fiorentina's matches that season.

Hysen says: 'That was a young team, and we did well to qualify for the UEFA Cup at a time when Serie A was even tougher than it is now. Sven was never afraid to give talented young players a break. He'd given Baggio his chance the previous season, and he also showed great belief in Dunga, who went on to captain Brazil at the World Cup.' Paul Elliott, the former Chelsea centre-half who was playing for Pisa at the time, remembers Dunga well. 'You never heard anybody say a bad word about him. He was very level headed and mixed well with the other players. I recall Eriksson saying in the newspapers that Dunga was 30 per cent of the football Fiorentina were playing, and I could see what he meant. He had a significant influence on the others. Not only did he have good skills, but he had qualities we considered more European. He was prepared to run and press, as well as play with the ball. Juventus were always keen on him, but Eriksson didn't want to sell.'

Only Aldo Serena (Internazionale), Careca (Napoli) and Marco van Basten (Milan) scored more goals in Serie A than Baggio's 16 that season, and Borgonovo was next on the list with 14. It was Benfica, however, who won the contractual tug-of-war, and by the summer of 1989 Eriksson was back in Lisbon, earning less but saying: 'Life here is more relaxed than in Italy. There are still pressures, but they are not so personal. My wife and I are happy here, and that is worth more than money.'

CHAPTER ELEVEN

BACK TO BENFICA

One of Eriksson's first signings for Benfica second time around was Jonas Thern, the Swedish international midfielder, who cost £800,000 from Malmo. Another was Aldair, the Brazilian centre-half, who joined from Flamengo. Young at the time, both were to enjoy lengthy careers at the highest level, and provide impressive testimony to the canny Swede's eye for a player. Of Thern, who later played for Roma and Rangers, Eriksson says: 'He had everything – the complete all-rounder. He was strong, but he was much more than that. He could run, pass, tackle and shoot. He was my Roy Keane. He is not the best player I have worked with, but he was very, very good.' Thern is modest about his achievements with Benfica, crediting the team and the manager for his success: 'In my time there, we had a lot of good players. I think we had a squad of 24, and every one of them was an international of some sort. You expected to win things with players like that around you. "Svennis" was good at bringing the best out of everyone and finding their best roles. He's very clever at moulding players so that they fit together to form the best possible team.'

Benfica's motto is '*E Pluribus Unum*', and 'All for one, one for all' was supposed to be the way of it in the 1989/90 season. This unity of purpose was not immediately apparent in their first match, a disappointing 1–1 draw at home to Guimaraes, but by 10 `September, with the season just two weeks old, they were back in the old routine, drubbing Beira-Mar 5–0. Mats Magnusson, a big, strong Swedish striker scored four that day, two more in the 4–1 defeat of Nacional that followed, and with three wins and a draw from their first four league matches, Benfica were handily placed, two points behind the leaders, Sporting, but with a game in hand.

Their first defeat, on 22 October, gave the top of the table a new look, for by beating Eriksson's team 1–0, Porto became the new front runners. Benfica hit back hard. The following week, Magnusson had another hat-trick in the 5–0 demolition of Portimonense, and then they went one, or rather two better, thrashing Hungary's Honved 7–0, for a 9–0 aggregate, in the European Cup. Magnusson scored two in the last two minutes there, his boots having been filled earlier by Cesar Brito (two), Abel and the Angolan striker Vata, with two in three minutes. On 5 November Benfica met Sporting in the Lisbon derby. Public expectation was stratospheric but the match could never do justice to its billing, and came nowhere near doing so. Sporting's early brio turned to discord when Thern rattled a post after ten minutes, and a tense scrap was

settled eight minutes into the second half, when
Abel got away and put over a cross which Cesar
Brito, fresh from his international debut for
Portugal, stabbed home.

At this stage in his managerial career, Eriksson
was not averse to varying the 4–4–2 which has
always been his stock in trade. He explained:
'Against the top teams, we played with four defenders and four in midfield, but against less
demanding opposition we'd use three at the back
and five in midfield. In Portugal, we only had two
real rivals, Sporting and Porto. The rest were either
quite easy or very easy! In Italy it was different.
There, it was not a case of two or three major teams
but six or seven.'

Magnusson did much as he pleased against the
'easy' opposition, and rattled in his fourth hat-trick
of the season against Maritimo. That 4–0 win was
followed by another seven days later, with Braga on
the receiving end, and by now the prolific Swede
was a contender for the Golden Boot.

Benfica were looking the part as title aspirants,
but ended 1989 on a flat note, their goalless draw at
home to Boavista slated by Eriksson as 'our worst
performance of the season'. There was only a point
in it, but Porto had the psychological advantage
of going into the new year as league leaders.
Magnusson took his tally to 19 in 15 games in a 3–0
win away to Uniao, then added two more as
Amadora were beaten 2–0 at the Estadio da Luz, but
February was to be a bad month. The first seismic
shock came when Setubal put Benfica out of the

Portuguese Cup, the follow-up took the form of a 1–1 draw at home to bottom-of-the-table Nacional, described by Eriksson as 'a very sad performance'. Porto were three points clear at the top after beating Sporting 3–2, and Benfica v Porto on 11 March was hyped as 'the match of the season'. A 0–0 stalemate, it was nothing of the sort, but the result did ensure that the advantage stayed with Porto.

Ten days later, after a 3–2 away win at Portimonense, Benfica were in European action, against Dnepr Dnepropetrovsk, of the former Soviet Union. Having won only 1–0 at home, the decisive away leg looked tricky, and at 0–0 it was still anybody's game at half-time. In the second half, however, Benfica scored twice on the break, through striker Adesvaldo Lima, before Ricardo added a spectacular third to make the final margin 4–0 on aggregate. Benfica then beat Sporting 2–1 in the derby, with Lima on target again, Magnusson weighed in with a couple in the 2–0 defeat of Chaves, and the season was firmly back on track.

Controversy reared its ugly head in the semi-finals of the European Cup, where Benfica were paired with Marseille. The French champions, who were appearing in the tournament for the first time for 17 years, outplayed Eriksson's side in the first leg, yet somehow won only 2–1. Benfica took the lead, after ten minutes, with a headed goal from Lima, but the French defender Franck Sauzée equalized after 13, from a corner taken by Chris Waddle. The England winger, who was outstanding throughout, put Jean-Pierre Papin through for the winner, just before half-time, and was unlucky when his free-kick struck the crossbar. Benfica, very much second best on the night, were fortunate to emerge only 2–1 down, with the away goal offering them every chance of progress. Nevertheless, the president, Joao Santos, was not happy. Why, he wanted to know, had the Marseille players not been subject to dope-testing? He would be insisting upon it for the second leg. The inevitable row ensued, and the suspicious Santos was formally reprimanded by UEFA on 11 April. In the return, a week later, it took Benfica 84 minutes to get the one goal that was all they needed, and there was a clear handball before it was chested home at close range by the Angolan striker, Vata. Television replays showed the illegal contact, after Magnusson had flicked on Valdo's corner, but whose hand was responsible was unclear. Before this scruffy decider, Benfica had not looked like breaking through.

Back home in the league, Eriksson's team were cracking up. They could only draw with Maritimo and Farense, while Porto were beating Tirsense and Uniao, and a 1–0 defeat away to Boavista on 29 April left them five points behind their northern rivals with five games to play. If they were going to win anything, it would probably have to be the European Cup. The final, in Vienna's Prater stadium, brought them up against Milan, who were looking to complete an Italian clean sweep, Sampdoria having already won the Cup-Winners' Cup and Juventus the UEFA Cup.

Benfica were poor and Milan not much better in

one of the less memorable finals. The Italian team was full of household names – Baresi, Maldini, Rijkaard, Gullit, Van Basten and so on, but Benfica had internationally celebrated players of their own. Defenders Ricardo and Aldair and midfielder Valdo were all in the Brazilian World Cup squad, and there were two notable Swedes in Thern and the mighty Magnusson, who finished the domestic season as Portugal's leading scorer, with 33 goals from 32 games. Benfica's names, however, were not from the same stellar firmament as Milan's and their cause was not helped by the absence of Lima, the Brazilian forward, who had scored in the semi-finals, but was now laid low by a leg injury. For all that, Eriksson said: 'We are not here simply to make up the numbers, we feel we can win – especially as Milan this year are not as strong as they were.'

In the first half, Benfica were marginally the more positive side, Thern's strong runs from mid-field threatening to embarrass Baresi, but for too long Magnusson suffered from a lack of support. Ricardo's run from deep set up a chance for Valdo, but his drive, from 25 yards, flew tantalizingly wide. That was it, Benfica had shot their bolt. Milan won it midway through the second half with the only goal of the game, when a typically deft flick from Van Basten enabled another Dutchman, Rijkaard, to score with the outside of his right foot. Benfica, once pre-eminent, had lost the European Cup Final for a fifth successive time.

Thern says: 'It was not a good game, neither team played well, but we felt a bit unlucky, coming so close. In the dressing room afterwards, Svennis came in and showed his disappointment. He told us: "You've come so close, and maybe you'll never have this chance again, because it's going to be even harder to reach the final of the European Cup in future." By that, I think he meant that the old knockout tournament was about to change into the Champions' League. Whatever he meant, he was right. For him, and for me, there hasn't been another European Cup Final. You could see that he was very disappointed. It's a big thing on a trainer's CV, to have won the European Cup.

'We had a good team, but at that time Milan were the best in Europe and maybe the best in the world, with Gullit, Van Basten, Rijkaard, Baresi and so on. It was always going to be very difficult to beat them, but we still have our memories. Of course, you want to win, but we can be proud of coming second in such a competition.'

In the league, Benfica finished strongly, with three successive wins, but it was not enough. They were runners-up, four points behind Porto.

For the 1990/91 season, their prospects were scarcely enhanced by the sale of Aldair, the Brazilian centre-back, to Roma for £3m. However, the Brazilian flavour was maintained by the acquisition of William, 23, from Vitoria Guimaraes, as Aldair's replacement, and Isaias, a 26-year-old striker from Boavista, who was to partner Rui Aguas, re-signed from Porto at the age of 30 for a third spell with the club. Eriksson also replaced the goalkeeper, Silvano, with Neno, 28, from Guimaraes, and offloaded midfielders Ademir and Chalana, to Boavista and Belenenses respectively, making way for Stefan Schwarz, the 21-year-old Swedish international, from Malmo.

Sporting Lisbon, a distant third the previous season, won each of their first 11 league games, but Benfica also got away well, winning eight and drawing one of their first nine, with Schwarz contributing four goals. Eriksson recalls 'Big Stefan' fondly. 'He was a good player to have around – versatile and very strong,' he told me. 'I used him at left-back, then left midfield – sometimes even left-wing. Unfortunately, he got a bad injury soon after joining us, and was out for months.'

The season's early days were not without controversy. In the first round of the UEFA Cup, Benfica were drawn against one of Eriksson's old clubs, Roma, and the aftermath of the first leg, in Italy on 19 September, brought high drama, and echoes of Marseille the previous April. The match was unremarkable, Roma winning 1–0 with a goal in the first minute from Andrea Carnevale, but four days later Carnevale and the Roma goalkeeper, Angelo Peruzzi, both failed dope tests and were banned for a year. The ban was lifted pending appeal (when it was confirmed), and both players took part in the return, after which Eriksson was the one with the problems. Benfica had been confident of turning around their single-goal deficit at home, but lost 1–0 again, with Giannini's 27th minute strike proving decisive.

Out of Europe and fourth in the league, the

natives were restless. Rumours of an imminent change of management grew stronger with a 2–0 defeat at Setubal on 4 November, but Eriksson weathered the storm, and it proved to be their only loss in the league all season. Others were not so lucky. It seems scarcely credible now, given his status as a maestro among coaches, but Marcello Lippi was sacked that January, with his Cesena team propping up Serie A, and Eriksson's old assistant and successor at Gothenburg, Gunder Bengtsson, was forced out at Feyenoord after a defeat by PSV.

Back in Portugal, the tide turned. Sporting lost 2–0 at Porto, then 2–0 at home to Benfica, for whom Isaias and Cesar Brito got the goals, and at the halfway stage Porto, whose attack was cleverly led by the Bulgarian, Emile Kostadinov, were top of the table, leading Benfica by two points and Sporting by six.

Eriksson and his team were ready to make their run. From 3 February they played a dozen league games and won the lot. Suddenly, he was hot currency again. In March, Fiorentina tried to lure him back to Florence to replace the Brazilian, Sebastiao Lazaroni, and he had talks with the United States Soccer Federation, about managing the American team at the 1994 World Cup. Most attractive of all, the Internazionale president, Ernest Pelligrini, wanted him to take over from Giovanni Trapattoni, but negotiations broke down over compensation. Meanwhile, Mats Magnusson's winner against Maritimo put Benfica through to the quarter-finals of the Portuguese Cup, where Porto hit back from a goal down to beat them 2–1. In the league, it was still nip and tuck in the third week of April, when Porto regained the leadership with a 2–0 win at Sporting, only to be dislodged by Benfica's 5–0 trouncing of Tirsense.

The coup de grâce came in the archetypal six-pointer (it was four then) on 28 April, when two late goals from substitute Cesar Brito brought Benfica a precious 2–0 win away to Porto. They stumbled and nearly fell in their next match, at home to Sporting, when they needed an 89th minute goal from Isaias to escape with a 1–1 draw, but then clinched their 29th league title in the penultimate fixture, away to Maritimo, with goals from William, the Brazilian centre-back, who was the only ever-present that season, and Rui Aguas, the league's leading scorer, with 25 goals from 37 appearances.

Having scaled the heights, Eriksson found there was only one way to go, and the 1991/92 season was easily the worst in his two spells in Lisbon. Before it started Ricardo and Valdo were sold to Paris St Germain, Fernando Mendes to Boavista and the experienced defender, Samuel, was transferred to Boavista. A London-based Israeli agent, Pini Zahavi, who was later to try to take Eriksson to Chelsea, had approached the club, and at his instigation Benfica moved away from the Brazilian influence and into the murky waters of Soviet football, signing Sergei Yuran, a striker from Dinamo Kiev, and Vasily Kulkov, a defender known as 'the Soviet Baresi', from Spartak Moscow. Later in the season they were to import a third international from the old CIS, taking Alexander Mostovoi, a 23-year-old midfielder from Moscow Spartak, who married a Portuguese girl to get around the immigration laws. Eriksson also promoted two 18 year olds to the first-team squad. Rui Bento and Rui Costa had both been members of Portugal's World Youth Cup-winning squad in 1991, and Rui Costa was recalled from Fafe, of the Third Division, where he had been loaned to gain senior experience. Another young player, Manuel Valido, a 21-year-old defender, joined from Gil Vicente.

In the league, Benfica got off to a terrible start, losing their first game 1–0 at home to Boavista, then managing only a scrambled draw against the minnows of Gil Vicente. A goalless stalemate in the derby against Sporting, who were much the better side on the day, saw Eriksson under pressure from supporters, who resented the departure of Valdo and Ricardo, and who, in increasing numbers, were calling for the coach's dismissal.

The first round of the new Champions' League, four days later, afforded a break from the pressure. Benfica were drawn against little Hamrun Spartans, of Malta, and won 6–0 away, with Yuran getting four, and 4–0 in the return for a 10–0 aggregate. But on the domestic front Porto were the best team in the league. They had a new Brazilian coach, Carlos Alberto Silva, whose reputation, unusually for his country of origin, was built on parsimonious defence. Kostadinov's success had been such that they signed another Bulgarian striker, Petre

Mihtarsky, but the emphasis was elsewhere, and in Carlos Alberto's first season in charge, Porto had the best defensive record in Europe, conceding just 11 goals in 34 league games. At one stage, Vitor Baia, their goalkeeper, kept 12 successive clean sheets.

When they were on song, Benfica played some lovely football, but they were inconsistent, too often passing the ball around self-indulgently, with no sign of penetration. Their best moments came in Europe. After coasting past Hamrun Spartans, they came up against George Graham's Arsenal, for a place in the lucrative group stage. Just before the first leg, in Lisbon, Benfica had gone top of the table in Portugal for the first time by beating Chaves 4–1, so Arsenal knew they were in good form, and Graham and his staff did their homework, watching them several times. Eriksson, however, outwitted them by keeping his most dangerous forward, Isaias, under wraps on each occasion. The Brazilian loved to run at defenders from deep, and Arsenal were clearly caught unprepared for this when a pass from Schwarz allowed him to break the most famous off-side trap of them all and open the scoring. Graham's response was to put Paul Davis on Isaias and tell Merson to tuck in deeper. That drew Benfica's sting, and a fulminating drive from Kevin Campbell brought Arsenal the important away goal which, at 1–1, left the tie tilted in the English team's favour. Graham, well satisfied with a good night's work, said: 'I was very pleased with our performance. The atmosphere was very intimidating and Eriksson surprised us with his tactics early on, but through hard work, skill and organization, we earned our reward.'

Before travelling to Highbury, Eriksson said: 'I went there with Gothenburg in the Cup-Winners' Cup and we lost 5–1. I will not lose 5–1 again.' He was as good as his word. Arsenal versus Benfica at Highbury on 6 November 1991 was a classic – a match those privileged to witness it will never forget. George Graham said beforehand: 'I remember from my own playing days that not all continental sides travel well, and I have told my players that in the opening 15 minutes we must test the will of the opposition. We have to mark them tightly and not give them the time and space to play. We will soon find out who amongst them wants to play and who wants to hide.' This little Englander's speech (and from a Scot) was the archetypal hostage to fortune. By the end of the night, it was Graham who was looking for a place to hide.

In the opening half-hour, Arsenal followed his instructions to the letter, denying Benfica the time and space to develop their slick passing game. Thern says: 'After the 1–1 draw in Lisbon, we knew it was going to be hard to go through, and in the first 20 minutes at Highbury I remember we hardly touched the ball. Arsenal were attacking from right and left, and the crosses were raining in. I thought to myself: "They're going to score a couple here before half-time," but somehow we managed to stay in the game.'

Campbell headed against a post after six minutes, and after 19 Paul Merson's 25-yarder was touched against the crossbar and over. From the consequent corner, Colin Pates, making his European debut at the age of 30, drove home his first and last goal for Arsenal, and all was going according to the managerial masterplan. David Seaman saved from Isaias, but at this stage Graham and company had no reason for concern. That all changed with 36 minutes gone, when Yuran headed through to Isaias, who ran through Graham's vaunted defence before beating Seaman with aplomb.

Benfica's passing was a delight to behold, light years beyond Arsenal's long-ball game, which they preferred to describe as 'direct', and England's right-back, Lee Dixon, was given a torrid time by Isaias and Yuran. 'In the second half,' Thern says, 'we showed how well we had been prepared. We kept on playing our game and Arsenal's performance level dropped – especially the physical aspect. We were better conditioned.' Yet still Graham's Gunners might have won it. In the 70th minute Merson, with the goalmouth gaping, lifted Alan Smith's inviting cross over the crossbar, and in extra-time Smith wasted a good chance from six yards. Such was the sublime quality of Benfica's football, however, that it would have been a travesty had they not prevailed, and justice was done ten minutes into the additional period when intelligent running off the ball by Yuran enabled Kulkov to score with a low drive into the corner. The away-goals rule meant that Arsenal, who were trailing 3–2 on aggregate, now needed to score twice to save the game. Tony Adams hit a post, but then Isaias left him for dead to settle the issue.

Thern says: 'In extra-time, we felt much stronger than them and knew we were the better footballing team. They had started at such a pace that it was impossible to keep it up for 90 minutes. If you expend a lot of energy at the beginning of a game, sometimes you suffer towards the end.'

Adams recalled a chastening experience as follows: 'After the 1–1 draw in Lisbon, the return was far from the formality many people expected. We took the lead through Colin Pates, but they came back strongly, hitting us on the break. As we went looking for the winner, I missed one of the biggest sitters of my career, scuffing a shot from about two yards out. Then they broke away and scored again. Behind, we were chasing the game and played helter-skelter football. Finally, Isaias nutmegged me and we were out. There was a lot of talk about them having better technique than us, but we certainly had the chances to win, whether they were more gifted or not.'

Graham, who had learned the hard way 'who wants to play', said: 'Their forwards were lovely to watch, but they had a big headstart on us in the skill factor. It was also very unusual to see opponents at Highbury look fitter than us, but Benfica did.' He had been particularly impressed by Yuran and Thern, and was later to sign Schwarz.

Eriksson is not so sure that stamina was of major significance. 'I always admired the English mentality, because you are so strong, so hard working,' he says. 'But we had the talent. Arsenal were physically stronger than us, and we were lucky they didn't score earlier, but we had the better technique. They had more of the ball than us, but when we had it, we did more with it, and created the better chances.'

England's champions had been given a master-class in the 'beautiful game', and nobody who saw it would have been at all surprised had Benfica gone on to win the tournament. At the group stage, they were bracketed with Barcelona, Sparta Prague and Dinamo Kiev, and Eriksson was confident of achieving the top-two finish needed if they were to progress. But that confidence was soon dented. In their first match, Benfica lost 1–0 in Kiev and Rui Aguas broke a leg, and in the second, a goalless draw at home to Barcelona left them with a lot of ground to make up. Two 1–1 draws, at home and away with Sparta, barely improved the situation, but a 5–0 drubbing of Kiev, in which Yuran scored twice against his old club, certainly did. With Barcelona losing 1–0 in Prague, it was now possible for Benfica to squeeze through, but only if they won in the Nou Camp and Kiev beat Sparta at home. It was a tall order, and it never looked like happening. Kiev did their bit, winning 1–0, but Barcelona went 2–0 up, and had the game won before Cesar Brito scored his fourth goal of the tournament. The pride of Catalonia won the group, with nine points from their six matches, three ahead of Sparta. Benfica, on five, missed out by a single point.

Further disappointment came in the Portuguese Cup, where they were beaten 2–1 in the semi-finals by Boavista, and then their league form fell away, too. They dropped nine points at home, which was unheard of, moving one of Portugal's leading sports journalists, Alberto Da Silva, to write: 'Just as Arsenal were deluded after their draw at Estadio da Luz, so were Benfica, despite their brilliant 3–1 victory at Highbury. Since that unforgettable evening of majestic football, the Lisbon Eagles have not produced anything consistent with their ambitions and the demands of their traditions. Having lost in Kiev and drawn at home to Barcelona, the Portuguese champions lost the chance of again becoming the masters of European football. This, however, could be understood, given the class and the determination of the opposition, were it not for the abysmal performances and results in the domestic league.

'Exceedingly poor results have removed Benfica from the leadership of the league, which is headed by Porto, a much more consistent and determined team. What has gone wrong? I watched Benfica in their recent games, and their attitude is quite simple. They only need to be there, and show the red shirts, in the hope that the opposition become terrified and allow themselves to be conquered. They only need to dance with the ball in midfield. But the web of passes leads nowhere. The illusion that their adversaries will surrender, or make a couple of mistakes, is all Benfica play for. They are not creating, not scoring.

'Benfica are not drawing the crowds as before, and grounds which used to be filled wherever they played are now half-empty. Naturally people are calling for Eriksson's head – something they have been doing for quite a long time in a campaign of resentment against tactics and his cold, studious approach. He had been given a new lease of life after Highbury, but it is hard to see how he is going to resist the pressure now.'

He couldn't. Porto winning 3–2 at the Stadium of Light on 27 March to clinch the title was too much for the president, Jorge De Brito, to bear. Benfica had won nothing, and second place was unacceptable. On 10 May, it was announced that they had recruited Tomislav Ivic, from Marseille, in succession to Eriksson, whose departure for Sampdoria was hardly a surprise. A few months earlier, on 24 January, it had been reported in Italy that he had signed an agreement to replace Vujadin Boskov at the end of the season.

CHAPTER TWELVE

DANCING TO MANTOVANI'S TUNE

It was all-change in Lisbon. Eriksson was replacing the 61-year-old Serb, Vujadin Boskov, at Sampdoria, and the following day, Bobby Robson signed a two-year contract with the Portuguese capital's other big club, Sporting. Some high-profile players were moving, too. Sampdoria's extra-time defeat by Barcelona at Wembley in the 1992 European Cup Final prompted the sale of Gianluca Vialli to Juventus for a world record fee of £12m. At the same time, Paul Gascoigne's protracted transfer from Tottenham to Lazio was finally completed.

Although they had reached the Champions' Cup Final, 'Samp' had finished a disappointing sixth in Serie A, and their president, Paulo Mantovani, bought Eriksson half a new team. Vialli and the 37-year-old Brazilian midfielder Toninho Cerezo went, the latter sold back to Sao Paulo for just £10,000, and in came Des Walker from Nottingham Forest, Vladimir Jugovic from Red Star Belgrade, Enrico Chiesa from Chieti, Mauro Bertarelli from Ancona and Michele Serena from Verona. David Platt, the former England captain who now works for Eriksson as manager of the England Under-21 team, was to join 12 months later. 'The team was being dismantled when Sven took over,' he told me. 'It had been a successful side, but the club decided that they needed to start another cycle. They were projecting figures and knew they couldn't afford to keep the likes of Vialli, Cerezo and some of the older players. If they didn't rejuvenate the squad, they would no longer be competitive in Serie A. They'd had their successful cycle, winning the league and getting to the final of the European Cup and Cup-Winners' Cup. Now they had to drop down a level and rebuild before they challenged again. While they did that, they couldn't hope to compete with the likes of Juventus and Milan.' So 1992/93 was to be a transitional season.

It started well enough, with Sampdoria winning England's annual Makita tournament, beating the hosts, Leeds United 1–0 in the final, but on 2 September they were eliminated from the Italian Cup in the second round, by Cesena. In the league, they were quickly into decent form, Jugovic scoring twice in a 3–2 win away to Ancona, then again as Udinese were defeated 2–1 on their own ground. A last-minute equalizer from stalwart defender Pietro Vierchowod gained another good away result, against Torino, after which, with five matches played, Samp were unbeaten and third in the table, with three wins and two draws. The first defeat, on 25 October, was a bruising one, Fiorentina scoring four without reply, but Eriksson's team responded well, by putting four of their own past Genoa in the derby, and the goalless draw away to Internazionale and 3–1 beating of Napoli that followed had them only four points behind the leaders, Milan, and still in good shape.

The dip that was to shape the season started at the end of November, when Faustino Asprilla scored the only goal of the game at Parma. After losing their next home match, 3–2 to Atalanta, Samp drew four in succession, with the result that they were down to seventh in the table at the start of 1993. They had found their level. They were good enough to beat ordinary opposition, but were found wanting by the better sides, getting a 4–0 drubbing from Milan and losing 3–1 to Internazionale and even, late on, 3–1 to Brescia. In the final table, they were seventh, and their record – won 12, drawn 12, lost 10 – said it all. They were just above average.

For Eriksson's second season, there was a major policy change, which brought in Platt, from Juventus, Ruud Gullit and Alberigo Evani from Milan, Fausto Salsano from Roma and Mauro Rossi from Brescia. Gullit and Platt signed on the same day (15 July), the Dutchman, who was deemed to be past his best, costing a paltry £500,000 and Platt £5.2m. Both proved to be inspired choices, Gullit a real catalyst. Explaining the club's new, money-no-object approach, Platt said: 'The president, Mantovani, was terminally ill, and knew he was dying. From a business point of view, he'd done well for Sampdoria, reducing the wage bill and putting the club on a sound base financially. But he wasn't enjoying finishing seventh in the league after the success he'd had, and Mancini persuaded him to go for it one last time. It was Mancini, the president's favourite player, who got him to sign me, Evani, and Gullit, telling the old man: "Let's go and have another crack at it."'

The opening game of the season, away to Napoli, got them off to a flying start, Platt scoring the first goal and Gullit the winner in a 2–1 victory. Platt missed the next two matches, away on international duty with England, but made a scoring return in a 2–1 win at home to Lecce, and when he did it again, in a 4–1 win at Atalanta, it had taken him just four appearances for his new club to harvest as many goals as he had managed in the whole of the previous season for Juventus. Gullit had contributed four already, and with six games played Sampdoria were only one point behind the leaders, Milan. Well though Platt and the clever Roberto Mancini were playing, Gullit was the star of the show. Drawing motivation from the way Milan had dumped him after six successful years, he proved that at 31 he could still be a matchwinner in any company, wonky knees or not. At half-time in the win against Lecce, Eriksson went up to him in the dressing room and said: 'Just keep that up, and we're sure to win. I haven't seen you play as well as this for four or five seasons.'

Gullit told me: 'At Milan, they'd said I had knees of glass, and that I couldn't play two games in a week any more. My answer to that was that because they wouldn't let me play that often, I couldn't prove that they were wrong. I wanted to play all the time.

Fortunately, Sampdoria wanted me, and I went there and played nearly every game. I had a fantastic season, and like to think I proved a few people wrong.' Gullit also remembers his manager in Genoa fondly, saying 'I was really charmed by him. He's a real gentleman. If you didn't do what he wanted, or just did your own thing, the way he is meant that it would only affect you. He was so nice, such a good man, in the way he treated people that it seemed rude, as well as silly, not to do what he asked. Because of the regard we all had for him, he never had to raise his voice to anyone. He would talk to you, one on one, in a very civilized way. He was genuinely interested in you, personally – not just what you were doing on the pitch.'

Platt warmly described those days of fond memory. 'The spirit in the squad was exceptional, Sven's training methods were interesting and enjoyable, he was – still is – an exceptional coach. The first thing I noticed about him was the way he could handle big-name players. There were some big egos, some big personalities in that dressing room. The quality of the players was of the highest class. Mancini was a genius. He could put the ball where he wanted, whenever he wanted. Pietro Vierchowod, at 36, was still remarkably good. Gary Lineker told me that he had never played against a better defender. Maradona called him "The Incredible Hulk" and Van Basten listed him as his finest opponent. Our goalkeeper, Gianluca Pagliuca, who played for Italy, was exceptional, Gullit continued to show why he had been at the very peak of his profession for so long, and Moreno Mannini has to be the shrewdest defender I've ever played with. I'd admired Attilio Lombardo when I was at Bari and Juventus, but until I trained with him every day I didn't realize just how good he was. He had everything – tactical knowledge, pace, dribbling ability and a marvellous temperament to go with it. He never once came to training without a smile on his face. Not only were these players blessed with tremendous ability, they were all extremely intelligent and receptive to new ideas.

'Sven handled them all very easily. Players like Gullit gave him great respect because of what he did on the training pitch and what he did in games. He could change our formation part-way through a difficult match to win it. In training we worked on tactics every day and a lot on fitness as well. We worked harder at Sampdoria than we did at Juventus. Sven worked on spirit and morale, individually, as well as collectively. Tactically, he prefers to work with a back four, but with the players we had that season he realized we were better suited to playing with a sweeper, or spare man, at the back. Mannini was the sweeper, with Vierchowod and Stefano Sacchetti marking. Lombardo was in midfield, with me, Chicco Evani and Jugovic, and up front were Gullit and Mancini. In reserve we had Giulio Nuciari, the former Milan goalkeeper, Michele Serena, a versatile player who had hardly missed a game the previous season, Salsano, who had returned to Sampdoria after three years with Roma, and a free-scoring centre-forward called Mauro Bertarelli.'

The style of play suited Platt much better than it had at Juventus, where everything had revolved around Roberto Baggio. 'There was Gullit, who didn't really want to play centre-forward, and Mancini, who didn't want to either, both dropping back off their markers, leaving space for me to get forward.'

Gullit says: 'I played centre-forward, up front with Mancini, but we were not what you'd call orthodox strikers, we'd go deep or wide a lot. We had our options, we could do whatever we felt was necessary. We had our freedom to go and do what we thought was best. Eriksson gave us that licence to think for ourselves, and we paid him back by working hard for the team. He is very knowledge-able about tactics, but he believes more in the individual. He knows that it is individuals who determine whether you win games or not.'

The date Gullit ringed in his diary on the day of his transfer was 31 October, and that balmy Sunday afternoon he exacted sweet revenge. A proud man, he had felt slighted by the way Milan offloaded him, and when Sampdoria travelled to meet the league leaders he was duly fired up. Samp were 2–0 down at half-time, to goals from Demetrio Albertini and Brian Laudrup, and seemingly set for defeat, when Gullit took charge. After Srecko Katanec had pulled one back, he 'won' a penalty for Mancini, then scored the winner as his new team fought back magnificently to inflict on his old one their first defeat of the season. The result put Sampdoria joint top of the table, but sadly, Paulo Mantovani did not live to see it. He died in October 1993, to be replaced by his 34-year-old son, Enrico. Anyway, pride was followed by a nasty tumble, Samp losing 2–1 at home to Cagliari next time out. Back-to-back victories over Foggia and Cremonese kept them in the hunt, but after Platt had scored yet again in the drawn derby with Genoa, there was a sizeable setback in the shape of a 3–0 defeat at Inter. Christmas, however, found Samp with every reason to be full of good cheer. Third in the league, three points behind the leaders, they were also making progress in the Italian Cup, where they had just beaten Roma on penalties.

Well into the new year they were widely regarded as credible title contenders, and all the more so after Mancini (two), Gullit and Lombardo had put four past Napoli. There was nobody to match them as far as goalscoring was concerned, and after Lombardo and Gullit had seen off Internazionale in the domestic cup quarter-finals, the most exciting forward line in Serie A cut loose, beating Lecce 3–0 and then hitting Udinese for six, with Jugovic and Mancini each netting twice. Yet to Eriksson's frustration, every time his team gained ground on Milan, they stumbled and lost it again. Gianfranco Zola's stoppage-time winner left them empty-handed at Parma, and although they bounced back strongly, with consecutive victories over Atalanta, Roma and Torino, it was by now apparent that they would have to win away to Milan on 13 March if they were going to overhaul them. Instead, Daniele Massaro scored the only goal of the game, after 26 minutes.

With Milan winning game after game, and now seven points clear, it was clear that Eriksson's best chance of putting a trophy in the table was in the Italian Cup. There, having needed penalties to overcome Pisa and Roma in the early rounds, it took a last-minute goal from Gullit in the San Siro to see off Internazionale in the last eight, and set up a semifinal against Parma, who were two points behind Samp in the league, in fifth place. In the first leg, in Genoa, Faustino Asprilla gave Parma a 1–0 half-time lead, but goals from Lombardo and Platt earned Sampdoria a slender 2–1 advantage to take to Parma two weeks later. As it happened, it was a cushion they didn't need. Gullit got the only goal in the return for a 3–1 aggregate win which took Eriksson and his team into the final, where they were odds-on favourites against Ancona, from Serie B.

Eriksson finally got his hands on his first piece of Italian silverware on 20 April 1994. The final was a mismatch. Sampdoria were about to finish third in Serie A, Ancona eighth in Serie B and the difference in class showed. Content to take the teeth out of the underdogs away, where they drew 0–0, Samp won 6–1 at home, Lombardo scoring twice, and celebrated in style. The abstemiousness for which Italian footballers are renowned was forgotten as the players drank wine with the fans in a bar at the stadium, then adjourned to a restaurant for a long night with family and friends.

The cup won, and the scudetto destined to stay in Milan, the bread and butter that was league football became a chore, and the last two games were disappointing – a draw with Reggiana and a 4–3 defeat against Lazio. 'Towards the end of the season,' Platt says, 'Gullit was going back to Milan, everybody knew it, and I think he took his foot off the pedal, and because of that everybody else did.' With 64 goals in their 34 matches, Sampdoria were easily the highest scorers in Serie A (the title was won with just 36), but they shipped 39, which was more than Reggiana, who were 14th.

Third place was the club's highest finish since their 1990/91 championship season, and Mantovani expressed satisfaction with a place in Europe, but Platt says: 'In fairness to Gullit, he said constantly throughout that season, that we had to have more belief. He said that was all we needed to win the league. He had been there and done it with Milan, and knew exactly what was required. Whereas a lot of us looked at it and thought: "We're not as good as Milan and Juventus", he knew that with a bit more belief, we could have won it. Looking back, we were good enough, it was only our mentality that was wrong. Milan, who had already won it twice in succession, had more belief than us.'

Gullit, who enjoyed a best-ever return of 15 goals, says: 'In the beginning, nobody thought we had it in us to do as well as we did. For the players, when it started to happen it was a case of: "What's happening here?" We worked very hard at tactics because for a long time we weren't convinced that we were good enough individually. To overcome that, we worked very hard at our collective game, and all of a sudden the improvement was incredible. We grew together and came on to our game throughout the season. We just got better and better. It's true that I felt, and said, that with a bit more belief we could have finished higher than third.' Eriksson accepts that Samp could, and should, have done better that year. 'Nobody at the club realized how good we were – and that includes me.' The experience accentuated his quasi-religious faith in the power of positive thinking. Pagliuca, Mancini, Evani and Lombardo all played for Italy that season but, surprisingly, Lombardo's ever-present excellence on the right flank did not get him to the 1994 World Cup.

On a personal level, it was in 1994 that Sven and Ann-Christin went their separate ways after 17 years of marriage, and Eriksson was seen at the World Cup, in the United States, in the company of another woman, Graziella Mancinelli. Eriksson blamed the pressures of football management for the marital breakdown, but his ex-wife is not so sure.

For the 1994/95 season, Sampdoria swapped goalkeepers with Internazionale, Pagliuca going to Milan in exchange for the experienced Italian international, Walter Zenga, 34, whose last appearance for Inter had brought him man-of-the-match honours in the UEFA Cup Final. Eriksson's other reinforcements were the Italian defender Riccardo Ferri, 31, also from Inter, Sinisa Mihajlovic, the 25-year-old Yugoslav midfielder, who joined from Roma, and the Parma striker Alessandro Melli. Gullit duly went back to Milan, for £1.3m. 'You make mistakes in life,' he says with a shrug. 'I realized very quickly that I had done the wrong thing, and put it right [he rejoined Sampdoria on 9 November]. What I liked about Genoa was that it was a different environment. In Milan it was very stressful. You have to win all the time – have to, have to. There was always that pressure on you. That wasn't the case with Sampdoria. The life there was different for me. I wasn't used to it, but it was very nice.'

Platt says: 'We'd lost Gullit and signed Melli, who was a different type of player altogether, which changed our game, and gave us a more clearly defined, less fluid formation. Melli was a good striker, but his style wasn't to pull wide or fill holes. So the change wasn't like for like. Gullit's particular characteristics had helped everybody else's to fit together. Sven saw that and changed to a more conventional 4–4–2. Melli didn't vacate the centre-forward's space for me as much at Gullit had done.'

The new-look team got off to the brightest of starts. A goal for Milan by Gullit held them to 1–1 in the Super Cup (the Italian equivalent of England's Charity Shield), but then Samp defeated Civenza 5–1 in the Italian Cup and routed Padova 5–0 at home in their first league game, with Melli and Mihajlovic both scoring on debut. Unfortunately for all concerned, it was a false dawn. In October they went out of the Italian Cup in the third round, losing 3–2 on aggregate to Fiorentina, could only draw 0–0 at home to Napoli, and lost 2–0 at Cremonese. Then Gullit, who had fallen out with Fabio Capello after only nine league games and three goals for Milan, telephoned Eriksson to engineer his return to Sampdoria, and a swap was promptly arranged which took Melli the other way. 'Something had happened at Milan, and Gullit, called me and said he wanted to come back,' Eriksson explained. 'He had lost his motivation. Unfortunately he never found it again.' Platt says: 'With Ruud coming back, we reverted to the old playing style, but he had lost what he had before, and it didn't really work. He wasn't the same player he had been that first year. It seemed he thought he didn't have anything to prove.' Gullit was told as much in the dressing room, where he had several confrontations with Mancini, the senior professional, who was an icon in Genoa. Their disagreements had a detrimental effect on the harmony Eriksson had worked so hard to create in and around the squad. 'It all happened in front of the other lads,' Platt says, 'with the result that we weren't as unified in the dressing room as we had been.'

On 27 November, Gullit and Platt were back in the old routine, with a goal apiece in Florence in a match in which Fiorentina's Gabriel Batistuta set a record by scoring for the eleventh consecutive league game. Next up was the Genoa derby, which Sampdoria won 3–2, followed by a goalless draw at Brescia and a 5–0 thrashing of Cagliari, with Gullit scoring twice. Lazio were beaten 3–1 and Padova 4–1, but there were bad results, too, against Inter (0–2) and at home to Bari (1–1) and Juventus (0–1), and by mid-season Samp were 11 points behind the league leaders, Juventus, and Europe, in the guise of the Cup-Winners' Cup, was already their main focus. Inauspiciously, they lost their first game in the tournament 3–2, away to the obscure Norwegian part-timers of Bodo-Glimt, only scraping through with a 2–0 home win for a 4–3 aggregate. Grasshoppers of Zurich, were more of a name, but less of a problem. It was a case of 'job done' after a routine 3–0 victory at home, which rendered the 3–2 defeat in the return academic.

The quarter-finals brought Platt up against Porto, and his manager from the 1990 World Cup, Bobby Robson. 'What a struggle that was,' Platt recalled. In the first leg, at home, Sampdoria were defeated for the first time in 23 European ties at their Luigi Ferraris stadium, when Sergei Yuran, whom Eriksson had once bought for Benfica, gave Robson's side a 1–0 lead to take back to Portugal. Platt recalls: 'Emerson, the Brazilian who later joined Middlesbrough, ran the show. They were so much better than us, they outplayed us. We came off the pitch thinking we were out of the competition. We were down on the floor.'

In adversity, Eriksson came into his own, earning his money and burnishing his reputation as an astute tactician and master of the art of man management. Platt takes up the story. 'Sven refused to accept that we were out, and three days before the second leg he took us away to a hotel near Parma, owned by a chef who used to travel with us. That was the best I've ever been prepared for a game in my life – not just tactically, but mentally, too. Sven worked us morning and afternoon, changing our formation and devising a plan to hit them from midfield, on the counter-attack. We trained hard, but we also had a bit of fun, being away together. The most significant thing, though, was the way we worked incessantly, for three days, on our game plan. Gradually, he persuaded us that we could win the game. He did it so successfully that we went out believing there was no way we were going to lose. He picked us up mentally, physically and tactically.

'We played with only one man, Mancini, up front, but with me, Lombardo and Jugovic all breaking from deep. Sven had two other midfield players holding, so it was more or less a 4–5–1, but with the clear understanding that nobody, not even Mancini, stuck to the same role throughout. Rotation was the key. Mancini would float and the three breaking midfielders would appear in attack from different angles. There was nobody set in any one position. We always had good interchanging anyway in that team. We all looked after each other's positions when people ventured forward.

'We all went there with deep belief in the training we'd done and the tactics chosen, and after 20 minutes, when we could see it all working, we knew we were going to go through.'

Three minutes into the second half, Mancini scored the goal that took the tie into extra-time, giving Sampdoria a mental advantage that was to survive Platt's sending-off, two minutes from the end. Of the first dismissal of his professional career, the former England captain says: 'A lad called [Fausto] Salsano gave the ball away in the centre of the field and Russell Latapy [the Trinidadian who played for Rangers in 2001/02] broke away with others in support. We had several players out of position, and I slid in for the ball instinctively, realizing immediately that I wasn't going to get it. It was a foul, and I deserved to be sent off because the thought in my mind was to foul him. Fortunately, there wasn't time for Porto to take advantage of the extra man.'

Still deadlocked at 1–1 on aggregate after three-and-a-half hours of play, it went to penalties, where an outstanding save by Zenga, from Latapy, and Lombardo's decider condemned Porto to their first home defeat of the season. Platt says: 'I remember thinking to myself at the time: "If I didn't rate this bloke as a coach before, I certainly do now." Sven is not a ranter and a raver. He doesn't throw teacups around, like some, because he knows that is usually done just for effect, when a coach can't get his argument across with words. He knows that when you are working at top level, with top players, you don't need any tub-thumping. He recognizes that top professionals have their own pride and self-motivation. He trusts his players to fire themselves up. If he has a point to put over, he'll do it in a quiet, meaningful way that creates a togetherness.

'When you speak to him, you think what a nice, reasonable, intelligent, studious person he is, but there's a desire and a drive inside him which isn't immediately apparent. You only detect that when you see him in a working environment. He hates losing, and you see a different emotional level when

Sven in 1979 – his first year as coach at IFK Gothenburg. The four fingers signify his switch to a four-man defence.

The Torsby FC team in 1967. Sven, aged 19, is second from the left in the front row.

It is 1971 and Sven, right, is playing for SK Sifhalla against Bengtsfors, challenging Bjorn Johansson for possession.

Ralf Edstrom, Sweden's World Cup striker of the Seventies, welcomes Sven on his arrival at Gothenburg in 1979.

Sven relaxes with his all-conquering 1982 IFK Gothenburg team, who did the league and cup double in Sweden and won the UEFA Cup.

Sven, doing his best to look chic, on the touchline in his Gothenburg days.

One of the most coveted young coaches in Europe after Gothenburg's UEFA Cup triumph, Sven is about to leave for Benfica.

A family group. Sven with his wife, Ann-Christin, and son Johan in June 1984, after Benfica had won the Portuguese league.

Sven and the best player in Sweden, Torbjorn Nilsson, after
Gothenburg had beaten Hamburg in the UEFA Cup final.

Above The family home in Torsby
where Sven's parents live. The
school he attended is just across
the road.
Left Sven's parents, Sven senior
and Ulla, pictured at home with
his brother, Lars.

An exultant Sven, in Lazio tracksuit, celebrates winning Italy's coveted scudetto at last.

Sven and the Lazio president, Sergio Cragnotti, after the European Cup-Winners' Cup victory over Real Mallorca in 1999.

Sven faces a phalanx of photographers at Villa Park, before his first match as England coach, against Spain.

Above The England team pose before their never-to-be-forgotten 5–1 drubbing of Germany in Munich in September 2001. *Right* The unbelievable scoreline in Munich, where German supporters were streaming for the exits well before the end.

Michael Owen completes his hat-trick with England's fourth goal in a stadium previously regarded as an impregnable fortress.

The England coaching staff enjoy the demolition of the Germans. Eriksson is backed up by Steve McClaren, Sammy Lee and Ray Clemence.

We've made it! David Beckham goes wild after his last-minute equaliser against Greece, which booked England's place at the 2002 World Cup.

The brains trust. Sven and his assistant, Tord Grip, pictured before the trip to Albania in March 2001.

Sven learned a lot from Bobby Robson during his formative years in coaching. In July 2001, Sir Bobby seems to be laying down the law again.

he's not happy. He controls his anger, but you know it's there.

'At Sampdoria, the squad would split into two groups for an eight-a-side game at the end of training. Sven would always insist on a competitive edge to it, and we'd have a side bet of 5,000 lire on the result which was doubled if one team lost by five goals. You wouldn't believe the rowing that went on. Obviously it wasn't about the money, which was roughly £2, but the players' competitive nature was such that we'd have a right pop at anyone we felt wasn't pulling his weight. Sometimes it would get a bit silly. Vierchowod would have a go at me, or maybe Gullit, and we'd be going at it while play went on. If it got a bit out of hand, Sven would blow his whistle and say: "We have two choices here. We can either carry on the argument in the dressing room, and I don't mind that, or we can play football." The pitch was for football, the dressing room the place if we wanted to have a go at each other. "This should be your fun, your enjoyment," he'd say. "If you'd rather argue among yourselves, we'll go in." It was like having your wrist slapped, and the players accepted that. If there wasn't total respect for the man, somebody would have said "Piss off" and just got on with what they had been doing, but nobody ever did. It was always a case of "Yes, you're right, we'll play football." It was the same at half-time if things were not going well. He wouldn't lose his temper, he would tell you what was going wrong in a very calm but firm manner.'

The semi-finals of the Cup-Winners' Cup saw

Eriksson renew old acquaintance with Arsenal, whom he had put out of the European Cup with Benfica, in 1991. Sampdoria would be without half their best team, with Platt and Mihajlovic suspended, Gullit ineligible and Ferri and Vierchowod injured, yet they were confident. Platt explained: 'Beating Porto had given everyone a tremendous boost. The players and management saw it as a springboard from which to rescue our season, and the supporters looked at it as an excuse for our disappointing mid-table position. A poor performance in the league was the price to pay for a successful run in Europe. Everyone felt we would now go on and win the trophy, because we had defeated the best team in the competition.'

In the first leg, at Highbury, where Eriksson's Benfica had won in such impressive style, Sampdoria played on the break, with their lone striker, Mancini, often dropping deep to clutter further an already claustrophobic midfield. Eriksson's main concern going into the game had been Arsenal's renowned height and power at setpieces, where he was without his tallest defenders to combat the threat. They could have done with Vierchowod and Ferri to counter Tony Adams, Steve Bould and the young John Hartson. Not that the goal with which Bould opened the scoring, midway through the first half, was anything to do with size, the centre-half lashing the ball home after a shot from his defensive partner, Adams, had been parried by Zenga. Bould's second however, five minutes later, definitely exploited that vertically challenged

defence, his near-post flick going in at the far upright
via Zenga's panicky fumble. 2–0 down at half-time,
Eriksson rallied his charges to tide-turning effect,
and although Ian Wright got a third for Arsenal, two
goals from Jugovic, both created by Mancini, left his
team with every chance in the return.

Platt, still suspended after his red card against
Porto, and Gullit, who was ineligible after playing
for Milan in the first round, were again notable
absentees, but 13 minutes into the decisive second
leg, the odds shifted in Sampdoria's favour when
Mancini scored, deftly lobbing David Seaman, and at
half-time, with the score still 1–0, the Italian crowd
were noisily optimistic. Their racket was stilled on
the hour mark, when Wright steered a Paul Merson
corner past Zenga – an away goal which looked like
the winner until the 83rd minute, when Claudio
Bellucci, a 19 year old who was on as substitute for
Ferri, deflected a Mihajlovic free-kick past Seaman.
As inspired substitutions go, this one really took the
Garibaldi, for almost immediately Bellucci struck
again. There were just four minutes of normal time
remaining when the teenager raced clear to make it
5–4 to Sampdoria on aggregate. The tifosi celebrated
as if the tie had been won, in the mistaken belief
that Arsenal now needed to score twice in the last
two minutes to burgle victory. How wrong they
were. In the dying seconds of normal time, Stefan
Schwarz, who had played for Eriksson at Benfica,
drove home a 25-yard free-kick to necessitate the
extra half-hour. After scoring five goals in a pell-mell
90 minutes, neither team could produce one in the

additional 30, and so, as in the quarter-finals, it all came down to the lottery of the shoot-out again. Against Porto, Sampdoria had succeeded with all five kicks, requiring Zenga to keep out only one. This time, the tension was such that neither Platt nor Mancini could bear to watch, both retreating to the tunnel, heads in hands, and beseeching the almighty. Lee Dixon went first and put Arsenal 1–0 up, then groans resounded around the ground as Seaman saved from Mihajlovic. But Eddie McGoldrick scooped his kick over. Now, if Jugovic could only . . . Seaman saved again. Hartson made it 2–0 to Arsenal before Riccardo Maspero finally got Sampdoria up and running. Adams widened the gap, Mannini closed it again. Zenga needed to pull off a save, and right on cue he did so, at Merson's expense. At 3–2 to Arsenal, it was up to Lombardo, who had scored the fifth and final penalty against Porto, to keep his team in the cup. He couldn't, denied by Seaman's reaching right hand. The England goalkeeper started the game with a rib injury and ended it as a hero, enveloped in a Union Jack.

Sampdoria and their fans were bitterly disappointed, and bad soon became worse. There was still an outside chance of qualifying for Europe again the following season through their league position, but if they were to have a chance of doing so, it was essential that they beat Fiorentina at home the Sunday after the semi-final. They went 2–0 up, only for Francesco Baiano's last-minute equalizer to deny them. Next came the local derby, Sampdoria v Genoa, with the latter en route to relegation. Platt headed home from a corner, but then missed a clear-cut chance which was to prove costly, as Genoa went on to win through a Tomas Skuhravy penalty. The supporters were distraught. In the space of two weeks, they had seen their team go out of the Cup-Winners' Cup, surrender a two-goal lead against Fiorentina and lose to the old enemy. The doriari, as the fans are known, sent a letter to the club captain, Mancini, demanding that the warm-up for the next home game, against Brescia, take place out on the pitch, instead of in the dressing room, as was the norm. Having endured the taunts of Genoa followers all week, they believed the team deserved the same, but felt it would be counter-productive to do it while the match was being played. Accordingly, at 3.30pm every Sampdoria player, including those not selected, went out with Eriksson and his staff and the president, Mantovani, to be abused for two minutes. At 3.32pm Enzo Tirotta, the leader of the 'ultras', took a microphone and told the crowd to whistle for another 30 seconds only, whereupon he led them in the traditional chant of 'Doria, Doria'.

After only three minutes, the fans must have felt like jeering again. Brescia, already relegated, took the lead, and in the second half only a penalty miss by Eugenio Corini prevented them from going 2–0 up. Cometh the hour, cometh the man. With four minutes left, Mancini was fouled for a Sampdoria penalty, with which Platt equalized, then right at the death Gullit's accurate helping on of a Serena cross enabled England's prolific midfielder to power home a headed winner.

With others slipping, Eriksson's team stayed in contention for a UEFA Cup place with a 2–0 victory at Cagliari, but a 1–0 defeat at Lazio left them needing to win their last game, at home to Internazionale. It was not to be. Gianluca Festa gave Inter the lead after five minutes, Vierchowod levelling after 25. In the second half, with the score 1–1, Delvecchio let fly with a shot that was goalbound until Platt stuck out a hand and saved it on the line. He was already trudging towards the dressing room by the time the referee produced the inevitable red card. Dennis Bergkamp failed with the penalty, and when Claudio Bellucci headed the ten men in front, after 66 minutes, Platt started to feel rather less culpable, only for Bianchi's 86th minute equalizer to wreck Sampdoria's European hopes.

Eighth place in Serie A was a hugely disappointing finish for a team rich in individual talent, and the failure to get into Europe was to have significant repercussions. The loss of revenue dictated that players had to be sold to balance the books, and Platt was among the departures, transferring to Arsenal for £4.75m in July 1995. Of that second season at Sampdoria, he said: 'It was poor really, but we should have won the Cup-Winners' Cup. We beat Porto, who I thought were the best team in the competition, in the quarter-finals, then lost to Arsenal when we shouldn't have done. I think we would have won it, had not Gullit gone back to Milan at the start of the season, which cup-tied him. That was a pity, but Ruud at that time was getting towards the end of his career, and Milan was a more appealing place than Genoa for him. You can't blame him, but as soon as he got there, he realized he had been happier at Sampdoria.'

Platt was not the only major departure that summer. Gullit decamped to Chelsea, Jugovic, Lombardo and Vierchowod all went to Juventus, Screna to Fiorentina and Maspero to Cremonese. Eriksson was to have another new team for the 1995/96 season. Platt's replacement was Clarence Seedorf, a 19-year-old Dutch midfielder of infinite promise, who cost £4.5m from Ajax. Christian Karembeu, a Frenchman from Nantes, brought enterprise and agility and the striker Chiesa, still only 24, was back for a third spell with the club, recalled from Cremonese, for whom he had scored 14 times in 34 Serie A appearances on loan the previous season. The other new recruits were Felippo Maneiro, a 23-year-old striker, and David Balleri, a 26-year-old defender, both from Padova, and Emmanuele Pesaresi, a 20-year-old defender from Ancona. Good, proven international players had gone, to be replaced on the cheap with youthful promise. 'We rebuilt with youth,' Eriksson says, 'and in Karembeu and Seedorf we had two of the best young midfielders in Europe. Christian had tremendous potential. He was athletic, never stopped running and was technically outstanding. He was dynamic – the sort of forceful player that makes things happen.'

There was still a strong backbone to the team when Zenga, Ferri, Mannini, Mihajlovic and

Mancini were all fit and available, but the back-up was thin, and it was difficult to see how the improvement desired was going to be brought about. More than ever, Eriksson was reliant upon 'Maestro' Mancini. 'He was a footballing genius and a natural leader,' the England coach says. 'He was able to assess the tactical changes needed while he was playing, and had the ability to turn any game around. The job would be easy if all players were as good as him.'

It was apparent from the outset that the likes of Vierchowod, Platt, Lombardo and Serena were going to be missed, and it hardly helped that Chiesa was out for the early part of the season, injured. Nevertheless, Samp made a decent start, drawing with Roma, Cremonese and Torino and raising expectations with an emphatic 3–0 victory over Parma. Karembeu, who had scored in an impressive debut against Roma, got two more against Parma, who were widely regarded as strong contenders for the title. As tends to be the way of it, however, a team lacking strength in depth was found wanting away from home. They lost 3–2 at Piacenza, by the same margin at Atalanta, and it took them until 3 December to record the first win on their travels, a Chiesa hat-trick accounting for Bari 3–1. Chiesa had hit a purple patch. He scored two more the following week, in a 2–0 victory over Juventus, then another two in the 6–3 defeat away to Lazio which signalled the start of a slump. After 15 games, Sampdoria were down in ninth place. It took Eriksson time to bed in so many new faces, which accounts for the fact that the best results came late in the season. With Chiesa finally fit and firing – he achieved the considerable feat of outscoring Gabriel Batistuta by 22 league goals to 19 and was called up by Italy for the first time in March – Sampdoria had four notable wins in succession, culminating in a 3–0 victory away to second-placed Juventus on 13 April. They then beat the newly crowned champions, Milan, by the same emphatic score on 5 May. This late spurt, however, was not enough to improve upon the previous season's eighth place, while in the Italian Cup, they got no further than the third round, where they were beaten 2–1 by Cagliari. Unsurprisingly, given all the comings and goings, the season had been spent marking time.

For frustrated supporters, the summer of 1996 must have been like *Groundhog Day*. 'Again we sold the family silver,' Eriksson says, 'getting £14m for Chiesa [transferred to Parma] and Seedorf [who went to Real Madrid]. At Sampdoria, we changed a lot every year.' As usual, he came up with a couple of gems among the replacements. Seedorf was replaced by 21-year-old Juan-Sebastian Veron, signed from Boca Juniors of Argentina for £4.5m, and in Chiesa's place came Vincenzo Montella, who had scored 21 goals for Genoa in Serie B in 1995/96, and was destined for a big future. Alongside Veron in midfield was Pierre Laigle, 25, from Lens, who was to prove a bargain at £2m, and another new arrival from France was the Paris St Germain defender Omar Dieng. For Veron, Eriksson broke one of the commandments of his personal catechism: 'Thou

shalt not buy a player without watching him first.'
Transfixed by a video of South America's newest
star lording the Boca midfield, he decided he had to
have him before another club stepped in. If it was a
gamble, it was one that paid off many times over.
The admiration soon proved mutual, Veron saying of
Eriksson: 'For me, the best coach is the one who is
best at building a relationship with his players, so
that they feel at ease, feel supported. When, sitting
on the bench, there is more than just a coach, a
friend too, you perform to the best of your ability.
There aren't many like that, but it is the mark of
Eriksson.'

Sampdoria were slow out of the traps, losing 1–0
away to newly promoted Perugia on opening day,
when Mihajlovic was sent off, but recovered quickly.
Goals from Veron and Mancini gave them a 2–1
victory over the defending champions, Milan, and
this was followed six days later by a thumping 4–1
win away to Roma, where Montella rattled in a second-half hat-trick. 'That season, I was lucky to find
the right blend very early,' Eriksson says. 'We didn't
do that the previous year. This was much more of a
team, less a group of individuals. They fought hard,
with good spirit. They felt they were a good team,
and I felt it, too.'

Veron and Laigle in midfield tandem had impressive debut seasons in Serie A, Mihajlovic made the
most of the licence he was given to roam, and
Montella and Mancini were both among the league's
top five goalscorers, with 22 and 15 respectively.
Not that it was all plain sailing, far from it. On

29 September, Samp lost 1–0 at home to Napoli, and the following week they were eliminated from the Italian Cup, when they were beaten 2–0 in a replay – by Genoa, of all teams. At this stage, Eriksson was undoubtedly under pressure. Losing to the old enemy, who were now in Serie B, was too much for the young president, Enrico Mantovani, to bear. Immediately offering to refund the fan's admission money, he said: 'Tonight we played very badly – like a team from I don't know what division. Everything is now up for discussion, and when I say everything I mean the coach, his assistant, the squad and the rest of the staff.'

The next match, in the league, brought another defeat, 2–1 at Bologna, and although the pressure was partially relieved by a 2–0 win against lowly Atalanta, Eriksson had been unsettled by the fans' criticism, and made up his mind that come the end of the season, it would be time to move on. In November he had to fight to keep his most important player. Mancini would have joined Internazionale but for the decisive intervention of Mantovani. Initially, he had approved the deal, but furious protests from the fans outside the training ground persuaded him to change his mind, and on 7 November, five days after his transfer had been agreed, Mancini said he would not be leaving after all.

During the same month, Eriksson ridiculed reports that Blackburn Rovers wanted to make him their new manager, in succession to Ray Harford, who had quit on 25 October. For public consumption, he was still dismissing the story as 'pure speculation' on 11 December, when he told Rovers' bankrolling benefactor, Jack Walker, that he would take the job, but that he could not come to England until June. Eriksson's behaviour then will be entirely familiar with Chelsea now. Meanwhile, Sampdoria's mediocre form continued. They had lost at home to Milan and Juventus, and on 16 December 1996 Blackburn announced that Eriksson had agreed to join them at the season's end.

Roy Hodgson comes back into the picture hereabouts. Hodgson, by this time with Inter Milan, who were above Sampdoria in Serie A, was offered the Blackburn job before Eriksson. He takes up the story: 'Blackburn contacted me in the November, and I was interested. Inter was a strange place. We were doing well, and yet I never got the feeling that things were right. My contract was due to run out the following spring, and I was ready to move on. After making contact, Jack Walker and Robert Coar [the Rovers chairman] flew over, and I met them at Linate airport. They offered me the job, but I said I couldn't commit until I'd spoken to Inter. I owed it to them to tell them that I wouldn't be resigning because I was going to Blackburn. Jack, typically, gave me a cheque and said: "There, you can pay that into your account as soon as you start working for us." I went to Massimo Moratti, the Inter president, and he went crazy. I thought there would be a few crocodile tears, and then he'd wish me well, but he said: "How can you? What have I done to deserve this? I want you to stay with me." He gave me a new contract and I had to ring Jack to say I wouldn't be coming after all. He was annoyed with me. He said: "I thought we had a deal."

'The next thing I knew, Sven was going to Blackburn, which really surprised me, because we knew each other well and he'd never mentioned it to me. Anyway, as far as I was concerned, that opportunity was gone, and as soon as I'd got my new contract, the usual thing happened. We hit a bad spell in February and March and drifted down the table. Now all the questions started. "Why did we give him a new contract?" and "Is he really any good anyway?" Meanwhile, Sven has done the opposite at Sampdoria. He can't stop winning and Lazio have come in for him, so he phoned Jack and said: "I'm not coming." At this stage, I was feeling a bit low. I was annoyed with myself for turning down Blackburn, and I didn't trust Moratti to come up with what he'd promised me. Then, out of the blue, Robert Coar rang and asked: "Any chance of you changing your mind?" I said: "Too right" and he replied: "That deal we agreed, is that still on?" I didn't have to think, I told him: "Yeah, we'll do it", and that was that.'

It was true that as soon as Eriksson had made up his mind to leave for Blackburn, results improved. The day before the decision was made public, Sampdoria came back from 3–1 down at the San Siro to beat Inter 4–3, Montella scoring twice. Milanese fury was such that stones were thrown at Roy Hodgson after the game. 'That match was a turning point,' Mancini says. 'After it, we went on a great run.' Two more goals from the prolific Montella brought a 2–1 win over Vicenza, which was followed by a dramatic 5–4 triumph at Udinese (Montella and Mancini scoring two apiece), a 4–1 victory at home to Cagliari (Montella two again) and a 5–2 drubbing of Perugia (Mancini's turn to get two). Sampdoria were now up to second, just two points behind Juventus, and the scudetto, which they had won only once before, in 1991, was very much 'on' after yet another high-scoring victory, 3–2 away to Milan, on 2 February.

Eriksson said at the time: 'In August, nobody expected us to be where we are now, and it's obvious that everything is positive for us at the moment. But the title is a long way off. When both Juventus and Sampdoria are at full strength, then we are a match for them, particularly at the moment, but Juve have a stronger squad than us overall.'

It was on 31 January that Lazio, whose Czech coach, Zdenek Zeman, was defecting to Roma, asked Rovers to name their price for releasing Eriksson from the letter of agreement he had signed, stating that he would join them on 1 July. Jack Walker had a personal fortune estimated at £370m, money was much less important to him than the success of his beloved home town club, and in broad Lancastrian tones, he told the Romans where to go with their compensation offer. But unfortunately for Blackburn and their fans, it was not as easy as that. Eriksson had set up home with a new love, Graziella Mancinelli, and for both of them the 'eternal city' held rather more appeal than the 'dark satanic mills' of England's industrial north-west. For 'personal reasons', as he called them, a move to Lazio suited him very well. On 21 February, he told Blackburn he would not be joining them after all, and three days later he announced that he would be leaving Sampdoria 'for another Italian club' at the end of the season. Walker was not happy. 'When a man gives his word, he should stick to it,' he said. 'We had every belief that he was coming, and that's why we haven't been buying players. You can't buy players when there's a new manager coming in.' Privately, however, Walker told a mutual friend: 'He wants to go to Rome, and who can blame him?' Suggestions that Walker reneged on an agreement that Eriksson could bring Mihajlovic and Mancini with him are rejected by Robert Coar, the Blackburn chairman, who told me: 'Jack did not renege on any deal about any players,' and added: 'Blackburn Rovers at no time sought or received compensation from Sven, or any other party.'

Within 48 hours, Blackburn had recruited Hodgson, from Inter. Eriksson is still embarrassed by what happened. 'I signed a contract with Blackburn, and I didn't feel right about breaking it,' he says. 'But they were aware of certain family problems. It was all very difficult. It is the one black mark on my CV. I still feel sorry about it, and it won't happen again.'

The news that their coach would definitely be leaving did nothing for dressing-room morale at Sampdoria, and their form collapsed, just as Lazio's was to do before Eriksson took up his appointment with England. On 16 February, their title hopes were punctured by a 2–1 defeat at home to Roma, the following week they could only draw 1–1 with Napoli, on 2 March they lost at home again, 2–1 to Bologna, and a 4–0 pasting by Atalanta on 9 March left them clinging on for a UEFA Cup place. Eventually, after a 4–3 win at Cagliari, they trailed in sixth, with a feeling of if only . . .

Well before the end of the season, Eriksson had one eye on events at Lazio where, on 27 April, the president, Sergio Cragnotti, announced that he had given up on the attempt to prise the world's best player, Ronaldo, away from Barcelona. Instead, on the incoming coach's recommendation, he bought Alen Boksic back from Juventus for £8m and the Argentinian midfielder, Matias Almeyda, from Seville.

Mancini was one among many who were sad to see Eriksson go. 'I learned many things from him,' the Sampdoria icon said. 'Before he came, we played defensive, man-for-man football. He gave us our freedom. He likes to play with the ball on the floor, and he is never scared. His way is to attack, and we did so, even at places like Milan and Juventus.' Veron was even more disappointed by the departure of his mentor, although the blow was softened when Sampdoria appointed an Argentinian, Cesar Luis Menotti, from Independiente, to replace him. 'Sven is a very good man,' Veron says. 'He was very important to me – almost like a father figure when I first came to Europe. Italy is similar to Argentina in some ways, but there are differences, and I had to get used to them. I had to live on my own for the first time, doing my own ironing and cleaning. Sven was a big help during that period [not as a 'char', presumably]. For the first six months, he protected me, particularly from the press. I wasn't having such a good time on the field, and he provided my base – a calmness for me to rely on. After that first six months, he started to see the best of me. In the second half of the season I did well.'

Well enough for this old acquaintance to be renewed before too long.

CHAPTER THIRTEEN

SCUDETTO LOST

Sven-Goran Eriksson got his chance at Lazio because Dino Zoff, Italy's legendary goalkeeper, was told by the relevant authorities that he could not be club president and coach at the same time. The World Cup-winning captain from 1982 was the 'chosen instrument' of the owner, Sergio Cragnotti, and had done both jobs the previous season, when he took over team affairs after Zdenek Zeman's sacking in January. It was not his first spell as coach. He had been Zeman's predecessor, in charge for four seasons, from 1990 until 1994, and pressed into service again, he had done well, lifting Lazio from the wrong half of the table to finish fourth. His reputation was such that in July 1998 he was put in charge of the Italian national team. Now, however, the Italian coaches' federation insisted that if he wanted to remain president, or rather if Cragnotti wanted him to, he would have to stop coaching.

Enter Eriksson. Against such a political background, it surprised nobody that he immediately set about surrounding himself with familiar, friendly faces. Apart from Boksic and Almeyda, he quickly

signed two of his Sampdoria 'old boys', Roberto
Mancini and Vladimir Jugovic. He felt he needed
not just allies (there are enough of those in Italy
when the going is good), but more importantly a
dependable and entirely trustworthy character to
back him up. There was only one man for the
job. Two decades after they last worked together,
Tord Grip was reunited with his erstwhile protegé.
'Tord was very important to me,' Eriksson explained. 'When you move to somewhere new, it's
vital to have someone you can rely on through
thick and thin.'

Their parting in 1976 came about because Grip
left Degerfors to work for the Swedish FA, running
the national Under-16 team, the women's team and
becoming assistant to Sweden's manager, Georg
Ericsson. Together, they took Sweden to the finals of
the 1978 World Cup, in Argentina. The following
year, Grip went back to manage one of his old clubs,
Orebro, in the First Division. The Swedish FA were
not prepared to lose him, and put him in charge of
the Under-21s, where Eriksson became his assistant.
That lasted until 1980, when Eriksson got the job at
Gothenburg.

Grip takes up the story: 'In 1981 I went to Malmo,
as assistant to an Englishman, Keith Blunt, and
when he left, after two years, I was put in charge of
the team. I was there for six years in all, the last two
as sports director, when I brought in Roy Hodgson,
after he had been sacked by Bristol City. He did very
well there. I thought I'd stay at Malmo for ever, but
then I got this offer from a Serie B club in Italy,

Campobasso, just south of Rome. I was there for only six months. They sacked me at Christmas – a nice present, eh?'

His reputation as a diligent and knowledgeable coach ensured that he was never out of work for long, and Norway took him on as their national team manager for 1987/88. It was not a job he enjoyed. 'I wasn't prepared for it, I wasn't ready to leave club football,' he told me. 'As a national coach in Scandinavia, you start the season in April and finish in October. Then, for the whole winter, you have no football at all. That was boring for me. I think my main contribution in Norway was stressing the need to improve their facilities. They have done that very well since.'

It was back to club football, and two years in Switzerland, with Young Boys of Berne. 'That was an interesting time – and another language to learn. I was in the German-speaking area.' At that time, Grip's wife, Siv, became terminally ill, and he went back to Sweden, as sports director at Malmo, so that he could nurse her. 'By the end, I was with her almost every minute of the day, looking after her.' He didn't like working with Bob Houghton, the Englishman who had taken Malmo to the 1979 European Cup Final, and left after a year, at the behest of the Swedish FA. From 1991 until 1997, Grip was the number two to Sweden's manager, Tommy Svensson. They took a good Swedish team to the semi-finals of the 1992 European Championship, putting out Graham Taylor's England along the way, and the 1994 World Cup, in the

United States, where Brolin, Schwarz, Limpar and company won the play-off for third place. After that, Degerfors renamed his road 'Grip Street', but he balked when it came to putting his name on a plaque in front of his house.

'Tommy was the manager and I was the coach,' Grip explained. 'Not that there is a lot of time for coaching with a national team. It's mainly a matter of tactics and organization.' All this time, Grip had kept in touch with his old friend. 'I visited him, with my wife, when he was at Benfica and at Roma. We were particularly close [in proximity, as well as personally] when I was at Campobasso and he was with Roma. We played each other in the Italian Cup once [Roma won]. He tried almost every year to get me first to Portugal and then to Italy, but I have to say I never thought that I would come to work with him again.' It finally came about when Eriksson joined Lazio and Grip was sports director at the Danish club, Odense. 'I'd been there a couple of months, working without a contract,' Grip said. 'Anyway, on the Monday the chairman came to me and said we should talk about something per-manent, and on the Tuesday Sven phoned and said: "I have a job here for you at Lazio, can you be here on Friday?" So I went back to Degerfors to collect my things, and on the Friday I was in Rome. I didn't have to think it over, I've never done that. If a good job has come up, I have taken it just like that [he clicked his fingers for emphasis].

'I helped Sven to coach the team. [Roberto] Mancini joined the coaching staff for the last season we were there, he'd been promised that by the president. Then we had too many coaches, but it wasn't a big problem. My responsibility was technique training, working with individual players, one on one. I devised exercises for shooting, shielding the ball, crossing and so on. Sven was there all the time. Managers in Italy are responsible only for the team, not for transfers, contracts or anything else, so he was there for training every day. We shared it between us – he'd say: "I'll take the warm-up today, you do the rest," or vice-versa. Sven gave the team talks, but he always discussed selection with me.'

Had Eriksson changed while they had been apart? 'Of course he had, having been in other countries for so many years. He had come to like Italian food and their way of life, and had taken on their sophistication, but his real personality was not that different. He was still very determined, still a winner.'

Eriksson's increasing savoir-faire was due in large part to the latest woman in his life, a socialite by the name of Nancy Dell'Olio, who, according to mutual friends, was responsible for a makeover which saw his teeth capped, designer spectacles replace workaday glasses and fashionable Italian suits complete the new image. They met in 1998 and lived together in Roman opulence on the Via del Corso, in a balconied residence overlooking the Piazza del Popolo. More recently they had a £2m house in London's West End built in the 18th century by the celebrated architect John Nash, where their neighbours included the pop star George Michael and the impresario Cameron Mackintosh.

On the field, Eriksson had an impressive array of attacking talent at his disposal, and with Boksic, Mancini, Pierluigi Casiraghi and club captain Giuseppe Signori to accommodate, he forsook his customary 4–4–2 formation for a more adventurous 4–3–3. It was to last less than a month. The first two rounds of Serie A were promising enough, Lazio beating Napoli 2–0 at home on opening day, then gaining a creditable 1–1 draw away to Milan. But a 1–0 defeat away to newly promoted Empoli in their third match did not go down well with the tifosi, and questions were asked about the team's defensive capability after a narrow 3–2 victory over Bari on 27 September. Early days these may have been for the new regime, but by mid-October Eriksson had a crisis on his hands. Losing 2–0 at home to unfancied Atalanta was such a shock that it provoked a group of wealthy fans to form a committee to campaign for Zoff's return as coach. A rethink was urgently needed if the situation was not to get out of hand, and good old 4–4–2 saved the day. Eriksson concluded that his team were conceding too much space in midfield, where the Czech playmaker, Pavel Nedved, had been sacrificed in favour of an extra striker. Nedved was recalled to the midfield, where he formed a highly effective partnership with Jugovic, and went on to become the club's leading scorer. Nedved, who moved on to Juventus in the summer of 2001, after five successful years with Lazio, says he did not get on with Eriksson at first. 'He didn't know much about me, and left me out of the team. Then, we went 4–4–2, he gave me the chance to show what I could do, and after that everything went well. The way he changed the formation like that was typical. Tactically, he's the best I've played for.'

Lazio were a much more solid unit with four men in midfield, and results picked up. The first game after the Atalanta defeat was the Rome derby, where Nedved was among the scorers, along with Mancini and Casiraghi, in a morale-enhancing 3–1 win, and the Czech was on target again in the 3–0 demolition of Sampdoria that followed.

Still not everybody was happy. Signori, the captain, and a huge favourite with the supporters after scoring 129 goals in five years, was the unlucky forward to make way for the extra midfielder, and neither he, nor his personal fan club, liked it. Eriksson took a bold decision. On 28 November 'Beppe', as he was known, was offloaded to Sampdoria. The inevitable protests that followed were fuelled by a 3–2 home defeat against Udinese, and 48 hours later, as Eriksson drove away from the Formello training ground, his car was attacked by the pro-Signori faction. It was another crisis, a bigger one this time, and Eriksson's handling of it evoked memories of his early days at Gothenburg. There was one significant difference. Instead of asking the players if he should quit, he went straight to the top, to the man who owned the club, Sergio Cragnotti. Eriksson picked up the phone and asked his boss for a meeting, at which he said: 'If you don't have confidence in my methods, let's tear up my contract and forget about the three-year development programme we agreed.' It was clearly a gamble, but the coach kept his job. 'You're not leaving, definitely not,' Cragnotti told him. 'You have my full confidence, do what you wish.'

Born in Rome on 9 January 1940, Sergio Cragnotti was an accountant turned businessman who worked in Brazil from 1970 until 1988, when he came home as the now-disgraced Enimont group's managing director. With a pay-off he received from Enimont, he founded Cragnotti and Partners, his own merchant bank, a venture in which he was helped by his friendship with Cesare Geronzi, the president of the Bank of Rome. Cragnotti became one of the big players in business, buying food-processing companies such as the government-owned Cirio, Bombril, Del Monte and Centrale Latte. With the support of his brother, Giovanni, who died the following year, he acquired Lazio for £15m in February 1992, from Gianmarco Calleri, president since 1986. In 1994, he gave up the presidency in favour of his own nominee, Dino Zoff, resuming office in 1998 – the year Lazio became the first Italian club to be floated on the Milan bourse (Stock Exchange). The flotation saw 49.5 per cent of the club's shares offered to the public, the majority remaining in the hands of the Cragnotti-controlled Cirio company which, with 11,000 employees, had a turnover of £740m in 1999. Shares in Lazio, originally priced at £1.45, were up to £9 at one stage. Eriksson says: 'I bought shares for 5,900 lire each. I remember one of my staff selling his for 19,000 lire each.'

Progressive and ambitious, Cragnotti presided over the expenditure of more than £200m on players in the next seven years. Eriksson accepts that he could not have had more staunch, or generous, backing. There was more evidence of this on 12 February when, just 24 hours after he had scored both goals in Chile's 2–0 victory over England at Wembley, Lazio paraded Marcelo Salas as their next signing at a news conference in Rome. Salas was in attendance as it was announced that the 23-year-old striker would be joining from River Plate at the end of the season, for £11m. Eriksson made no mention of his vote of confidence from Cragnotti until 23 February, the day after Lazio had beaten second-placed Internazionale 3–0, with goals from Fuser, Boksic and Casiraghi, to extend their unbeaten run to 15 matches. By that stage, Eriksson's team were second in the table, four points behind Juventus, and Zoff was having to play down increasingly feverish talk of the scudetto coming to Rome. 'The next month will be decisive in league and cup,' he said. 'I know everyone is excited, but we've got to just wait and see how we get on.' A goalless draw away to Atalanta was something of a dampener, but on 8 March Lazio defeated Roma 2–0 in the big derby, in front of 69,450 fanatics, with Boksic and Nedved on target, and the fans' joy and expectations knew no bounds. The Roma coach, Zdenek Zeman, had now lost four successive derbies, and was in crabby mood. Of Lazio's 4–4–2, he sniffed: 'It's nothing new. I saw one of the minor clubs play like that 20 years ago.' Eriksson chuckled

at that. 'If it's old-fashioned football, it's keeping us
on course for the UEFA Cup, the Italian Cup, and in
the contest for the title,' he said. 'That makes it fine
by me!' Three days later, Nedved scored twice
in three minutes as Lazio, who had won the first
leg 1–0 away, drew 2–2 at home to Juventus in
the decisive leg of their Italian Cup semi-final to go
through to the final 3–2 on aggregate. When they
trounced Sampdoria 4–0 in Genoa on 14 March,
Fuser getting two, the treble was very much 'on',
and expectation was further raised over the next
couple of weeks. On 19 March, Lazio became the
first Italian club to apply for listing on the stock
market, on 27 March they spent another £8m on
Dejan Stankovic, a midfielder from Red Star
Belgrade and the following day they won 2–0 away
to Udinese.

It was then that the wheels came off, the victory
over Udinese proving to be the last league win of
the season, even though there were still seven
more games to play. A 1–0 defeat at home to their
main rivals, Juventus, on 5 April, broke their spirit
and convinced them that they could not win the
championship, and after that they lost to Vicenza
and Parma, and reached their nadir on 2 May
when they were beaten 1–0 at home by relegation-
bound Lecce. Further defeats followed in their last
two league games, 4–1 at home to Fiorentina and
2–1 at Bologna. Having been title contenders for
so long, Lazio trailed in a demoralized seventh, a
massive 18 points behind the champions, Juventus.

The defeat at home to Juve had destroyed their

confidence. After it, an emotional Sergio Cragnotti had accused the man who was to become known as the world's best referee, Pierluigi Collina, of bias towards the team from Turin, and José Chamot, the Lazio defender, was banned for one match for giving Collina an 'overly firm' handshake. Eriksson says: 'When we lost at home against Juventus, our players realized that they could no longer win the league, and their motivation just evaporated. Our last seven league matches said it all – six defeats and a draw.' In Italy, coaches and their teams are judged almost entirely on their achievements in the league. Almost, but not exclusively. There was consolation to be had in the cup competitions, where Lazio did manage to last the course. In the Italian Cup, they had beaten Napoli, Roma and Juventus to get to the final, where they defeated Milan 3–1 on aggregate to ensure that they did not go empty-handed at the end of a season that had promised so much. 'Winning the cup was a great success for Lazio, who hadn't won anything for years,' Eriksson says. 'There was champagne afterwards, and although we still had important games to come, there was a feeling that the season was over.'

Of greater importance than the Italian Cup, in the eyes of all concerned, was the UEFA Cup, and Lazio's first European final. They had enjoyed a fairly undemanding run to the last four, beating Vitoria Guimaraes of Portugal, Russia's Rotor Volgograd, Rapid Vienna and Auxerre without too much difficulty before coming up against Atletico Madrid in a tough semi-final. There was one goal over the two legs, Jugovic scoring it in the Spanish capital to take Lazio through to meet Internazionale in Paris in an all-Italian final.

Sergio Cragnotti's delight at his club reaching their first European final was enhanced by a successful stock market launch, which went so well that trading had to be stopped for a time because the huge demand for shares caused a computer crash.

Inter had accounted for Neuchatel Xamax of Switzerland, Lyons and Strasbourg of France, Schalke 04 of Germany and Moscow Spartak of Russia en route to the final, where their coach, Simoni, elected to field only three Italians in a cosmopolitan line-up. Eriksson said he was more relaxed than the last time he came up against Milanese opposition in a European final, in 1990, when Milan beat his Benfica team in the European Cup Final.

He was without Alen Boksic, who was injured, and played with Casiraghi, supported by Mancini, up front. Inter were the stronger team anyway, having been runners-up in Serie A, 13 points ahead of Lazio. The duel between Ronaldo, the world's best striker, and Alessandro Nesta, the best central defender in Italy, was expected to be decisive, but it was Inter's other South American striker, Ivan Zamorano, who set the tone, running like the wind to beat Lazio's offside trap, and goalkeeper Luca Marchegiani, to put his team in front. Possession was shared equally, but Inter were more assertive with it, and might have doubled their advantage midway through the first half, when Ronaldo rattled the frame of Marchegiani's goal from 25 yards. Lazio managed only one noteworthy attack in the first half, and then Casiraghi headed over. Simoni had correctly identified Diego Fuser, wide on the right, as the source of Lazio's attacking inspiration, and Zanetti's mastery of him was the key. Nevertheless, while there was only one goal in it, Lazio were still in contention, and Eriksson's introduction of Matias Almeyda to the midfield maelstrom, after 49 minutes, had the desired effect, perking them up considerably. The Argentinian provided the physical challenge that had been lacking, and a more direct service to the strikers. Unfortunately for those of the blue and white disposition, Almeyda's combative attitude saw him booked for disputing a free-kick, then sent off three minutes from the end for a second yellow card, after fouling Ronaldo. Moments earlier, Taribo West, Inter's Nigerian defender, had also been dismissed, for elbowing Casiraghi, so it was ten against ten, but by this stage it hardly mattered. By now it was 3–0, and all over as a contest. First Zamorano diverted a long cross from Ronaldo for Zanetti to score from 25 yards, then the Lazio back line hesitated fatally, expecting an offside flag that never came, and Ronaldo, who was named man of the match, strode through for the third.

Looking back, Eriksson says: 'It was the first goal that did it. We didn't expect to concede so quickly. After that, we were always chasing the game, and they caught us on the counter-attack. The longer the match went on, the more risks we had to take and the more space we left. Inter were a strong side and deserved to win.' Simoni said: 'We were very keen to score the first goal, and that's why I started with three forwards. Scoring so soon gave us the opportunity to dictate the game, and the longer it went on, the stronger we looked. Lazio did not have the same physical edge, but then they'd had the Italian Cup to distract them. They got a great result there, and maybe they paid the penalty against us.' Eriksson does not argue with that assessment. 'In the final in Paris, the team just couldn't get going. We were mentally dead, and Inter won easily.'

The disappointing denouement had helped Eriksson to come to an important conclusion. He explains: 'Lazio used to lose to certain opposition despite the fact that we were the better team. The only possible explanation was that the players had a mental block, that psychologically and sub-consciously they accepted that they were going to lose, despite appearing outwardly confident. It was as if the club had defined its role, which was a class below the great Italian teams, like Milan and Juventus. It was important for us mentally to change that role, otherwise it was going to be impossible to achieve real success.' Eriksson knew he was going to have to change personnel in order to transform the team's mental characteristics, and decided a clear out was necessary. Cragnotti had reached the same verdict, and was thinking of changing more than the team.

On 17 June 1998 Lazio offered Marcello Lippi, of Juventus, a three-year contract, worth £5m, when his existing engagement in Turin expired the following summer. In effect, Lippi had been offered Eriksson's job. It was a worrying time until on 6 July Massimo Moratti, the president of Internazionale, announced that Lippi would be joining Inter at the end of the season.

Meanwhile, the dressing room at Formello was given a revolving door, Cragnotti spending another £72m to create what *World Soccer* magazine labelled 'the most expensive team in history'. Apart from Salas and Stankovic, whose transfers had been agreed in the spring, in came Sergio Conceicao, from Porto, Fernando Couto and Ivan de la Pena from Barcelona, Sinisa Mihajlovic from Sampdoria, Igor Protti from Napoli and the piece de resistance, Christian Vieri, from Atletico Madrid, for a cool £19m. Deemed surplus to requirements were Pierluigi Casiraghi, who went to Chelsea for £5.4m, José Chamot and Vladimir Jugovic, sold to Atletico Madrid, Diego Fuser, who went to Parma and Alessandro Grandoni who left for Sampdoria. To complete a summer of unending upheaval, on 23 July Dino Zoff replaced Cesare Maldini as Italy's national coach.

Eriksson's modus operandum is to have a cadre of three will-of-iron characters, 'winners' is his description, capable of carrying the team with them through sheer force of personality whenever the going gets tough. For the 1998/99 season, these were Alessandro Nesta, Sinisa Mihajlovic and Christian Vieri. Mihajlovic is a controversial, some would say unsavoury character, who caused international offence when he publicly declared his support for

Arkan, the Serbian racketeer-cum-warlord, who was wanted by police all over Europe before he was shot dead in Belgrade in January 2000. Despite his choice of friends, however, Mihajlovic the footballer has always been an Eriksson favourite. The coach says of him: 'He always wants to win everything, even in shooting practice. He doesn't believe he can lose, and even if he does, it makes no impression on his confidence. In every match he plays with exactly the same attitude, he's going to win, and his will-power seems to spread through the rest of the team. Vieri is the same. He has enormously high ambitions, but doesn't worry if something goes wrong. He always maintains the same high level, and is not afraid of doing what he wants, regardless of how the match is going. And when the match is over, well, it's over in his mind. When the final whistle goes, he won't waste energy blaming himself, or senselessly looking for mistakes. Nesta was another with this fantastic ability to take the team with him in a positive direction always. With all three of them, their competitive spirit was as impressive and important as the quality of their play.

'I would say you need a core of three players with these qualities in a team. It's natural for many to become hesitant and defensive if the team suffers a setback. Your core group then has to function as a counterbalance, to stabilize things.'

For a club with such high hopes, Lazio's start to the new season was something of a downer. Three successive draws against unfancied opposition (Piacenza, Bari and Perugia) was hardly the stuff of

potential champions. The 5–3 win away to Internazionale on 18 October was much more like it,
with Salas and Conceicao (two) both getting their
first goals in Serie A, but a 1–1 draw at home to
Vicenza and a 1–0 defeat away to Salernitana had
'the most expensive team in history' scuffling
around in mid-table. Roberto Mancini, who was 34
at the time, and the sage of the team, says: 'We were
over-confident early in the season, and that's why
we got off to such an inconsistent start. Nothing
seemed to go right.'

There were two more successive defeats, away
to Venezia and Milan, before the first derby of the
season, when the concession of three goals to
the old enemy, in a 3–3 draw, provoked an inquest
into what was going wrong. 'After that game, we
talked things out in the dressing room,' Mancini
says, 'and I moved back into midfield, behind Vieri
and Salas. Then things improved.' Took off would be
a better description of what happened next. On 6
December Lazio won 1–0 away to the defending
champions, Juventus, beginning a barnstorming run
of nine consecutive league victories. They remained
unbeaten for 16 games in Serie A, winning 13 and
drawing the other three.

Suddenly, in the eyes of the Italian press, who
could give Fleet Street's finest lessons when it comes
to fickleness, Eriksson could do no wrong. Fulsome
where they had previously been vitriolic, the new
mood was typified by the daily newspaper *Il
Messagero*, where the following Cartlandesque nonsense appeared: 'Her [Nancy's] caresses have melted

the heart of the icy magician of football. Love helps the coach. The "avocatessa's" friends are whispering that if Lazio continue to win, the fans will build a monument to Nancy. Sven, since falling in love, communicates even better with his players.'

In March 1999 a Swedish journalist, Thomas Sjoberg, visited Eriksson in Rome, and saw Lazio, who were league leaders, beat Salernitana 6–1, with Vieri scoring twice. Sjoberg wrote: 'One of his little tricks is the ability to relax when he needs to. He has learned to control his sleeping patterns, so that whenever he wishes he can take a nap. "I just switch off. 30 seconds is all it takes and I'm fast asleep. It does me the world of good, and the players are green with envy."'

Sjoberg described Nancy as: 'One of those classic Latin beauties with a thick crop of raven-black hair. People say Svennis is eager to keep a distance between his private life and the journalists, but he has not been able to prevent the Italian newspapers unleashing the paparazzi to hunt down the spectacular couple.'

After the match, Sjoberg dined with Eriksson at his favourite Rome restaurant, Celestina ai Parioli. Of Nancy's entrance, he said: 'A black, deep décolleté top and tight jeans reveal that she's not the kind of woman who's afraid of showing her femininity and Svennis, maybe in the heady aftermath of the day's runaway victory, is certainly not afraid of showing off his new girlfriend.' The path the evening follows shows another side of Eriksson, not the stolid Swede but Sven the bon viveur. 'A whole bottle of Glenmorangie is polished off by just three people – one of them Svennis,' Sjoberg says. 'Nancy makes no effort to hide her affections. She gives little hints about trying to get her Italian viking to loosen his grip on that famous self-control of his and set his passions free. Svennis smiles at her without the slightest intimation that he will bow to her will. He pours more wine and whiskey into our glasses, lights a cigar and enjoys life.'

At the beginning of April, Eriksson was still enjoying it. His free-scoring team were top of the table, seven points clear of Milan with eight games to play. This surely was it, pay-off time for 'Croesus' Cragnotti. But wait. The title was effectively decided in the next three matches. On 3 April, Lazio were held goalless at home by an ultra-defensive Milan, then horror of horrors, two goals from Roma's Delvecchio and a third from Totti condemned them to a 3–1 defeat in the most frenetic and fractious of derbies, which saw Mihajlovic and Nesta both sent off. The attitude had been wrong. Somebody (Eriksson insists it was not him) had crowed before the game that Roma could win the derby, Lazio would be satisfied with the league. Such arrogance served only to aid the motivation process for Roma who, although less technically accomplished, looked much hungrier on the day. The defeat undermined Lazio's confidence and, angered by the statement that had so 'wound up' the opposition, Eriksson imposed a media blackout, which was counter-productive in that it only intensified the tension that was invading the players' minds.

A restorative victory was needed to banish the demons, but Nesta and Mihajlovic, for their red cards, and Giuseppe Pancaro, for accumulated bookings, were all suspended for the visit of Juventus on 17 April, when two goals by Thierry Henry helped Juve to a 3–1 win. Suddenly, that seven-point lead over Milan had been whittled down to one, and Lazio had the tougher run-in. Both teams won their next three games, Vieri scoring against Sampdoria (1–0), Udinese (3–0) and Bologna (2–0), but then the penultimate round of matches took Lazio to Fiorentina, who were unbeaten at home that season, and although Vieri was on target yet again, Gabriel Batistuta's early goal earned the Viola a 1–1 draw. Milan, meanwhile, were drubbing bottom of the table Empoli 4–0, with an Oliver Bierhoff hat-trick.

Trailing by one point on the final day, Lazio had to beat Parma, and still needed Milan to slip up at Perugia. The first half of the equation worked out right, thanks to two goals from Salas, but Bierhoff's winner against Perugia gave Milan the scudetto by a single point. It was enough to make strong men weep, and Mihajlovic and Vieri broke down and cried in the Olympic stadium, while George Weah, Paolo Maldini and Boban cavorted in triumph elsewhere. 'Milan Win Lazio's Title' wailed the headline in *Il Messagero*. Rubbing salt into the wound, Alberto Zaccheroni, the Milan coach, said he had not been looking to win the title in his first season in charge. He had thought Lazio and Parma were both better equipped.

Again it was left to the cup to cheer. On 19 May, four days after their fateful draw in Florence, Lazio played Spain's Real Mallorca at Villa Park, in the last final of the old European Cup-Winners' Cup. As in the UEFA Cup the previous year, their path as far as the semi-finals was scarcely a minefield, although they made unnecessarily hard work of seeing off Lausanne, of Switzerland, on away goals and Partizan Belgrade 3–2 on aggregate before rattling seven, without reply, past Greece's Panionos. In the last four, they came up against Lokomotiv Moscow, and Boksic's late equaliser in the drawn first leg in Russia proved sufficient, the subsequent 0–0 draw in Rome taking Lazio through on the away-goals rule.

Eriksson's team had always been expected to get to the final, not so Mallorca, who were in their first season in European competition. Along the way, they had beaten Hearts, of Scotland, 2–1 on aggregate, Belgium's Genk on away goals, Varteks of Hungary (3–1) and Chelsea in the semis, 2–1. Their Argentinian coach, Hector Cuper, said: 'Right through the second leg against Chelsea I was going crazy, but I had to try to keep a straight face for the sake of the team. When we got through, I wanted to wave flags and do crazy things out there, but I had to wait until I was in the dressing room.' The Spanish team were underdogs, but Lazio came to the final with a warning from the Barcelona captain, Pep Guardiola, who said: 'Mallorca have beaten us three times this season, and they've probably got the best defence in Europe. Breaking them down will be a real challenge.'

It didn't seem that way when Vieri headed in a long cross from the right from Pancaro after only seven minutes, but Dani equalized after 11, and then it became a dour battle of attrition, with Mallorca preoccupied with defence and Lazio unable to profit from a near-embarrassing share of possession. Vieri, Salas and Mihajlovic all threatened at one end, while Nesta was required to head out from under his own crossbar at the other. Marchegiani had only one save to make all night, denying Lauren spectacularly, but with 80 minutes gone it was still 1–1, and anybody's game. One more score was always going to be decisive, and it was Nedved, a bargain buy at £1.5m in 1996, who finally settled the issue, spinning and half-volleying home a goal fit to win any final after an initial thrust by Vieri. Nedved was substituted three minutes later, and came off to a hero's reception.

Lazio had won their first European trophy, and Cragnotti had a dividend on that Gettyesque investment. The surrender of a seven-point lead in the championship had not been forgiven, but it could be forgotten while the cup overfloweth.

CHAPTER FOURTEEN

EMPEROR OF ROME

In the summer of 1999, Sven-Goran Eriksson put his job on the line by telling Lazio's endlessly ambitious owner, Sergio Cragnotti: 'Buy me Veron and I will deliver the scudetto.' After the agonizing near-miss of the previous season, it was an offer Cragnotti couldn't refuse. Not only did he pay Parma £19.8m for Veron, an Eriksson protegé at Sampdoria, he invested another £11m in Piacenza's Simone Inzaghi, the younger brother of Juventus' Filippo, and made sure Veron would feel at home by signing two more Argentinians, Nestor Sensini, also from Parma, and Diego Simeone, from Internazionale. Simeone's arrival was part of a deal which took Christian Vieri, Lazio's principal goal-scorer, to Inter for a world record £31m.

Members of Italy's so-called G7 elite (Juventus, Milan, Internazionale, Parma, Roma, Lazio and Fiorentina) had just signed massive new television contracts with one of two digital stations, TelePlus or Stream, in addition to which four of them (Milan, Lazio, Fiorentina and Parma) were all aboard for a ride on the gravy train that was the newly expanded

Champions' League. The rich were getting richer.

The loss of Vieri, who had scored 12 times in 22 league games, was seen as a major blow, and Lazio tried, unsuccessfully, to sign Nicolas Anelka, from Arsenal, before deciding that they could get by, for the time being, by perming two from Salas, Boksic, Mancini and Inzaghi. In midfield, Eriksson was more than happy to use the newcomers, Veron and Simeone, in the centre, with Nedved and Sergio Conceicao wide, with back-up provided by Almeyda and Stankovic. To the defensive unit that had served him well the previous season (Marchegiani in goal, protected by Negro, Nesta, Mihajlovic and Pancaro or Favalli) he added the utility defender Sensini. The squad now had real strength in depth, enabling Eriksson to select his teams on a horses-for-courses basis. His favourite alternative to the conventional 4–4–2 became 4–5–1, with a lone striker, who tended to be Inzaghi, in front of a packed midfield.

Vieri, who has a habit of flitting from club to club, wherever the money is best, insisted that he hadn't wanted to leave this time, but Inter trebled his salary, to an annual £3.7m after tax, and Cragnotti cried all the way to his bank, via his stockbroker. News of the deal leaked before it was done, and within minutes Lazio's share price was up by 7.1 per cent. In a classic case of pot calling the kettle black, the carpetbagger Vieri said: 'Cragnotti sold me to make money. He bought me for 50 billion lire and sold me for 90 billion. It's very difficult to say no to an offer of that kind, but what I didn't like was that he criticized me personally, to justify his decision to the fans. It would have been better for him not to attack me as a person, especially as he doesn't even know me. In a whole year, we met only once. I was sad to leave because Lazio were building a great team, and I was sorry to leave my friends, Mihajlovic, Pancaro and Negro.'

With an expanded squad, designed to cope with the extra workload of the Champions' League, Eriksson was about to introduce a policy of rotation, or 'turnover', as he calls it. It was an innovation not readily accepted by a dressing room full of big names and even bigger egos. 'In the beginning,' he says, 'turnover was not easy, because it is difficult for great players, who were not used to sitting on the bench, to accept it, or sometimes to accept having to stay at Formello and train rather than go and take part in a big match. Gradually, though, players learned to accept it, because they under-stood that you can't play 65 big matches in a season and always be at your best. Of course it helped that we were winning!'

The rigours of the Champions' League were a concern. 'To win the Cup-Winners' Cup, we'd had to play nine games. To win the Champions' League you had to play 17 – half a Serie A season. Basic ideas about automatic first-team choices had to change, because apart from the goalkeeper, no player can be expected to cope with the physical and mental stress of 60-plus matches at this level. We had to plan care-fully, and make maximum use of our resources. The real problems came in the second half of the season.

That's when we needed all our players. In the first stage of the Champions League we were drawn against a pretty tough set of opponents. Bayer Leverkusen were one of the best teams in Germany, with a good European record. Dinamo Kiev were tried and trusted and would be very competitive. The fourth club were Maribor Tetanic, from Slovenia, who I knew nothing about, other than the fact that they had knocked out Lyons, of France, in the preliminary round, so they had to be useful. But despite all that, I was optimistic. We were strong, and expected to get past the first round.'

Was there life after Vieri? It was immediately apparent that there was, Eriksson getting his hands on one trophy before the domestic season had even started. On 27 August 1999, Lazio and Manchester United met in Monaco for the inconsequential bauble that is the European Super Cup, and in ront of just 15,223 spectators Salas, who was on as substitute for Inzaghi, scored the only goal. The United team was a clear indication of the level of importance they attached to the fixture, with reserves like Raimond Van der Gouw, John Curtis, Jonathan Greening and Jordi Cruyff all given a run out. Lazio were at full strength.

Serie A was the priority, of course, events in Monte Carlo serving as little more than an aperitif for opening day, when Veron was on target after only five minutes and Inzaghi also scored on debut in a 2–1 win at home to Cagliari. A goalless draw away to Bari was followed by a 3–0 victory over Torino in Rome, with Veron and Inzaghi both scoring again, and a 2–1 win at Parma, where Almeyda got the decider. Lazio were off to a flyer, with what was billed as the 'revenge match', against Milan, to follow.

Milan, champions the previous season, and Lazio, the team they had pipped for the title by a single point, met in the Olympic Stadium on Sunday 3 October, and produced what Italian observers described as the best Serie A match for a decade. It finished 4–4, with outstanding performances all over the pitch, one of which installed Ukraine's Andrei Shevchenko in calcio's Hall of Fame. In a heart-stopping rollercoaster ride, which saw Milan twice come from behind to lead 4–3, Shevchenko's hat-trick made him the man of the match.

Veron opened the scoring after 18 minutes, only for Mihajlovic to put through his own net after 34. The Milan goalkeeper, Christian Abbiati, promptly did likewise, making it 2–1 to Lazio, and when Salas struck next, after 38 minutes, the Milanese must have feared the worst. Enter Shevchenko. His three goals, between the 45th and 69th minutes, turned the game on its head again, leaving Lazio happy with the point saved by Salas' second. Shevchenko, making only his fourth appearance in Serie A, had to take pride of place, but there were plaudits, too, for Abbiati, who atoned for his own-goal with a series of top-notch saves, for Salas, who showed that a striker doesn't have to be tall to be deadly in the air, for the stunningly inventive George Weah and for Mihajlovic's dead-ball expertise.

Internazionale, under their new coach, Marcello

Lippi, were top after five games, but next came Roma and Lazio, both two points behind with identical records. Eriksson's team brimmed with conviction now, confident that they could score heavily without Vieri, and after the four against Milan they won 3–0 at Udinese, 4–2 at home to Lecce and put another four past Verona, without reply. After eight games they were unbeaten, and had taken over at the top of the league, one point ahead of Juventus and three clear of Milan. If they were proud, however, they were heading for a fall, the first derby of the season bringing them down to earth with a nasty bump.

Roma's manager, Fabio Capello, had a cunning plan. He decided that hitting Lazio early was the key to success, and that the way to do it was to turn their flat back four with long, raking passes. On this occasion, there was to be no slow, methodical build-up. Instead, 50-yard long balls would cut out Veron and company and drop like howitzer shells behind their defence. Eriksson's team, who approached the old foe on the back of a 16-match unbeaten run, were 4–0 down and in total disarray after just 31 minutes. Mihajlovic and Nesta were turned, according to plan, allowing Marco Delvecchio and Vicenzo Montella to use their pace to score two apiece. Next morning, the *Corriere Dello Sport* carried the headline 'Sols La Roma', or 'Only Roma', and said: 'In a derby the like of which has never been seen, Roma took only half an hour to wipe out a non-existent Lazio.' At Formello, angry fans broke into the training ground and on to the pitch to abuse the players, provoking the mild-mannered Mancini into kicking balls at the invaders.

The psychological scars took time to heal, and Lazio were uncharacteristically tentative in their next two games, in which they laboured to overcome a poor Marseille team in the Champions' League and could only draw 0–0 at home to Juventus. Eriksson was worried, and said: 'There was no point denying it, after that result in the derby we weren't the bold team we had been up to then, and I was happy with the draw with Juventus. At half-time, I was tempted to put on another striker, which I would normally have done, but then I realized it wasn't time to take risks and unbalance the side. You always want to win, but sometimes it is more important not to lose.' Now Lazio were joint top with Roma, who had won 2–0 at Udinese for their fourth win in five away games.

There were welcome signs of recovery in December, with three successive 2–0 wins, away to Perugia and at home to Fiorentina and Piacenza, but then on 5 January Lazio were defeated on a frost-bound Isola Sant'Elena pitch in Venice. Taking advantage of the mid-season transfer window, Eriksson had signed Fabrizio Ravanelli from Marseille, but the 'White Feather' was disappointingly ineffective on debut, and it was Venezia's new recruit, Maurizio Ganz, on loan from Milan, who was the matchwinner. He scored the first goal, by getting to a cross in front of Nesta, and made the second for Filippo Maneiro. Juventus were on top at the season's mid-point, three points ahead of Lazio, after beating Verona 1–0.

Eriksson convinced his players that the treacherous conditions underfoot had been their downfall in Venice, and they seemed to be back on track with a 3–0 victory over Bologna, Ravenelli opening his account for the club in the last minute. But successive goalless draws, with Reggina and Cagliari, left them with one win in four league games and towards the end of January, Cragnotti was not a happy man. His message to Eriksson was unequivocal: 'Win something, or you'll be sacked in June.' The jitters spread to the training pitch, and much was made in the local media of an exchange of opinions, and blows, between Couto and Simeone. There was speculation, too, about the imminent arrival of another striker – either Valencia's Claudio Lopez or Edmundo, aka 'The Animal', from Brazil. Despite all the soul-searching, however, the fact remained that Lazio were the only Italian club still in contention for the classic treble: Serie A, the Champions' League and the Italian Cup, where they had just defeated Juventus, on away goals, in the quarter-finals.

Into February, and they were still challenging strongly for the scudetto after beating Bari 3–1 and Torino 4–2. On 10 February, as if to prove their overwhelming superiority on a decent surface, they thrashed Venezia 5–0 in the first leg of their Italian Cup semi-final, but supporters were on tenterhooks again when a goalless draw at home to Parma was followed by a 2–1 defeat at Milan, for whom Zvonimir Boban scored both goals. Juventus, unlike Lazio, were not slipping, their consistency exemplary, and Eriksson and his team had to nail the accelerator pedal to the floor just to stay in touch. They beat Udinese 2–1 at home, won 1–0 at Lecce and showed the fighting spirit that is the hallmark of champions when, two goals down at home to Internazionale with only seven minutes left, they hit back hard to draw. Then, disaster. On 19 March unfancied Verona came to Rome's Olympic stadium and won 1–0. After 26 games, Lazio were nine points behind Juventus. 'I thought it was all over,' Cragnotti admits.

Eriksson drew deep on his upbringing and told himself everything would work out. 'And if it didn't, it wouldn't be the end of the world.' He says: 'In critical situations, like that one, you have to calm things down while you explain to your players that there is still a chance of succeeding. It was extremely important to spend extra time talking to my most important players – the ones that could take the whole team with them. In pressure situations, you have to expect the younger players to hang back, in fear. As a coach, you can't put too much pressure on them.'

The cadre of strong characters Eriksson relied upon comprised Nesta, Mihajlovic, Simeone, Veron, Mancini and Lombardo. Nesta, who made his debut as an 18 year old, in 1994, was a big man in every sense, a formidable centre-half blessed with peerless positional sense and such a powerful personality that Cragnotti dubbed him 'the symbol', and made him part of the club's off-the-field administration. In England, Simeone will forever be associated with the play-acting which got David Beckham sent off in the 1998 World Cup, but the Argentinian midfielder has proved his worth in European club football over more than a decade, in Spain as well as Italy, and will be remembered in Rome for entirely positive reasons, as a box-to-box grafter who could be relied upon when the going got tough. Veron was younger than the rest, but a key element in the team. Apart from his marvellous range of passing and explosive shooting, from open play as well as at free-kicks, he was, through force of personality, 'a natural team leader', Eriksson felt. Mancini, at 35, was the senior professional, and an outspoken one, who would express his opinions in forceful terms, to the extent that it would occasionally make him unpopular with his teammates. Animated and argumentative, his views carried such weight that he later joined Eriksson's coaching staff.

Mihajlovic had been Eriksson's strong right arm, or rather trusty left foot, since they first worked together, at Sampdoria. No more than ordinary in midfield when he first arrived in Italy from Red Star Belgrade, the Yugoslav (he is from a mixed family, his father Serb, his mother Croat) improved out of all recognition when Eriksson moved him back into defence, first at left-back, then at centre-half. But he was much more than a defender. In his first season with Lazio he scored eight goals, including a hat-trick of free-kicks against his old club, Sampdoria.

Eriksson tells a story about a day at Formello in August 1999 when Mihajlovic was practising his dead-ball shooting, standing in one penalty area and aiming at the other goal, 80 yards away. 'I'll bet you 10,000 lire you can't put one over the fence and out of the ground,' the coach said, joking. The challenge was accepted, and at the second time of asking Vukovar's favourite son clubbed the ball fully 120 yards into the countryside, and ran off to the dressing room to applause all round. His politics may have left a lot to be desired, but as a footballer Mihajlovic was a man's man and a major influence.

Finally, there was Lombardo, another of Eriksson's Sampdoria alumni. 'A good team man,' his old coach says. 'He was really a winger, but I got 17 good games out of him in centre midfield that season.' These, then, were the players Eriksson called upon to galvanize the rest, and none of them let him down. 'The turning point came at Chelsea, in the Champions' League, on 22 March,' he says. 'We had to win there to get into the last eight, and I thought to myself: "If we lose, I'll have to settle for seeing out the season and then getting the sack." On the outside, I didn't show my feelings. I knew that the players were playing with a knife at their throats, under extreme mental pressure, but I also knew that their problems were in their heads, not in their legs. If only we could get our concentration back, I knew we were capable of beating anyone.'

Chelsea had not lost at Stamford Bridge in 33 European ties, and looked set to make it 34 when Gus Poyet gave them the lead. 'After the first half, things looked pretty bleak,' Eriksson says. 'We were 1–0 down, but even so the players didn't lose belief. The team showed character, they really wanted to fight, and we came back to win 2–1.' Inzaghi equalized a minute into the second half to raise morale, and Mihajlovic supplied the winner, after 66 minutes. Lazio were even able to survive a late red card, for Fernando Couto.

It was a watershed. As if sensing that the initiative was changing hands, Juventus lost 2–0 at Milan three days later, Shevchenko scoring both, and on 25 March Lazio won the Rome derby 2–1, with goals from Nedved and Veron. Everything was set up nicely for the summit meeting, Juventus versus Lazio at the Stadio delle Alpi on 1 April – a match Eriksson's team had to win. They did, with a goal midway through the second half from Simeone. 'Suddenly, everything had changed,' Eriksson says. 'The force was with us now. I could tell beforehand, in the dressing room, that the team was ready. I noticed it especially when we got together after our warm-up. When we were right, everyone was in an attacking frame of mind, everyone believed in himself. It felt like the dressing room was going to explode. This was no guarantee that you'd win, but it was a guarantee that everybody was really committed to winning. In critical situations, the spirit in the squad can be decisive. A good atmosphere is not something that can be built up in a short time. It takes work and patience. I always try to instil a "we" feeling among the players. I believe mental attitude is even more important during the final stages of a season, because then it's too late to change your tactics. Success in sport is largely a matter of psychology. That psychological difference can determine whether you win or lose. Of course, you need a bit of luck as well. Then the impossible can become reality.'

Hitting their straps as they approached the final furlong, Lazio beat Perugia 1–0, took a point from a thrilling 3–3 draw away to Fiorentina, which saw Mihajlovic and Gabriel Batistuta both score in the last 90 seconds, and won the first leg of the Italian Cup Final, against Internazionale, 2–1, with goals from Nedved and Simeone. After 30 league matches, with four to play, Juventus still held a five-point lead over their Roman rivals, but now it was Lazio who kept on winning to maintain the pressure, reeling off four consecutive victories. On 30 April, Juventus were beaten 2–0 at Verona, reducing the gap at the top to two points with two games left.

On the penultimate day, Juventus beat Parma 1–0 while Lazio won 3–2 at Bologna, but the scores don't tell half the story. In the Juventus match the referee, Massimo de Santis, disallowed a last-gasp equalizer from Parma's Fabio Cannavaro which, had it stood, would have sent the top two into the last day level. Nationwide outrage ensued, with the renewal of age-old allegations of refereeing prejudice in favour of Juve. De Santis claimed he had blown for full time before Cannavaro's 'goal', but endless television replays showed that he had whistled after Cannavaro had headed the ball, but before it entered the net.

Everybody now assumed that Juventus would go on to win their last match, against little Perugia, and wrap up their 26th league championship. Cannavaro said: 'There will be shadows over Juve's title. My goal was valid. If I was a Lazio player, I'd have to think that someone always gives Juventus a helping hand.' It was a view shared, and given bitter articulation, by Sergio Cragnotti, who argued that his team were the 'moral victors', and promised legal action. He said: 'Other clubs keep on winning the title year after year, but my team, on the field, have proved themselves the best in Italy over the last two seasons. We proved it against Juventus when we won there last month. But, yet again, sporting fair play has gone missing. A lot of work needs to be done at league and federation [FA] level, because it is simply not acceptable that you invest millions and then find yourself face to face with suspicious incidents.'

Enraged Lazio fans rioted outside Rome's police headquarters, demanding an investigation, and were only dispersed with the use of tear gas and baton charges. On the last day of the season, believing their team's chance had gone, they staged a funeral procession to the Olympic stadium, complete with a black coffin bearing the words: 'Football Is Dead'. Their only hope was that Perugia might somehow hold Juve to a draw. Then, if Lazio beat Reggina, it would necessitate the first title play-off since 1964. There was encouragement from the Perugia president, Luciano Gaucci, who made a public promise that his team would not be 'compliant', and warned his players that if they lost to Juventus, they would be locked in training camp until the end of June.

Whether it was Gaucci's influence or divine intervention, the denouement was extraordinary. Lazio set about their task with a will and were leading Reggina 2–0 at half-time in Rome, Inzaghi and Veron the scorers. Meanwhile, Juventus were the embodiment of nervousness throughout a goalless first 45 minutes at Perugia, at which point a monsoon-like thunderstorm broke over the Renato Curi stadium. The pitch was flooded during the interval, and when the referee, Pierluigi Collina, trotted out, complete with umbrella, to see if the ball would bounce on such a surface, it plopped into the mud and stuck fast. Play was impossible. Juventus pressed for a postponement, Collina played for time. In Rome, too, the resumption was held up. The plan had been to synchronize the start of both second halves, to avoid any suggestion of skulduggery, but after a delay of three-quarters of an hour, the referee in the Olympic stadium, Gennaro Borriello, decided that he could wait no longer. Lazio went out and scored again, through Simeone, to win 3–0. By the time their game was over, play was ready to resume in the Perugia mire, and five minutes into the second half, the impossible happened. A misplaced clearance by the Juventus captain, Antonio Conte, allowed a Perugia defender, Alessandro Calori, to lumber forward and score. Despite Herculean efforts, Juve could create nothing in the mud, but after a week of controversy over the Parma equalizer-that-wasn't, they were probably beaten by stress, as much as the conditions.

After the debate that had preceded the finale, the majority feeling seemed to be that the real winner had been Italian football. There was widespread agreement with the Perugia president, Carlo Mazzone, who said: 'This result is proof that our football is clean, despite all those who say otherwise.' In a front-page leader, the *Gazzetta dello Sport* declaimed: 'Juventus have lost a title that, after all the squalid mysteries of the last week, would only have made the number 26 look sad. Lazio have won a title that has become the redemption of Italian football.'

By common consent, Lazio's superior fitness had been key. They had chased Juventus since February, dropping nine points behind before staging a valiant comeback, highlighted by their 1–0 win at the fortress that was Stadio delle Alpi in April. They kicked on in the final furlong when Juventus had looked jaded, losing four of their last eight games. Lazio were fresher, despite their commitments in the Champions' League and Italian Cup, which was handsome testimony to the efficacy of Eriksson's rotation policy. He says: 'There were times that season when it seemed that I was the only person who believed that we could still win the title. Well, perhaps not quite the only one. The team proved that they believed it as strongly as me, if not more so.'

Not only had he won the scudetto that had become his holy grail, he had done the double. 2–1 up on Internazionale from the first leg of the final, Lazio completed the task of winning the Italian Cup with a goalless draw in Milan in the return. Only in the Champions' League was there disappointment. Lazio had won their section, this time by one point from Chelsea, and after the second stage Inzaghi was joint leading scorer in the competition with eight goals. But in the quarter-finals Lazio came up against Valencia, and were overwhelmed 5–2 in the first leg, in Spain. 2–0 down after only three minutes, they were torn apart by Lopez, who rattled in a hat-trick. Veron scored the only goal in the return, but long before the kick-off in Rome the overall outcome had been rendered a foregone conclusion.

'We really got hammered in the first leg,' Eriksson says. 'We'd conceded two goals before I'd had time to take my seat on the bench. It came about because of our demanding programme of games beforehand, and my mistakes. Before Valencia, we'd had Chelsea away, and won a hard one 2–1. Then we played the derby against Roma. They'd beaten us badly in November, and we needed to take revenge. We won 2–1. Then we had our biggest game of the season, against Juventus, who were top of the league, and we managed to win 1–0. The players had no problem finding the mental energy for these matches, because we played with a knife at our throats in all three. But they were not able to maintain the same level of concentration for the match against Valencia, which they saw as important, but not decisive. They'd got it into their heads that if it didn't go well, there was always the home leg to put it right, and so they weren't as charged up as they had been.

'As the coach, I should have had the courage in that situation to change several players – not because they weren't good enough, but because I should have been able to foresee that some of them wouldn't be able to keep their concentration and intensity.'

No matter, the domestic double would do nicely. Eriksson believed he was at last rid of the sobriquet bestowed on him by the Italian press 'Perdente di Successo', which translates as 'The Successful Loser'.

CHAPTER FIFTEEN

PARADISE LOST

Sergio Cragnotti was a happy man at last, but resting on his laurels was never an option. He bathed ecstatically in the reflected glory of the scudetto, but he also had a business to run, and if turnover means squad rotation to Eriksson, it means profit to his Midas of an employer. Champions or not, he sanctioned another £110m-worth of transfer activity in the summer of 2000, taking his personal investment in Lazio to a mind-boggling £225m.

We had dinner together once, in London's Connaught Hotel, when Dino Zoff was also present. Cragnotti's philosophy is as follows: 'In Italy, football is seen as the plaything of the rich, and not as part of the entertainment industry. This is an old-fashioned mentality which, fortunately for us, continues to prevail. I say fortunately because otherwise we [Lazio] would not have been able to overturn the established order. In an era of globalization, when people have ever more leisure time, football is the most global business of the lot. You tell me another product that is bought off the shelf by three billion consumers. Not even Coca-Cola comes close.'

To stimulate further interest in his 'product', Cragnotti paid a scarcely credible £56m for two more Argentinians, Parma's Hernan Crespo (£37.5m) and Claudio Lopez, from Valencia (£18.5m). Lazio had now bought six Argentina internationals for a total cost of £90m. Crespo and Lopez were not the only newcomers that summer. Angelo Peruzzi, the Internazionale goalkeeper, was another recruit, and agreement was reached with Barcelona over the acquisition of Holland's Boudewijn Zenden, only for the Spanish club to back out after selling another winger, Luis Figo. Departures included Matias Almeyda and Sergio Conceicao, both to Parma as part of the Crespo deal, Marco Ballotta to Inter and Alen Boksic, who went to Middlesbrough for £2.5m. The sale of Sergio Conceicao and the failure to get Zenden to replace him was to have serious repercussions, depriving the team of width. The Portuguese international had been a fundamental part of the best midfield in Serie A, a right-winger who could also play on the left.

Looking back on the last spate of hiring and firing in which he was to be involved, Eriksson says: 'I took Crespo to Rome in the biggest deal in the history of Italian football, and that first season he was "Capo Cannonieri" [the top scorer in Serie A], with 26 goals. He is a fantastic, natural goalscorer, and a wonderful all-round player. Unfortunately, Lopez was injured during my last few months. Since then, he has been back to the marvellous form he showed at Valencia.'

Lazio's start was steady, rather than spectacular.

In the Italian equivalent of English football's Charity Shield, they beat Internazionale 4–3, with Claudio Lopez off to a promising start with their first two goals. On opening day, however, they needed a late equalizer from Inzaghi to gain a point in a 2–2 draw away to Atalanta, and although they then beat Perugia 3–0, with Crespo opening his account, the 2–0 defeat at Verona that followed was a disturbing result. Inzaghi scored twice in a 2–1 victory over Brescia on 1 November, and after the first four games Lazio were in sixth place in the table with seven points, the same as Juventus, but three behind the early pace setters, Udinese and Atalanta, and two behind Roma.

It was on the eve of the Brescia match that Eriksson's appointment by England was confirmed, and there was no trace of antagonism shown towards him, just the opposite. He was given a warm round of applause as he took his seat. The fact that Lazio won did no harm. The reaction from the cognoscenti was almost entirely positive. Cesare Maldini, Italy's coach at the 1998 World Cup, said: 'This was a very prestigious offer, and one fully deserved by a man like Eriksson, who has given so much to football – and not just to Italian football. The fact that he is the first foreigner to coach the England national team says all you need to know about Eriksson and the honour bestowed on him.' These sentiments were echoed by two other men who had coached Italy, Arrigo Sacchi and Azeglio Vicini.

Cragnotti dismissed a few calls for Eriksson's

immediate departure as 'just plain stupid'. The president said: 'In today's football world, the world of showbusiness, I see nothing wrong with the fact that Eriksson is at a press conference in England in the morning and at training at Formello in the afternoon. A winning cycle with Eriksson is coming to an end, but that end is next June, and between now and then both he and the players are determined to win more trophies.'

The fans were prepared to go along with that, but only as long as their team kept winning. There were no complaints when Lazio beat Bologna 2–0, with goals from Nedved and Crespo, nor when Salas earned them a 1–1 draw away to Juventus. But when they lost 2–0 at Parma on 26 November, a banner appeared bearing the words 'Go Away Eriksson'. After eight games, Lazio were a disappointing eighth in the league and, horror of horrors, Roma were top, nine points ahead of them. The situation in Serie A improved a little, after successive victories over Reggina (2–0) and Vicenza (4–1), Crespo and Salas scoring in both games, but December degenerated into a terrible, cataclysmic month.

The Rome derby was bigger than ever, featuring the league leaders, Roma, against the defending champions. There were more than 80,000 shoehorned into the Olympic stadium to see it, and it was shown on television in over 200 countries. Lazio lost 1–0, the goal being put through his own net by poor Paolo Negro. To make matters worse, Eriksson's team had made a dreadful start to the second phase of the Champions' League. They lost their first game, away to Anderlecht, 1–0, and were then beaten at home by Leeds, 1–0 again, on 5 December 2000. It is a date Eriksson is unlikely to forget, his divorce from Ann-Christine was finalized the same day. Next, Lazio crashed out of the Italian Cup, to Udinese. Surely it couldn't get worse? It did. The year closed with reports that police were preparing charges of 'incitement to racial hatred' against Mihajlovic over a clash with Arsenal's Patrick Vieira in the Champions' League match at home to Arsenal on 17 October. The day after the game, European football's governing body, UEFA, initiated an investigation into allegations by Vieira that he had been racially abused by Mihajlovic throughout the 90 minutes. Arsenal's French mid-fielder said: 'He called me a fucking black monkey, and when you are playing, you are not happy to hear that from another player. What is really surprising is that it came from a player who is a foreigner in Italy. It is the worst abuse I have ever heard, and it never stopped, from the moment the teams were shaking hands at the start. I told him he'd said enough. You could see in his eyes that he was really thinking about what he said. It was very hurtful and difficult to accept. When fans do it, you can do something about it. They can be identified. But when a player says it to you on the pitch, it is difficult to prove, I feel I have to speak out about this and do something.' In response, Mihajlovic told reporters at Formello: 'What Vieira says is not true. I didn't call him a monkey. It's true that I did call him a black shit, but that's not the same as calling him a negro shit, is it? He called me a gypsy shit and that was my way of replying. I'm not a racist, and I've nothing against blacks, but if he is going to start dishing it out, then he's got to be ready to take it, too.' After that admission, Mihajlovic was suspended for two European matches by UEFA, and Lazio made him read out an anti-racism statement before the 5–1 victory over Shakhtar Donesk the following week.

To their discredit, a large proportion – some would say the majority – of Lazio fans sided with Mihajlovic. The club's support has a deserved reputation for being rabidly right-wing, and drove out Aron Winter, their Dutch international of Surinamese origin. In the derbies against Roma, the Lazio 'ultras' routinely abuse their rivals' black players, and on one occasion they unfurled a giant banner in the Olympic stadium reading: 'Black squad, Jewish home end'. As a consequence the club was fined £190,000 and ordered to play their next home game on a neutral ground. The few black players they have signed have hardly been immune. In 1992, Winter arrived from Ajax to be greeted by the spray-painted welcome: 'Jew go home', and swastikas and racist graffiti are commonplace on the training ground walls. Eriksson says: 'Some clubs have it worse than others, and unfortunately Lazio are one of the worst. It's not just boring, it's disgusting. If there are still people who think like that, it is all wrong.'

Meanwhile, the English media were camped

outside Formello, expecting the end to come any day, but they were made to wait for their story. Cragnotti stayed staunch in trying circumstances, and told Eriksson that they would ride out the storm together. It was a nice thought, but one that went out of the window almost as soon as 2001 began. Eriksson finally got his replacement for the departed Sergio Conceicao on 5 January, when Karel Poborsky, the former Manchester United winger, arrived from Benfica for £1.6m, but it was much too late. Two days later, Lazio started the new year with a wretched 2–1 defeat at home to relegation-bound Napoli, and everybody decided enough was enough. Eriksson resigned on 11 January – the day Lazio played the Chinese national team in Rome as part of the club's centenary celebrations. Zoff stepped into the breach once again, and before the match the two men shook hands on the pitch, accompanied by Sergio Cragnotti. All three made speeches to the 35,000 crowd, and for those with an interest in augury, an eclipsed moon hung over the stadium as everybody said their farewells. As befitted the most successful coach in Lazio's 110-year history, Eriksson was greeted with appreciative applause, and a giant banner was draped behind one of the goals, reading: 'Victories brought us together, the good of Lazio tears us apart. Good luck Mister Sven, a stylish champion.' Poborsky made his debut, Mancini his final appearance. He had followed Eriksson from Sampdoria, now he would quit with him. For what it is worth, Lazio won 6–3, with Ravanelli scoring twice.

Now that the players' minds were focused fully on football, free of all the speculation about their coach, Lazio won their next three games, scoring ten times in the process. They were to finish third in Serie A, six points behind the champions, Roma.

Veron provided the most perceptive postscript to Eriksson's final season in Rome. 'It was as if having the scudetto badge woven into their shirts gave the players the right to keep winning,' he said. 'Football is not like that. Real Madrid and Manchester United had what we didn't have: the hunger to keep winning. The great clubs have a certain mentality. If you don't perform, they sell you or leave you on the sidelines. That's the difference between, say, Juventus and Lazio.'

Giorgio Chinaglia, a former president of the club, and a legendary Lazio player, believes the announcement that Eriksson was to leave to manage England rendered his position in Rome untenable. 'I spoke to Sven when the news came out, and he told me how badly he felt about the timing of it. He had hoped to be able to continue a lot longer before news of his new job became public knowledge. He told me he felt let down. It made it almost impossible for him to go on. When he lost a couple of matches, everybody here said his mind was with England, and it was probably true. Even Sven would have to accept that.'

He did. Eriksson said: 'Every time you are criticized, you start to doubt yourself. You ask if you should have done things differently, if you could have done a better job. I have made many mistakes. It was a mistake not to resign at Lazio the minute I agreed to become England's coach. I should have said "Thank you, and goodbye" there and then, but I was a bit stupid because I thought I could handle the situation. I wanted to win the Champions' League, but I lost the confidence of the Lazio players. There was too much talk of England.'

Of the experience of coaching in Italy, he says: 'I tried to discuss team selection with the players, as I had done in Sweden, but it didn't work. They didn't want responsibility for decisions of that nature. The coach had to bear all the responsibility. If things went well, fine. If not, I got fired. It was difficult to be a player or a coach in Rome. There were so many commentators, so many opinions among the media, so many people who thought they were experts. Generally speaking, the media played too big a role.'

He hadn't seen anything yet.

CHAPTER SIXTEEN

ENGLAND'S BOSS

England's first foreign manager thought it was some sort of joke when the job was first mentioned to him. He explained that he was informed of the vacancy, and his suitability for it, by his agent, Athole Still. 'It was just after Kevin Keegan quit. Athole phoned and said: "Would you be interested in England?" I laughed and replied: "Are you having a joke? Have you ever heard of a foreigner being manager of England?" He insisted he wasn't joking, and I said: "Who wouldn't be interested in that job?"' Still flew to Rome to discuss it with him, and the rest is ground-breaking history.

Eriksson started work in London on 11 January 2001. He was to say later that everybody was 'extremely positive' about his appointment, and 'very welcoming', but that was not strictly true. On his first day, he arrived at the Football Association's offices in Soho Square to be greeted by an ex-policeman in a John Bull outfit carrying a placard which read: 'Hang your heads in shame. We all wanted Terry Venables.'

The man himself accepted the xenophobic

reactions all in his customary measured stride. He says now: 'I was never worried about what people were saying. You know in football that if you win games, you will be accepted. If you don't win games, you will be criticized whether you're English or Swedish.' He took charge with England bottom of World Cup Group Nine, with just one point from their first two qualifiers. It was exactly the same start as they had made to Euro 2000, when they had to win a play-off against Scotland to qualify.

Eriksson's first match was a friendly fixture at home to Spain on 28 February 2001. With Wembley decommissioned, it was to be played in Birmingham, at Villa Park, which is where, five days earlier, he had announced his first squad. By way of the meticulous, no-stone-unturned preparation that was to become his trademark, Eriksson had watched 25 league matches in 41 days, casting his net far and wide. Tord Grip, who had been in England longer, had seen 47 games, and it was he who was responsible for the first rabbit pulled from the managerial hat. Working with a clean slate, and no pre-conceived ideas, Grip had been much impressed by the Charlton Athletic left-back, Chris Powell, who at the age of 31 had never been considered, or mentioned, in international terms.

Grip told me: 'When I arrived, I was led to believe that there weren't any left-backs. No, not just full-backs but left-footed players in general. We [Eriksson and Grip] talked to the club managers and were told: "We just can't find any here, there aren't any." Then I looked around, and it was a case of there's one they never thought of [Powell], and there's a good young one [Arsenal's Ashley Cole]. They looked good – very good – so now there were some good left-footed players available, after all. I saw Powell play as a wing-back in a 3–5–2 formation and as a left-back in a 4–4–2. Then I took Sven with me so that we could have a look at him together. He was the one who jumped out at me. To be fair, we'd been told that Ashley Cole was the one coming through.'

Powell was the biggest surprise, but not the only one in an unusually large squad of 31 players (25 is the norm). Gavin McCann, the Sunderland midfielder was an unheralded selection, in for the first time, as was Michael Ball (then with Everton), and Ugo Ehiogu, with Aston Villa at the time, was back after five years. There were six uncapped players in the 31, including five left-backs, and the average age was 28. Notable absentees included Alan Shearer and Tony Adams, two erstwhile captains who had announced their retirement from international football, Paul Ince and Dennis Wise, who were pensioned off, Martin Keown and Steven Gerrard, both injured, and the Leeds United pair, Lee Bowyer and Jonathan Woodgate, who were both persona non grata pending the outcome of their prosecution for grievous bodily harm and affray after an incident outside a Leeds nightclub.

Eriksson said: 'I am not looking to start a revolution, just to do things my way. I know I may have made some errors in my 31. It would be remarkable if I hadn't. You cannot judge players properly on the evidence of one or two games.' He had been overwhelmed by the warmth of his welcome. 'Everywhere I've been, I've felt at home, and I would like to say "thank you" to everyone, from the car park attendants to the chairmen, at every club I've visited. They have treated me as a friend. Thank you also to the fans. From them, it is always "Good luck", and "Come on, Sven, we're behind you." It has been like a honeymoon. I don't know if it's over yet.'

It was, of course, the honeymoon period every new manager enjoys. The media, one or two extremists apart, were not about to consign him to the compost heap before his first game. In truth, English journalists, none of whom knew him or had worked with him before, were not sure what to make of the newcomer. There were blank looks all round after this first squad announcement. The 'Ice Man's' smile was impenetrable. All questions, routine or barbed, were met with a uniform blandness. When the subject raised was not to his liking, he hid behind his unfamiliarity with the language. He was never going to talk himself into trouble, as so many of his predecessors had done. For the tabloid 'rottweilers', there were no easy pickings on offer. This was going to be hard work.

Only the best is good enough for England's millionaire footballers, and their 'digs' for the Spain match was the New Hall at Sutton Coldfield. A former AA Hotel of the Year, which dates in part from the 12th century, it is the oldest inhabited moated manor house in the country. By the time the players assembled there, on the Sunday before the game, three midfielders had withdrawn, injured the previous day, and a fourth was unlikely to be fit in time. Eriksson had lost Ray Parlour, Kieron Dyer and Steve McManaman, and would not have Michael Carrick. Welcome to international management.

As soon as he had them at his disposal, the new manager called the players together for the first of a series of meetings at which he spelled out precisely what he required from them, on and off the field. Ground rules were laid down, standards set. Looking back and recalling his first impressions, David Beckham says: 'One of Sven's greatest strengths is setting things out clearly and organizing the team. That worked well before the first game, even though we were together for only a couple of days. The back four, the middle four and the front two were set up well, and the game plan worked perfectly. The manager has got a lot of experience when it comes to coaching, and he is very good at getting his ideas across. He spoke to us more than once as a group, and did a few one-on-one talks as well. He sees good communication as essential to success. An international manager has to be good at that because he sees his players so infrequently, and in that respect he was excellent from the start. It's also important, of course, that he's got a good eye for football and for players. There were a lot of people surprised when Chris Powell was invited to join the squad, yet he came in and did very well.'

Another key England player, Rio Ferdinand, remembers those early days as follows: 'He [Eriksson]
immediately came over as someone different, out
of the ordinary. He's so cool, so calm. He doesn't
rant or rave or come in swearing his head off. I've
played my club football for managers who shout a
lot, and look to get their point across forcibly that
way. Sven's not like that, not at all. To be honest,
I thought it was strange when he got the job. It
seemed funny, if you know what I mean. Mind you,
when I heard that England had appointed a foreign
manager, I wasn't one of those who thought: "I
don't want a foreigner in charge." My feeling was:
"As long as he's going to take the team by the scruff
of the neck, sort it out and make us a force in world
football again, then I'll be happy." But then when
it came to his first meeting with the players, I did
think to myself: "I wonder what his ideas about
football are going to be like?" We didn't know what
to expect.'

In retrospect, Ferdinand chuckles at his appre-
hensions. He told me: 'He came in, stood there in
front of us, and said: "Listen, it's a simple game. I
want to play 4–4–2, which you are all used to. At
certain times we might use a different formation, but
basically this is how I want you to play." He then
went through all the positions in the team, explaining what he expected from them. When we came
out of that meeting, I turned to Frank Lampard and
said: "Bloody hell, man, he has just made the game
sound so simple." I went in there thinking he would
make it complicated, and start talking intricately, but

he told us that the game on the other side of the world had no secrets. There was not a lot of difference. It was exactly as we saw it, only played by different people. I came away thinking: "I didn't expect that. It was good."'

Lampard, similarly impressed, told me: 'He [Eriksson] spelled out very clearly what he expected from the squad. He told us how he expected us to behave. He said: "I'm not going to lay down a lot of rules and regulations, just act like good professionals." He's a polite man, he treats players with respect, which is a good thing. It helps him to get respect back. He doesn't tell you a million and one things and clog your brain up. He keeps it simple, and when he speaks, what he's saying makes sense.'

Happy with their new boss, England gave him the start he wanted. A new-look starting line-up, featuring David James in goal, Chris Powell at left-back, Nicky Butt in the midfield holding role and Andy Cole up front recovered from a dodgy start to win 3–0. Spain, clever and accomplished, looked capable of spoiling Eriksson's big night early on, when their passing was purposeful and cohesive, but when they fell behind they seemed to remember that it was 'only a friendly', and suffered a collective loss of will. Nick Barmby, bright and incisive on the left of midfield, scored the first goal of Eriksson's managership – just as he had done for Glenn Hoddle in Moldova, in 1996. Emile Heskey and Ugo Ehiogu, who were among seven second-half substitutes, were the other scorers.

After the match, as the players left the dressing

room, Eriksson asked David Beckham for his shirt, and had him sign it for his daughter, Lina, who was 14 at the time. 'It was her who chose the England captain,' he said, smiling. Eriksson then went through all the usual media conferences: television, then radio, then soundbite newspaper stuff for overnight use, in-depth comment for follow-up purposes and finally Sunday newspapers. Each time his responses were the same – it was a good start, he was very proud when the national anthem was played (although he didn't know the words) but the real task, qualifying for the World Cup, lay ahead. By the time he got to the Sunday correspondents he was very much in 'Is there much more of this?' mode, and was overheard asking Paul Newman, who was the FA's head of communications at the time, 'Why am I doing all this?' It was soon to become apparent that the new manager was not willing to follow precedent when it came to media access. In future, there would not be so many briefings.

Hugh McIlvanney, the doyen of British sportswriters, wrote in *The Sunday Times*: 'Everything Eriksson has done since taking up his appointment has confirmed the advance reports that he would be guarded and skilful in working with the media, more inclined to manipulate than be manipulated. His post-match sessions on Wednesday represented a masterclass in stonewalling with a smile. He displayed a marked talent for talking freely and charmingly without saying much. And always the agreeable countenance beneath the domed forehead was lit by a friendliness that made it hard for even the most single-minded interrogators to object aggressively to the polite obfuscations. Predictably, there was much sighing and groaning subsequently over the dullness of what had emerged.'

The real thing started the following month, when England played back-to-back World Cup ties at home to Finland on 24 March, and against Albania in Tirana four days later. For the Finns' visit Anfield was the venue, which created pre-match concern over how Liverpool fans would react to the presence in the team of a strong contingent from the old enemy, Manchester United. The squad had a full week in which to prepare this time, and their base was the Carden Park Hotel, just outside Chester, where the main topic of conversation when Eriksson met the media on 20 March was David Beckham's worrying dip in form. The manager was unequivocal. 'He [Beckham] is my captain – hopefully for a long time. I am not worried about his form, but I am not worried about taking him off, either, if I have to. There is no question of leaving him out of the starting line-up. Some players are more difficult to rest because of their personality. Even if Alessandro Nesta, my captain at Lazio, did not have a good game, it was difficult to leave him on the bench the next time.'

There was no question of trying to change England's best player in any way. 'Beckham should play football as Beckham can, and not try to do things he didn't do before. It would be very stupid of me to ask him to do other things. He is his own person, and it is the same with me. I can't be like

Giovanni Trapattoni [the manager of Italy]. I can't whistle and shout from the bench and so on, and I don't think Beckham can be like Tony Adams. Beckham shall be Beckham, Trapattoni shall be Trapattoni and Eriksson shall be Eriksson.'

Beneficially, he was able to assess his captain from an opponent's perspective. 'When I was manager at Lazio and we played Manchester United, I told my left defender: "Don't let him cross." That makes life more difficult for him, because crossing is an enormous weapon, but he is not just good at that. He is good at passing, shooting, corners and free-kicks. I think Finland would be very happy if I left David on the bench.' Beckham, reassured, said: 'Mr Eriksson has told me to come inside a bit more than I have done in the past, so that I can be involved on the ball more.'

Steven Gerrard, an increasingly influential figure in England's midfield, had missed the Spain game with one of his all-too-frequent injuries, and Eriksson was delighted to have him back. 'He is an enormous talent, the complete midfielder. He is an all-rounder who can do everything. He can pass, attack, defend, shoot and head the ball. He has everything the modern midfielder should have. You can play him as the defensive midfielder, more offensively inside, or as an outside-right. He could play almost anywhere.'

The next day, Wednesday, the press again had acres of space to fill. This time their chosen line was supposed cliques in the squad, with the Liverpool and Manchester United players not mixing. Eriksson dispatched that one like the slowest of full tosses. 'I pick the line-up when we play, not when we eat,' he said. 'It's normal to have tea or coffee with a clubmate. I can't order Paul Scholes to have tea with Sol Campbell. If Scholes and Beckham want to have dinner together, why shouldn't they? They have known each other a long time and practically live together at their club. Of course it's that sort of closeness that I want in my team – the kind which exists between Scholes and Beckham.'

Eriksson had been to watch Steve McManaman play for Real Madrid, and dropped an early hint that the scouse maverick would be asked to fill England's problem position, on the left side of midfield. 'Playing for Real,' he said, 'has given Steve experience of, and knowledge about, Spanish and European football, which means a lot. I've gone to see him twice, and he's done very well in those games.'

On the Thursday, Kevin Keegan broke a long silence on England matters to back the new regime. Qualification for the World Cup was definitely 'on', he said. 'The players are certainly good enough, and in Sven they have a coach with a tremendous knowledge of European football. I won't be there on Saturday, but I'll be with them all in spirit, cheering them on and kicking every ball. I was an England fan as a boy, an England player and then England captain. Finally, I ended up being England manager, and I wouldn't have missed a minute of it. I'll be cheering them on all right, and I do believe the players are good enough to do it. Sven is a coach I admire tremendously, and he also happens to be a nice guy.'

Grip agreed with Keegan about England's prospects. 'There is more potential in this team than the Swedish side that finished third in the 1994 World Cup,' he said. 'Sweden had good teamwork and outstanding individual ability in Tomas Brolin, but there are more players to pick from in England, and the standard overall is better. We can get to the World Cup, and if we get the right draw we can do well.'

Friday brought the sort of fun story that every newspaper loves, although Eriksson was not amused. Mike Maguire, a radio DJ who had successfully hoaxed Kevin Keegan on air a couple of months earlier, struck again, deceiving the hotel switchboard operator into believing that he was Keegan, and getting put through to Eriksson's room at 7.30am. 'He could have waited until I'd had a glass of water, at least,' Eriksson said. 'I think 8.30am would have been better.' There was a serious side to the mimicry to consider. He explained: 'When I phone the club managers, a lot of them give one-word answers and say: "Can I phone you back in ten minutes?" They want to check if it's me or not, and that's not very nice. Maybe we'll have to use code words.' The FA withdrew the accreditation and cancelled the match tickets allocated to the radio station in question, Century FM, of Manchester.

Eriksson likened his first World Cup match to club championship deciders he had experienced in Sweden, Portugal and Italy. 'Many times I've gone into a big game telling myself: "I've got to win this one" and this was the same. In terms of the number of supporters counting on my team, it was my biggest game yet. In Benfica's case, there could up to 120,000 fans, but that's nothing compared with the number behind England.' Unlike all his predecessors since Graham Taylor, he had faith in Andy Cole, and would give him a second successive cap for the first time. 'He was a very experienced player, playing in the Champions' League nearly every other week. He was scoring and playing skilfully for Manchester United, so why shouldn't he do it for the national team? I couldn't think of any reason why not. He and Michael Owen had played well together against Spain.'

Eriksson gave his last team talk at the hotel, at 12.30pm on the day of the game. Gary Neville says of the build-up: 'The one thing that struck me about Sven in the run-up to the match was that he let Steve McClaren and Peter Taylor do most of the talking. While Terry Venables, Glenn Hoddle and Kevin Keegan all got quite heavily involved in the coaching, Mr Eriksson tends to stand on the sidelines and watch everything very closely. But of course he is the one who speaks at team meetings. He goes through the system we will be playing and the disciplines needed for that system, and he talks about the opposition's style of play. It comes down to trying to instil in us what is expected of the team, and its individual departments. He is very thorough about all that. Every detail is covered, from positions at setpieces to situations that may arise in the flow of play. The idea is that we won't be surprised by anything that confronts us. There is nothing worse than being completely taken aback by what you find the opposition doing, and not being able to do anything about it until half-time. By then, it might be too late.'

For all the planning, come 3.27pm on Saturday afternoon Neville was certainly 'taken aback' when woeful marking at a corner created chaos in the England goalmouth, and the ball ended up ricocheting off his knee and past David Seaman for a horrible own-goal. The Finns, strong, determined and organized, were no push-overs, and the roar which greeted Michael Owen's equalizer, just before half-time, was one born of relief as much as celebration. The winner, five minutes into the second half, brought the house down. Beckham, who was treated as an honorary scouser, rather than a pariah throughout, chose a welcome time to score his first international goal from open play, driving the ball home hard and handsome after clever approach work by McManaman and Scholes. Cole should have made it 3–1, but fired wildly over when it seemed easier to score, condemning England to a nervy finale in which Jari Litmanen would have ruined their day but for a top-notch save by David Seaman.

Looking back, Eriksson says: 'It was hard work, and they had chances to get a draw, but it was a very important win, because of our situation. If we hadn't beaten Finland at home, we would have had to forget about the World Cup. That was our first step towards the finals.' After three games apiece, England were up to second place in Group Nine, but the Germans, with their 100 per cent record, were still five points clear, and odds-on to win it. And so to Albania, the land that time forgot. The Balkan countries were in conflict, and there was some doubt as to whether the match would take place, with what amounted to civil war raging in neighbouring Macedonia, but the Foreign Office finally advised the FA that it was safe to travel on the Monday after the Finland game. Dirt-poor after half a century of hard-line communism, the green shoots of social democratic recovery are only just beginning to sprout in the land that once offered the throne to C.B. Fry. Beggars abound in Tirana, and even those residents lucky enough to have a telephone will rent it out on the pavement in the never-ending struggle to make ends meet. The England players, as ever, were cosseted away from conscience-churning reality, in the one really luxurious hotel in the city.

It was Eriksson's first visit, and a real eye-opener for the erstwhile radical. When not on duty, he occupied his mind by reading *The Second Most Important Job In The Country*, a book that traces the fate of the nine England managers, from Walter Winterbottom through to Kevin Keegan. Turning to more immediate matters, he had lost Gerrard, injured again, but knew he had a capable deputy in Nicky Butt. Of the Manchester United midfielder, he says: 'He's a ball-winner, a very tough player. I would think he's unpleasant to play against, because he's always there, at you. But he's a good passer, too. He has improved a lot there.' Butt replaced Gerrard in the starting line-up, and there was one other change. After a competent start against Spain, Chris Powell had been found wanting at Anfield, and 20-year-old Ashley Cole was given his debut at left-back.

The match had an element of the surreal. Norman Wisdom, an icon in Albania (I did say the country was backward), was chased around the pitch by police, doing his 'Mister Grimsdale' routine, before the kick-off and at half-time. For a long time, England were not all there, either. Ashley Cole, eager and adventurous, played well throughout, although there was something positively Wisdomesque about the way he collapsed after being hit by a lipstick thrown from the crowd. After an instantly forget-table first half, England improved sufficiently to win 3–1, scoring all their goals in the last 18 minutes. Owen and Scholes got the first two and then, in the dying seconds, Andy Cole got his long-awaited first at international level, on his 13th appearance. Elsewhere that same night, Germany beat Greece 4–2 to maintain the status quo at the top of the group.

Eriksson's start had been better than he had dared to expect. 'I didn't expect to win my first three games, but we were pretty convincing in all three, I think. We deserved to win them all.' He was missing the day-to-day involvement of club football, but had 'known what it would be like beforehand', so he couldn't complain. He also had a little dig at those who had opposed his appointment. 'I was criticized for taking the job, but we now have six points from two qualifying games, which is a good start. I don't think those people had doubts about me as a manager, they had doubts because I was a foreigner, but I'm here and I'm not going away.'

His critics had fallen silent now, temporarily. Newspapers tend to be black and white, in every sense, and praise was heaped upon the 'Swedish Messiah' – as it will be on any manager who is successful. On the Friday after the game, the *Sun* carried the banner headline 'Eriksson Has Proved He's The Man For The Job', beneath which they quoted Gary Lineker as follows: 'You can already see this guy knows his stuff. OK, he didn't know all of our players when he took over, but it was a great time to come in, with three games in which he could afford to experiment a little and still get the right results. That was the perfect scenario, but you have to be impressed with the start Eriksson has made. He is clearly very intelligent, articulate, and tactically he is very sound. In an ideal world, of course you would want an Englishman in charge, but so long as he keeps on winning that is not going to be an issue, and I've thought that way from the moment he was appointed. If he takes us to the World Cup, I'm convinced we will do really well.'

There was more in the same vein. The same paper pointed out that Sir Bobby Charlton and his brother, Jack, and Gordon Taylor, of the Professional Footballers' Association, had been against a foreigner managing England. Bobby Charlton had said it was 'a disgrace' not to appoint an Englishman, Jack had called the break from tradition 'a terrible mistake' and Taylor had forecast 'tears at the end of the day'. Now Taylor said: 'That was then and this is now. I've spoken to him [Eriksson] and been very impressed. He could have been difficult, but he wasn't. You can't fail to be impressed by the way he has handled himself, his assurance and the way he has given players a chance. Both the senior and junior players say the atmosphere is better.' Bobby Charlton said: 'I've been impressed with how he [Eriksson] has done so far. Everyone should unite and back him now.'

From within the squad, the players' view was articulated best by David James, who said: 'Sven must have been a cub scout when he was younger, because I've not met anyone with his devotion to being prepared.' Eriksson's attention to detail had lifted the players' confidence, 'so much so that when we were losing to Finland and drawing late on in Albania, we knew that things would turn our way if we stuck to the plan,' said James.

There was a ten-week hiatus now between World Cup games, but Eriksson remained in the full glare of the limelight. Seclusion was a thing of the past. In late April, when he took Nancy on holiday to Barbados, it made the front page of the *Sun*. Beneath the headline 'Look Who Sven's Got On The Bench', the paper carried two pages of pictures of Eriksson in swimming shorts and his partner in a bikini. In what could have been a send-up of their own inimitable style, the *Sun* devoted page seven to a series of holiday snaps. Below one which showed Nancy sunbathing with her bra straps undone, the caption read: 'Sven always prefers playing with a big pair up front.' In another, picturing Eriksson doing press-ups with Nancy laying beside him, the comment was: 'Nancy watches Sven get into a really good position, but his effort is sadly wide of the target.'

Eriksson, unused to such treatment in Sweden, Portugal or Italy, didn't like what he regarded as an invasion of his privacy. He says: 'I've never been angry with the press for talking about football. If my team plays badly, I deserve to be criticized. It's the other things, personal things, that I don't like. I always have difficulty accepting that, but this is England, so you have to accept it, and laugh about it sometimes.' Nancy wasn't laughing. She wanted to sue, and had to be dissuaded, on the grounds that the consequent publicity would be even worse.

By way of preparation for their next World Cup match, away to Greece, England played a warm-up friendly against Mexico at Pride Park, Derby on 25 May. To Eriksson's amusement, mass media interest focused on David Beckham's new mohican hairstyle. 'All the discussion about it was a little bit surprising to me,' he says. For those of us more interested in the football, the West Ham prodigy, Joe Cole, was given his first cap, as a second-half substitute for Beckham, Robbie Fowler started, in partnership with his Liverpool teammate Michael Owen, and in the second half Emile Heskey became the latest player to be offered the short straw that was the left side of midfield.

The match coincided with Kevin Keegan's return

to football, as manager of Manchester City, which surprised Eriksson less than some others. Of the managerial fraternity, he said: 'Football is like a drug to us. If I should lose my job, it wouldn't take me even one month to want to get back into it. Anyone who has tasted this life wants it to carry on for as long as possible. We wouldn't change jobs with any-one in any other walk of life. The only problem with being England coach is that there are not enough games. I miss the stress of a match every Saturday. You just want to be in there – winning, losing, being criticized and reading in the papers that you don't understand football. As coaches, we're all the same. We go away on holiday at the end of the season, and after two weeks we miss the stress. I love the battle, the challenge of trying to beat my oppon-ent on the other bench. After a game, I can never sleep. Win or lose, my stress level has gone up so much that I can't rest. Sometimes I hear the criticism after a bad result and think I can live with-out it, but none of us wants to be out of it. That's why it's like a drug.'

Mexico regularly appear above England in the FIFA rankings, often in the world's top ten, but the strength of the opposition they play, in Central America and elsewhere, is not up to European standard, and their rating gives a false impression of their true worth. They were easily beaten, 4–0, at Pride Park, England scoring through Scholes, Fowler, Beckham and Teddy Sheringham. Eriksson was delighted with the performance. 'We played very good football. Excellent. Couldn't be better,' he said. He had been particularly pleased by the way Gerrard, fit again, had dovetailed with Scholes in midfield. 'They are a complementary pair, and two very good footballers,' he enthused. 'They have good technique on the ball, they pass it well, their shooting is formidable and they are hard workers, too. They are two very modern midfielders who can do everything. One can attack while the other defends. In the teams I've had in the past, I've rarely had two such excellent footballers who can defend, as well as attack. I know Scholes is better at attacking than defending, but he can do both. If Gerrard moves out to the right or left, Scholes will cover in the middle. That's when he's not drifting wide himself. They are a very good pair, and Gerrard is very powerful going forward. We must hope he stays fit.'

The two strikers, Fowler and Owen, had also looked good. 'They know each other's game very well and work well together,' Eriksson said. 'I knew that they could do that. I'd seen them do it a good many times for Liverpool.' Heskey had not been entirely convincing in unfamiliar territory, on the left, but he had satisfied his manager. 'He had an important role, and I liked him there. I can understand that he wants to play up front, but I think he'd rather do this job than sit on the bench.' Generally, as well as individually, he was 'well pleased' with England's progress. 'I think we have a team that can be even better because there are so many young players in it. Gerrard is very good and will get even better – if he stays fit, of course. Then there are other players who seem to have been around for a long time, like Beckham, Scholes and Owen, who are still young, and can still improve. In the second half, after all the substitutions, we struggled a bit, but you could see the players saying "Come on, come on" to each other. They wanted to solve their problems. It was a team that had never played together, or even practised together before, but slowly they came together and created chances.' Sheringham, that cleverest of conduits, had been the key to this gelling process.

The players were given the weekend off, then the squad flew out to La Manga, the golf-orientated leisure resort in south-east Spain, for a week, to acclimatize and prepare for the World Cup tie in Athens on 6 June. It was the first time Eriksson had had his players together for so long. Did he discover anything new? 'You learn a bit more about how they react in practice and how they are in private. You learn more about that every time. We used the week to work on tactical things – offensive and defensive play, setpieces and so on. We also had a lot of team meetings, focusing on exactly how we wanted to play. I didn't push to get to know how they are in private, I don't believe in that, but it came naturally, from talking to one today, a couple of others tomorrow. There was a growing realization that we were a good team and could get even better. Good enough to get big results. I can't compare, because I don't know what the ambience was like before I took over. I can only say that the atmosphere was marvellous, and the spirit excellent. The players worked extremely hard. It was the end of the season, but there were no complaints about the heat or the blisters they were getting on their feet on the hard ground. I was very happy with their attitude.'

By this time, Eriksson sensed that the players had faith in him. He had won over the sceptics, inside and outside the dressing room, and had the respect of one and all. 'This was important,' he said. 'We had to grow together. You need a very strong and united group to get anywhere. That's especially true the first time you lose a game. Then you have to pull together, and the coach's job is to defend the team – all of them – against the world outside the group. That's important.'

In the sunshine of La Manga, the players were allowed time to relax, as well as work, and some very respectable golf was played by the low handicappers, against the likes of Kenny Dalglish and Gordon Strachan, both of whom have holiday homes at the resort. Eriksson did not take part. 'I don't play golf, I haven't the patience,' he says. 'The ball is too small, and it isn't moving when you hit it. It's a bit like taking free-kicks. I was no good at them, either.' Preferring to concentrate on football, he released two of England's most promising young players, Joe Cole and Michael Carrick, both of West Ham, to play for the Under-21s, who also had a match in Greece, in their case an important European Championship qualifier. 'Long term,' Eriksson explained, 'they are going to be part of the senior team, but they were needed in the Under-21s this time.'

Looking back, Eriksson said the week in La Manga was time particularly well spent. 'We had to get together, either in England or somewhere abroad, for intensive practice. We chose Spain because the climate was very similar to Greece's. That time also enabled us to get to know each other a lot better. The new players who were coming into the squad needed that.' Playing Greece in their own backyard is never easy, but Eriksson was always optimistic, and when the squad flew from Murcia to Athens on 4 June they were in particularly good heart, Germany having slipped up for the first time by drawing 2–2 with Finland two days earlier. Greece had also played on 2 June, beating Albania 1–0 in Crete.

On arrival in Athens, it was nudging 100°F, and the Greeks were amazed when England elected to train in the heat of the afternoon, rather than at night, which was the local custom. Eriksson wanted his players prepared for any extreme. 'We had to take a lot of water and sports drinks all afternoon, before the game and during it,' he recalled. The match took place the night before Tony Blair's second triumph in the General Election, but this was no landslide. It took 64 minutes to find a way through the Greeks' labyrinthine defences, Phil Neville and Emile Heskey setting up Paul Scholes at close range for his third goal in successive internationals. And Greece were still in it until three minutes from the end, when a mind-bending free-kick from David Beckham put the issue beyond doubt.

It had been a workmanlike performance. 'A good

job, well done' was Eriksson's preferred description. Unremarkable? 'Not brilliant football,' he agreed, 'but good, solid work. A manager is happy when he sees his team playing that way, not playing at their absolute best, but still getting the job done.' Five wins from his first five matches had put Eriksson in the record books. It was a feat none of his predecessors had managed with England. 'I heard a lot about that at the time,' he says. 'I was happy about it, of course, but much more so about the three wins in the qualifying series. They were the important ones. We'd taken a big step towards at least the play-offs, and maybe even winning the group.' The players' attitude had been 'absolutely top class', he said. 'From the day the squad came together, three days before the Mexico match, they were superb. In the first practice I took it was "Come on, we want this." All the training was excellent, and they were very professional about everything – eating, drinking, relaxing, whatever. I could see no difference from Italy, where I was working before.'

Special praise was reserved for the last of the Mohicans. 'David Beckham behaved like a captain from the first,' Eriksson says. 'From day one with me, he was extremely good on the pitch. He's not the type to stand on the table to address the team, but you can see that he is concerned about everything that happens within the squad. He'll always come to me if there's the slightest problem with any of the players. He communicates with me and with the rest of the staff, like a captain, and he's got better at it with experience in the job.'

Germany had won the same day, 2–0 in Albania, but England were on a roll, still six points behind, but with a game in hand. Now if they could just squeeze out a 1–0 in Munich . . .

CHAPTER SEVENTEEN

MUNICH MAGIC

Sven-Goran Eriksson always insisted that England could win in Germany and turn the group on its head. After the match in Athens he said: 'We have to go there [Munich] thinking we have nothing to lose. If we want to qualify directly for the World Cup, it's a must to win the game. If we don't, we'll be runners-up, but I think we can do it. If Germany could win in England, why can't we beat them there? Then it will come down to a question of goal difference. Everything is possible. We've taken maximum points from our last three games, and we still have the chance to finish top of the group. Let's take a holiday now, and then go again.' He was looking forward to adding two midfield reinforcements, Lee Bowyer of Leeds and Newcastle's Kieron Dyer, to his squad, but unfortunate circumstances would deny him both.

The make-or-break match in Munich was on 1 September 2001 – a time of year when England, traditionally, do not play well. In need of a testing rehearsal, they arranged a friendly against Holland at White Hart Lane, Tottenham, on 15 August.

Eriksson says: 'It was a strange time to be playing an international, before the Premier League season had started, but it was important to have it as preparation for Germany.' With no league matches in which to check on his players' form and fitness, he did the rounds of the training grounds. 'I talked to the managers and watched them work with their squads. That also helped me get to know everybody a bit better.' And there were, of course, pre-season friendlies. The day after returning from holiday in Portugal, Eriksson watched Fulham play Sparta Prague, and 24 hours later he was spotted at Newcastle's Intertoto Cup match against Lokeren in Belgium. It was still more than a month before the big kick-off in the Premier League, but he said: 'If Newcastle are playing, then the English season has started.'

Conscientious to an extraordinary degree, Eriksson took in another Intertoto tie, Aston Villa v Slaven Belupo, on 22 July, then attended Arsenal v Kocaelispor in Austria on 25 July, and the following morning caught a 10.30am flight from Innsbruck to Amsterdam to see Liverpool play Valencia in another friendly tournament. It was an uncomfortable journey in a small, turbo-prop aircraft with no business class option. The England coach, dressed casually in jeans and trainers, consumed the chicken sandwich and orange juice that passed for an inflight meal while scanning the Italian sports newspaper *Corriere dello Sport*. He stayed for the whole of the Amsterdam tournament, including Ajax v Milan, and on 29 July travelled to Rotterdam for Feyenoord v Southampton, returning to Austria the next day for Arsenal v Real Mallorca. After Manchester United v Celtic on 1 August, he was as well prepared as it was possible to be.

There was a brief, unwelcome distraction when Eriksson, acting on legal advice, accused *Hello!* magazine of an invasion of privacy over a five-page feature on his new London home. There were lavish interior photographs of the imposing Georgian house near Regents Park which Eriksson and Nancy Dell'Olio had bought for £2.5m. The article, published on 19 June, gushingly described the property as: 'the ideal urban base for a dazzling couple with a glittering lifestyle'. It included a close-up of Eriksson, sitting in an armchair at an Italian hotel, but he was conspicuously absent from any of the pictures of his living room, bedroom, dining room, bathroom and study. The article noted that Eriksson guards his privacy jealously, and his lawyers claimed costs and damages, on the basis that the photographs were obtained without his authorization, and therefore represented a breach of privacy. Phil Hall, the editor of *Hello!*, said the pictures were supplied by the previous owner of the property and denied that they had been taken from an estate agent's brochure.

The Holland game brought an emphatic end to Eriksson's 100 per cent start with England. In fairness, it was always going to be a difficult test. The Dutch brought a coruscating array of household names – Stam and Van Bronckhorst, Zenden and Van Nistelrooy, Kluivert and Overmars – so outstanding that Edgar Davids could only make the bench. England, on the other hand, were without the likes of Seaman, Campbell, Ferdinand, Gerrard, Heskey, McManaman and Butt, and Eriksson had assured the managers of the top clubs that none of their players would be required to play more than 45 minutes at a stage in the season when they were not completely match fit. In weakened circumstances, he promoted Owen Hargreaves from the Under-21s, offering him the poisoned chalice that was the left flank.

Hargreaves is an interesting character, who was qualified by birth and residence to play for Canada and Germany, as well as England. He had caught the eye with compelling performances for his club, Bayern Munich, in the Champions' League, first against Manchester United and then in the semifinal and final, against Real Madrid and Valencia respectively. Eriksson had watched him closely, and was much impressed. He had done well in distinguished company, but could he play out on the left? The answer was no. The novice floundered, neither fish nor fowl. He accomplished next to nothing going forward, and was unable to provide sufficient cover for his full-back, Ashley Cole, who was given the run around by Zenden. Hargreaves and Cole were not the only England players to suffer as the Dutch, who were also struggling to qualify for the World Cup, gave a technical masterclass. Their slick passing and instinctive rotational movement rendered Jamie Carragher inadequate in the midfield anchor role, and the pacy, intuitive interplay of Van Nistelrooy and Kluivert set the tone for what was to be a desperately disappointing season for Wes Brown. Nothing went right for England from first to last, their evening epitomized when David James, who had come on at half-time for Nigel Martyn, was carried off within three minutes of his introduction, having sustained serious knee damage in accidental collision with Martin Keown. Holland won convincingly, and might have had more than their two goals, scored by Mark van Bommel and Van Nistelrooy.

As preparation goes, it was scarcely ideal for Munich; the only positive spin that could be put on the result being the fact that the players had been brought down to earth with a bump. Eriksson was criticized by the media, but it was powderpuff stuff. No swedes and turnips – yet. 'It's always interesting to see what happens when you lose, always an experience,' Eriksson observed. 'But I didn't read everything. To save yourself grief, you should read everything when you win and as little as possible when you lose. You'll sleep better that way. If Holland had been a qualifying tie, and we'd played like that, I would have expected the critics to have been much harder, and that's fair.' After a week's reflection, he said he would have been much more concerned had England been at full strength. Should he not have been firmer with the club managers, and insisted on all his best players being available, and for more than one half? 'No. It will never be my way to go pushing people around. You can't go looking for a fight with the club managers, you just can't do the England job that way. You must try to be as diplomatic as possible – even if it means we lose some friendly matches. Through compromising like that, I hope to get all our players for the competitive games, and win when it matters. I don't think we should risk players who are important to their clubs in friendlies.' Diplomacy was an essential requirement for the job. 'It is very different to that of the club manager. The players are only yours on certain occasions. If I'd been convinced that it was right for England, and good for the future of the England team, to have all my players, I would have insisted on it, but I wasn't convinced of that.'

He had wanted to pick Lee Bowyer, but had been told by the Football Association that the Leeds midfielder was not available for selection, pending the outcome of the court case in which he was accused of grievous bodily harm and affray after an incident outside a nightclub in January 2000 (he was subsequently acquitted).

Free of the historical and emotional baggage the English bring to clashes with Germany, Eriksson was always upbeat about the fateful trip to Munich. 'I think if you are frightened going into a game, you've given the opposition a 1–0 lead before you start – maybe 2–0. I knew we had a good team. A very good team. We hadn't shown it against Holland, but the ability was there. I think we were all roughly at the same level – England, Germany, Holland and so on – and it all came down to attitude. Who was in good shape, mentally, and who had their best players available. When we have that, we can compete with anybody.'

One aspect of his job, at least, was easy. 'In games like that one, there's no need for me to say anything to motivate the players, it's an automatic thing. The danger is that they become too tense to play at their best, so we had to try to be relaxed. When you run out in the Olympic stadium in front of 80,000 people you know the importance of the game all right, so it was a case of trying to take it as easy as possible mentally beforehand, while still working properly to prepare for the game.'

Reminded before departure that the Germans had lost only one World Cup qualifier in 60, Eriksson showed surprise for once. 'In 60? Oh, Jesus,' he exclaimed. 'That's a big plus in their favour, to have that record in the bank, but I still think we have possibilities there.'

As ever when England play Germany, it was hyped by the more hysterical sections of the media as the match of the century. Much was made of the fact that the England squad's hotel was adjacent to the biggest beer hall in Munich. The tabloids were outraged that the players' sleep would be disturbed (in reality, the sound-proofing was so good that when I visited the hotel at midnight you could have heard an umlaut drop), and the *Sun* sent an oompah band of their own to the Germans' hotel, where they promptly got themselves arrested. 'We were only obeying orders' was their classic retort.

With a strange sense of timing that had the conspiracy theorists crying 'fiddle', FIFA decided to make the draw for the play-offs now, before the participants were known. Either England or Germany

(whoever finished runners-up in the group) would
play Ukraine or Belarus from Group Five. The draw,
unscheduled, took everybody by surprise, Eriksson
said. 'I only heard about it on the bus, on the
way from the airport to the hotel. I suppose it was
done so hurriedly to give all the countries who could
finish second as much time as possible to arrange
things.' England booked Old Trafford, on a pro-
visional basis, 'just in case'. Eriksson had thought
about coming second, then? 'Of course, it was
always a possibility. If you'd asked me at the outset if
I'd have been happy to settle for that, the answer
would have been yes.'

On the Tuesday before the match, when the
squad assembled, he had made a point of including
the match at home to Albania eight days later in
his opening remarks. 'I spoke to the players about
it because there was a risk that it would be all
"Germany, Germany, Germany", and the Albania
game couldn't be forgotten. It wasn't as glorious as
Germany, but it was just as important.' Playing the
two big matches back to back, in the space of five
days wasn't a problem. 'The Germans had started
their league season two weeks before us, which was
an advantage for them, but physically our players
could handle the two games.'

There was a scare over the fitness of David Beckham, who was troubled by a groin injury which had
prevented him from training at Manchester United,
but come the big day, Eriksson was able to field the
team he wanted. 'That was a good thing, of course,'
he says. 'The ideal is to have a national team like a

club one, with eight or nine playing always.' A full-strength team included Gary Neville, Sol Campbell and Nick Barmby, who had missed the previous qualifier, in Athens. Barmby was given another shot at left midfield, allowing Emile Heskey to partner Michael Owen in attack, in preference to Robbie Fowler.

'I felt lucky on the day of the match,' Eriksson says. 'For the first time, I had all 25 players originally selected in the squad fully fit and available. No player had to go on the pitch in a position he didn't normally play for his club. Heskey was in because he is the perfect player for a manager to have. If I asked him to play as the left defender he would do it without a word of complaint. But I know he wants to play up front, and a player gives of his best when he plays in the position he likes and normally plays for his club.'

At his pre-match press conference, the coach was confidence personified. 'Beating Germany is something very few players have achieved, and we are going to do it,' he said. 'To win, we have to do everything more or less perfectly, but we have a good opportunity to win our group and go to the World Cup automatically, so we are going out to beat the Germans, and I know we can do it.' As the conference ended, somebody shouted 'Good luck'. Eriksson turned, smiled and said quietly: 'Thank you. We will need it.'

And despite the eventual scoreline, they did need it. The atmosphere on a balmy evening in the Olympic Stadium had the hairs on the back of the neck standing to attention even before the anthems were played. There were English flags, banners and shirts everywhere, turning what was expected to be a hostile environment into a home from home. Even for those of us who have reported on international football all over the world for more than 25 years, it was an 'I was there' occasion. 'Eriksson's Army', as the travelling hordes called themselves, had caught his mood. England expected.

In his team talk, the manager told his players: 'We're here for all three points; a draw's no good to us. Don't be afraid, go out and play your football. Don't think they're a better team than we are, because they're not.' Then, before they left the dressing room, the captain, Beckham, went to each player in turn, wishing them 'good luck', telling them that Germany 'were beatable', and to 'relax and enjoy the game'. The start, however, was anything but enjoyable, an explosion of Teutonic joy greeting the goal with which Carsten Jancker gave Germany the lead after only six minutes. England's defending was poor, Michael Ballack's short, lofted centre from the left bisecting Rio Ferdinand and Ashley Cole for the smallest player on the pitch, Oliver Neuville, to nod the ball down for Jancker to score with a deft touch from eight yards. First blood to the Germans, how would England react? They needed to respond quickly if heads were not to drop, and after 13 minutes they did so. This time Germany's defence was at fault, failing to clear Beckham's free-kick from the right and paying the price when Gary Neville's nicely cushioned head through was transferred by Barmby to Owen, who made short work of a sidefooted finish.

At 1–1 it was anybody's game, and the outcome might have been very different had Sebastian Deisler regained the initiative for the Germans, as he should have done when, all alone in front of goal, he somehow contrived to scoop the ball over from a central position, eight yards out. It was a horrendous miss and one which, when allied to the outstanding save with which David Seaman denied Jorg Bohme, constituted a turning point. Instead of going in at the interval a goal down, England were 2–1 up, Steven Gerrard beating Oliver Kahn just before half-time with a fulminating drive which had both power and accuracy, after the ball had been laid off by Rio Ferdinand.

Gerrard told me: 'We'd got into it and were starting to dominate the game. It was a good time for me to score, so that we went in ahead at half-time, but I wasn't thinking about how long there was left. I just saw bodies coming towards me and thought: "If I lose it here, we're wide open to a counter-attack" so I checked and shouted to Rio to set the ball up for me. He did, and I just hit it.' Eriksson had said very little during the break. 'All the lads were buzzing,' Gerrard recalled. 'Our goals had given us our self-belief and confidence back after a ropy start, and we were able to go out and build on that platform in the second half. Sven just said: "Keep doing what you were doing for the last 25 minutes. The bad start is out of the way now, just keep playing, and make sure you start the second half the way you finished the first." He's so cool. I've never seen him raise his voice over anything. Because he's dead calm, he handles anything that happens really well, even when the pressure is on. In Munich, in a high-pressure game, I looked across at him when we were a goal down and he was sitting there straight-faced on the bench, very calm and relaxed. He does all his talking in his meetings during the build-up, then he'll have a chat with the lads immediately before the game, and I think he feels that's enough. He's not one to leap off the bench, shouting orders. Even at half-time he has just a quiet word.'

Eriksson explained that at the interval it was a case of 'Keep playing the same way, and we'll be all right.' England did, and they were. The third goal, which gave them control, came three minutes into the second half. Gary Neville's long ball down the line from halfway found Beckham, who delivered a poor cross but set a captain's example by diligently retrieving possession to have another go, this time with his left foot. At the second attempt he found Heskey who, from near the penalty spot, laid the ball off to his right for Owen to strike a textbook volley, which went in off Kahn's body at his near post. To their credit, the Germans hit back, and Jancker was desperately close with a header from eight yards. But the game was put beyond their reach midway through the second half, when Gerrard won the ball in midfield and played it through in the inside-right channel, where Owen advanced, took a couple of touches and scored with a pulverizing shot which was said to have left scorch marks on the face of the world's best goalkeeper. An England striker had a hat-trick against Germany; shades of 1966 and all that. And Sir Geoff Hurst was there to see it.

Forearms were black and blue everywhere from onlookers pinching themselves, but still England were not finished. Ferdinand and Scholes combined to send Heskey striding away from Marko Rehmer, and the man they call 'Bruno' supplied the coup de grâce with a resounding shot into the corner. As Heskey mimed an easy putt by way of celebration, there was the astonishing, unprecedented sight of German fans heading for the exits with more than a quarter of an hour to play. Germany just didn't lose qualifying ties at home. It was a historic result and the margin fantastic in the true meaning of the word. Eriksson was undemonstrative at the final whistle, just as Alf Ramsey had been 35 years earlier. He shook hands with his coaching staff, then made for the tunnel, only to be stopped on the way by Adam Crozier, who embraced him as he offered his congratulations.

In the immediate aftermath, Eriksson sat calmly amid the debris of the dressing room and said: 'People everywhere will read this result and say "Wow", but I don't know exactly what this means for England yet. It has been a great party, and it is important for the points gained and for the confidence of a young team to know that we can do this. But the most important thing is that we get to the World Cup finals, and we're not there yet. If we do make it, I think the squad we have can do well but remember, I have not said that we will win it. Coming back from a goal down here shows that we are strong, mentally, but we had a little luck in scoring just before half-time. Going in 2–1 up, rather than 1–1, made a great difference. The reason we could come back into the game was that the players believe we can achieve big things. If you don't believe it, it doesn't matter how good you are. Always, you must start in the head.'

Looking back months later, Eriksson said: 'You never forget a game like that. Those goals – beautiful goals, all of them. How can I describe the feelings I had? Sitting on the bench, seeing 1–1, 2–1, 3–1 and so on . . . It was unreal – and extremely nice. We were in Germany, in Munich, the referee blew his whistle, the match was over and we'd won 5–1. Amazing. To be honest, it was incredible that they didn't score to go 2–1 up. But they didn't take their chance and we took ours to go 2–1. They should have done it, whereas we did it. We were lucky there. In any football match, when it is near the end of the first half or at the beginning of the second and you go from drawing to being in front, that advantage means a lot, mentally. The opposite is also true, and Germany definitely suffered.' Michael Owen recalled: 'The first thing I was asked by the media was: "Did it really happen?" If they couldn't believe it, imagine what the players were like. I don't know how long it took to sink in – maybe it still hasn't. Maybe at the end of my career I'll look back and still think: "Did we do that?" When I equalized, I think the whole team fancied it then. Going 1–0 down, the thought occurred: "Uh-oh, here we go, we're going to lose to this lot again," but as soon as we hit 1–1 I knew there was no way we were not going to score again. We were causing them problems every time we went forward.'

It was a triumph stamped 'Made On Merseyside'. All five goals had been scored by Liverpool players, and each of Owen's three came from final passes delivered by clubmates. Under Eriksson, however, the old tribal rivalries, which had seen previous teams split into Manchester United and Liverpool camps, were a thing of the past. The captain, Beckham, said: 'The way we celebrated the goals showed that. It didn't matter who scored, or what club they came from. I think it was a turning point in the way fans see England players. We're not separate groups from different clubs, we mix well. That showed when we played Germany.' There were no wild celebrations. Beckham explained: 'There wasn't any jumping around and opening champagne in the dressing room because we knew we hadn't qualified yet. I just sat there and thought: "What was that?" I turned to a couple of the lads and said: "What's happened there?" It was just an amazing experience.' While Owen, the hat-trick hero, took most of the plaudits, there was praise, too, for David Seaman, and that vital, top-drawer save from Bohme at 1–1. The veteran goalkeeper recalled: 'It was strange afterwards, because you wanted to go out singing and dancing and having a few beers, but we had another game coming up on the Wednesday, against

Albania, which was really important as well. There was so much emotion there, and although you were just dying to let it out, because it was such a fantastic result, you couldn't. You had to keep it in.'

Rio Ferdinand was another player in wonderland. He recalled 'sitting there thinking: "We've just beaten Germany 5–1 in their own backyard." How is that possible? After all the times they'd beaten us, it was just a blinding result. I didn't realize the euphoria that surrounded it until we got back to England and everyone was going mad. It lasted a couple of weeks, everyone talking about it. We'd set ourselves a benchmark. Now we had to keep up to it.' Ferdinand, like Owen, had feared the worst when the Germans took the lead. 'When we went a goal down so early, I thought: "What's going on here?" But when you look around our team, and see the quality players we have there, you never think: "We're not going to score." Their goal kick-started us. We weren't playing well at the start, but that livened us up. We came flying out of the traps, expressing ourselves a lot more, and put a few past them.'

It was not only the England players who deserved praise. The English fans were well behaved, and the Germans, without much practice, proved remarkably good losers. Everywhere visiting celebrants went in Munich that night – and some of us were at it until breakfast time – it was 'congratulations' and 'well played' from the locals. Two nationalities forever portrayed as 'traditional enemies' mixed like brothers. Franz Beckenbauer, the most celebrated

German footballer of all time, said: 'I have never
seen a better England team. When they scored
their third goal, they started to play football that
would have beaten anyone in the world. Owen
was unstoppable.' Dietmar Hamann, the Germans'
matchwinner at Wembley 11 months earlier, said:
'England beat us with a bit of the Liverpool style.
They played long balls which made it difficult for
our defenders to deal with the pace of Owen and
Heskey.'

Back home, the reaction was ecstatic. They
danced all night in Trafalgar Square, and the result
dominated all the newspapers – front, middle and
back. It all but filled the *News of the World*, pushing 'Posh's Anorexia Nightmare' and 'Sam Fox: A
Lesbian In Love' off the front page. The *Daily Mail*
hinted at a knighthood for the man they had
greeted as an 'unwelcome alien'. All that stuff about
'designer Scandinavians' and 'selling our birthright
down the fjord' was forgotten under the headline
'Will Eriksson become the Swedish Sir Alf?' Sadly,
they could not leave it at that. Just three days later,
they carried an 'exclusive' in which John Barnwell,
the chief executive of the League Managers'
Association, 'stood by his opinion' that Eriksson's
appointment had been 'an insult'.

Insulting or not, England were now just three
points behind the Germans, and with a game in
hand.

CHAPTER EIGHTEEN

BECKHAM'S MATCH

On their triumphal return from Munich, England set up camp at the Slaley Hall Hotel, near Hexham, 25 miles west of Newcastle, to prepare for the Albania match at St James' Park, on 5 September. Sven-Goran Eriksson may have wanted it otherwise, but only three days on, the talk was still of that seismic result in Germany. Verbal bouquets were still being sent from every direction. Arsenal's Arsene Wenger, who might have had Eriksson's job, said 'England are the best of the up-and-coming teams, and I can see them as world champions. It was a pleasure to see them do so well, but I warned the Germans last week that I believed England would win. England are now a team with young players developing well, and up front they have Michael Owen, who is on fire.'

Claudio Ranieri, the Chelsea manager, who knew Eriksson from their days in Italy, said: 'If you can coach there, you can coach in hell. I know Sven and I know his work. I knew he would be a success with England and I thought they would win in Germany. We had a sweepstake at Chelsea, and I got the result right but the score wrong. I said it would be 2–0. Sven is an "Ice Man", like they say. He never lets his emotions show. He is a typical English gentleman in that respect, and maybe that's why he is doing so well. He has been blessed with a lot of good, young players who already have plenty of international experience. At this moment, Michael Owen is the best striker in the world.'

Gianluca Vialli, who had played under Eriksson at Sampdoria, said: 'When he took over, Sven took risks and chances. This shows he has "big balls". His decision to call up young players and leave out the older ones was very brave.' Liverpool's Gerard Houllier weighed in with: 'I think this generation will reach its full potential in 2004 or 2006. But already Eriksson has been able to give his team confidence and real unity. As proof of that, I give you the camaraderie that now exists between the players from Liverpool and Manchester United. David Beckham speaks to me about my players as if they were from United. Eriksson's experience is priceless, and he has improved the mindset of the players.'

The players spoke in similar vein about the man who had transformed their fortunes in under a year. Michael Owen's hat-trick against Germany had taken his tally to 19 goals in his last 12 matches for club and country. Of Eriksson's influence, he said: 'Under previous England managers I was not exactly the flavour of the month, and I suppose you could trace this run I'm on back to the Spain game [Eriksson's first]. I wasn't having the best of times before then, but I started that game and did well, and since then I've gone from strength to strength.'

David Beckham was more expansive. 'The captain and the manager have always got to have a good relationship. The results have obviously helped with me and Mr Eriksson, but I've had a good relationship with him from his first game. It's hard to bridge that divide between getting on well with the manager and the players, too. Fortunately, I've got a good relationship with both. I don't think the players feel I'm being a snitch when I'm talking to the manager. I don't think they are worried about having a conversation with me and it all getting back to him. To my mind, the important thing the manager has given us is the way he has brought the best out of the team and also out of each individual. He has a lot of experience, and the players realize that. He trusts all of us to do our job, and every one of us has got massive respect for him. That's a vital thing for a manager.'

Of Eriksson, the person, Beckham said: 'He is extremely calm. We all got excited about the Germany result, but the first thing he said to us in the dressing room afterwards was that we had another big game on the Wednesday. It was: "Well done for tonight, but now we focus on Albania."'

Unsurprisingly, there was a vote of confidence for the players who had done England proud in Munich. Announcing an unchanged team, Eriksson said: 'The team that played on Saturday deserves to play again.' The media were still up on cloud nine. At a press conference on the eve of the match, the man who had gone from unwelcome immigrant to messiah in the space of seven games looked understandably embarrassed when he was asked: 'Are you surprised that you have reached God-like status?', then: 'Do you realize you are the most popular man in the country?' Sensibly, he ignored one tabloid's attempt to present him with a trophy 'containing the ashes of German football'. To redtop frustration, he wasn't giving them the headlines, or the pictures they wanted. In response to comments about his retiring manner, he said: 'I am not the type to explode with emotion,' before adding with a smile, 'Mind you, I do hope to do it in June next year.' Winning in Germany had been 'just one small step towards the top of the mountain'. Some newspapers had been talking in terms of double figures against Albania, but no team could score five goals or more every time they played, and he was looking for a 2–0 win. 'The players are very focused,' he said. 'If we want the chance to be a great team, we have first to win the next two games [the last two qualifiers, against Albania and Greece]. A great team doesn't go out and play a great game every now and then. A great team hates to lose. Fortunately, in every game we seem to get better and better. The short-term target is to qualify for the World Cup, but we have a good, young team that can improve in the future, and stay together for five to seven years.'

The near-hysterical heroes' welcome when the team bus arrived at St James' Park beggared belief. 'It wouldn't have happened in any other country,' Eriksson said. 'We hadn't even qualified for the

World Cup yet, but you would have thought we had won it. I saw it in Italy, but only once, and that was when Lazio won the league. There is such a passion here. I said to my captain, David Beckham: "Not even Manchester United get a reception like that."'

After such scenes, the match was never going to be anything but an anti-climax. Far from running riot, England made hard work of overcoming stubborn opposition. Despite yet another goal from Owen just before half-time, when he fastened on to a long through-ball from Paul Scholes to score with a dextrous volley from eight yards, the outcome was in doubt right up to the 88th minute. Then Robbie Fowler, on as substitute for Heskey, gained possession 35 yards out, evaded two defenders, drew the goalkeeper and then stroked home a goal of the highest class. England were on top of the group, albeit only on goal difference, and nobody much minded if it had been a bit of a scramble to get there. Certainly Eriksson was not surprised by the contrasting performances in the space of five days. 'We were always in a dangerous situation,' he said. 'You are up in the skies, with people saying and writing nice things about you, and then you have to play Albania at home. Of course the tension is much less, and the danger is that you don't go out there fighting, prepared to kill off the opposition, like we did in Germany.'

Owen offered much the same view. 'It was hard, playing another important match, just four days after being emotionally drained in Germany. I've never felt so tired in my life. I don't think it was a physical thing, more a case of having done so well in Munich and then having to start all over again. We know we didn't play well, but the important things is that we got the three points.'

In hindsight, should Eriksson have changed and freshened up a team depleted in terms of physical and mental energy? 'Maybe, but the performance in Munich was not just a win, it was a big, big event, so I listened to my heart, as well as my brain. The same 11 players all deserved to start the home game, and receive the supporters' thanks. But we paid a price for that. By the second half we needed to change more than three players, which is not allowed. Then, we were a little bit tired, and lost our confidence. For 15 minutes it reminded me of Holland. We cannot afford to drop the pace, we have to play a high-tempo game. When we do that, we are a very good team.'

By this time, Beckham was talking the talk, as well as walking the captain's walk. 'Eleven months ago,' he said, 'there was a dream. We have worked so hard to live it, and now it is within our grasp. There's no better place to finish the job than Old Trafford [where England were to play Greece on 6 October]. From the day I took over as captain, it has been an unbelievable experience. We were in a pretty desperate position at the time, but we have all grown together as a team since then. I don't think anyone realized just how much Saturday's game in Munich had taken out of us, mentally and physically. It wasn't a great game against Albania, but we ground out a result, and it means just one more win and we're at the World Cup. We were a bit critical in the dressing room afterwards, but the general feeling was: "Thank God for that."'

Of Beckham's ever-expanding influence, Eriksson said: 'He is a wonderful player and an inspirational captain, and I am very proud of him. Peter Taylor should be congratulated for making him captain, as well as for giving a chance to other young players. That made it easier for me when I came in. Beckham is more than just a good player, he is becoming the symbol of a team that is growing match by match. He is now, I believe, the complete player. Every time we come together, he seems to have grown in stature a little bit more. The World Cup is never the same without players like him.'

No manager is ever entirely happy with his squad, there is always room for improvement, and in the run-up to the Greeks' visit Eriksson spoke about 'some players on the outside who are very close to getting in'. Pressed for names, he said: 'Don't forget Keown. He's not out of it, absolutely not. He can be a very important player for us.' In the younger age group, there was Newcastle's Kieron Dyer, injured at the time, but still a World Cup contender. 'If he's the player I think he is, he'll be involved,' Eriksson said. On the left, possibly? 'I don't know about that. Bobby Robson says yes, but of course I want to see it for myself, and before I can do that, Dyer has to be fit and playing football.' Meanwhile, the endless search for perfection would continue. 'I'm not concerned, because the team is doing extremely well, but I do have to go on travelling and looking to see if I can find anyone better than we already have. Mind you, it won't be easy.'

Ominously, the talismanic Michael Owen was unavailable, injured, as were two centre-halves, Sol Campbell and Wes Brown, for the visit of Greece. David Seaman was 'highly doubtful' with a shoulder injury which was to keep him out until well into the new year, and Frank Lampard was dropped for disciplinary reasons after some drunken mis-behaviour at a Heathrow hotel. Chris Powell was another absentee, having fallen by the wayside as Ashley Cole made the left-back position his own. The replacements were Teddy Sheringham, Martin Keown, Ugo Ehiogu, Nicky Butt and the uncapped Trevor Sinclair.

Their plea for leniency on grounds of diminished chords having been accepted by the German police, the *Sun*'s oompah band were back, and heading for the top ten with the imaginatively titled 'Sven, Sven, Sven'. But all was not sweetness and harmony as England gathered at the Marriott Hotel in Worsley, just outside Manchester. Steven Gerrard, injured again, had been given permission to fly to France for treatment by an osteopath before joining up with the squad the following day. To his, and the England management's, considerable embarrass-ment, he was seen drinking in a Southport bar at 2am. Not only was he spotted, but some nark, as is their wont, tipped off the newspapers, and the *Sun* was soon devoting the whole of its back page to Lampard's 'short, sharp lesson' and Gerrard, whose '2 am booze shock' had left Eriksson 'let down

again'. The manager was accused of 'double standards' for dropping Lampard, who was dispensable,
and forgiving Gerrard, who was not. Worse, he was
called 'a bottler' by a couple of tabloid papers for
failing to attend that afternoon's press conference
to explain his actions. The *Daily Mail*, anxious to get
in first with his views on the matter, quoted a report
compiled on the habits of young footballers for the
League Managers' Association, in which Eriksson
had said: 'Drinking is a matter of culture. As northern Europeans, we are used to alcohol being a part of
our lives. In Italy, it is viewed as being part of the
experience of eating. You dine and you take wine. It
does not matter in southern Europe whether you are
a sportsman or a lawyer, it is not the done thing to
be seen around late at night the worse for drink.'

The following day, Friday, Eriksson still refused to
answer questions about Lampard and Gerrard, who
by now had been joined in the dock by Robbie
Fowler and Steve McManaman, both of whom had
been 'shopped' to the media for being on licensed
premises, when they were having an innocent, and
and sober, night out. 'My intention today is not
to answer questions outside football,' the manager
warned his inquisitors, wearing the sort of steely,
fixed smile that brooked no argument. 'I don't think
this is the right time to be talking about other things.'
When the man from the *Daily Star* asked if Gerrard
owed him a performance, Eriksson's reply was: 'No,
he doesn't. I hope he will play well, and I'm sure he
will, but it's not a question of that. I don't think any
of the players I have picked have let England down.

They have been very professional, they have been working hard and their spirit is good. And that's it. Football questions, please.'

In April 2002 he was finally prepared to elaborate on the alcohol issue. If a player wanted to take a glass of wine with his meal, it was not a problem, he said. 'As long as they don't for a . . . what do you say in England? A session? Sessions are very bad.'

Back in October 2001, there was a danger, Eriksson warned, of the right result against Greece being taken for granted. How right he was. Come the morning of the match the *Sun*, under the head-line 'Crisis, What Crisis?' said of Michael Owen's absence: 'Sven could pick Lineker and Hurst, and we'd still beat the Greeks by two', adding 'England really will face Greeks bearing gifts this weekend.' Eriksson, of course, was at pains to gainsay that school of thought. 'Listening to people, they seem to think that we're already in the finals, and we're not,' he said. 'We need another very good 90 minutes to get there. To think any other way is a dangerous attitude. When we played Germany away, there was no need to motivate the team because everyone knew it was going to be difficult. This time, especially after Greece lost 5–1 in Finland [the night England were winning in Munich], it's easy to think that we don't have to work very hard to win the game. But for us to think like that would be a big mistake.

'It's certainly not a trap I have fallen into. The preparation has been exactly the same as it was in Germany, done with the same spirit and in the same atmosphere. On the training pitch, it has been exactly the same work as we always do, with careful emphasis on the organization of the defence. I haven't changed anything, and the preparation has been very good. We must play with a lot of patience, like we did against Albania and Greece away. We can't expect to score in the first minute. We're talking about 90 minutes' work – hard work, difficult work. Only after 90 minutes will we have won the game.' He expected Germany to beat Finland in their last game, in Gelsenkirchen, which meant England needed all three points to win the group. 'The Germans had a very bad result against us, but they are at home again, and they won't repeat that.'

It was the biggest occasion in his entire career, yet he was not nervous. 'This is much bigger than anything I've done at club level. Qualifying for the World Cup is something I've never done as a manager, and certainly not as a player. So for me, it is very big and very beautiful. If you love football, the World Cup is the biggest party of all. You know all the world is joining in, watching at home or in the stadiums, and it's marvellous. It will be so good to be there. We shall go out tomorrow all together and make sure that England will be there in June. I hope that after the game we can say "thank you" to each other. Personally, I've slept very well all week. I will be surprised if we don't play well tomorrow. To win, you have to work hard, and we will.'

England showed three changes to the team that had played Germany and Albania. Nigel Martyn took over in goal from David Seaman, whose shoulder was still troubling him, Martin Keown came in for Sol Campbell, who was nursing a damaged ankle, and Robbie Fowler deputized for Michael Owen (hamstring). The *Sun* had promised 'We Can Win It Without You, Owen', but against all forecasts, and to the dismay of an expectant crowd, Greece were clearly the better side in the first half, and deservedly led 1–0 at the interval, Angelos Charisteas having scored with a powerful, angled drive after the right wing-back, Christos Patsatzoglou, had rounded Ashley Cole and left him for dead. It was goalless at half-time in Germany, which meant that if the scores stayed the same, it would be England suffering ordeal by play-off.

In response to the gathering crisis, Eriksson sent on an extra striker, Andy Cole, in place of Nick Barmby for the second half, and this first sub-stitution would quickly have had the desired effect but for a save at close quarters by Antonis Nikopolidis. At this stage, with the Greeks 1–0 up, it took an heroic intervention by Nigel Martyn to pre-vent their captain and best player, Theo Zagorakis, from doubling the margin. It was a key moment. Had England fallen two goals behind, the corrosive effect on their morale would probably have been decisive. Instead, they hit back hard, Scholes and Beckham both testing Nikopolidis.

Meanwhile, over in the Ruhr, the Germans were also going through agonies. Oliver Bierhoff, recalled to the team as captain after six months out, might have had a hat-trick, but hit first the crossbar, then the legs of the Finnish goalkeeper, Antti Niemi, and finally a post. They call Old Trafford the 'Theatre of Dreams', and this time the drama threatened one twist too many. Karagounis brought another notable save from Martyn, and it was increasingly apparent that England were in trouble.

Cometh the hour, cometh the man. Sensing that it was all in danger of going terribly wrong, Beckham took up the baton and ran with it. Suddenly, the captain was everywhere, on a one-man crusade. The right side of the field is his normal area of operations, but now he popped up all across the line. There's Only One David Beckham? It was as if there were three. He still needed help to turn the tide, however, and midway through the second half Eriksson sent on his close friend and erstwhile Manchester United teammate, Teddy Sheringham, in place of Fowler. The canny 35 year old was just what England needed. Within seconds of his introduction he re-directed a Beckham free-kick with the deftest of back-headers which carried the ball over Nikopolidis and into the roof of the net, and with 68 minutes played England were level.

Now, surely, the crowd could relax at last. Unfortunately, so did England, and within a minute Greece were ahead again, Themis Nikolaidis turning adroitly before beating Martyn from near the penalty spot. Beckham chivvied and chased, charging hither and thither, but the sands of time were running away. The scoreboard clock showed 4.37pm when Beckham drove another of his free-kicks into the side netting. In the same instant, Michael Ballack was going desperately close for the Germans. Some

12 minutes later, the game in Gelsenkirchen finished goalless, and the news that England were still losing 2–1 prompted celebrations 700 km away. Too soon, they started singing too soon. At 4.53pm, Sheringham was deemed, dubiously, to have been fouled by Kostas Konstantinidis, and Beckham stepped forward for what everybody knew was England's last chance. It seems scarcely credible now, but the captain had tried, and failed, with six previous dead-ball strikes, and Sheringham, who had scored with a belter against Mexico, wanted to take this one. Fortunately, as it transpired, Beckham pulled rank, and from a central position, 28 yards out, he curled a never-to-be-forgotten beauty into the nonplussed goalkeeper's top right corner. As the vital goal went in, two-and-a-half minutes of stoppage time had been played. Just over a minute later, the final whistle signalled an explosion of relief that threatened to bring down the walls of Old Trafford – a triumphant yell that was echoed all over the country. Appropriately, after his colossal individual contribution, it was Beckham who was in possession when the end came. He picked the ball up, kicked it as high as he could into the air, and fell into the jubilant embrace of Rio Ferdinand, who hoisted the hero aloft.

In Gelsenkirchen, the distress was pitiful to behold. As the German players filed down the tunnel, believing they had qualified on the back of an English defeat, they spotted a TV monitor which showed that play was still in progress in Manchester. Defender Marko Rehmer takes up the story: 'We saw that the England match had not finished, after all, so four or five of us gathered around the screen to watch. We saw David Beckham score with his free-kick, and of course we knew what it meant. The place just fell totally silent. Everybody was so stunned, nobody knew what to say.' Oliver Kahn, Germany's captain, burst into tears, and then, back in the dressing room, questioned whether his teammates had wanted victory enough.

It was the first time the Germans had failed to qualify automatically for any major tournament. They had been so confident of doing so again this time that they had already arranged friendly internationals away to South Korea and Thailand on the play-off dates. These were hurriedly cancelled and filled with the home and away play-offs against Ukraine, which eventually saw them through to the finals on a 5–2 aggregate.

Back at Old Trafford, as the celebrations spilled out into Sir Matt Busby Way, someone told Eriksson that his team had been just 85 seconds away from Kiev, and the Ukrainians, when Beckham scored. Typically, his initial reaction was analytical, rather than exultant. 'We knocked the ball forward with the heart, rather than the brain,' he said. Anatomically, this was impossible of course, but his audience got the drift. By way of explanation, he added: 'Our passing was not as good as usual. Maybe we were nervous and tense.' Of Beckham, he said: 'He is a big, big captain, and he showed that with his performance and with his ice-cold goal when

I thought the game was up. I have seen only one other player who could produce a free-kick like that, and that was Sinisa Mihajlovic, with his marvellous left foot. Beckham is the best taker of free-kicks in the world today.'

Months later, having replayed the game, and its dramatic denouement, time and time again in his head, Eriksson reflected on it all as follows: 'I was sitting on the bench, knowing that Germany had drawn, thinking: "Jesus, can't we even get a draw against Greece at home?" And then suddenly Beckham goes bang! Of course we were lucky that we drew with a goal in the dying seconds, but on the other hand, it wasn't luck that Beckham scored with that free-kick. It was a great goal. Mentally, as well as technically, Beckham showed that he is something special. That was real pressure. Everybody knew our World Cup ticket depended on him scoring, and he did it.' Unusually, the manager had been taken by surprise by the opposition. 'Greece were much better than I had expected them to be. I'd seen all the games they'd played before in the qualifying series, and they never came close to playing as well as they did against us. Of course, the better they played, the more the pressure was on us, and players who are among the best in the world suddenly couldn't pass the ball five yards. It was very frustrating to see that. I thought about changing some players, but you can't change ten.'

All's well that ends well. It had been an agonizing afternoon, but England were there, and the bookmakers immediately installed them as 7–1 third favourites to win the World Cup, behind only Argentina and France.

CHAPTER NINETEEN

THE LUCK OF THE DRAW

The task of qualifying for the World Cup had been successfully accomplished, but England still had to stay in trim and prepare for the tournament, and one month after the Greece match they were back at Old Trafford, for a friendly against Sven-Goran Eriksson's native Sweden. Those wanting to point up the issue of divided loyalties did not have to wait long for the opportunity. There were fireworks on 5 November when the coach announced his squad *in absentia*. Breaking with custom and practice, he did it not at a press conference, where he could be questioned about his selections, but over the internet. The reason was that he was in Stockholm, receiving Sweden's Personality of the Year award. The English press did not take kindly to his absence, a typical reaction being that of the *Daily Telegraph*, where Henry Winter wrote: 'Disappointingly, Eriksson's views on yesterday's squad were obtainable only via the FA's website, the increasingly presidential coach continuing to remove himself from the media. England's eager fans, who deserve a more detailed explanation of the squad chosen to represent them, will have to wait until Eriksson descends from on high to address the masses.'

With no precious points at stake, the squad in question was an experimental one. Missing, for a variety of reasons, were David Seaman, Ashley Cole, Sol Campbell, Wes Brown, Nick Barmby and Andy Cole. In were Ian Walker, Chris Powell, Frank Lampard, Darren Anderton, Trevor Sinclair and Kevin Phillips. A notable absentee who would have been chosen, had he been fit, was Newcastle's Kieron Dyer.

On the Wednesday before the match, Eriksson faced the press at the squad's base, which was again the Marriott Hotel, in Worsley. He had warned the players that unless they improved on their lack-lustre performance against the Greeks, they could forget all about the notion of winning the World Cup. The coach revealed: 'I got them together and the first thing I said was: "Welcome, and once again congratulations on getting to the finals." But then I told them: "I don't want to take a team all the way there just for three games. We have to stay there as long as possible – hopefully until the final. Yes, you should be happy that you have made one step towards the big target, but now you must go on and try to do better and better." I reminded them that they had to play much better than they had against Greece if they wanted to stay the distance in Japan and Korea.'

On the Thursday, there was more media interest in whether Eriksson would sing either or both national anthems before the kick-off than in Steven

Gerrard's latest withdrawal because of injury. 'Maybe it's better if I don't sing either,' the coach said, smiling. 'I'm a good listener. Seriously, it's nice to meet Sweden, but my job is to manage England, and so of course I want to beat Sweden. I'm a supporter of Sweden in every other game, but not this one.'

Michael Owen, like Gerrard before him, failed a fitness test, allowing Sunderland's Kevin Phillips a rare start in attack, where Emile Heskey was his partner. Sinclair was also in the team, for his international debut, and Jamie Carragher and Gareth Southgate were given the chance to prove their worth. The match was a disappointment, a dull, if diplomatic, 1–1 draw. Sinclair, who was otherwise anonymous, took a dive for a penalty which David Beckham tucked away, but the Swedes gave as good as they got throughout, and deservedly equalized through Hakan Mild.

Once again, Eriksson was disappointed. 'We should be able to read the game better,' he said. 'When you play Sweden, you should be much more direct. If you wait 15 seconds before you send the ball forward, you have to beat a minimum of eight players, because it's in their DNA that when they lose the ball they get back behind it. I don't think that by passing four times in the midfield you necessarily get a better chance to play the ball forward well. Against Sweden, you have to do it quickly, before they organize. It's not about playing it long, it's about a defender playing it to a midfielder and a midfielder to a striker. We need to be able to adapt better.

'Some of the goals we scored against Germany were examples of how I like football to be played. You win the ball, with your second touch you play it forward, and when you have Owen up there, the pace of it is perfect. That was how we scored the fourth against the Germans. Gerrard won the ball and played it to Owen who went "Bang". Goal. You can't always play fast, one-touch football, but you should be capable of it when the chance occurs.

'If you look at the statistics in big club games or internationals, more than 80 per cent of goals are scored with fewer than five passes. If you talk about Real Madrid and Barcelona, the biggest teams in Europe, they are able to keep possession, and are very good on the ball, but they can also win it and give it, and we should be able to read when to do that.'

It all sounded sensible enough, but this tactical dissertation was not to every critic's liking. The most implacable of them all, Jeff Powell, wasn't at the press conference concerned, but was put in mind of another bête noire, Graham Taylor. Powell wrote in the *Daily Mail*: 'Eriksson started to talk like a throwback to the old school of the long ball. And just for a moment, the Swede sounded ominously like The Turnip.'

'Turnip' or not, Eriksson received the UK Coach of the Year award from the Princess Royal on 16 December. Then all eyes turned to the World Cup draw, held in Busan, South Korea. The day before the ceremony, there was an eye-opening indication of the colossal interest in England and their

Messianic coach when Eriksson arrived at the Marriott Hotel there. Italy's Giovanni Trapattoni created a minor stir among the international media massed in the lobby, but when Eriksson tried to check in, it was the full-blown circus. It would have been easier to get through the All Blacks' scrum. He had arranged to meet the English journalists at 5pm, but word of this press conference spread like wildfire, and the FA had to change the venue at the last moment to prevent their coach from being mobbed. To considerable amusement, the FA's director of communications, Paul Newman, switched Fleet Street's finest to Murphy's Irish theme bar, in the hotel basement, and asked them to enter in groups of two and three, rather than mob-handed, to avoid alerting the locals. Amid diversionary scenes reminiscent of *The Great Escape*, somebody asked if we should tunnel down, dispersing the dirt displaced through our trouser legs.

Comical or not, the ruse worked. For the consumption of English ears only, Eriksson said there were three teams he wanted to avoid in the draw the next day – Argentina, France and Italy. He was to be out of luck. Not only did England get Argentina, they were also dealt Nigeria and Sweden in what was immediately dubbed 'the group of death'. Afterwards, a rueful Eriksson said: 'I hope we have more luck in June than we had tonight.' It was the most difficult group of the eight, he felt. 'We've got the best team from South America, maybe the best from Africa and a very good European team, so we will have to be in good shape right from the start. There's no place to hide. When there was just one team left to complete the group, I smiled and said to Adam Crozier, who was sitting next to me: "We only need Nigeria now for the set," and out they came. We're going to have to play exceptionally well, but we can do that.'

When it was pointed out that if England were runners-up in the group they would probably have to play the world champions, France, at the second stage, he sighed and said: 'You see what a lucky evening it was? It would have been difficult to get a worse draw. No team would like to swap with us.'

Eriksson spent Christmas in Torsby, with his parents, then took Nancy for some winter sun in Mauritius. He routinely switches off his mobile phone when he is on holiday, but leaves a number on which he can be contacted in emergency, and was greatly concerned to learn on 8 January that Tord Grip had been hospitalized after a heart scare. He had been driving to the FA's offices in Soho Square when he felt pains in his neck and down one arm. At the Chelsea and Westminster Hospital they performed all the usual tests and deduced that there was nothing wrong with Grip's heart. 'It was some kind of inflammation, maybe in the neck,' Grip said. 'Nothing serious.' On a safety-first basis, he cancelled a trip to Mali later that month, when he had been due to run the rule over Nigeria in the African Nations Cup.

It was no more than a scare, but one which left Eriksson reflecting on his own health. He said: 'In Italy they have a very good rule. As a manager, you have to have regular check-ups every six months, otherwise you're not allowed to sit on the bench. Every summer, and again at Christmas, you have to show that you are fit – the heart, the lungs, the blood, everything. It's something I've spoken to Adam Crozier about for the future.'

By the end of January, the England coach and the FA hierarchy were on the move again, this time to Oporto, to attend the draw for the 2004 European Championships, in Portugal. The balls fell rather more kindly this time, leaving Eriksson and his team in Group Seven, with Turkey, Slovakia, Macedonia and Liechtenstein. England were as fortunate here as they had been unlucky in Busan, and it must have been difficult for the coach to keep a straight face when he trotted out the time-honoured cliché about there being 'no easy games in international football'.

England's next match was the preparatory friendly against Holland in Amsterdam on 13 February, but before choosing his squad for that, Eriksson was assailed by a frenzy of tabloid speculation about his future. Little more than 12 months into a five-year contract with the Football Association, he was repeatedly linked with his old club, Lazio, and the managership of Manchester United. On 2 February, the *Sun* covered their back page with the headline: 'Lazio In Bid To Grab Sven'. It was only when the story turned deep inside the paper, tapering into a small single column on page 61, that the true seriousness, or otherwise, of the situation was revealed. The Lazio president, Sergio

Cragnotti, was 'preparing the way for a takeover by Eriksson after 2006'.

Next it was Manchester United, who were searching for a new manager for the 2002/03 season, Sir Alex Ferguson having announced his decision to retire. On several occasions the media had made Eriksson favourite for the job – when they weren't showering favouritism on Ottmar Hitzfeld of Bayern Munich, Fabio Capello of Roma, Louis Van Gaal, formerly coach of Barcelona and Holland, Martin O'Neill of Celtic or David O'Leary of Leeds United – and each time he had claimed disingenuously, that he was 'not interested'. United DID want Eriksson, and substantial contact was made through third-party agencies, as it had to be to avoid accusations of breach of contract or 'poaching'. The England coach, who has frequently admitted that he misses the 'day-to-day involvement of club management', was definitely interested, and at one stage United were certain that they had their man. Ferguson said: 'I think they'd done the deal all right. I'm sure it was Eriksson, and I think they'd shaken hands. They couldn't put anything on paper because he was still England manager. I think Eriksson would have been a nice, easy choice for them. He doesn't change anything. He sails along and nobody falls out with him. He comes out and he says: "In the first half we were good, second half we were not so good. I am very pleased with the result." I think he'd have been all right for United – the acceptable face.

'Carlos Queiroz [Ferguson's former No 2 who

went on to coach Real Madrid] knows him because he [Eriksson] was at Benfica and Carlos is from Lisbon. Carlos says, what he did well was that he never fell out with anyone. He was best pals with the president, and the press liked him. I think he does that. The press make a suggestion and he seems to follow it.'

What had happened was that Ferguson and his advisers, had misjudged the situation. They thought Peter Kenyon and the money men on the Old Trafford plc would move heaven and earth to keep the most successful manager of them all, and would offer Ferguson whatever it took to get him to stay. It was only when it became apparent that the club were instead going for Eriksson, and that they would get him, that Sir Alex and his clan performed their hasty U-turn and announced that his retirement was not set in stone, after all. Once that news was carefully released, public pressure ensured that Ferguson got a lucrative three-year extension to his contract.

It was a close call, and one which required some careful news management by the FA. The story was broken by Harry Harris of the *Daily Express*, who wrote that: 'There have been talks between United and Eriksson for the past four months. United used one of their most influential overseas representatives as the conduit between themselves and Eriksson.' This was outrageous, blustered the spin doctors of Soho Square. There had been no contact. Eriksson issued a statement to the effect that he was 'deeply disturbed' by the 'untruth'. He said: 'I can categorically state that at no stage have I been involved in any negotiations with United, either directly or indirectly.' The FA spoke of taking legal action on his behalf, but none was forthcoming.

The story was to surface again in late April, when the *Daily Mail* serialized a book entitled *The Boss: The Many Sides Of Alex Ferguson*, by Michael Crick, in which the author wrote: 'What nobody knew at the time was that the [United] board was within hours of sealing an agreement for a new boss to take over at the start of the 2002/03 season. And the man whose services they were about to clinch was England coach Sven-Goran Eriksson, who was set to move to Old Trafford after the World Cup in Korea and Japan.'

Crick went on to quote an unidentified 'senior source' at the FA as saying: 'United offered the job to Sven, and he was very keen to do it, all set to go. It's amazing in some ways, but I don't think Sven enjoys being England manager that much.'

My information is that Crick's source was the FA's technical director, Howard Wilkinson, who is a long-standing friend of Ferguson's. The United manager was kept in the dark throughout by his bosses at Old Trafford, but Ferguson certainly believes Eriksson was approached, through a third party, and various members of the FA's international committee, including David Dein, of Arsenal, insist there was contact. Ulrika Jonsson, who was privy to Eriksson's thoughts and deeds at the time, said much later: 'He wanted in at Manchester United, and established a dialogue with their chief executive Peter Kenyon. He was frustrated at not managing a club, with weekly matches, and having to deal with the bureaucratic FA.'

Turning his attention to more pressing matters, Eriksson decided on an experimental squad for Holland, regarding it as his last chance to hold auditions, with the World Cup finals only four months away. As was his wont, the emphasis was to be on youth, with half David Platt's successful Under-21 team promoted to the seniors. Those advocating the return of Alan Shearer or Graeme Le Saux, both of whom were in excellent form at the time, were disappointed. Instead, Eriksson turned to the other end of the age spectrum, springing two major surprises by calling up Bolton's Michael Ricketts, 23, and 21-year-old Darius Vassell of Aston Villa. These two young strikers, with 15 and nine goals respectively, were selected ahead of Teddy Sheringham, Robbie Fowler and Andy Cole, all of whom were stood down with an assurance from management that their exclusion was a temporary expedient, to enable Eriksson to assess the cover available. Also in for the first time were Southampton's left-back, Wayne Bridge, and Ledley King, the Tottenham central defender, and there was a recall for West Ham's midfield prodigy, Joe Cole.

Apart from the strikers who were 'rested', the squad needed to be viewed in the light of the unavailability of 13 players. A good team could have been fashioned from these: David Seaman, Danny Mills, John Terry, Jonathan Woodgate, Martin

Keown, Ashley Cole, Lee Bowyer, Jamie Carragher, Michael Carrick, Kieron Dyer, Steve McManaman, Nick Barmby and Alan Smith. To make matters worse, between the announcement of the 23, on the Saturday night, and their arrival in Amsterdam, on the Tuesday, Eriksson lost three more players. Sinclair, who would have played on the left side of midfield in Dyer's continuing absence, Anderton and Owen all withdrew, with various ailments, and were not replaced. For the first time, there was real friction between the coach and English journalists, who were not happy about the way the squad had been named, or his unwillingness to discuss its composition until the day before the game. Eriksson broke with custom and practice by having the squad announced on the Saturday night, after he had watched Aston Villa's 1–1 draw with Chelsea, in order to make an eleventh hour check on Vassell. He declined to speak to reporters at Villa Park, and left it to the FA's media department to disseminate the names of the chosen ones, which they did much later than had been the agreement, thereby causing the story to miss the early editions of the Sunday papers. The dailies' noses were also put out of joint when Eriksson was unavailable for comment on the Sunday and Monday, and chose to delay his press conference in Amsterdam on the Tuesday until just after 7pm, again too late for the early editions. All the travelling correspondents were miffed, the common view expressed best by Paul Hayward, of the *Daily Telegraph*, who returned to a recurring theme as follows: 'Over the past few days this news-paper, in common with all media outlets, would have liked to convey some of Sven-Goran Eriksson's thoughts on tomorrow's friendly against Holland, but so far the England coach has said nothing publicly, and if we left a blank space you might demand your money back. The more successful he becomes, the less he appears willing to engage in a meaningful dialogue with those who relay his thoughts to the fans. A concern of some of our lead-ing constitutional experts is that New Labour have smothered parliamentary scrutiny of Government policy. The England camp are careering along the same path.'

Eriksson's response, which changed nobody's opinion, was that he didn't think the public wanted to read his comments day after day, ad infinitum. Among certain correspondents, the feeling in Amsterdam was that a defeat would be timely, and not just because it would serve to keep the players' feet firmly in touch with terra firma. Eriksson needed to be acquainted with the rules of man-ager–media relations, and the scolding that would follow a bad result would do the job nicely. It didn't happen, of course. The coach picked an experimen-tal team, tried a new formation, and still came away with a very creditable 1–1 draw. Trying out 4–3–3, for use as Plan B at the World Cup, Eriksson gave Bridge his debut at left-back, with both Ricketts and Vassell winning their first caps in a front three completed by Heskey. A midfield trio comprising

Beckham, Gerrard and Scholes is just about as good as it gets, and they were as powerfully competitive as one might have imagined.

Bridge had a excellent game, or 45 minutes to be strictly accurate. He had to come off at the interval, injured, but such was the quality of his play that one half was all it took to install him among the World Cup probables. Ditto young Vassell, whose eager-beaver running and gobsmacking equalizer, à la Denis Law, immediately thrust him to very near the head of the strikers' queue, ahead of Kevin Phillips and Andy Cole. The only disappointment on an encouraging evening was Ricketts, whose close control and hold-up play was not of international standard.

Eriksson felt it had been important for England to be rid of the memory of how the Dutch had outplayed them at White Hart Lane seven months earlier. 'Important for me personally [at that stage, it was his only defeat], but more so for the team. The game at Tottenham was the worst we'd played, and this showed that we could take on the same opposition away and be good enough to win, which we would have done with just a bit more luck. Holland didn't create many chances, and the goal they scored was a scrappy one. They were playing their first game for a new manager [Dick Advocaat], keen to impress him, and yet we created more. That was good for the players' confidence.'

No sooner was Eriksson back in England than he was off on his travels again, for the Champions League matches between Bayer Leverkusen and

Arsenal, and Nantes vs Manchester United the next night, then on to Japan on World Cup reconnaissance.

The coach was back, at White Hart Lane for an FA Cup quarter-final which saw Chelsea thrash Tottenham 4–0. More significant than the result, in terms of the bigger picture, was the dismissal of Graeme Le Saux, who was sent off for the ugliest of fouls on Mauricio Taricco. The previous Friday, Le Saux had told me, as he had told other friends, that he was at a loss as to what to do to catch Eriksson's eye. Capped 36 times under other managers, he felt he was playing as well as ever, and could not understand why he had not been called upon under the new regime. Here was the answer. His suspect temperament had undermined his cause yet again after an otherwise impressive performance, embellished by a good goal.

Without mentioning Le Saux by name, Eriksson left no doubt as to his reasoning when he said: 'I don't want to make examples, but in general I think that if we are talking about a young player, for whom there are big hopes, he can change. But if a player over 30 behaves like that, then you have to forget him. In Sweden, we say: "Don't even try to teach an old dog how to sit."'

On the same Sunday, Lazio were thrashed 5–1 by Roma in the Rome derby, and on the Monday the players had to lock themselves in their dressing room as 400 angry fans invaded Formello, calling for the dismissal of Alberto Zaccheroni as coach and Eriksson's return. Sergio Cragnotti gave the pot a stir by saying he should never have let him go in the first place and Eriksson, somewhat disingenuously, gave an interview to *Corriere Dello Sport*, in which he said 'Lazio and the Cragnotti family are still in my heart, and it's not hard for me to picture myself once more on the Lazio bench', then expressed his surprise when English papers carried headlines like 'Sven: I'm Going Back To Lazio'. In fairness, en route from Italy to what used to be Fleet Street his comments were given a fair amount of spin. What he actually said was: 'I don't rule out the possibility of returning, but I sincerely don't see any chance of me abandoning my post with England. I don't want to fool anyone – especially not Lazio fans – because at the moment I see myself only as the England coach, ready to do battle for the World Cup against Brazil, France, Argentina and Italy. I made a commitment to the most prestigious football association in the world, and the only people who will get me to leave are the English themselves, if they choose to sack me.'

If his treatment bordered on misrepresentation on that occasion, it has to be said that on others he asked for trouble. On 15 March, the football correspondents of the various national newspapers assembled in west London for a press briefing with Eriksson at which they expected to press him on his long-term future, and discuss the squad he was about to announce for the friendly international against Italy. Instead, they were told that football questions would not be entertained; the media had been invited only to promote the launch of two Playstation games the coach was promoting. It was a public relations gaffe. The exploiters do not take kindly to being exploited, and while the publicity the computer games received was negligible, the headlines Eriksson attracted were not. He was portrayed, not without reason, as a money-grabber. The *Sun*, claiming 'Sven's More Popular Than The Queen', said Eriksson would net 'an incredible £1.3m' from commercial deals in the run-up to the World Cup, and under the headline 'Sven Is Selling His Soul', the ascerbic Martin Samuel wrote in the *News of the World*: 'A five-year contract worth £2.5m annually should be enough to keep the wolf from the door, even in Regents Park. Sadly not. There is no bundle so big it can distract the modern football manager from pursuing a career as a salesman, the erudite Eriksson included. On Friday, the man normally so reluctant to engage in question-and-answer sessions that he releases his squad details by e-mail, was singing like a canary on the grounds he had a computer game to sell.'

My colleague at *The Sunday Times*, Rob Hughes, gave the subject a balanced perspective. He duly reported what others did not, that on the same day Eriksson made an unpublicised visit to Great Ormond Street Hospital, where as patron of one of their fund-raising schemes, he spent 90 minutes brightening up the lives of sick children.

The squad for the friendly international against Italy at Elland Road on 27 March, was announced after Eriksson had watched Arsenal beat Newcastle 3–0 at Highbury – the match in which France's

Robert Pires sustained the knee injury that kept him out of the World Cup. There was much speculation about whether Jonathan Woodgate would be included, the Leeds defender having completed the 100 hours of community service to which he was sentenced, for affray, for his part in the beating of an Asian student, Safraz Nejeib, outside a Leeds nightclub. The then Leeds chairman, Peter Ridsdale, told me on the Monday before the squad was named that the FA did not 'have the bottle' to pick Woodgate, which he thought was 'disgraceful'. Ridsdale, a member of the FA board, explained that the player had served the punishment deemed appropriate in court, and had already served a two-year international ban while the case was tried and retried. He felt it was time for the prodigal to be welcomed back into the fold.

Eriksson agreed. He told his Under-21s manager, David Platt, that once the judicial process was over, Woodgate's selection ought to be a footballing decision, and on those grounds he deserved to be in. The FA saw it differently. This was not a black-and-white case, it was clouded in shades of grey. Adam Crozier, the chief executive, pointed out three potential pitfalls. The first was that the Nejeib family, dissatisfied with the penalties imposed at Crown Court, had briefed their lawyers to institute civil proceedings against Woodgate. This conjured the ghastly vision of a player being served with a summons while England trained. Second, Woodgate's early rehabilitation would leave the FA open to accusations of double standards. In their fight against hooliganism, they had reorganized the old England Members' Club so that anybody with the same conviction as Woodgate, for affray, could not travel to support the team. One rule for the players and another for the fans would reek of hypocrisy. Finally, the FA had intelligence reports to the effect that activist groups were planning protest demonstrations at the team's hotel, at the training ground and before the match if Woodgate was present. To have the England players running the gauntlet would do nothing for morale, and would be a PR disaster. Eriksson had envisaged hostility only from certain sections of the press, which he was prepared to handle, but the rest he could do without. After much persuasion, he backed down and Woodgate was excluded.

The decision was a sensible one, but the way the news was disseminated left a lot to be desired. To borrow Ridsdale's phrase, the FA did not have the 'bottle' to come straight out with it. Instead, the announcement of the squad was handled in unprecedented cloak-and-dagger style. The chief correspondents of the various Sunday newspapers were told to ring the FA's head of communications, Paul Newman, on his mobile phone between 5.00pm and 5.30pm on the Saturday, for an informal, off-the-record briefing. There would be no statement and no quotes were to be used. The gist of this was that Woodgate had not been selected, for the above reasons, and that he would not be going to the World Cup. End of part one. The names of the 27 players who were selected came more than two hours later, via the FA's website. In their release, there was explanation from Eriksson about the absence of David Seaman and Steve McManaman, among others, but not a word about the Woodgate issue. That was delayed until a press conference at Anfield the following day when, before watching Liverpool beat Chelsea 1–0 to go top of the Premier League, the England coach insisted, disingenuously, that the decision had been his. 'I am the only one who can have the last word,' he said. 'If I had wanted to do it differently, I am sure Adam would have supported me.' For once he was wrong. Crozier was never going to allow a squad player to cause him so many problems.

On a more positive note, Michael Owen was back after injury and Owen Hargreaves was promoted from the Under-21s, having caught the managerial eye with a strong performance for Bayern Munich against Manchester United in the Champions' League. Danny Mills returned on his home ground, having completed the domestic suspension that kept him out of the Holland game. The only uncapped player in the party was Tottenham's Ledley King, who would have had his debut in Amsterdam but for an untimely bout of tonsillitis. David Seaman was rested, but Teddy Sheringham and Robbie Fowler were recalled. Absentees with cause for concern, with the World Cup drawing ever nearer, included Steve McManaman, Chris Powell, Jamie Carragher and Kevin Phillips. Andy Cole was not available for selection because of a domestic suspension.

No sooner had the squad been announced than there was the usual crop of withdrawals. Steven Gerrard, with groin trouble, was the first to go, followed by Rio Ferdinand, Paul Scholes and Kieron Dyer. His midfield resources severely depleted, Eriksson called up Liverpool's Danny Murphy as cover.

The FA feared trouble on the night from the pro-Woodgate faction, but there was none. Eriksson's starting line-up was the strongest available, with one exception. He wanted to have a good look at Mills, so Gary Neville was on the bench. The match was a bore, neither side getting out of second gear, and England made 11 substitutions after a goalless first half. Fowler, on for Owen, gave them the lead after 63 minutes with a top-class finish, but Montella equalized with an even better one, after Joe Cole had committed the cardinal sin of giving the ball away. Montella then won it for Italy with the very last kick – a coolly taken penalty. The matchwinner was well known to Eriksson, who had signed him for Sampdoria, from Empoli, as a 22 year old. 'I had wanted him even before that, when he was at Genoa, but they wouldn't sell to us. Then, when he moved to Empoli, I had my chance. He has always been a tremendous finisher – one of the best I have ever worked with.'

One of Eriksson's predecessors, Bobby Robson, complained that by making so many substitutions he had excessively devalued the exercise. 'The second halves in England friendlies have become an absolute farce,' Robson said. 'Friendlies are a time to experiment, but Sven's tendency is to over-experiment. He uses too many players. I never did that. I would throw on four or five substitutes, but I would never use 22 players in one match.' The FA's answer was that Robson had the job before the clubs' commitments in the Champions' League necessitated an agreement with the managers that their players would be used for one half only. Without that understanding, their release would be irregular, interrupted by spurious injuries.

Eriksson's second defeat in 12 games left him undismayed. 'I don't like to lose football matches at all, even friendlies,' he said, 'but it wasn't a problem. It was a very strong Italian team and we had important players missing.' Hargreaves, Fowler and Wayne Bridge had come out of it in credit, but Joe Cole had played, according to *The Times*, 'as if someone had set his shorts on fire', doing himself no favours. He knew it, and said the following day that there would be no tears from him if he failed to make the plane. He was young, and there would be other World Cups.

A fortnight later, on 10 April, Sir Alex Ferguson was uttering exactly the same words about the one man England could not afford to lose. The fact that David Beckham's World Cup place was in extreme jeopardy after breaking a bone in his left foot was the lead item on the BBC News, ahead of the Palestinian crisis, both that night and the following morning. The England captain had been injured by an Argentinian, Aldo Duscher, after 15 minutes of United's Champions' League victory over Deportivo la Coruna, and the nationality of his assailant, who was booked for a two-footed tackle, gave rise to the inevitable conspiracy theories. These were fed, it must be said, by Argentina's own media. Rodrigo Calderon, editor of the *Buenos Aires Herald*, said Duscher had been 'trying to help Argentina'.

As Eriksson looked on, aghast, Beckham was taken straight to hospital by ambulance, where his foot was encased in plaster. Ferguson said his season was over. Recovery was expected to take from six to eight weeks. 'It's a terrible blow for United, and for the lad, but he's young, and there will be other European Cups and other World Cups for him,' said the United manager.

To nationwide relief, the healing period was revised downwards the following day, when it was revealed that Ryan Giggs had suffered the same injury and played again in 36 days. On the Friday, sanguine as ever, Eriksson said he was confident that his captain would be fully restored in time. Fitness, fatigue and fixture congestion had become the managerial F-words. He wanted to field the team he had in mind to start the World Cup in the friendly against Paraguay at Anfield, but injuries and club commitments were such that he got nowhere close. With a world-weary, 'What can I do?' expression on his face, he threw up his hands and looked to the heavens.

On Saturday 13 April, after watching Tottenham draw 1–1 at home to West Ham, he named a 25-man squad for the Paraguay game, then sat back and waited for events to change it the following day. Already without Beckham, Ashley Cole, Rio Ferdinand and Emile Heskey who were all injured, he drafted in the Blackburn Rovers striker Matt Jansen for his first appearance at senior international level, was delighted to be able to choose Kieron Dyer, after 12 months of trying, and recalled David Seaman and Jamie Carragher. Both FA Cup semi-finals were being played on the Sunday, one in the afternoon, the other in the evening, and Eriksson had the look of a man who had driven over a whole litter of black kittens as he sat watching one England player after another go lame. Graeme Le Saux's early departure on a stretcher in the game between Chelsea and Fulham did not bother the coach unduly, for the player many still rated the best left-back in the country had no part in his plans, but the loss of Arsenal's Sol Campbell and Ugo Ehiogu, of Middlesborough, was a problem. Two centre-halves light, he called up Martin Keown, himself newly recovered from a broken leg.

It was becoming increasingly apparent that friendly fixtures had been devalued to the extent that they no longer served any worthwhile purpose, and Eriksson wrote to all the Premier League managers, informing them that in future, England would be playing far fewer friendlies. Instead, midweek training camps would suffice. It was an initiative applauded by Bobby Robson, who said: 'It is a good idea because almost all his best players will be involved in the Champions' League next season, and do not need any extra games. Certainly I wouldn't want to lose Kieron Dyer for too many friendlies during a season when we will probably be in Europe. Players like Dyer, who have had injury problems, need proper rest between games. One of the reasons Sven has done this is to forge better relationships with the Premier League managers. He knows how difficult it is for us when our best players get taken away for friendlies, and he wants to help us do well in Europe.'

Over lunch with Eriksson at the FA, the conversation turned to a back-page 'exclusive' in the *Sun*, headed 'We Reveal World Cup Squad'. The squad for the tournament had not been picked, and the man who would be picking it was intrigued to read that Carragher would definitely not be in it. 'I left him out last time, but he has been playing very well since,' Eriksson told me. He went on to reveal that he was interested in playing two left-backs, Arsenal's Cole and Wayne Bridge of Southampton, together, with Bridge, rather than Cole, seen as a possible answer to the recurrent left midfield riddle.

The small talk took in Sven's younger brother, Lars, who lives in Lisbon and had been negotiating the purchase of a hotel. The sale had fallen through, Sven said, but there was no danger of sibling unemployment. Lars had an executive position with a sports promotions company, and would have his hands full with a sporting complex on the Algarve which was due to be up and running in 2003. 'Lars is using my name for it, but it's his business,' Sven explained. 'I'm nothing to do with it really.'

For the Paraguay match, England set up camp at the Carden Park Hotel, near Chester – the same

base they had used for the qualifying tie against
Finland at Anfield 13 months earlier. Eriksson met
the media in the clubhouse the day before the game,
when he announced, to universal surprise, that
Michael Owen would be Beckham's stand-in as
captain. Rio Ferdinand or Sol Campbell would have
had the job, had either been fit, and in their absence,
the press had expected the honour to go to David
Seaman or Gary Neville. Explaining his choice,
Eriksson said: 'There are many reasons. One small
one is that Michael is playing on his home ground.
More importantly, he is the current European
Footballer of the Year, and one of the most famous
players not just in England but all over the world.
He is a good ambassador for English football. He is
also very popular, both in the country and in the
squad. Remember, this is just for this game. If
Beckham is not fit next time, we'll think again. But
as I see it, Owen has all the other qualities – now
it's up to him to show that he can be a good leader,
as well.'

On the collective level, the coach was keen that
England should 'pick up' their form. He accepted
that their performances had, for the most part, been
disappointing since Munich, and said: 'I want us to
start having the right attitude again, like we had
before we qualified.' What had been wrong since?
'It hasn't been easy for the players. They have been
playing friendly games for me while they have had
important ones, and a lot of pressure on them, at
their clubs. I understand the difficulty there, but this
is the last game we play in England before leaving

for the World Cup, so I should like to see a bit more fire from them on the pitch.'

On the Tuesday night, 24 hours before the main event, England's Under-21s played Portugal at Stoke, where Eriksson intended to check on Wes Brown, Manchester United's young defender, whose season, and career progress, had been interrupted by injury. To their mutual frustration, however, the jinx that had already claimed Ferdinand, Campbell and Ehiogu struck again, and Brown was ruled out when an accident in training left him with blurred vision. In his absence, nobody staked a claim for early promotion in a match England lost 1–0.

On the day of the Paraguay match, there was yet another withdrawal, Jansen having been taken ill. Eriksson confirmed that he would have had his first cap had he been fit to take part. The vacancy created by Beckham's injury was filled by the simple expedient of moving Steven Gerrard out to the right, with Nicky Butt coming into centre midfield, along-side Paul Scholes, and Dyer on the left. Elsewhere, Martin Keown and Gareth Southgate deputized for the regular centre-halves, Wayne Bridge was given another opportunity at left-back and Darius Vassell partnered Owen in attack.

Eriksson had called for a higher tempo, and a bit more 'fire', and was delighted with the response. England flew out of the traps and were ahead after only three minutes, when Owen headed home a cross from Gerrard that showed normal service was possible from the right, even without you-know-who. England's crisp passing and overall control was such that they should have been three goals to the good by half-time. Gerrard was the dominant figure in midfield, the pacy Vassell buzzed around the Paraguayan defenders like a particularly pesky wasp, and when the second goal came, the only surprise was that it had taken until the 47th minute to arrive. Eriksson had made six substitutions at half-time, and two of the replacements, Joe Cole and Robbie Fowler, set up another, Danny Murphy, for a shot deflected in off Carlos Gamarra. Vassell was similarly fortunate for England's third, and when the fourth went in off Celso Ayala, the poor Paraguayan goalkeeper had really been beaten three times by his own men. That said, England fully deserved their convincing margin on a night when nearly all the 21 players Eriksson put on the pitch advanced their cause.

Joe Cole, whose cat-on-a-hot-tin-roof perform-ance against Italy seemed to have played him out of the World Cup reckoning, was right back in it after repeatedly tricking and running past opponents with a facility unmatched by any England player since Paul Gascoigne. Bright, imaginative and delightfully clever on the ball, he looked like the ideal man to bring on to turn a tight game. Vassell, quick in mind and feet, had cemented his place in the squad and Murphy had made a strong case for his retention. Eriksson was surprised how well Vassell had taken to international football. 'He is doing very well – better than I expected. When he gets a chance he is not shy, he is quick, good on the ball and he scores goals – two in three games. Not bad, eh? If he goes on like this, I'll be very happy.'

The only downside was a disappointingly ineffective contribution from the much trumpeted Dyer, who did nothing to suggest that he was the answer on the left. Eriksson, however, had made up his mind, and was not about to be swayed. Asked if Dyer was always going to be in his World Cup squad, regardless of how he played against Paraguay, the coach replied: 'I guess so. He's a very good footballer. I've seen him play better, but that's not a problem.'

England looked much better when they sustained a brisk pace and played a high-octane, pressing game. I suggested to Eriksson that this would be difficult in the heat and humidity of Japan and Korea. 'I can't be sure that we can do it, but why not try?' he said. Would he rotate his strikers, given the workrate he expected from them? 'That's a good question. We have three games to start with, and it's almost a life-or-death situation straight away, so there's no room for rotation. If somebody is really tired, or is carrying a knock, it could be necessary, but I don't think you can go to the World Cup and say: "We'll play our strongest team in the first game and then change five or six players." I don't think any team can afford to do that. If we win our first match, I certainly won't be changing half the team.'

Ability would not be the sole criterion when he allocated the last two places still up for grabs in the World Cup squad. 'When you pick the last two or three, under normal circumstances they won't start the tournament, so you need players who will accept that situation. It would be awful to have people who, after two games, were not happy to be there, so that's definitely a consideration. Mind you, they have to be good enough to be considered in the first place.'

CHAPTER TWENTY

THE HALO SLIPS

'The girlfriend of Gillingham chairman Paul Scally found herself standing alone in the Highbury board-room before this season's FA Cup tie against Arsenal, but she was soon engaged in conversation by a suave, sophisticated gentleman with designer glasses, who also kept catching her eye during the match. Not a big football fan, she pointed out her charming admirer to Scally, and asked whether he knew who he was. He told her it was England coach and Romeo-in-chief Sven-Goran Eriksson.'

Daily Mail diary item, 1 May 2002.

That Eriksson is a ladies' man, there can be no doubt. On one occasion when I was with the coach, in his office at Soho Square, Paul Newman sat with us fielding calls from Nancy Dell'Olio. This was at the height of the Ulrika Jonsson affair, and it was clear that Eriksson did not want to speak to his common-law wife. It was before his liaison with the TV celebrity became known, and I found his behaviour strange at the time. It is, of course, much less so in retrospect. Before joining the FA, Newman had been a BBC television newsman, and had covered the Gulf War. That had been a cakewalk compared to Eriksson's love life, he told me.

At least two female journalists sent to interview the England coach came away feeling that there could be rather more than words on the agenda. Christa D'Souza, of the *Daily Telegraph*, said: 'The meeting didn't start auspiciously. On the surface, he appeared to be just as you would expect – a rather humourless ice man. As he led the way into the bar of the hotel where we met for a cup of tea (being a bit of a health nut, he loathes coffee), I recall wondering how I was going to keep the conversation going. And yet, within a matter of minutes, it was clear that I had misread the man. Not only was he a perfectly good interviewee, he was also surprisingly attractive up close, bearing a passing resemblance to Kevin Costner – and spent a good part of the interview checking out my legs.

'I found myself charmed, and was touched when, at the end of our meeting, he not only kissed me goodbye but slipped me his personal mobile number. I was even more touched that, when I called him a couple of days later to check a few facts, he wondered whether I might join him for lunch at his favourite restaurant, San Lorenzo. Perhaps I am flattering myself, but I felt sure that the invitation did not extend to Nancy as well. Anyone who is baffled by the effect the England coach appears to have on women shouldn't be. He's what they call "A Quiet Storm".'

The storm had been a long time brewing. From his teenage years, well before he developed an eye for a player, Eriksson always had an eye for the ladies. His manager in his playing days at Torsby, Sven-Ake Olsson, remembers him for scoring off the field, rather than on it. Olsson, a retired baker, says: 'The girls would always flock around him when the team went out to the dancehall on a Saturday night.' The man himself has described Nina Thornholm, a blonde beauty contestant he met on his 18th birthday, as 'the cutest of all'. Now 53, Nina recalled her old beau fondly. 'He was a very good dancer, very sweet and well-mannered, and I just fell for him straight away.' After a year, they moved into a flat together, but they were too young to settle down. 'Yes, I loved Sven, but we never discussed marriage,' Nina said.

Ann-Christin Pettersson, daughter of the principal at his teacher-training college, took Nina's place, and all the dating was supposed to stop when they married, on 9 July 1977. But friends and associates, including Morgen Oldenmark in Torsby and Dave Mosson, the Scot who succeeded Eriksson as coach at Degerfors, say Sven never lost his rakish ways. Rolf Wanggren, who worked with him in a local social security office, says: 'He was always very popular with women when we were young because he was good-looking and because he was a nice guy. He was popular at parties, and we used to party hard. He was always nice to his friends and nice to the girls we met.'

Infidelity is a matter 'Anki', as his ex-wife is known, is not prepared to discuss, saying only that Sven is 'an excellent father' to their two children, Johan and Lina. It is a fact, however, that while he was coaching in Genoa he met Graziella Mancinelli, a voluptuous divorcee. Their chance meeting (they were near-neighbours and their respective sons attended the same school) led to a conversation over coffee, then to dinner at the Scandelin restaurant. Ms Mancinelli is now 52 and a lecturer in marine biology at Genoa University. Explaining how Eriksson left Ann-Christine for her, she said: 'His wife may want to believe that I split them up, but if something like that happens, it is because you want it to. Sven was ready to leave home, and I just came along. The timing was right. We had a special chemistry, and it was a wonderful relationship.'

She had known Eriksson for a year before their affair began, in September 1993. At first, they would rendezvous in secret at the Astor Hotel in Nevi, near Genoa, but by early 1994 their relationship was out in the open. Sven had told Ann-Christine that their marriage was over, and it was Graziella who accompanied him to the 1994 Word Cup finals, in the United States. Upon their return, they rented a four-bedroom cliffside villa in the small village of Mulinetti, just outside Genoa.

Ms Mancinelli said: 'I do not like to say too much about the beginning of our affair because I do not want to upset Sven's ex-wife, for whom I have great respect. I felt a tremendous responsibility for what he had done, but I genuinely thought we were for ever. When I met Svennis, I thought he was the man I would grow old with. I lost my mind for him because he was so kind. He was so thoughtful and attentive. He would take care of you like you were a child. You felt safe and protected in his love for you. Looking back, I would say he was selfish. It is football before women. His priorities are in strict order: number one, his children, number two, his parents, number three, work, number four, love, number five, friendship. But when you are in his world, you feel like a queen.

'In private, he was a very passionate man, but he is different in public because he is Swedish. I'm Italian, I don't hide my feelings, so for instance, if we were walking along the seafront, I would go to take his hand or show affection, and he wouldn't like that. But he was so caring in so many ways. Sometimes, he would come in and say: "Relax, I'll cook the dinner for you tonight." Even if he'd had an awful day, he would not mention it. He had great self-control, and wouldn't disturb other people with his problems. He believed that the house was sacred, and it should be tranquil. He would leave problems outside the front door.

'He is a humble man who likes the simple things in life. He loved being alone and relaxing quietly. He liked sailing, sunbathing on a deckchair and an afternoon nap in our garden. He loves to read, mainly books on ancient history, and enjoyed listening to music. We would fall asleep with the stereo playing quietly in the background – usually something by Queen, or Celine Dion. Our song was "The Power of Love". He had very few close friends and would prefer to have them to dinner in the garden, rather than go out. Tord Grip often came.

'The Sven I know likes simple, plain things, and although he's always been very conscious about his appearance, he was never interested in designer clothes. The only thing that was important for him was if it was practical and comfortable. Obviously, if he had to dress up he would know how to, and would, but the fact that he always looks nice is because he has an inbuilt sense of style. What would please him most was to sit in our garden, over-looking the sea, with a plain bowl of spaghetti with tomato sauce, then steak with salad, followed by fruit salad with a scoop of vanilla ice cream. Give him that and he feels like a king.'

It was Nancy, apparently, who gave him the celebrity makeover, sharpening his hairstyle, choosing his cologne and putting him into suits hand-stitched by their friend, Franco Aldini.

Graziella's final summer holiday with Sven, three years after they had set up home together, was a visit to Eriksson's parents, in Torsby. His move to Rome, to coach Lazio, spelled the end. 'Obviously I didn't see so much of him, but we were still together,' Graziella said. 'Then, in December, I found some notes at his flat in Rome. I knew then that there was someone else. A couple of months later, I read an article about his birthday party in Rome, which had been organized by Nancy. I saw a picture of her smiling for the cameras and knew then that it was her. At first, he denied it, and we kept seeing each other until May 1998. But by then I knew that he had fallen truly in love with Nancy. I have read that Sven was single when they met, but that is not true. I was there. I was part of his life and had been for years. The truth is, my clothes were still hanging in his flat in Rome when she moved in. But we remain friends.

Friends with Eriksson, yes. With Ann-Christin's mother, Mait Pettersson, most definitely not. 'We still hate that woman,' Mrs Pettersson says. 'She got her claws into Sven. She invited him round for coffee one day and flipped his head. Until then, my daughter and Sven seemed as if they would live happily together for ever. At first, I was angry with him, but in the end we broke down in tears and hugged each other. We now treat him as one of the family again.' Ann-Christin says only: 'This all happened a long time ago, and we've moved on.' She now lives in a £2m villa in Florence, with an American art school director and Sven's daughter, Lina.

Eriksson met Nancy at a Lazio function. Aged 37, she was a married lawyer, with a degree from Rome university, specializing in handling property deals for wealthy clients as far afield as Manhattan. She was born in New York, where part of her family still resides, but her mother is Jewish-American and Nancy has spent much of her life toing and froing between Italy and the United States. 'I completed my studies at New York University before returning to Rome in the early 1990s,' she says. 'I did some

consulting, PR and lobbying, working for private
and public companies that wanted contacts with
the political world.' When her romance with
Eriksson was first revealed, in 1999, it surprised
the Italian newspapers, not so much because Nancy
was married, to a wealthy lawyer nearly twice her
age, but because they regarded the Lazio coach
as a stereotypically dour Swede. 'Latin Fire Melts
Scandinavian Ice', was one, fairly typical headline.

Nancy told the new man in her life that she was
not prepared to deceive her husband, Giancarlo
Mazza, and that if they were to carry on carrying on,
he would have to be told. Eriksson was in need of
all his renowned charm when he did the telling.
A mutual friend, Maurizio Salticchioli, explained:
'Nancy asked Sven to come to their house and tell
her husband that he was in love with her. He is a
very shy man, and it was not easy, but he went to
see the husband and explained. Mazza held up his
hands and resigned himself to the situation.'

The marriage broke up, and the lovers set up
home together in a £2m apartment on Rome's
fashionable Via del Corso, where they enjoyed
views of the Vatican. Previously known by the
Italian press as 'Il Gentiluomo', or 'The Gentleman',
Sven now had a new sobriquet. He and Nancy were
called the King and Queen of Rome. They were
pictured together regularly on the gossip pages, and
Nancy attended all Lazio's home games (the fans
dubbed her 'La Dama Nera' – 'The Dark Lady'),
where they would exchange messages in a hand-
signed code. Barbara Palombelli, a well-known

commentator on the Italian social scene, said: 'After each goal, Sven would turn to her with his hands held high, as if dedicating it to her, like a bull-fighter. You always notice her immediately. Dark and blond, they were easily spotted, and became top celebrities.' Nancy said of her soulmate: 'His sensitivity is extraordinary. He is a very gentle man. I could never betray him. I don't like betrayal and I hope it will never happen. Our relationship needs a lot of work, and I put in everything I have to defend it.'

Prescient words, for it seems this lothario of a leopard was not about to change his spots. On Friday 12 April 2002, Eriksson was due to meet his assistant, Tord Grip, to discuss the World Cup squad, and how the friendly international against Paraguay the previous Wednesday had affected it. He expected the usual speculation in the morning papers – should Joe Cole be in or not and would he take four strikers or five? Instead, that impassive countenance creased and reddened over the muesli as the front page of the *Daily Mirror* broke the news of 'Sven And Ulrika's Secret Affair'. Rumours that the two Swedes were becoming close friends had been doing the rounds in media circles for some time (I was first told to 'keep an eye on them' by a mutual friend at Sky TV when we were in Amsterdam, for England's match against Holland on 13 February), and the first paper to 'stand up' the story was the *News of the World*, who had a team of reporters logging the movements of both parties before the *Daily Mirror* first got wind of it.

The *Mirror* beat them to the scoop through the timely intervention of their editor, Piers Morgan who, aware that the Sunday paper were about to run the story, struck a quick deal with Ms Jonsson's agent, Melanie Cantor. Her client had a choice, Morgan said. She could co-operate and have the revelations handled 'sympathetically' by the *Mirror*, or have the public learn first of the affair in shock-horror fashion, in the Sunday paper for whom lurid tales from the bedroom were something of a speciality. Caught between a rock and a hard place, Ms Cantor succumbed to Morgan's blandishments, and under the headline 'Svensational!', the *Mirror* informed the world of the liaison as follows: 'It has got to be the most extraordinary love match we've ever come across, and we could hardly believe it ourselves, but gorgeous TV beauty Ulrika Jonsson is having a passionate romance with England coach Sven-Goran Eriksson. We understand that both parties are besotted with each other.' Adhering to their side of the bargain, the paper avoided anything remotely censorious.

The following day, the other papers were playing catch-up. *Express* journalists, to their embarrassment, had to admit that it had all started right under their noses. Beneath the headline 'Couple Met At Our Party', they wrote: 'Sven and Ulrika first met in December 2001, at the *Daily Express* Christmas party. The pair were introduced by Alastair Campbell, director of communications for the Labour party. The glittering event was organized by Richard Desmond, chairman of Northern and Shell, which owns the *Daily Express*, *Sunday Express* and *OK!* magazine. The party, held at the Roundhouse in Camden, north London, attracted a host of top names from the world of showbusiness. These included Barbara Windsor, Harrods owner Mohamed Al Fayed, TV host Tania Bryer and TV stars Richard Madeley and Judy Finnigan.'

Chris Williams, editor of the *Daily Express*, said there was an immediate attraction between Sven and Ulrika. 'I was there on the night they met, and it was clear that there was an instant chemistry which went beyond the fact that they are both Swedish,' he said. Vanessa Feltz, an *Express* columnist who attended the party, seemed unaware of the party line regarding how Eriksson and Ms Jonsson met. Describing how Ulrika tapped the England coach on the shoulder and introduced herself (not a spin doctor in sight), Ms Feltz said: 'Ulrika came back to her seat glowing. She said Sven was charming, and Nancy had given her some truly evil looks.' Ulrika had told her: 'I think I am in love.'

The *Sun*, sensitive as ever, led their front page with 'Did Ulrika Get Her Kit Off For Sven?', while the *Daily Mail* found Nancy in combative mood. 'It's the biggest load of shit, without a doubt,' she told their reporter. 'It just makes me want to laugh. There will be an official denial. We are living together happily, and we love each other immensely. Sven doesn't even know this woman. We will be suing, and the money we win, I will give to my favourite charity.' No legal action was forthcoming however. Meanwhile, *The Times* was assured that it had nothing to fear from m'learned friends. Ms Cantor told them: 'We will not be issuing a denial. Don't worry, if you repeat everything that's in the *Mirror* we won't be dragging you down to the High Court to sue you for libel.'

Chelsea's match at home to Manchester United that afternoon was a media fun-fest. Eriksson was always going to attend, to run his World Cup rule over borderline cases like Wes Brown and Frank Lampard. What nobody expected was that Ms Jonsson would turn up at Stamford Bridge, too, in a car driven by Angus Deayton, a friend and United fan. A cast list more in keeping with a French farce than a major football match was completed by Stan Collymore, one of the lovely Ulrika's exes, who was working as a summarizer for Radio Five.

All eyes were on Sven as he climbed out of his chauffeur-driven Mercedes on arrival at the ground. How would fans, not noted for their delicacy in such matters, react? We did not have to wait long to find out. The stentorian greeting 'You lucky bastard' broke the ice, and Eriksson was in no way discomfited by choruses of 'Ulrika, Ulrika'. At this stage, Adam Crozier, the Football Association's chief executive, returned the call I had made from the press room at Stamford Bridge, and confirmed that the two men had discussed the situation, and had decided Eriksson's position as England coach had not been jeopardized. The party line would be that it was purely 'a private matter'. They would 'ride out the storm'.

Once inside the stadium, Eriksson sat in a

different stand to Ms Jonsson, next to Holland's coach, Dick Advocaat. There was applause, but no chanting of any sort when spectators spotted him, and when he left ten minutes from the end, to rejoin Nancy at home in Hyde Park, he thought it had all gone surprisingly well. Putting on a united front, the couple dined out that evening at the San Lorenzo restaurant, in Knightsbridge, a favourite haunt of celebrities, and therefore the paparazzi. Only those of infantile naivety would contend that they did not expect their picture to be all over the papers.

Unfortunately for the supposedly happy couple, what also appeared, all over the first five pages of the *News of the World*, was the 'Eriksclusive' that Ms Jonsson's nanny had 'Caught Sven At It With Ulrika', with the further headline news that 'They Were Romping Naked In The Middle Of The Day'. The good old '*News of the Screws*' was in its element. Not only had the nanny, Michelle Smith, 'walked in on them while they were naked on a bed at Ulrika's home', but 'Pint-sized Eriksson left his built-up shoes outside Ulrika's bedroom door to warn the nanny that he was inside, having sex.' There was more – pages more. The *News of the World* had 'discovered' (it did not say how) that 'Sven speaks only in Swedish on the phone to Ulrika, and conned his live-in partner, Nancy, that he was talking to his assistant, Tord Grip.' He had 'promised Ulrika that he would give Nancy the boot – but only after the World Cup, because he didn't want his England preparations disrupted'.

Ms Jonsson's mother, Gun Brodie, was quoted as saying: 'I think they have a future together. Why not? I know they've been seeing each other. Ulrika has spoken about him quite a bit. I'm happy for them.' Eriksson's mother, Ulla, sounded as if she had heard it all before. From sleepy Torsby, she said: 'You can teach a child how to walk, but you can't decide which way they go in life. But he hasn't committed a crime.'

Over the weekend, the theory that only the British press took such prurient interest in such liaisons dangereux was exploded as the story crossed frontiers. In Sweden, the mass-circulation tabloid *Expressen* carried three pages, and the headline 'Sordid Sven Kept His Romance With Ulrika Secret', while *Aftonbladet* devoted page one to the nanny's tale: 'I Caught Sven and Ulrika In Bed.' In Italy, *La Repubblica* told all with 'Calcio, Amore, Politica, Scandoloso Mr Eriksson', or 'Football, Love and Politics; The Scandalous Mr Eriksson', while *Il Messagero* used a picture of Ms Jonsson and spoke of: 'The Irresistible Charms That Helped Sven Succumb.'

Come the Monday, the eternal triangle was still front-page news. With Ms Jonsson, or at least her unnamed 'friends' on board, the *Mirror* continued to make the running, with a banner headline which posed a question on her behalf. For them, 'What Kind Of A Man Are You, Sven?' was the burning issue of the day, and one which came with its own answer. He was a 'lying cad', according to Ulrika. The gist was that she was 'furious that the England coach had failed to get in touch since the news broke on Friday – and took her rival, Nancy, out to dinner on Saturday night'. She accused Eriksson of 'behaving like the worst kind of Tory politician caught with his trousers down'.

The *Express* chose another tack. Dominated by a large picture of a smiling Nancy, done up to the nines in evening wear, their front page screamed: 'EXCLUSIVE: I've Beaten Ulrika Says Sven's Girl'. Inside the paper, she said nothing of the sort. A two-page spread was notably short on attributed testimony, relying heavily on unidentified 'friends' and 'sources close' to the principals. All Nancy said, in fact, came by way of angry response. Asked if she and Sven were still together, she replied: 'I think it's a really stupid question. Definitely. Yes. More than ever. The facts are much, much clearer.'

The *Sun*, up to speed by now, carried a front page picture of Eriksson and Ms Jonsson at a charity breakfast in Manchester. 'Fancy A Roll?', it had Eriksson asking, adding that the snap was taken the morning after the couple had spent the night together in a hotel after Manchester United's Champions' League match against Bayern Munich on 13 March.

At 4pm on Monday 22 April, the coach had a long-standing commitment to appear in London, at Burton's headquarters off Oxford Street, to launch the England World Cup suit. Those who predicted cancellation on a pretext did not know him. Facing the music was no problem for a man who had just put out his own *Classical Collection* on CD. Hardened newshounds confidently expected to break him down. First to bare her teeth was the woman from the *Mirror*, who led off with: 'Who is your first choice for selection – Nancy or Ulrika?' Eriksson took a deep breath and blocked a googly he had seen coming with a bat of Boycottesque straightness. 'That is a question which is private,' he said. 'The England squad is not private. You will know on 7 May who is going to be picked or not picked, but my private life – I prefer to keep that private. It is not easy, as I have seen in the last three or four days, but I never had any intention of commenting on my private life. I won't do it today and I will not do it in the future.'

How much of a distraction had the furore been? 'Well, my concerns are about other people in this country, in Sweden, in Italy. I am talking about parents, ex-wife, my children – a lot of people. That is my concern, and I am sorry for that. But I will get on with my job as usual, and try to do my best for England, even if I have to use violence, more or less, to get in the car in the morning.'

How stressful had the past few days been? 'Professionally, I have got on with my job. I have watched football and I was in the office today, doing normal things. It is not pleasant to be followed 24 hours a day, and not by one person, but by 20. But I can't do anything about it.'

Because of the intrusions, might he reconsider his position with England after the World Cup? 'I have never thought about it and I have never talked about it. As you can see, I am sitting here today in my England suit, and my intentions are to go on like this.'

The man from the *Sun* wanted to know: 'Do you still love Nancy?' With a thin smile, Eriksson replied: 'Private is private. I'm sure you will find out – you are parked outside my house.' The same reporter wondered whether the man of the moment had any complaints about press inaccuracy. 'If I have complaints, I will tell you. But I have not complained.'

There was much more in the same vein, Eriksson handling the inquisition with such cool, unflustered dignity that he was given a round of applause at the end. The verdict was that he had coped remarkably well. The *Sun*, having given it their best shot and got nowhere, hailed a worthy adversary with the front-page headline: 'He's Got Balls', while at the back of the paper their chief sportswriter, Steven Howard, wrote: 'All I can say is that if Eriksson's players show half as much resolution and grace under fire as their boss did, then Argentina could well be put to the sword in June.' In *The Times*, the sports columnist of the year, Simon Barnes, said: 'I hope Rio Ferdinand is as composed at the back in six weeks' time. Against all the odds, Eriksson came out with his dignity intact.'

For those of goodwill, who liked and admired the man, there was a more important issue here than 'Did he or didn't he?', or even, given Ms Jonsson's track record, 'How could he?' The concern was the extent of the damage done to the transcendent esteem in which he was held by his players. Managerial authority is easily undermined, especially by smutty gossip. How would the squad react, inwardly, the next time Eriksson saw fit to remind them of their behavioural responsibilities off the field? How could the Football Association justify blackballing Jonathan Woodgate, on the grounds that his selection would cause a 'media circus', when their head coach had done precisely that?

It was also becoming apparent that Eriksson, as well as enjoying a nice pair of legs, is also fond of a cheque. Having said at the outset that he would not be exploiting the commercial potential of his position until after the World Cup, he was suddenly endorsing everything from Playstation games to Sainsbury's and music CDs, and holding press conferences to promote them at which football questions were banned. Represented in football matters by Athole Still, an agent of the old school in his sixties, he milked his success for England for all it was worth by signing up with the International Management Group, whose worldwide stable includes Tiger Woods. Under IMG's avaricious auspices, he was soon earning more from commercial activities – their sole concern – than he was from the FA. The Playstation and PC games he was paid to promote would bring him £1m, he received £200,000 for a walk-on role in a television advertisement for Sainsbury's, and a similar sum for ads for Cirio Del Monte pasta sauces. A triple CD set entitled *The Sven-Goran Eriksson Classical Collection* was worth another £50,000, and his numerous public speaking engagements bring in £20,000 a time. At the time of writing, lucrative deals with

Volvo, Ikea and Ericsson – all Swedish companies – had been mooted, and Lars Sternmaker, the Scandinavian head of IMG, said: 'We are talking about a very popular name. With such a marketable individual, you'd expect him to earn at least £15m through long-term deals.'

My colleague at *The Sunday Times*, David Walsh, offered a new perspective on Eriksson shortly before the World Cup, when he wrote: 'He now stands before us a little more human, more like the rest of us. His players have talked of the authority he brings to the dressing room, and of his impenetrability. Now they will feel they know him a little better, and the sense of awe is diminished.' Walsh spoke of 'the vague sense that he isn't quite the man he has been cracked up to be', adding: 'It was a feeling that surfaced some weeks back. Seeing Eriksson promote Playstation, I thought of posters in libraries promoting the joys and benefits of reading. Tony Adams is one of the football people used in that campaign. It is what you would expect of Adams. Why should England's coach lend his name to Playstation? Because the monetary return was sufficient, that is why. Ah well, you say, that's the nature of the game. It would be nice, though, if Eriksson's £2m-a-year contract with the FA were enough. Nice, too, if he promoted reading, not Playstation.'

As the 'Ulrikagate' saga rolled on, day after day, it was revealed that Ms Jonsson was writing an autobiography which, with juicy serialization rights, was expected to fetch £1m. The news prompted the Arsenal manager, Arsene Wenger, to speak out on Eriksson's behalf. Wenger himself had endured rumours about his private life in his early days at Highbury. Now he said: 'Sven is not married, he can do what he wants. In Latin countries, there is a different type of mentality. Such a reaction wouldn't happen in France, for example. In other countries, even if a guy is married they say: "OK, it's his business." In England, it's a different culture. I wasn't shocked at all when I read the reports. It's his private life, he can do what he wants. He has the right to live like he wants, with the girl he wants. It's down to him. If he comes home and spends all night watching TV and smoking, it can be more harmful to his job than going out with a girl and going to bed at 12 o'clock.

'As managers, we are judged on our results and our consistency, but everybody has a different way to find a balance in life. Only Sven can answer whether what's going on is a problem or not. Certainly I don't have a problem with it. I think Sven is orientated towards preparing for the World Cup, and considers this a minor incident.' With a mischievous smile, Wenger added: 'I don't think it will affect the respect he receives from the players – if anything, it could help it.'

By Wednesday, after six silly days, it was all over. Ms Jonsson, realizing she was fighting a losing battle against a more ringwise opponent, issued a statement. She said: 'In the hope of dispelling any further rumours about my relationship with Sven-Goran Eriksson, I would like to make it clear I have never issued him with any ultimatums. Like everybody else, I wish Sven the very best for the World Cup, but I also have a job to do, both as a mother and professionally, and would like to be allowed to continue to do my job without any further speculation involving me and this relationship. I am no longer a part of this relationship.' Ludicrously, as if to point up the absurdity of the media's treatment of the affair, Sky TV's political editor, Adam Boulton, broke off from his coverage of Prime Minister's question time to read the statement.

Sven and Ulrika were front-page news for one more day. On the Thursday, newspapers had more fun with the outcome. Under the scoreline Nancy 1 Ulrika 0, the *Sun* carried a huge picture of a grinning Nancy with the heading 'I've Won The World Cup Willy'. Across pages four and five there was the tongue-in-cheek headline: 'Six Days That Shook The World.' Even the *Mirror*, which had been identified with Ms Jonsson throughout, had to concede that their girl had taken a beating. 'Ciao, Ulrika' was their front-page headline, complete with a picture of the smiling Nancy waving to the crowd at Highbury, where she had accompanied Eriksson the previous night to make the most of her triumph. To her delight, the full house, assembled to see Arsenal beat West Ham and close in on the title, greeted her with a warm round of applause.

On Sunday 28 April, showing off a new diamond ring, Nancy announced that they were engaged to be married. She was wrong, of course. Ulrika Jonsson, meanwhile, was all over the *News of the*

World again. Under the headline 'Ulrika Drove Me
Wild With Passion In A Lay-By On The A59 To
York', it was reported that the 'TV sex bomb' had
'seduced three other household-name celebrities'
before 'bedding' Eriksson. The two-page spread
went on to say that Eriksson had 'apologized' to her
for his part in their affair on the Friday.

If he thought the story would go away, he was
wrong. The following Wednesday, Lynda Lee-
Potter, the doyenne of columnists, wrote in the
Daily Mail: 'Nancy Dell'Olio is being seen as a smart,
sassy female warrior who has won her man. I suspect Sven-Goran engineered it because he wanted
his girlfriend to retain her dignity. Also, being a disciplined chap, he can't face a bust-up before the
World Cup. However, I predict that later this year a
press statement will be issued which says: "Sven and
Nancy wish to announce the end of their relationship. They remain friends, no one else is involved in
the separation and the decision is mutual."

'All three statements, almost certainly, will be
false.' Exactly two years later, with the relationship
then still ongoing, Nancy laughed when she was
reminded of the prediction. 'What is it about the
English and sex?' she said. 'Originally it was the sex
lives of your politicians that obsessed you, then it
was show business personalities and now finally it's
sportsmen. I think these people who are so interested in other people's sex lives must have none of
their own. It's very sad.'

She had sympathised with Victoria Beckham
after it was alleged that David had enjoyed a

dalliance or two in Madrid. 'It's not true that I contacted Victoria, offering a shoulder to cry on, but I
did feel for her, as I have been put through it myself.
And what a waste of everyone's time that was, too.'

CHAPTER TWENTY-ONE

THE SQUAD

The England coach gladly turned his full attention to football again, not that there was any relief from stress there. While at Highbury, watching Arsenal beat West Ham 2–0, his mind was dragged 200 miles north by the news that a second regular in his starting line-up had fallen victim to the same injury as David Beckham.

Playing for Manchester United, in the first leg of their Champions' League semi-final against Bayer Leverkusen, Gary Neville had come out of a tackle on Ze Roberto with a fractured metatarsal. One club suffering two such freak injuries in as many weeks was virtually unheard of, the coincidence compounded by the fact that Neville and Beckham are best friends. The crucial difference was that England's captain was already on the mend. His teammate had been hurt a fortnight nearer to the World Cup, and the six weeks he would need to recover took him past the first match at the finals, against Sweden on 2 June. England's first choice right-back was out, and it was to get worse. Much worse.

Attention focused on potential replacements, with the resurgent Wes Brown moving up in the queue. Eriksson travelled to Germany to watch him play in the decisive second leg of the European semi-final, which put United out, but a so-so performance from the young defender left the coach unconvinced. On his return to London the following day, he postponed the announcement of his squad by 48 hours, from 7 May to 9 May. The explanation given for the delay was that two Premier League matches had been rearranged for 8 May – Manchester United at home to Arsenal and Liverpool against Blackburn – when half his players would be at risk. In reality, the coach wanted to make one last check on Brown and Blackburn's Matt Jansen.

Before that, the FA Cup Final, between Arsenal and Chelsea, was played at Cardiff, where Ray Parlour and Frank Lampard both made late, unavailing bids for World Cup places with strong, eye-catching performances, outshining France's Patrick Vieira and Manu Petit in midfield. Eriksson, who attended the final with Nancy Dell'Olio, was more interested afterwards in Freddie Ljungberg, who scored a solo goal of the highest class. The coach readily acknowledged that the Arsenal midfielder was an obvious threat to England in their opening match in Japan, against Sweden on 2 June. On current form, Eriksson said, Ljungberg was the best player in the Premier League.

On the day before the squad was named, Eriksson made a last-minute decision to travel to Anfield, to run the rule over Jansen, and dispatched his trusty assistant, Grip, to Old Trafford for the title decider, which was being billed as the Premiership's 'match of the decade'. The plan was for the two to rendezvous afterwards at Knutsford Services, on the M6, and to use the journey back to London, in the same chauffeur-driven car, to make any late adjustments to the squad that were deemed appropriate.

The events and consequences of that night were misinterpreted, causing something of a kerfuffle. Jansen, who was aware of Eriksson's presence, scored for Blackburn and was told at half-time by his manager, Graeme Souness, that he had 'made it' and was 'in the squad'. Eriksson insists that this was merely Souness's interpretation of the situation and that he had given no such indication. However, what the FA had done the previous week, at the coach's request, was ask Blackburn to postpone the hernia operation Jansen was due to have at the end of the season, 'just in case'. Having learned of this, the *Mail on Sunday* carried a two-page article on 5 May, forecasting the player's inclusion in the World Cup squad.

A combination of this confident newspaper prediction and Souness's words to him during the interval of the game against Liverpool left Jansen distraught when he was not in the 23 chosen the following day. Instead, the surprise inclusion was Martin Keown, who had been left out of Arsenal's Cup Final team only five days earlier. Some observers, the *Mail on Sunday* foremost among them, drew the conclusion that after an outstanding performance by Keown at Old Trafford, Grip had persuaded Eriksson that he had to take the Arsenal centre-half, and that Jansen should be the man to make way. It sounded a plausible enough explanation, but was a case of putting two and two together and making five. From my discussions on the subject with the coach and his number two, I can reveal that it was Grip who first pushed Jansen's credentials, and who promoted his cause all along. Eriksson was the Keown fan, who had to have him once he was back in the Arsenal team. He explained that he felt there might be games when he needed the country's best man-marker to 'take out' a particularly dangerous opponent, and others when Keown would be invaluable as a substitute, sent on to defend a lead.

Before the squad was announced on the Thursday, Eriksson and Nancy attended a Variety Club of Great Britain charity lunch, at which the piece of paper on which he had jotted down his 23 names was auctioned for £5,000. Tongues wagged when Eriksson was introduced to speak at the lunch not by Gabby Yorath, ITV's glamorous presenter, as was the original intention, but by a last-minute replacement, Steve Curry, of the *Daily Mail*. Later, at the main press conference at which Eriksson made his squad public, at the Cafe Royal, in London's West End, Curry asked a question which, in the light of subsequent events, bordered on the clairvoyant. 'Given the injury record of Steven Gerrard and Kieron Dyer,' the *Mail* man wondered, 'were you not tempted to take another midfielder, rather than an extra defender?' Eriksson had 'thought about it', he said, but if he had 'tried to be clever' that way, he might have had 'more defenders injured'. At a 'certain stage during the past few weeks', he had decided to take two players for each outfield positions, to be 'properly covered everywhere'.

The question and answer session went as follows:

Q: What was the thinking behind choosing four centre-halves, plus Wes Brown?
Eriksson: It is to have two men for every position. Also, don't forget that Gary Neville would have been in the squad, if he'd been fit.
Q: So is Wes Brown in for Neville at right-back?
Eriksson: Yes, he's a natural there.
Q: Is Danny Mills your first choice?
Eriksson: No, I didn't say that. I have two to choose from at right-back.
Q: Do you go to the World Cup with a sense of trepidation or optimism?
Eriksson: Optimism, of course. I've been looking forward to this for over a year now. It's the biggest stage you can be on. I've never been there before, so I look forward to it all the more.
Q: Was Steve McManaman one of five or six players not chosen who you thought deserved a phone call this morning?
Eriksson: Yes. I left him a message. I think he was out training when I called him. I don't want to comment on when I decided to leave him out.
Q: Why did you postpone the announcement of the squad, from Tuesday to Thursday?
Eriksson: Just because of the possibility of injuries

in the two games that were played on Wednesday.

Q: Why has Danny Murphy been put on standby?

Eriksson: I think Murphy is the complete midfielder, who you can play almost anywhere. He played well again last night, especially in the first half, and he is cover for David Beckham and Nicky Butt, in case either of them fails to recover from injury in time.

Q: In the cases of Owen Hargreaves and Joe Cole, were you attracted by their technical ability, as much as their youth and potential?

Eriksson: Their technique was most important. A footballer these days needs many qualities, and technical ability is obviously among them. You must be clever out there, whether you are attacking or defending, and you have to be able to run and run. With Joe Cole, technique is definitely one of his strengths.

Q: Generally, you have discarded the old guard since you took over. Have you been keen to put your own stamp on the squad and to go to the World Cup with your own men?

Eriksson: I haven't picked anyone just because he's young, or new. I have picked them because they are good. Joe Cole, Owen Hargreaves, Wes Brown, Ashley Cole, Wayne Bridge – they are in because I think they are good enough to represent England at the World Cup. I have always said that there are good, young footballers in this country. Now we'll see if they are good enough.

Q: What roles do you envisage for Teddy Sheringham and Martin Keown?

Eriksson: You hope that your players who are over 30

will act as leaders, and not only on the pitch. They have valuable experience, they have been there before, and that can help the rest of the squad, especially the young ones. Teddy Sheringham has much more World Cup experience than I have. I don't remember when I first saw Martin Keown play, but it was probably when I was at Benfica. He is always standing firm, always blocking shots, always containing centre-forwards, always doing a good job. If you look at the Keown of ten years ago and how he played yesterday, you can't see much difference.

Q: The managers of Sweden and Argentina will pinpoint our weaknesses as left midfield and right-back. Would you agree with them?

Eriksson: I hope to answer them after the games, not now. Let's hope they're wrong. I think the players we have in those positions have enough experience to cope.

Q: Andy Cole has announced his retirement from international football after being left out, yet at one stage he said you were the only England manager who ever really believed in him. Has he lost his way?

Eriksson: First of all, I feel sorry for him. I really do. But not only for him, for a lot of players who didn't make it. It's never nice to phone people and say: "You're not in this time." It's a part of the job I could easily live without, but you have to do it. For Andy Cole, yes I'm sorry, but I had to make my choice.

Q: Did all the players you spoke to about leaving them out understand and accept your reasons?

Eriksson: I didn't ask them if they accepted or understood. That's not the right way to do the job. I told them: "I'm sorry, I can only pick 23 and that's it."

Q: This is the second time it has happened to Phil Neville, and he has been in every squad you have picked up to now. Did you feel particularly sorry for him?

Eriksson: Yes, but it's really the same for all those players who did a great job for us during the qualification games. Of course I feel for them.

Q: There has been a lot of speculation that you won't stay on as England coach after the World Cup. Is it your intention to carry on?

Eriksson: I don't know about that speculation, because at a certain stage during the last few weeks I decided it was better not to read it. But I have a contract, and I've always said that I want to continue as manager of England after the World Cup.

Q: In yesterday's match at Old Trafford, Keown and Scholes would both have been booked, or even sent off, by a World Cup referee. Does their physical style worry you?

Eriksson: No, I'm not particularly worried about that. Martin Keown has a lot of experience, and knows what a World Cup is like.

Q: You have one-for-one cover in all positions, but how important is versatility, and the ability to slot into difference roles unexpectedly?

Eriksson: It's very important. Remember the Greece game? We had Teddy Sheringham on the bench and he came on and improved things dramatically in ten minutes. He scored a goal and was awarded the free-kick from which Beckham scored. To have players who can come on and change things like that is extremely important. Sheringham has proved that he can do it, and I think Joe Cole can, too. We can bring him on and he's very lively, and can beat opponents.

Question: What was wrong with Graeme Le Saux – can you give a reason why he failed to impress you and Tord Grip, when he seems to have impressed everybody else?

Eriksson: If I was to think hard, I might do that, but I shouldn't, because if you start to give reasons why one or two players are not in there, it will never end. And it's not fair. I have made my choice after watching a lot of matches and talking to a lot of scouts and club managers, and that's it, right or wrong. I don't expect every England fan to have the same opinion as me. That way, football would be very boring.

The squad was announced as follows:

David Seaman (Arsenal). Age 38, caps 68. The passé ponytail only underlined the fact that he was slightly past his prime, but he remained England's best goalkeeper, and was always going to reclaim his place for a third World Cup, if fit.

Nigel Martyn (Leeds United). Age 35, caps 21. He had the chance to establish himself as number one when Seaman was absent, injured, but was never as convincing at international level as he was for his club. Shots eluded his grasp to embarrassing effect against Sweden at Old Trafford and Holland at White Hart Lane.

David James (West Ham United). Age 31, caps 7. On his day, he looked like the best English goalkeeper in the Premier League, but those days were interspersed with too many dodgy ones for the East End bleach boy to threaten the two men ahead of him in the queue. The penalty he conceded in the friendly against Italy hardly helped his cause.

Danny Mills (Leeds United). Age 25, caps 5. That volatile temperament and horrible disciplinary record made him a gamble, and one deemed too risky to take until Gary Neville's injury forced Eriksson's hand. In the final analysis, his ability to cover in central defence was the clincher.

Wes Brown (Manchester United). Age 22, caps 4. Like Mills, he got his foot in the door when Neville broke his. Long lauded by Sir Alex Ferguson as potentially the best centre-half in the country, he has struggled to live up to that extravagant billing, but recovered from injury just in time to creep in on the back of his ability to cover at right-back.

Rio Ferdinand (Leeds United). Age 23, caps 20. A shoo-in who had only to stay fit to go. His move from West Ham to Leeds, and elevation to the captaincy, accelerated his maturing into a dependable, as well as skilful, centre-half. An Eriksson favourite, he would have deputized for David Beckham as captain against Paraguay had he not been forced out by injury himself.

Sol Campbell (Arsenal). Age 27, caps 44. In contrast to Ferdinand, the transfer away from the club with whom he had been associated for so long – in his case Spurs – caused him grief, precipitating a temporary loss of morale and confidence. Class will out in the end, though, and a commanding performance in the FA Cup Final dispelled any lingering doubts.

Gareth Southgate (Middlesbrough). Age 31, caps 47. On his own admission, 'Steady Eddie' thought for a long time that he had no place in Eriksson's plans, but when opportunity knocked, courtesy of injuries to others, he grasped his chance with eager alacrity, rising from nowhere to first reserve centre-back in the space of six months.

Martin Keown (Arsenal). Age 35, caps 41. England's best man-marker seemed to have been put out of contention when he broke his leg, but he fought back with characteristic determination and came through with a strong late run.

Ashley Cole (Arsenal). Age 21, caps 7. The young Gunner quickly saw off Charlton's Chris Powell, but just as he seemed to be here to stay, as England's left-back for the next decade, injury struck, keeping him out for four games. During his absence, Wayne Bridge took to international football like the proverbial duck to water, leaving Cole facing a real challenge for his place.

Wayne Bridge (Southampton). Age 21, caps 3. Derided by the Graeme Le Saux lobby when he was selected for the first time, against Holland, he had some of us breakfasting on our words after an impressive debut in Amsterdam. A more reliable defender than Ashley Cole, he was a genuine contender for the left-back spot, and was viewed by Eriksson as a possibility for the left side of midfield.

David Beckham (Manchester United). Age 27, caps 49. Universally regarded as England's talisman, and all the more so after his heroics against Greece to secure qualification. Irreplaceable as one of only three players in the team blessed with skills of unarguable world class. But would that damaged left foot stand up to the strain?

Steven Gerrard (Liverpool). Age 22, caps 10. A key component at the hub of the team, almost as important as Beckham. The precocious scouser's dynamism and range of passing was fundamental to the high-tempo game Eriksson wanted to play, and his telepathic understanding with Michael Owen and Emile Heskey was essential if optimum use was to be made of their pace.

Paul Scholes (Manchester United). Age 27, caps 42. 'The complete, modern midfielder', as Eriksson called him. A high-class finisher, good enough to have scored a hat-trick for England (against Poland in 1999), and further blessed with high endurance energy. The perfect partner for Gerrard in the centre, he could also fill in on the left, or even as the support striker.

Kieron Dyer (Newcastle United). Age 23, caps 9. Eriksson had waited all season to have him fit, after which his reappearance against Paraguay was a real letdown. Seen as the answer to England's problem on the left in midfield, he instead looked exactly what he was – a right-footer playing out of position. Too good to leave out, but where to play him?

Nicky Butt (Manchester United). Age 26, caps 18. The perfect understudy for the midfield anchor role, for club and country. Never likely to be man of the match, but a reliable ball-winning grafter, unlikely to let England down.

Owen Hargreaves (Bayern Munich). Age 21, caps 4. After an unsuccessful trial in the 'black hole' that was left midfield, the footballing equivalent of Greg Rusedski seemed to have missed his chance, but caught the managerial eye again in the nick of time by demonstrating in the Champions' League that he had a valuable second string to his bow, at right-back.

Joe Cole (West Ham United). Age 20, caps 4. The wild card in the pack. He seemed to have played himself out of contention with a poor performance against Italy, then demanded inclusion with a 45-minute cameo against Paraguay that was evocative of the young 'Gazza'. Chosen with a match-winning, or turning, role as substitute in mind.

Michael Owen (Liverpool). Age 22, caps 34. Pace like fire and top-class finishing made him, more than Beckham, the England player the rest of the world were worried about. If he could avoid those pulls and strains to which he has always been susceptible, anything was possible.

Emile Heskey (Liverpool). Age 24, caps 22. An Eriksson favourite, on the basis of his speed and workrate, but his first touch was not up to international standard, and was reflected in the sort of goals-per-game ratio that used to be held against Ian Wright: just three in 22 for England.

Robbie Fowler (Leeds United). Age 27, caps 24. The best finisher of them all, and terribly unlucky to be restricted in the main to substitute's appearances. England's match-winner in waiting.

Darius Vassell (Aston Villa). Age 21, caps 3. A real rabbit from Eriksson's hat when he was promoted from the Under-21s for a scoring debut against Holland in Amsterdam. Quick, willing and confident, he was in with a view to harassing tired defenders as a second-half replacement.

Teddy Sheringham (Tottenham Hotspur). Age 36, caps 45. Intelligence and experience personified. The second striker as playmaker is not a role that fits in Eriksson's preferred version of 4–4–2, but the coach acknowledged that there had to be a Plan B, and 'Steady Teddy' was the ideal man to bring order to unforeseen chaos.

First replacement: Danny Murphy (Liverpool). Age 25, caps 5. As a high-energy, adaptable midfielder and a free-kick expert, he was unlucky not to make the original 23, especially after his impressive, scoring appearance as a substitute against Paraguay in the final match before the squad was picked.

Second replacement: Trevor Sinclair (West Ham). Age 28, caps 3. At one stage he came to be regarded as a cert for the 23, because of his ability to play on either flank. Unfortunately, when he was given his chance he never rose above the mediocre, and was left reliant on the misfortunes of others to get in.

The big, setpiece media conference over, Eriksson relaxed and spoke about the squad, and his hopes for it, on a more informal basis. Blackburn were saying that they had been told the previous night that Jansen was in. 'That may be true, but it wasn't by me, and who was in a position to tell them but me?' From the tone of Eriksson's response, it was clear that his question was rhetorical. He had talked to Gerard Houllier and to Graeme Souness about their players, 'but I didn't say to either of them who I was going to pick or not pick'.

In an interview for *The Sunday Times*, Gerrard had told me he thought England could win the World Cup. Would Eriksson be telling them that they could do it? 'Yes, I will be saying that to them. It is essential in football not to be afraid, whoever you play. It doesn't matter if you're at home or away, or who your opponents are. It's when the opposition are less strong that you should tell your team to be careful. Why should England think they are going to lose to any team in the world? It might happen, of course, but thinking it will definitely won't help. I will be encouraging belief like Gerrard's. If you don't believe in yourself, you'll never win anything.'

Conventional wisdom held that a core group of

five or six world-class players was a prerequisite for success at this level. Did England have them? 'One is Beckham, another is Michael Owen,' Eriksson said. 'We also have an extremely good midfielder in Steven Gerrard. Which team in the world wouldn't want him? And Paul Scholes is the same. There are others, but I would say these four players are world class. I hope people around the world will say it of more of our players after the tournament.'

Injuries were now his 'big enemy', he said. 'That's the biggest concern I have. If it happens now, there will be very little recovery time. If someone was to get injured on Saturday, at least I'd be able to select from everyone at home. If it happens later, we'll have to look to the Under-21s [playing in the European Championship finals in Switzerland] for replacements, because the other senior players will all be away on holiday.'

Eriksson was right to worry, of course. On the Saturday, the last day of the Premier League season, he went to Highbury, to share in the champions' champagne celebrations. By the end of the game, however, he was in no mood to partake of the bubbly. News quickly filtered through that Kieron Dyer had been carried off on a stretcher during Newcastle's inconsequential finale at Southampton, his left knee wrecked by a dreadful challenge for which Tahar El-Khalej was sent off. And poor Dyer was not alone in his anguish. Gerrard was again hors de combat at Anfield, substituted with groin trouble. First reports indicated that Dyer's condition was the more serious of the two, and that Gerrard had been withdrawn for precautionary reasons. It was not until the following morning that the extent of Eriksson's problems became known. Over breakfast he took two hammer-blow telephone calls in quick succession. Dyer's knee ligaments were damaged and Gerrard had aggravated a long-standing groin complaint, which would now need surgery. Barring miraculous recoveries, both were out of the World Cup.

In the circumstances, it was a surprise that Eriksson opted only for a black tie and not the full sackcloth and ashes for his next media briefing, at Arsenal's London Colney training ground on the Sunday afternoon. Murphy and Sinclair would both now accompany the squad to Dubai the following day. 'It's very bad news,' the coach said. 'Dyer is out. The doctors and physios agree that it will be at least four weeks before he can start working properly. The other problem is Steven Gerrard. We thought it wasn't too bad last night, but now I'm told he has to see a surgeon to decide whether he'll be operated on at once or not. It's much worse than they thought. From what Gerard Houllier told me today, Liverpool have been worried about his groin since February.

'To wake up in the morning and get two phone calls like that . . . it could have been a better Sunday morning, without doubt. Certainly I wasn't prepared for it. Remember, we'd already lost Gary Neville, now Gerrard and Dyer, too. They are three top players – three of our first eleven.' He had talked to Dyer, who was taking it 'very badly'. They had agreed to speak again the following Friday 'in case there has been a miracle'. Eriksson did his best to put a brave face on what was a desperately disappointing turn of events, trying hard to sound convincing when he spoke of opportunity knocking for others. 'I'm not the sort of person to sit down and cry over our bad luck,' he said. 'If you wake up crying, it will never be a good day. I feel sorry for the players who are injured, and a bit for myself, but you will not hear any more from me about it after today because to do that would be negative thinking. We'll go there with 23 players and still have a good World Cup. Of course it's a pity if we're missing Gary Neville, Gerrard and Dyer, they are big players for us. But now someone else has to play as well as they would have done.'

The squad had assembled at the Sopwell House Hotel, near St Albans, to attend a party held by the Beckhams prior to flying out to Dubai from Luton airport the following afternoon, with their families, for five days' rest, recuperation and acclimatization. How had the players been affected by news of the injuries? 'They were surprised and disappointed, because we were talking about two of their friends, as well as important members of the team. But once we get out there, I don't think we'll ever discuss it. Many times in football, the door closes on injured players and others come in and do well, so who knows? I hope we can do well, and I'm sure we can.'

'The curse', as it was becoming known, even extended to the Under-21s, and the young players there that Eriksson had one eye on as possible replacements in the event of more withdrawals. 'Among the defenders, there's Ledley King,' the coach said. The Tottenham centre-half dropped out within a matters of hours, with ankle trouble. In midfield he identified Blackburn's David Dunn as 'one who could do it', adding 'I've always liked him', while the attacker he would call on, in extremis, was Jermain Defoe, of West Ham.

CHAPTER TWENTY-TWO

HERE WE GO . . .

When Trevor Sinclair was asked to go to Dubai in place of Kieron Dyer, he felt like Cinderella, finally making it to the ball. He received the call to join the squad on the day before its departure, while he was out playing golf with his next-door neighbour. At first he refused to believe that the voice on the other end of his mobile phone was Sven-Goran Eriksson's. It had to be another of those hoaxers he had read so much about. Eventually convinced, he dropped everything, including the family holiday he had been planning, and was wafted to paradise from Luton airport. His wife had no complaints. The Football Association were footing the bill for the 23 players to take their partners and families to the palatial Jumeirah Beach Club. In all, there were 123 in the party, occupying 35 individual villas. Two were bigger and better than the rest. One went to Eriksson and Nancy Dell'Olio, the other to David and Victoria Beckham.

The trip was to be six days (five nights) of rest and recreation, with occasional training to work off any dietary, or nocturnal excesses. It was made clear that the press corps would not be welcome, and would be denied access to management and players if they turned up. This was a PR gaffe. Instead of having to deal with the specialist correspondents, England put themselves at the mercy of the newshounds dispatched by various newsdesks to fill the space.

Any newspaperman worth his salt could have forecast the consequences, and many of us warned Adam Crozier well in advance of what a blanket ban on football writers would bring. It should have come as no surprise, then, that within 48 hours of the squad's arrival in Dubai, two papers reported that seven of the players had gone into town for what became a late night out. They had gone with Eriksson's blessing, so much so that they were ferried to and fro in chauffeured limousines. There was no excessive drinking or bad behaviour, but it was made into enough of a 'story' for rentaquote ex-players to deplore it.

Football reasserted itself, with the news that Bobby Robson had telephoned Eriksson with an impassioned plea on Dyer's behalf. The miracle was 'on', Robson said. Contrary to the original diagnosis, the midfielder's knee ligaments were not badly damaged, and he was able to run again – albeit only in straight lines. The Newcastle manager was a compelling advocate. He had taken England to two World Cups, in 1986 and 1990, so he knew all about the requirements and the timescale involved. He insisted Dyer could still make it, and Eriksson accepted his word. Dyer flew out in time to join the squad in Dubai on the Saturday, meeting the other players at the airport as the wives and children left for home. With the benefit of hindsight, the decision was a mistake. Eriksson was never sufficiently confident of the midfielder's fitness to use him as more than a bit-part substitute.

The foot-in-the-door merchants weren't finished. The *Sunday Mirror* 'exclusively revealed' that a bar bill had been left unpaid by the players when they checked out. There was talk of a sum in excess of £100,000, whereas in reality the figure was less than £20,000, but even that made it sound like Bacchanalia Beach, until it was remembered that 23 players, their wives or girlfriends and children were in residence for six days in one of the most expensive resorts in the world, where a soft drink costs £5. The FA, who picked up the tab, also pointed out that there were other extras involved – laundry, for example – but the explanation cannot have impressed the average fan, left wondering why players earning £60,000 a week could not pay for their own round of drinks, or dry cleaning.

Neither Eriksson nor a squad now expanded to 24 liked these stories, and the atmosphere was a little strained when England and the media were reunited on the idyllic Jeju Island, off the coast of South Korea, on Sunday 19 May. This gorgeous spot, a favourite with honeymooners, was to be their base for a week, during which they were to play a warm-up friendly against South Korea, who had just beaten Scotland 4–1. At his first media conference on World Cup territory, held al fresco, against a backdrop of palm trees and fishing boats, Eriksson faced a phalanx of television cameras and countless snapping photographers. He played a characteristically straight bat to a lively bouncer from Garth Crooks, of the BBC, who inquired about the 'cavalier' treatment of Sinclair. Was he in the squad or not? If not, it was unfair to keep him hanging around. The coach shrugged and wore that serene smile. Sinclair was happy to wait and see, shouldn't we all do the same? In reality Sinclair wasn't happy, as the coach was soon to find out.

After the TV cameras had gone, Eriksson took questions from the Korean media. The interpreter, who sat alongside him, was a strikingly attractive woman, So-Young Min, and the appreciative glances she kept getting from the England coach may not have been entirely down to her linguistic skills. Steve Howard penned a spoof postcard from Sven to Nancy for the *Sun*, in which he wrote: 'The interpreter today was awful – I don't know where they got him from. But Jeju is beautiful. Fantastico. They call it the honeymoon island. For some reason, I am feeling even more romantic than usual today. Could you send me my tape – *Sven's Classical Love Songs*?' Accompanying the piece was a picture of Eriksson paying rapt attention to So-Young. Afterwards, told that the England coach was establishing something of a reputation with the ladies, she said she was not surprised. She had found him 'a really charming man'. More seriously, it was revealed that Beckham's injured foot had swollen again and Dyer was making only slow progress. The team would not be at full strength against the Koreans, or in the last of the preparatory friendlies, against Cameroon in Kobe, Japan on 26 May.

For the game against the co-hosts, injury deprived England of Nicky Butt and Robbie Fowler, as well as Beckham and Dyer. Eriksson tried 4–3–3 again, with the first-choice back four (Danny Mills, Rio Ferdinand, Sol Campbell and Ashley Cole) behind a midfield of Danny Murphy, Owen Hargreaves and Paul Scholes. The front men were Darius Vassell, Michael Owen and Emile Heskey. The first half went reasonably well, Owen opening the scoring from close range after 25 minutes. After the interval, however, the introduction of eight substitutes stripped England of all cohesion, and their passing deteriorated to such an extent that the Koreans deservedly equalized when Ji Sung Pat scored with a diving header. Sinclair, on in place of Murphy, was so horribly profligate with possession that he apologized in the dressing room straight after the match, and said he wanted to go home. He told reporters that his 'nightmare' performance had shattered his confidence, and that he was no longer sure that he was good enough for international foot-ball. 'I didn't do well,' he said. 'I found it tough. I felt I had a lot to prove and couldn't do it.' After such an unusually frank admission, Eriksson felt compelled to grant his request, and let him go.

The coach was sympathetic, saying that Sinclair had not let down his country. 'I could understand that staying and feeling he was the 24th man in a squad of 23 was not nice for him. To have him on call at home was fine by me.' Beckham needed another X-ray and Dyer was nowhere near fit. It was tempting to replace one of them, at least, but Eriksson denied that their selection had been too much of a risk. After all, he had been prepared to take an even bigger one. He explained: 'The Sunday before we left England, when I got the phone call from Liverpool, withdrawing Steven Gerrard, I said to Gerard Houllier: "I'm willing to gamble – let me have him and we'll see." But Houllier wouldn't do it. Gerrard was out, and that was it. I didn't agree with that. When you go to a big tournament, like the World Cup, you should take your best players and leave the decision about their fitness as late as possible. I told Liverpool that, but they wouldn't have it.' Eriksson would go no further on the subject, leaving it to other sources at the FA to confirm that he was 'very upset' about the circumstances in which he had lost one of the four England players he regarded as 'world class'.

Liverpool had nursed Gerrard through the season since February, when he first reported his groin problem. The feeling in the England camp was that he could have been nursed through the World Cup, had he been rested for the last Premier League game. Alternatively, the operation Gerrard needed could have been performed in February. After the tournament, in mid-July, the player himself admitted he could have gone with England and 'played through the pain barrier', but added that, in his opinion, he could not have done himself justice.

By Thursday 23 May, the injury situation had

gone from bad to worse. Just before the end of training, Murphy went up for a header and felt a sharp pain when he landed. He had heard an ominous crack, and an X-ray confirmed his fears. Uncannily, the break was in exactly the same place as Beckham's, and Gary Neville's. The Liverpool midfielder, in as Gerrard's replacement, was also out of the World Cup. Trevor 'Air Miles' Sinclair, who had booked to see the Tyson–Lewis world title fight, had to cancel his trip to Memphis. He was back in the squad. Did Eriksson regret allowing him to leave? 'In one way, yes, but in another way no. He wanted to go home, and I understood why. To be the extra man, waiting for one of his friends to drop out, was not a pleasant situation, but he was very happy to get called back.'

England left Jeju for Japan on a BA charter flight on Saturday 25 May, and were visibly surprised by the scale and warmth of the welcome they received at Osaka–Kansai airport. The Japanese had adopted them as their 'second team', mainly because of David Beckham's huge popularity, and a crowd some 800-strong created hysterical scenes reminiscent of 'Beatlemania' when the players strode from the arrivals hall to the bus that transported them to their hotel on Awaji island.

The following day, England played their final warm-up friendly, against Cameroon. David Seaman (groin) and Ashley Cole (knee) had joined Beckham, Dyer and Butt among the walking wounded, so the team was again at half strength. Nigel Martyn and David James shared the goalkeeping duties, one half apiece. Wes Brown and Wayne Bridge were the full-backs and the preferred 4–4–2 formation also had Joe Cole making his first start, on the right of mid-field, with Emile Heskey deep on the left and Darius Vassell in as Michael Owen's striking partner.

Cameroon, the African champions, were always expected to provide a stiff test, and so it proved. They took the lead after only five minutes, when Martyn misjudged a cross to present Samuel Eto'o with a tap-in, and although Vassell equalized, with his third goal in five internationals, it was no great surprise when Geremi, the Real Madrid wing-back later to join Chelsea, beat James with a 25-yard free-kick for 2–1. England, unimpressive again, could not have complained had it stayed that way, but Robbie Fowler, on for Vassell for the last 15 minutes, burgled a draw in injury-time.

Eriksson felt that in these last two friendlies, the established players had merely gone through the motions, intent on 'looking after themselves', and that only Owen Hargreaves had in any way advanced his cause. 'It was understandable that half a dozen of them, who knew they were going to be in the team anyway, just did as much as they had to do,' the coach said. 'The opposite was true of Hargreaves. He improved a lot, really matured, going into the tournament.'

There was welcome news on the Tuesday, when Eriksson said that both Beckham and Dyer had been able to play a full part in training for the first time, along with Seaman, Ashley Cole and Butt, who were all deemed medically fit. As if by way of celebration, the squad had a barbecue that night at their luxurious seafront retreat. The following day, however, there was a cautionary note introduced by England's Italian fitness coach, Ivan Carminati, who forecast that Beckham would not be properly match fit for 12 days. 'At the moment,' he said, 'David and Kieron Dyer are able to work only with the physiotherapists.' Dyer would not be ready in time to start against Sweden and Beckham, in Carminati's opinion, was only 'fingers crossed' for the second game, against Argentina. 'The doctors tell me that maybe, from Monday, I can start work with David. Then, I hope we have enough time. I'm not thinking about the first game, but maybe the second. He is a real professional and he works out twice a day with the physios. The next step is to test him in contact with the ball. He needs to do that training hard, but for short periods.' Events were to prove Carminati's prognosis spot on.

That same day, Gareth Southgate made another prescient prediction, when he said England would not be able to maintain the high-tempo game that suited them best in the oppressive heat and humidity they would encounter in Japan. He told me: 'There's no way we're going to be able to do it for 90 minutes. In international football, you've got to keep the ball, and in the conditions we're facing that's going to be paramount.' For once, the headlines were being made elsewhere, with two Swedes, Ljungberg and Mellberg, fighting during training, and Roy Keane walking out on the Republic of Ireland squad after a spat with the manager, Mick

McCarthy. 'We've been on the computer, seeing what has been going on,' Southgate said. 'Sven says we're a dull lot by comparison.'

Over the weekend, the newspapers were full of stories raising fresh doubts about Beckham's fitness, and even his participation in the World Cup. The *Sunday People* headline, 'Bye-bye Beckham', was fairly typical. Eriksson pooh-poohed the speculation. 'I don't know where you got all that from,' he said. 'For me, he has never been 50–50 and he has never been out. The doctors, the physios and the masseurs who have been working with him have always thought that he would be fit in time for the Sweden game, and if not, for Argentina at the worst.' It was now largely a case of mind over matter. 'He has to believe that an ordinary tackle won't break the bone again and put him out for the tournament, and maybe for months after that. As long as he believes that, there shouldn't be a problem. He may have a little discomfort, but he can live with that.'

A decision on whether to replace Beckham or Dyer, or conceivably both, had to be taken before the Sweden game, but in truth, Beckham was never going home. Eriksson admits that the sight of the captain leaving would have been a psychological blow of catastrophic proportions. Dyer's case was much less clear cut, and Alan Smith, of Leeds, and Blackburn's David Dunn, were put on stand-by.

Eriksson never grew tired of talking about Beckham, saying, 'Of course there are a lot of questions about him, but you have to understand that he

DAILY Mirror

Friday April 19 2002

NEWSPAPER OF THE YEAR   32p

3am EXCLUSIVE

SVEN & ULRIKA'S SECRET AFFAIR

SEE PAGES 8 AND 9

Yes, we know it's amazing.. read this astonishing story

The story that melted the 'Ice Man' image. News that Sven was having an affair with Ulrika Jonsson gobsmacked the football world.

Sven, looking uncomfortable, does his best to weather the Ulrika storm, in the company of his then live-in girlfriend, Nancy Dell'Olio.

Sven, the ladies man, with the Atomic Kitten pop group, at the launch of T-Mobile in London.

Sven and Adam Crozier, the Football Association's chief executive at the time, meet Prime Minister Tony Blair at Downing Street in May 2002.

All England holds its breath. Playing for Manchester United in the Champions League, David Beckham sustains the broken foot that threatened his participation in the World Cup.

Sven models England's World Cup suit in London in April 2002. At the press conference that followed, he was grilled about his love life.

There was much criticism of Sven's money-making ventures before the World Cup, such as this launch of two Playstation games.

Sven and his daughter, Lina, swimming in a Swedish lake during a family holiday in 1997.

Happy days in Rome. Sven, in a Lazio tracksuit, is pictured with his parents and daughter Lina, and some of her friends.

Above Just smile and tell them nothing. Sven addresses the world's media in Japan.
Right Concern mounts as David Beckham battles for fitness at England's pre-tournament base, on Jeju island.

Danny Mills, who had a good World Cup as Gary Neville's replacement, won this tussle with Brazil's Roberto Carlos.

Michael Owen lifts the ball deftly over Marcos to open the scoring in the quarter-final against Brazil. If only...

Disaster strikes. Ronaldinho's long-range free-kick loops over David Seaman, and England are on their way out.

Never reluctant to voice his opinion, Sir Alex Ferguson was unhappy about England's insistence on taking the injured David Beckham to Dubai in 2002.

Back home, in Stockholm, Sven takes part in a question and answer forum. The big one is: How long will he carry on with England?

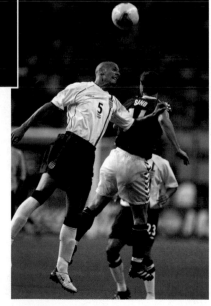

Rio Ferdinand was England's best player at the 2002 World Cup.

England 1 France 0, Euro 2004 group match, and a chance to put the game out of reach with a penalty. Barthez's save from the England captain was a portent of things to come.

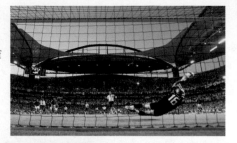

Rooneymania hits town, as the star of the championships slots in a cool second goal against Croatia.

It all had to end in tears. A frustrated Sven consoles Darius Vassell, another England missed-penalty victim, as Portugal end English dreams.

As if the football wasn't bad enough, the England manager's private life was soon to come under the microscope again. Sweet FA.

is one of the leading figures in world football today. I'm not sure who is the most famous – him, Zidane or Ronaldo. He's on that level, so it's big news whatever he does.' He added that only one player under his management had ever attracted similar levels of interest: 'Falcao at Roma in 1984. When he was injured, his fitness was a concern for maybe half the world.'

By Thursday, the players knew the team that would be starting the tournament against Sweden. They had not been told, but it was apparent from the eleven who were practising in yellow training bibs against the rest. For public consumption, both Beckham and Dyer had yet to prove their fitness, but it was made plain through the 'usual channels' that the captain was playing and that the Newcastle midfielder would be among the substitutes. No extra players would be summoned before the deadline for replacements.

Eriksson admitted that Beckham was 'only 95 per cent fit' (that proved to be a major exaggeration), but added 'Beckham at 95 per cent is not bad.' It was an acceptable risk to play him. 'I don't think I'm gambling with David. Maybe with Dyer, but when you're talking about a top, world-class player who can make that difference and win a game for you, you should give him every chance.'

The coach had watched countless videos of his countrymen in action, in draws with Greece, Switzerland, Norway and Japan, and a 4–1 defeat by Paraguay, whom England had beaten 4–0 at Anfield in April. What he had seen only buttressed his opinion of the Swedes as 'a team that always plays the same way, 4–4–2, and works very hard'. Their traditional characteristics had remained unchanged for years. 'Normally, they play a diamond shape in midfield and put a lot of pressure on the opponent on the ball. It is difficult to get past their midfield, and even harder to get behind their back line, because they defend so deep. They are very compact, and possibly the quickest around at getting at least eight players back goalside when they lose possession. They are extremely good at doing that, and that's why it is so difficult to counter-attack against them if you're not very quick up front.' Michael Owen's pace would be key. 'It would be hard to find anyone faster,' Eriksson said. Beckham's reaction to the first tackle was also important. 'But he mustn't think about that. If he does, he'll pull out of the challenge, and if you do that, the chances of getting injured are even greater. From what I've seen in training, he's not afraid at all.'

Some said Beckham was whistling in the dark, still unsure of the hidden dangers lurking in that first stray boot, but the man himself went into the match in bullish mood. Leading England out in the World Cup would be his proudest moment in football. 'I'm a patriotic person,' he said, 'and it is going to be a special occasion for me.' Beckham also felt that England were better than they had been in 1998. 'In the past, there have been times when players have gone out on the pitch feeling nervous. With this team, there's no nerves.' Eriksson had played his part in that respect. 'The manager definitely helps,' his captain said. 'Around the hotel, he is very laid back, and makes all the players, and everyone who comes into contact with him, feel at ease.'

CHAPTER TWENTY-THREE

'CHEER UP, IT'S NOT A FUNERAL'

The opening game in the World Cup is, by tradition, a sterile stalemate, with both teams more interested in avoiding defeat than winning, but there are exceptions, and on Friday 31 May 2002 the tone was set for the 'Tournament of Upsets'. France, beginning the defence of their title in Seoul, against Senegal, were odds-on favourites to win the game, despite the absence through injury of two of their best creative players, Robert Pires and Zinedine Zidane. How badly they were to be missed was soon to become apparent.

France had not had to travel far to check on the opposition from their erstwhile colony – 21 of the 23 players in the Senegalese squad earned their living in the French league – yet still the defending champions appeared to be caught unawares by the skill and verve of the Africans who, before an enraptured audience of 62,651, won 1–0 with a goal scored by Pape Bouba Diop. It was reminiscent of Italia '90, when the opening game saw the champions, Argentina, laid low by another unheralded African country, Cameroon.

On Saturday 1 June, in Niigata, Japan – the Cameroon of 2002 – went 1–0 up against a Republic of Ireland side shamefully deserted by their captain Roy Keane, but the Irish staged a fighting comeback in the second half and Matt Holland earned them a deserved and creditable draw. Elsewhere, in Sapporo, Germany put eight past a shambolic Saudi Arabia and Denmark beat Uruguay 2–1. The World Cup was up and running; meanwhile England waited and hoped that David Beckham would be, too.

Eriksson said that he had no problem trying to plot the defeat of his homeland. It was 'odd', but it hadn't troubled him. 'I wasn't worried about it more than any other game,' he insisted. 'Not at all.' He was more concerned by the mood in the dressing room before the game. 'In the World Cup,' he said, 'you have to be in the dressing room at least an hour and a half before the kick-off, which is a long time.' Time for all sorts of negative thoughts to invade his players' minds. 'I wanted to see some smiles and a few little jokes in there. Not worried faces. If you worry for an hour and a half, you'll use up a lot of mental energy.' I told him Beckham had said the England team were too young and too confident to be nervous. 'Did he really say that? I think one or two may have been nervous, but generally he is right. As a team, they just wanted to get out there and perform. They couldn't wait for their World Cup to start. To the young players, who hadn't played much international football, I said: "Don't be afraid, go out and play football as I know you can. I know what you can do – that's why I picked you."'

The dressing-room joker, who eased the tension, was England's consultant physician, Dr John Crane. With 20 years in the job, he was able to regale the players with tall tales of bygone days. 'He is a very good story-teller,' Eriksson said, smiling. 'He helped to put everybody at ease.' There was a time for laughter and a time for seriousness, however. 'Just before the team goes out to play,' Eriksson said, 'there are no more jokes. It is time for this [he screwed up his face and shook a clenched fist, knowing the actions would express his feelings better than words]. All of them do it, and it's good to see the players who are on the bench joining in and wishing good luck to those who are starting. That's team spirit.' He could always tell if his players were 'up for it', explaining: 'During the warm-up on the pitch, and back in the dressing room after the warm-up, you can feel if it's a good day and everyone is right.'

The pre-match routine never varied. 'Fifteen minutes before leaving the hotel, we have a team talk,' Eriksson said. 'There's a lot of repetition in that, to ingrain things. Things like how we attack while keeping our shape, how we defend with the midfield players getting behind the ball and the most important facts about the opposition. That takes a maximum of ten minutes. Then we leave for the stadium, and once we get into the dressing room I go round giving some last advice to individuals. I talk to them all, to some for less than 30 seconds, maybe two minutes to others, it depends on what they need. When there is a new player in for the first time – a Joe Cole or Darius Vassell – of course I talk to them a bit more. Then, as they run out, I'll say "Good luck" and two or three other words. It's always like that.'

For the game against Sweden, the extra words were 'Don't be afraid.' Eriksson explained: 'That was going to be very important. I didn't want them afraid of the occasion, the crowd, or the many millions watching the match on television. I told them: "It's just a football game – go out and play football, enjoy yourselves." The 23 players were our 23, and it was a great honour for all of them. They were representing a great football country. I told them: "Whether you play for the full 90 minutes in all the games or for two minutes in one, you're out here, playing in the World Cup. It doesn't get much bigger than that – the biggest event in football."'

Eriksson felt it was vital England got off to a good start. 'We had to be big at once. I mean, Sweden, Argentina and Nigeria – where was the easy one there? I couldn't find it. If we started slowly, our World Cup could be over very quickly. Our quality had to show through right from the start. Tactics and physical conditioning were important, but without quality a team won't survive.'

The starting line-up for the first match saw Hargreaves preferred to Butt as the midfield 'anchor' and Heskey given first crack at the problem position on the left. Vassell, impressive in the preparatory friendlies, would partner Owen in attack. Sweden, like England, had a late scare over their key midfielder, but Freddy Ljungberg, who had injured a hip during training, was passed fit to play in a team featuring seven players who earned their living in Britain.

ENGLAND 1 SWEDEN 1

Saitama, 2 June.

England: Seaman (Arsenal), Mills (Leeds United), Ferdinand (Leeds United), Campbell (Arsenal), A Cole (Arsenal), Beckham (Manchester United, captain), Hargreaves (Bayern Munich), Scholes (Manchester United), Heskey (Liverpool), Vassell (Aston Villa), Owen (Liverpool). Substitutes: Dyer (Newcastle United) for Beckham 62 minutes, J Cole (West Ham) for Vassell 73.

Sweden: Hedman (Coventry City), Mellberg (Aston Villa), Jakobsson (Hansa Rostock), Mjallby (Celtic), Lucic (AIK Solna), N Alexandersson (Everton), Linderoth (Everton), Magnus Svensson (Brondby), Ljungberg (Arsenal), Allback (Aston Villa), Larsson (Celtic). Substitutes: A Svensson (Southampton) for Magnus Svensson 76 minutes, A Andersson (AIK Solna) for Allback 72.

Referee: C Simon (Brazil).

It was like a home game for England, whose huge popularity with the Japanese public gave them more than 80 per cent of the support in a noisily enthusiastic crowd of 52,721. The heat (84°F) and humidity (40 per cent) were oppressive, despite the 6.30pm kick-off, but the Swedes were not used to the conditions either. England began well, passing the ball around crisply, and were rewarded for their superiority after 25 minutes, when Campbell rose above Olof Mellberg to head in Beckham's corner from the left. Ashley Cole, shooting from 25 yards, and Ferdinand, from another Beckham corner, threatened to improve the lead, and after half an hour England seemed well set for the win they needed. In the ten minutes leading up to half-time, however, the initiative changed sides. Beckham, said to be 95 per cent fit, was clearly well short of that, and tired badly, and Hargreaves also ran out of steam, enabling the Swedes to take charge in midfield.

Eriksson had strong words with his players during the interval, telling them in no uncertain terms what the consequences would be if they continued to cede the midfield and defend on the edge of their 18-yard area. Unfortunately, nobody took heed, and the longer the game went on, the more England missed the organizing skills of Gary Neville, whose underrated abilities include chivvying the back four to push out.

In the second half, England were always a poor second best, and there was an air of inevitability about the Swedes' equalizer, after 59 minutes, when Mills' maladroit clearance fell nicely for Everton's Niclas Alexandersson, who cut inside and beat Seaman with the sort of shot that brooks no intervention. England's shape and form disintegrated to an alarming degree, their only response to mounting adversity to entrench in a penalty area that began to resemble the Alamo fortress. Their cause was hardly helped by a couple of baffling substitutions, Eriksson swapping one half-fit crock for another by sending on Dyer in place of Beckham, then withdrawing Vassell, when it was Owen who was plainly out of sorts.

With bad going to worse, it needed a couple of top-notch saves by Seaman, both from Teddy Lucic, and a profligate miss by Celtic's Henrik Larsson, to spare England from a potentially calamitous defeat. The mood in the dressing room afterwards was funereal, all the players staring forlornly at the floor, avoiding each other's gaze, too shocked by their inadequacy, both collective and individual, to speak. Eriksson was worried by the atmosphere, which was negative to the point of depression. It was a time to coax, not to criticize. 'What's wrong in here?' he said. 'This isn't a funeral. You haven't lost, you've got a valuable point. You can go on and qualify from here.'

The players weren't so sure, and neither were the press. Some well-respected critics rushed to judgement. Paul Hayward, the sportswriter of the year, wrote in the *Daily Telegraph*: 'This was an English performance not to sadden but to enrage. For 45 minutes it was crude, regressive and redolent of many previous doomed foreign adventures. What we saw here last night was a spectacular failure of philosophy or intelligence.' The *Daily Mail*'s Jeff Powell, never an Eriksson fan, wrote: 'He looked utterly lost, rather than his usual, inscrutable self. The manager's tactical inertia was in conspicuous contrast to the commercial eagerness with which he is advertising enough products to open his own department store. Unless Eriksson can invest his day job with equal variety, not to mention urgency, then the lasting image of England's World Cup 2002 will be that of a travelling salesman scratching his head in bewilderment.' The *Sun* joined in with the front page headline: 'It's Not The End Of the World (It Just Feels Like It).'

Looking back on the match, Eriksson told me: 'When we had problems in the second half, we lost a little bit of our faith in what we were doing. At the final whistle, if you looked at the two teams, it seemed like Sweden had won an important game and that we'd lost. The fact was that it was 1–1, and one point each. Coming into the dressing room, there was not a word said, and all the heads were down. It was important to overcome that as quickly as possible. It wasn't all over after Sweden, we weren't going home. We had two more games to get it right. They were a sad team when they came off, and that's not good. I was worried until they started to pick up as we travelled back to the hotel. I had a good reaction from them at practice the next day, and the confidence came back. I don't remember exactly what I said to them, but I know I mentioned that with one point from one game, it was up to them. They could still win the group, but only if they kept their heads up.'

What had gone wrong in the second half? 'It's very difficult to say why it happened. Sweden were a bit more aggressive, and we couldn't handle it. When you can't keep the ball, everything breaks down.' There had been widespread criticism of England's long-ball game, but Eriksson insisted that this was a case of effect rather than cause. 'You must have options to pass it short. A defender needs good options, otherwise he can't pass into midfield because the risk of losing possession is too great. Our defenders didn't have those options, or at least very few of them. We played it through the midfield in the first half, but couldn't do it in the second.'

He had told the players at half-time that they were defending too deep, so why had they persisted? 'It wasn't a case of going out there and not following instructions. They tried, but sometimes your opponents make things too difficult for you, and if you can't keep the ball, everything else falls down. If you want your defence to push up, you have to keep possession, otherwise they can't. If you lose the ball again and again in midfield, it makes those playing in the back line reluctant to come out as quickly as they should.'

Beckham's fitness was a cause for concern, with the captain never more than a peripheral figure against the Swedes, but Eriksson had thought that another five days would see an improvement in the second game, against Argentina. He said: 'Considering he had been out for seven weeks, I think he did well in the first half. He kept the ball and his passing was good.' Nevertheless, it was disturbing that he had shown a marked reluctance to run with it.

Butt was to be brought in against Argentina, and given an important part to play. 'Like Beckham, he was coming back after injury, and I thought it was too dangerous to pick more than one player like that. He was much fitter by the Friday.' The South Americans, favourites with France to win the tournament, were a much different proposition. 'They're not as aggressive as Sweden, and they don't play that same direct football,' Eriksson said. 'They present other problems. They are very talented individually. They have a lot of skilful players, and some quick ones, too.' Veron was a particular favourite, having played for him at Sampdoria and Lazio. 'Veron can do everything,' his old mentor said. 'He is the complete footballer. People forget that he can defend extremely well, sitting in front of the back line. He is prepared to do that, but his best skills are his vision and his passing. When I saw him playing for Manchester United, for the first couple of months I thought he was fantastic.'

There were other 'danger men', of course, and Eriksson reeled them off. Of Gabriel Batistuta, a prolific striker of worldwide renown, he said: 'I never had him play for me, but I know him very well from Italy. He is a great goalscorer, who can get them from any angle and every position, and a good header of the ball. He is strong and powerful, and if he is challenged by a defender, he won't be moved. He's like a block of granite coming at you.' Hernan Crespo was 'technically better than Batistuta', his 'extra movement' making him a potent threat, and Claudio Lopez had 'incredible pace'. Ariel Ortega was similar – 'he's very quick and can beat his man' – while Beckham's bête noire, Diego Simeone, was 'a hard worker, tactically excellent'.

Although he made them sound invincible, Eriksson always thought England could beat them. 'There were negative aspects to their game which I knew we could exploit.' First, however, he had to raise his own players' spirits. 'That was even more important than playing 4–4–2, 4–3–3 or keeping the ball. If you don't have the right mentality, if you go out there feeling like a loser, then you're going to lose.' There was work to be done on the training ground, but first there was a day off. 'It was organized before the Sweden game, and you can't just talk, think and practise football for 18 hours every day. That won't make you play any better.'

Some went shopping, others played golf, then together they all went for a meal at the Hard Rock Café. 'It was an amazing experience,' Joe Cole said. 'We were just out having something to eat, and there were people screaming and crying at us. A lot of it was for "Becks", but it's nice to think that maybe a little bit of it was for you.'

When training resumed, Eriksson used a tape of the Sweden match to show his team where they had gone wrong. 'It was instructive to put the video on, show the Swedish goalkeeper taking a goal kick and pause the film to show the players their positions on the field. Often they were in the wrong place, and you can't argue with a video. Everyone agreed with what I was telling them, we had a talk about it, and then we went out to work on it on the pitch.'

Specifically, and crucially as it turned out, he had asked for more movement from Michael Owen, who had been too static, and therefore too easy to contain, against the Swedes. 'I talked to Michael about it, reassured him that he was 100 per cent fit and free of injury, and said he could do the job like he used to, when he was at his very best. In fairness, it's not easy for him to play up there when the ball is up in the air all the time. That's not Michael Owen's game.'

Nobody had looked forward to the Argentina match more eagerly than the England captain, who had been sent off against them at the 1998 World Cup, in France. 'That haunted me for a while,' Beckham said. 'It was the biggest downer of my career. [Diego] Maradona said in an interview the other day that they weren't better footballers than us, they were just more cunning, and I think maybe that's right.' The heat was on, in more ways than one, but he could handle it. 'When pressure is thrown at me, I can kick it straight back. I feel proud to be England captain, and to know that there are so many people back home willing us on to do well. Everyone is patriotic about the national team, they've proved that since we qualified. The atmosphere in the country has totally turned around since, and rightly so.' Beckham was confident of his team's chances. 'If we get through the first stage, anything could happen. We've got a good team, and our expectations are high.'

The Argentinians' mood bordered on arrogance in Sapporo, where they shared the Sheraton hotel with the English media. Both Gabriel Batistuta and Juan-Sebastian Veron refused to acknowledge my greeting when we met in the lift, and other guests complained of the same disdainful attitude. This surliness was typified when a wedding reception was held at the hotel, and the bride and groom were kept waiting, behind a phalanx of security guards, while the Argentina squad sauntered in from the team bus after training. There was a danger, presumably, that Veron and company might be injured by confetti. It was not only England who had their free days, when they could do as they pleased, and the Argentinians spent the Monday before the match at the beach, with wives and family. Matias Almeyda, who had played for Sven-Goran Eriksson at Lazio, said: 'As ever, England will never give up, and we're expecting a tough game. They're quick and good in the air, but we're trying not to think too much about them and focus on ourselves instead.'

Elsewhere, the surprises continued in what was becoming known as the 'Wobbly World Cup'. On 5 June, a remarkable 3–2 victory by the United States over Portugal stole the limelight from the battling Irish, who had gained a 1–1 draw with Germany, courtesy of Robbie Keane's injury-time equalizer.

The following day, a crowd of 250-plus, most of them screaming schoolgirls, greeted the England squad on arrival at their hotel outside Sapporo. Eriksson and David Beckham were presented with large bouquets of flowers by hotel staff. Keiko Tokita, a hotel receptionist, who made the presentation to Beckham, said: 'It is a day I will never forget. He did not speak to me, but he smiled. I will remember it forever.'

Over at the Argentinian hotel meanwhile, the team's manager, Bielsa, was telling a press conference that he had noted Sol Campbell's aerial prowess at setpieces. 'We'll have to deal with the ball in the air,' he said. 'They're good at crossing and heading. It is going to be a physical battle, but we are fit for that.'

CHAPTER TWENTY-FOUR

REVENGE

ARGENTINA 0   ENGLAND 1

Sapporo, 7 June.

Argentina: Cavallero (Celta Vigo), Pochettino (Paris St Germain), Samuel (Roma), Placente (Bayer Leverkusen), Zanetti (Internazionale), Simeone (Lazio), Veron (Manchester United), Sorin (Cruzeiro), Ortega (River Plate), Batistuta (Roma), Gonzalez (Valencia). Substitutes: Aimar (Valencia) for Veron half-time, Crespo (Lazio) for Batistuta 60 minutes, C Lopez (Lazio) for Gonzalez 65.

England: Seaman (Arsenal), Mills (Leeds United), Ferdinand (Leeds United), Campbell (Arsenal), A Cole (Arsenal), Beckham (Manchester United, captain), Butt (Manchester United), Hargreaves (Bayern Munich), Scholes (Manchester United), Owen (Liverpool), Heskey (Liverpool). Substitutes: Sinclair (West Ham) for Hargreaves 19 minutes, Sheringham (Tottenham) for Heskey 56, Bridge (Southampton) for Owen 80.

Referee: P Collina (Italy).

It was with some relief that England learned of the appointment of Italy's Pierluigi Collina, the best referee in the world, whose expertise was going to be invaluable in a match in which there was going to be so much going on, both on and off the ball.

The usual rituals were observed, both sets of supporters booing their opponents' national anthem, and so on, before what was billed as the Great Grudge Match finally got under way.

Gabriel Batistuta had just been booked, for bowling over Ashley Cole, when England were forced to make a substitution which turned out to their advantage. Owen Hargreaves had not begun well in midfield, and when injury forced him to withdraw, after only 19 minutes, the consequent reshuffle brought about a significant improvement. Trevor Sinclair, on for Hargreaves, went to the left, which meant Paul Scholes moving into centre midfield alongside Nicky Butt. Eureka! Scholes and Butt together made short work of subduing Veron, their Manchester United teammate, so much so that Argentina's captain and playmaker suffered the indignity of being substituted at half-time.

England, meanwhile, were more than holding their own, and midway through the first half Michael Owen, whose darting pace was worrying the Argentinian defence to the point of distraction, rattled a post, shooting from right to left. Batistuta and Kily Gonzalez threatened David Seaman, but it was no more than England deserved when they went ahead just before half-time. Owen, on yet another menacing run, was brought down just inside the penalty area by Mauricio Pochettino, and Beckham strode forward to take the kick. Collina, surprisingly, allowed the Argentinian goalkeeper, Pablo Cavallero, and Beckham's old adversary, Diego Simeone, to get away with some protracted gamesmanship before the England captain was finally able to beat Cavallero with a nerveless, straight shot.

Argentina replaced Veron with Pablo Aimar for the second half, and the substitution had the desired effect, enlivening their midfield, but England's confidence was up, and they might have scored again before eventually being forced into what-we-have-we-hold mode. Owen was inches wide, Scholes brought a notable save from Cavallero, Beckham fired into the side netting and then Teddy Sheringham, on for Emile Heskey, was desperately close to scoring what might well have been the goal of the tournament. Applying a volleyed finish to a glorious passing move, he was denied by Cavallero's reaching fingertips.

Argentina, cranking up for a big push, sent on Hernan Crespo and Claudio Lopez for Batistuta and Kily Gonzalez around the hour mark, but England continued to defend as if their lives depended on it, with Rio Ferdinand and Sol Campbell in unbeatable form, and wave after wave of increasingly frantic Argentinian pressure broke upon these twin rocks.

At the final whistle, you would have thought England had won the cup. After observing the traditional niceties by offering to swap shirts (the Argentinian players brusquely declined) and saluting their fans, Beckham and his team sprinted down the tunnel to their dressing room whooping and hollering words to the effect: 'That's for St Etienne and four years ago.' There were two incidents after the match, one amusing, the other rather less so. As

Scholes stood talking to English journalists outside
the dressing rooms, two Argentinian players deliberately barged into him from behind, one muttering
the word 'bastardo'. Then Sinclair, still up on cloud
nine, mistakenly boarded the Argentina team bus.
'I was rushing around a bit late – I was one of
those routinely drug-tested after the game – and
charging out of the stadium, I walked straight on
to their coach. Their guys were all on there and
there wasn't too much smiling going on, so I made
a sharp exit.'

It was a tremendous, historic result – the first
tournament victory over Argentina since the fabled
year of 1966. An omen, perhaps? Of the winning
penalty, Beckham said: 'It was the sweetest moment
in my career.' Invited to elaborate, he explained:
'After what happened last time, that game meant
so much to me, and to my family. To the whole
country, in fact. As a footballing nation, we'd been
waiting for that result for a long time, and it was
so nice that it came at the World Cup finals.' How
did it compare with the 5–1 drubbing of Germany
in Munich? 'It definitely beat that. Germany was a
massive result for us, but there is a lot of history to
England v Argentina.'

There were heroes everywhere, Owen, Butt,
Scholes and the much-maligned Danny Mills among
them, but first among equals was Ferdinand, who
had played the game of his life. I interviewed him
straight after the game, when he said: 'The players
all agreed that we had to dig deep and get a win,
considering Sweden had beaten Nigeria [2–1] earlier

in the day. We really had the bit between our teeth. There's a lot of history to this fixture. We're not the sort of lads to mock them, the way they rubbed our noses in it four years earlier, but revenge was definitely sweet. We always thought we had a chance to do well in the tournament, and beating the favourites can only enhance that feeling.'

During the preparation, Eriksson had concentrated on ingraining the need for positional discipline. 'We didn't have the right shape in the second half against Sweden, and that was the main reason why we didn't do well,' Ferdinand said. 'Sticking to our shape and organization was the difference against Argentina. They squeezed us, but we stayed hard to break down. We knew we could do it if everybody worked as a team, rather than as individuals.' He confirmed that there had been some wild scenes in the immediate aftermath of victory. 'You can imagine what it was like,' he told me. 'Everyone enjoyed it, but it stopped short of getting out of hand. We've got to enjoy moments like this. You could tell, coming off the pitch and in the dressing room afterwards, what it meant to the senior players who played in that game at St Etienne. It's nice just to pause and let it all soak in.'

Beckham revealed that he had warned his teammates what to expect from the Argentinians just before they went out to play. 'I said it was going to be hostile out there, and that there would be certain provocative things going on. You saw that when we got the penalty. They played a few little tricks on me then [Cavallero told him where to place the kick and

Simeone tried to shake his hand], and it was nice to see the ball go in the back of the net.' What had gone through his mind during the interminable delay? 'Different flashbacks from four years ago,' he said. 'I have to admit it was an emotional time when the ball went in. Our fans deserved it more than anyone because the whole stadium seemed to be full of England supporters.' Danny Mills, the combative Leeds full-back, whose temperament had been questioned before the tournament, had not only played well, he had been a model of restraint. Afterwards, he revealed the extent of Argentinian provocation. He said: 'When you're wiping phlegm off your face for a second time, having been hurt by a stray elbow only minutes earlier, it takes a fair degree of discipline not to lose your cool.'

The footballing perspective was provided best by the *Daily Telegraph*, whose correspondent, Henry Winter, wrote: 'This was an enchanted evening when England eschewed the long ball for the intelligent one, for the pass that kept the ball in England's possession. This, ultimately, was a victory for Eriksson, whose order to his players to press, press and press again ensured Argentina never settled on the ball. Some people had questioned Eriksson's tactics and his selections – indeed his suitability to manage England. But, showing remarkable sang-froid under pressure, the Swede confirmed why Adam Crozier, David Dein and the Football Association were so right to employ him. His calmness ensured that the players never panicked, despite Sunday's disappointment against

Sweden. His coaching nous prepared them perfectly.'

Eriksson was reminded of the fact that at Munich and Sapporo he had, in the space of nine months, led England to two of their biggest results for years. 'They were two very good victories,' he said, with typical understatement. 'It wouldn't be easy for any team to go to Germany and win 5–1, and Argentina were the favourites for the World Cup when we played them. You just had to look at their bench to see how strong they were. They had Crespo, Lopez, Chamot, Ayala and Almeyda among their substitutes.'

His renowned composure had deserted him for once during the heart-in-the-mouth closing stages. 'I can tell you I wasn't calm at all for the last ten minutes, even if it seemed like I was. Balls were coming into our penalty from everywhere, Argentina were pouring forward and we were tired.' His third and final substitution, sending on a full-back, Wayne Bridge, in place of Owen, reflected the need to relieve a hard-pressed defence. 'I was sitting there, knowing I had one more sub, and Argentina were all over us, so I had to make the midfield stronger. Maybe I let them come at us even more, because they no longer had Michael's pace to worry their defence, but it turned out to be the right decision. If they had equalized, of course, then I would have been wrong.'

The contrast between the performances against Sweden and Argentina had been marked. The question now was: had the Swedes made England look bad, or had England played that badly? 'It was a combination of the two,' Eriksson said. 'In the second half against Sweden we lost our positional discipline and our shape and ended up playing 4–2–4. I told the players that if they were going to do that against Argentina, it would be better not to play the game, because they would murder us.' The response had been excellent. 'The players did exactly what I'd asked of them.' He had been particularly pleased with Owen's contribution. 'That was the real Michael Owen – the way we want to see him play always. Not just waiting up there for the ball, but dropping off and going left and right . . . It's difficult to play against Michael Owen if you don't know where he is going to pop up next. If you know he is only going to stay up there, fighting for the ball with a big centre-half, then it's much easier. He played really well, and could have had a couple of goals with a bit more luck. He was everywhere, and every time he was in one-against-one situations, he took advantage.'

Argentina now had to play Sweden in their third game, and could easily run into the same difficulties England had experienced against them. 'It is a tricky one for both teams,' Eriksson said. 'It's not easy against Sweden, they don't let you play your football.' For England, the decisive third match was against the demoralized Nigerians, who had lost their first two games, to Argentina (1–0) and Sweden (2–1), and were already out. England, with four points, almost certainly needed only a draw to go through, but Eriksson was taking nothing for granted. 'Because of their situation, it is difficult to say how Nigeria will approach the game, but like all other footballers they have their pride, and they won't want to go home with no points. Often it is easier to play with no pressure. They've got nothing to lose, so they can go out and have fun. We've got to be on our guard, because there have been some strange results in this World Cup.' As if to prove his point, Italy promptly went out and lost 2–1 to Croatia and Japan made history with their first win at any finals, beating Russia 1–0.

Hargreaves would not be available for the Nigeria game, because of the damage to his shin. Eriksson, however, was increasingly upbeat as the squad moved on from Sapporo to Osaka. Anything was possible if England got through the so-called 'Group of Death', he said. 'And I mean anything. You never know what might happen. All the games are very tight, and as all the teams get more and more tired, anything can happen.' In manager-speak, this meant England could go all the way, and his comments were relayed under headlines such as 'Sven: We Can Reach The Final'.

Nigeria made all the right noises before their farewell appearance. 'The England game is very important for our people and our pride,' said their captain, 'Jay-Jay' Okocha, who was to retire from international football after the game. The coach, Adegboye Onigbinde, agreed, saying there was no question of using the match to give his reserves a taste of the World Cup. Had he done so, we would hardly have noticed the difference.

NIGERIA 0   ENGLAND 0
Osaka, 12 June.
Nigeria: Enyeama (Enyimba), Yobo (Marseille), Okoronkwo (Shakhtar Donesk), Okocha (Paris St Germain, captain), Udeze (PAOK Salonika), Christopher (Royal Antwerp), Sodje (Crewe Alexandra), Aghahowa (Shakhtar Donesk), Akwuegbu (Shenyang Haishi), Obiorah (Lokomotiv Moscow), Opabunmi (3SC Ibadan). Substitutes: Ikedia (Ajax) for Opabunmi 86 minutes.
England: Seaman (Arsenal), Mills (Leeds United), Ferdinand (Leeds United), Campbell (Arsenal), A Cole (Arsenal), Beckham (Manchester United, captain), Butt (Manchester United), Scholes (Manchester United), Sinclair (West Ham), Owen (Liverpool), Heskey (Liverpool). Substitutes: Sheringham (Tottenham) for Heskey 68 minutes, Vassell (Aston Villa) for Owen 76, Bridge (Southampton) for A Cole 84.
Referee: B Hall (United States).

England have never lost to African opposition, and that record was in no real danger here. It was hot (93°F) and humid, but the conditions were no problem at the sedate pace at which the game was played. The Nigerians 'huddled' interminably on the pitch before the kick-off, their show of unity beginning to look like a weary reluctance to start. Again, it was like a home game for England, the stadium decorated with flags and banners from the football hotbeds of Crawley, Bexhill, Kettering and Swindon.

A desultory first half saw Scholes shiver a post from 25 yards and Owen have a goal-bound shot deflected wide while Benedict Akwuegbu came closest for Nigeria. But there was more interest in the news from the other game, where Argentina were drawing 0–0 with Sweden at half-time. It suited England's purpose to have the Swedes put out Argentina, and after an hour the gleeful chant '1–0 to the Sweden' rang round the ground, in response to the news than Southampton's Anders Svensson had opened the scoring in Miyagi. England and Nigeria, meanwhile, had settled for a draw, and were doing little more than play out time. A left-wing cross from Ashley Cole that ran along the cross-bar was the nearest anybody came to a goal, and Eriksson's intentions were plain when he started counting down the clock by means of hand-signalled gestures to his team. It all became rather less cosy and comfortable when Crespo equalized for Argentina, after 88 minutes, which meant that if Nigeria scored, England would be out. Mentally, however, the Africans were already on the flight home, and were not about to cause trouble. A goal-less bore was never pretty, but it was effective. England had safely negotiated 'The Group of Death' and were through to the knockout stages, as runners-up to Sweden. Eriksson was unapologetic. 'It was a comfortable game,' he said. 'Getting through to the next round was our target, and we knew 0–0 was OK, so we didn't attack too much and risk losing the ball unnecessarily. That would have been crazy. I was kept informed throughout the match by Paul Newman about what was happening in the other match. Obviously the score in Miyagi had an impact on our game.'

Argentina, the favourites, were out, as were the holders, France, beaten 2–0 by Denmark at Incheon the previous day. Beckham, echoing Eriksson's comments about his team's potential, said: 'Two of the biggest threats have gone out, which has opened it up a lot.' Suddenly, anything really did look possible.

Going into the tournament, conventional wisdom had it that if England were runners-up in Group F, they would play France, who were expected to win Group A. But there was nothing conventional about this World Cup. The French were out, having finished bottom of their group, without a goal in their three games. Denmark, who had sealed the holders' fate, were to be England's opponents, and deserved the utmost respect. Apart from France, they had beaten Uruguay 2–1 and drawn 1–1 with Senegal. Like Sweden, their Scandinavian neighbours, the Danes' team spirit and belief in an uncomplicated method somehow made the whole add up to more than the sum of its parts. History was on England's side (of 14 previous matches between the two countries, they had won eight and lost only one), but nobody was taking anything for granted – especially not Eriksson. He expected such a tight game that, for the first time, England practised penalties in their last training session, in readiness for extra-time and a shoot-out. The five chosen men were David Beckham, Michael Owen, Paul Scholes, Rio Ferdinand and Teddy Sheringham. In the dress rehearsal, Sheringham was the only one who missed.

Denmark's success in winning their group was founded on the reliable goalkeeping of Sunderland's Thomas Sorensen and a nicely balanced midfield, which had a ball winner (Bolton's Stig Tofting) and a box-to-box grafter (Thomas Gravesen, of Everton) flanked by two flying wingers, Dennis Rommedahl (PSV Eindhoven) and Jesper Gronkjaer (Chelsea). Rommedahl, who had clocked 10.2 seconds for the 100 metres, had caught the eye time and again during the first three games, as a productive source of supply for the renascent Jon Dahl Tomasson, a striker who had struggled to hit the proverbial barn door during a depressing sojourn at Newcastle before coming good at Feyenoord.

In the two days before the match, Eriksson warned his players of, and paid particular attention to combating, the pace and incisive directness of the Danes' wingers. There was a danger that Danny Mills and Ashley Cole would be pegged back by Gronkjaer and Rommedahl. 'We couldn't let that happen,' he said. 'We couldn't afford to be apprehensive. At the knockout stage, you can become afraid to let the other team score, but I told the players that they had to play their football. We weren't going to change anything. We were getting better and better as the tournament went on.' At this stage, Owen had yet to score at the World Cup. 'I was asked a lot about him, his fitness, his mood and so on,' the coach later recalled. 'I was never worried about him, and always thought he would do it against Denmark.' Owen had shared Eriksson's confidence. 'I'd always had a good record against Thomas Sorensen,' he said.

The Danes had gone into the match playing the underdogs' card for all it was worth, their coach,

Morten Olsen, saying: 'England are the bigger team and must be the favourites.' It has to be said that if 'brave little Denmark' was their approach, then the FA played into their hands. At the press call to preview the match, the Danes put up all 23 players for interview, England not one. The Danish press were more surprised and put out than their English counterparts, who had become accustomed to such scorn. When the *Daily Telegraph* protested, they were told, haughtily: 'Yes, but Denmark have no stars.'

DENMARK 0   ENGLAND 3

Niigata, 15 June.

Denmark: Sorensen (Sunderland), Tofting (Bolton Wanderers), Henriksen (Panathinaikos), Laursen (Milan), Helveg (Milan), Gravesen (Everton), Gronkjaer (Chelsea), Tomasson (Feyenoord), Sand (Schalke 04), N Jensen (Manchester City), Rommedahl (PSV Eindhoven). Substitutes: Bogelund (PSV Eindhoven) for Helveg 7 minutes, C Jensen (Charlton Athletic) for Tofting 58.

England: Seaman (Arsenal), Mills (Leeds United), Ferdinand (Leeds United), Campbell (Arsenal), A Cole (Arsenal), Beckham (Manchester United, captain), Butt (Manchester United), Scholes (Manchester United), Sinclair (West Ham), Owen (Liverpool), Heskey (Liverpool). Substitutes: Fowler (Leeds United) for Owen at half-time, Dyer (Newcastle United) for Scholes 49 minutes, Sheringham (Tottenham) for Cole 80.

Referee: M Merk (Germany).

What was expected to be a tight, tense game turned out to be anything but. In the new Swan Stadium, purpose-built for the World Cup (Niigata didn't even have its own team), the Danes were dead ducks before half-time. England were gifted a flying start when, after five minutes, Sorensen made such a dreadful hash of defending a corner that he dragged the ball into his own net. Beckham took the kick, on the left, and although Ferdinand got up well at the far post, his header was a poor one, and was going wide until the keeper's maladroit intervention. In mitigation, he had been surprised, and forced to readjust his position, by the inaccuracy of what Ferdinand called 'a shit header'.

Own-goal or not, England were up and running while the Danes had sustained a demoralizing body-blow. Before they could clear their heads and recover, they took another, when Milan's Thomas Helveg, an experienced mainstay of their defence, was injured, and had to be substituted after only seven minutes. After such a start, the initiative was very much with England, and Owen and Heskey might have improved the lead before the second goal arrived, midway through the first half. Sinclair played a full part, in the inside-left channel, but it was Butt's deft flick-on that enabled Owen to keep up his record against Sorensen, controlling the ball with his right foot before scoring, from eight yards, with his left.

To their credit, the Danes rolled their sleeves and fought back with great spirit, and the outcome might have been different had Ebbe Sand pulled one back, as he should have done, after 27 minutes. His miss, from routine range, was a bad one, and instead of being back in contention, his team were out for the count just before half-time when Heskey, from the edge of the penalty area, found Sorensen wanting again, with a low shot that went under the keeper's body. The score now 3–0, the game was as good as over.

Peter Schmeichel, a legend in Denmark and one of the world's great goalkeepers, said: 'Our players were so consumed with tension, they forgot to play as a team. Thomas Sorensen was at fault for the first goal, but communication in the defence was very poor, and blame for the defeat did not rest on his shoulders alone. Defensive frailty was to blame for the second goal. Trevor Sinclair was given far too much space, allowing him time to play a dangerous ball into the heart of the penalty area. Nicky Butt then showed great vision in picking out Michael Owen for the goal. I played with Nicky for years at Manchester United, and it amused me when people commented on how well he was playing. Nicky was playing the way he always played. He is world class.

'A lot of people blamed Sorensen for failing to stop Emile Heskey's goal, but he was let down by others around him. He is a very good goalkeeper and has nothing to be ashamed about. The frustrating thing for Denmark was that minutes earlier Ebbe Sand had a wonderful chance. Danny Mills defended very well, dropping back to block the far post, but I expected a player of Ebbe's quality to score. It was a critical time for Denmark, and had the score gone to 2–1, who knows what might have happened. To win games at the World Cup, you have to be focused, committed and lucky. Denmark lacked focus and luck while England had all three.

'A lot of credit had to go to Rio Ferdinand, who had grown up as an individual and as a player, leading Leeds through a difficult season. He is now a truly world-class player at the heart of a solid defence. I had thought Mills and Ashley Cole would have been exploited by the speedy Danes, but the full-backs were a revelation. England played well within themselves, never reaching the intensity that marked their performance against Argentina.'

Victory had not come without a price. Three England players – David Beckham, Emile Heskey and Michael Owen – had been injured, and although it was the captain's troublesome left foot that received most attention from the media, it was Owen's groin strain that was to prove the real problem. Straight after the match, he played it down, insisting his substitution at half-time had been for precautionary reasons, but time was to tell a different story.

In the quarter-finals, England were to face the winners of the second-round clash between Brazil and Belgium, played at Kobe on the Monday 17 June. There was some debate between Eriksson and his staff as to whether the England players should attend the match, the case against being based on the feeling that they might be intimidated by the special aura that surrounds all Brazilian teams. Good sense prevailed – the players went and were encouraged by what they saw.

Belgium, superbly organized and inventive, did Europe proud, and the outcome hinged on a

perfectly good goal by their excellent captain, Marc
Wilmots, which the Jamaican referee, Peter Pren-
dergast, somehow disallowed. Wilmots outjumped
Roque Junior to head firmly past Marcos, the
Brazilian keeper, only to be penalized for a non-
existent push. After watching a television replay of
the incident at half-time, the referee admitted his
mistake, but his apologies were no good to Belgium.
Their fluent, co-ordinated football merited the lead.
Undeterred, Wilmots was back again and again,
his energetic persistence in the heat and humidity
belying his 33 years. Twice around the hour mark
he demanded notable saves from Marcos, and at
this stage there was a certain novelty value to the
story of a Brazilian goalkeeper keeping them in the
tournament.

Well into the second half, Eriksson and his players
were turning their thoughts to ways of countering
Belgian discipline, economy and cohesion, but then
lightning struck, in the svelte shape of Rivaldo. With
his back to goal, Barcelona's favourite adopted
son jumped high, controlled the ball on his chest
and let it drop to his left foot. With a deft flick and
a 180-degree turn he was facing the right way, his
dexterity granting him the time to allow the ball to
bounce before he struck it sweetly goalwards. For
all Rivaldo's masterful execution, Geert De Vlieger,
the Belgian goalkeeper, might have denied him,
but for a deflection off the outstretched boot of
Timmy Simons.

Rivaldo had now scored in each of Brazil's first
four games, and with Belgium forced to push

forward in search of equality, Ronaldo was to match this feat with three minutes remaining. The scoreline, 2–0 to Brazil, looked convincing but the performance was not. There was much sympathy, and quite right, too, for brave Belgium – especially for Wilmots and the goal that got away. Eriksson left the ground confident that England's midfield was more than a match for a Brazilian unit in which Juninho cut an ephemeral figure, and that Michael Owen could trouble Roque Junior, a central defender who had 'weak link' written all over him. The problem, of course, would be bottling up the mercurial talents of the three Rs – Rivaldo, Ronaldo and Ronaldinho.

The second round was not yet complete, however, and there was another major shock still to come. The day after the Brazil v Belgium match, South Korea played Italy in Taejon and won 2–1 with a 'golden goal' scored 25 minutes into extra-time. The Italians had gone the way of France and Argentina. Now, if only England could get past Brazil . . .

CHAPTER TWENTY-FIVE

BRAZIL

And so to Shizuoka, some 400 miles from Kobe. England and Brazil had both wanted to make the journey by the famous 'Bullet' train, but while the Brazilians were successful in booking a compartment for their exclusive use, England were unable to do so, and therefore elected to fly. However, England then scored what was deemed to be a more important point in the psychological battle when, as the designated home team, they exerted their right to have Brazil wear their change strip, blue, instead of the famous canary yellow.

For his part, Eriksson had bigger things to worry about, particularly Owen's troublesome groin. It quickly became apparent that his reaction straight after the Denmark game ('it's nothing really') was born of bravado. It was something all right. The most potent weapon in Eriksson's attacking armoury was unable to train for four days, and would not be 100 per cent fit.

Ironically, as it would turn out, much of the pre-match talk, from the English media, was of the enduring excellence of David Seaman in goal.

Eriksson, as is his wont, preferred to talk about the team, rather than individuals. 'We have a very good defence,' he said, 'but that's credit not only to the goalkeeper and the four defenders, but also to the other players, because the defence can't do well if they don't get cover from the midfield.' In this respect, nobody was contributing more than Butt, who was to be singled out later for special praise.

England were going to need all their defensive solidarity, the coach admitted. The 'Three Rs' would be the ultimate test for England. 'Every time Brazil get over the halfway line, it smells like they will score a goal,' he said. 'We have to be very compact and work as a unit. If we don't do that, and we give them room, they'll kill us.'

Respect was a two-way street. On the eve of the game, Pele said: 'England are the most difficult opponents left. Their defence is the best in the World Cup, yet those defenders are also young enough and fit enough to support the attack. Brazil possess the two finest strikers in the world in Ronaldo and Rivaldo, and it is important that they live up to their reputations because I fear for Brazil's defence under pressure from David Beckham's crosses, with Michael Owen so quick around the penalty area. Brazil have played England three times in the finals before, have never lost, and each time we have gone on to win the World Cup. If we beat England again, we can win a fifth title, no matter who else comes through the quarter-finals.'

The day before the match, Eriksson finally confirmed that Owen would be in the starting line-up.

His reasoning remains unchanged today. 'It was a game for Michael Owen. He lives for the really big games, they are the highlights of his life.'

ENGLAND 1   BRAZIL 2
Shizuoka, 21 June.

England: Seaman (Arsenal), Mills (Leeds United), Ferdinand (Leeds United), Campbell (Arsenal), A Cole (Arsenal), Beckham (Manchester United, captain), Butt (Manchester United), Scholes (Manchester United), Sinclair (West Ham), Owen (Liverpool), Heskey (Liverpool). Substitutes: Dyer (Newcastle United) for Sinclair 58 minutes, Vassell (Aston Villa) for Owen 80, Sheringham (Tottenham) for Cole 80.

Brazil: Marcos (Palmeiras), Cafu (Roma, captain), Lucio (Bayer Leverkusen), Roque Junior (Milan), Edmilson (Olympique Lyons), Roberto Carlos (Real Madrid), Gilberto Silva (Atletico Mineiro), Ronaldo (Internazionale), Rivaldo (Barcelona), Ronaldinho (Paris St Germain), Kleberson (Atletico Paranense). Substitutes: Edilson (Cruzeiro) for Ronaldo 70 minutes.

Referee: R Rizo (Mexico).

It was a big occasion, with a setting to match. The stadium in Shizuoka, like the rest of the World Cup venues, was state-of-the-art new, again causing English visitors to reflect ruefully on the protracted attempts to replace Wembley, and the bucolic back-drop could scarcely have been bettered. Imagine Newcastle's St James' Park in the middle of the New Forest and you have it. The weather, a sunny 86°F, was a delight for the England players' wives and families, who had been flown out by the FA the pre-vious day. They were not the only late arrivals. Eriksson's 15-year-old daughter, Lina, had travelled from Florence in time for the match, after completing her school exams. She sat alongside her brother, Johan, 23, and Nancy Dell'Olio. The heat was less agreeable for the players, of course, who were at a disadvantage against South American opposition much more accustomed to such conditions.

David Beckham led his team out for the warm-up (a misnomer if ever there was one) to encouraging applause from a crowd of 47,436, which again had a clear English bias. As he clapped back in appreciation, the England captain thought to himself: 'This is my time.' The players were tense, and Eriksson did everything in his power to put them at their ease, hiding his true feelings by laughing and joking with one of his coaches, Steve McClaren, on the touchline while another, Sammy Lee, supervised the preparations on the pitch.

When the line-ups were announced by public address, even the Brazilians in the crowd applauded Beckham's name, reinforcing his feeling that it was going to be his day. Down in the tunnel, before the teams made their entrance, Danny Mills was a fearsome sight, shouting, grimacing and kicking the wall in search of maximum intensity, both personal and collective. Another England full-back, Stuart Pearce, used to go through exactly the same routine. As the anthems were played, the television cameras panned to Prince Andrew, who was next to Brazil's Joao Havelange, the former FIFA president, in the VIP box.

England began well. There was an early indication

of what was to come when Brazil cut them open
through the middle for Ronaldo to get in a shot,
comfortably saved, but after 23 minutes Pele's
musings about his team's defence, and the threat of
Owen, were called to mind. Lucio took his eye off
the ball when moving to cut out a long pass from
Heskey, gifting possession to Owen who, from near
the penalty spot, lifted his shot over the advancing
Marcos with dead-eyed expertise. 1–0. English joy,
as they say, was unconfined. Cue 'Here We Go'.
There was a nasty moment when Seaman, making
a good catch under pressure, landed badly and
knocked himself out, but he recovered his senses
after treatment, and a substitution was deemed
unnecessary. For the rest of his life, he will wish he
had come off.

Brazil were enjoying the lion's share of possession, but England were defending competently and
confidently, shutting out the 'Three Rs'. If only they
could get to the sanctuary of half-time with their
precious advantage intact, surely all would be well.
It wasn't to be. Just before the interval, at the most
damaging moment psychologically, a bewitching
piece of Brazilian magic unhinged them. Beckham,
it must be said, was horribly at fault at the inception
of the move, jumping out of the way on the touchline as two tacklers converged, surrendering possession. It was an act that called to mind Eriksson's
comments before the Sweden game, when the
coach said that Beckham had to believe that his foot
could survive an ordinary challenge. The captain's
initial error was compounded when Scholes then

slipped when he had the chance to kill the danger in midfield. Nevertheless, there was cover in place as Ronaldinho started his run through the middle. It was spirited away by a sleight of foot known as a step over – a manoeuvre simple yet smart at the same time. It bewildered Ashley Cole, and meant that when Ronaldinho slipped the ball to Rivaldo he had half a yard on Sol Campbell, which was all he needed to beat Seaman with a left-footed shot, curled past the keeper's right hand.

England had suffered a crushing body-blow, and some uplifting oratory was needed at half-time. Unfortunately, the inspirational stuff is not Eriksson's forte, and the players were disappointed when he let his assistant, Steve McClaren, do most of the talking. As one of the defenders (to identify him would be to risk the termination of an international career) put it: 'We needed Churchill but we got Iain Duncan Smith.' In April 2004, Eriksson finally responded to that criticism, saying: 'I have been angry sometimes with the players, but I cannot be Winston Churchill in the dressing room. That would not be me. Every manager has his own way to do things, and I won't change.'

Short of managerial stimulation, the players were still trying to raise their own spirits when they were flattened completely by a freak goal, just five minutes into the second half. Ronaldinho continues to claim that the long-range free-kick that sailed over Seaman's head was a deliberate goal attempt, but Juninho says his friend confessed to him straight after the game that it had been a mishit. Deliberate act or not, Ronaldinho's strike made a complete fool of Seaman who, caught off his line, was left powerless as the ball looped over his head and under the crossbar, evoking memories of Nayim's goal from an improbable distance in the 1995 Cup-Winners' Cup Final.

England were reeling, but the smelling salts came from the most unlikely direction. Before the tournament, the lottery would have seemed a better bet than Danny Mills being assaulted by a Brazilian forward, but after 57 minutes Ronaldinho was sent off for an over-the-top challenge that could have broken the full-back's ankle. England had 33 minutes against ten men in which to pull back one goal – the odds had to be in their favour. What followed was depressing in the extreme. The way to make such numerical advantage count is to keep the ball and run it at the opposition. Instead, England repeated their witless second half against Sweden, hoofing it forward ever higher and longer. Never was Steven Gerrard more noticeably missed, for his ability to pass, rather than kick the ball over 40 yards and for his steely mentality. Not for the first time, Eriksson's substitutions were baffling. The situation cried out for Joe Cole, the one England player with a trick to beat a man, but it was the convalescent Kieron Dyer who was sent on, in place of Sinclair. Owen, never fully fit, was withdrawn after 80 minutes, at which stage Eriksson sent on Darius Vassell and Teddy Sheringham in a move which smacked of desperation, rather than tactical nous.

England were kicking the ball, not passing it, but

instead of using the technical area to issue corrective instructions, Eriksson sat rooted to the bench, like a rabbit caught in headlights. He could, and should, have done more. Mills had a shot deflected over and Scholes was tantalizingly wide with an 89th minute header, but these were no more than half-chances. To their damning discredit, in the 33 minutes in which they played against ten men, England failed to test Marcos even once. The poverty of their tactics was such that the suspect Brazilian defence held out without difficulty, and at the final whistle, English supporters all around the ground stared at one another in shocked disbelief.

The dressing room was like a morgue. Nobody moved, nobody spoke. The players were traumatized. They'd had a glimpse of immortality and let it slip. Some might get the chance to redeem themselves, others – notably Seaman – certainly wouldn't. The goalkeeper was distraught, inconsolable. Seeing his tears, Beckham embraced him on the pitch, and did his best to be of comfort, but Seaman was 'in pieces', as the captain put it, in the dressing room afterwards, and broke down again when he tried to give an interview on his way out of the stadium. Before crumpling and being led away by Joanne Budd from the FA's media department, he said: 'I just want to say sorry to all the fans, sorry to all the people I've let down today. I blame myself for this result because they've scored their winning goal from a free-kick that was hit from a long way out. I was expecting a cross, and I'm sure he meant it as a cross, but he mishit it, I misread it, and it ended up as a goal. I know it will go down as a goalkeeping error, but the main thing is to apologize to the England supporters, because they've been absolutely tremendous. All the players were fantastic at the final whistle, telling me to forget it and that I'd kept them in the tournament.'

Cruelly, Seaman is destined to be remembered for this one mistake, rather than the excellent service he had given his country over nearly 14 years. Ronaldinho was sympathetic. 'It moved me,' he said, 'to see such a great goalkeeper as David Seaman in tears. The English people should never forget all that he has done for the national team.'

Back at the hotel, Seaman called his friend and goalkeeping coach at Arsenal, Bob Wilson, for moral support. Wilson was not found wanting, absolving his protegé from blame. Then Terry Venables took the phone and coaxed the demoralized keeper into a better mood. 'Forget it – now,' he said. 'You've been the best goalkeeper in the tournament, so get your head up.'

Seaman's teammates defended him to a man, with David Beckham and Rio Ferdinand to the fore. The captain said: 'Making a scapegoat out of "Seamo" would be a disgrace. He has been the best keeper at the World Cup. Brazil scored a fluke winner from a cross that somehow turned into a goal. It wasn't even a mistake by David, and nobody blames him.' Ferdinand added: 'I had to go to doping control after the game and Ronaldinho was also in there. I asked him if it was a shot at goal and he laughed and said "Yes." I just told him: "No way." The first time I thought about it going in was when it hit the back of the net. Nobody on that pitch thought it was David Seaman's fault. It never even crossed our minds. I think David has been very harsh on himself. He took the blame, but he got beaten by a freak goal.'

Freak or not, England were out. As Ferdinand, their star of the tournament, packed and headed for home, he captured the mood of the nation. 'We were so, so close,' he muttered. Carefully packing his prized CD collection, he added: 'We tried to keep our thoughts in check, and think all those things you are supposed to think, about taking each game as it comes and not getting carried away, but you couldn't help dreaming of lifting the World Cup. Every day that went by, we could see the belief growing in each other's eyes. We talked about what it would be like. We knew what others were thinking without saying it. Here was a great chance to win it for the first time for 36 years. Now it's going to be 40 years, at least. That's a hell of a long time, and so much harder to take when you know you had a real chance. We are so sorry it didn't happen, but we tried our very best. I don't think anyone could argue about that, despite the disappointment.'

CHAPTER TWENTY-SIX

LET'S GO HOME

The Westin Hotel, on Awaji Island, had been England's base in Japan for four weeks. Now, suddenly, they were on their way home, beaten 2–1 by Brazil in the quarter-finals, and the shock of their exit, and their lack of preparation for it, was apparent in the chaos of their packing. The players threw clothes and the accumulated detritus of a month's stay into bags, chivvied by Football Association staff. They had a plane to catch.

Eriksson, was urging Nancy Dell'Olio to hurry. The extra baggage from expensive shopping trips with the wives of David Dein, the FA's vice-chairman, and David Davies, the governing body's executive director, was proving problematical, and Eriksson would be mortified if he was last on to the bus, having kept the players waiting. His agent, Athole Still, had journeyed from Kobe, 45 minutes distant, to check whether he was interested in alternative employment, only to be told his client was 'unavailable'. Their discussions were not urgent, in Eriksson's view, and could wait until they got back to London.

Leaving Nancy to fold and cram, Eriksson walked next door, to the hotel's conference centre, and put on a brave face for the media (after keeping reporters and TV crews waiting for two hours, he answered questions for barely ten minutes before being hustled away by Paul Newman, the FA's communications director), but his true feelings were betrayed by snatched press photographs of him on the team bus, where he was a picture of gloom and despondency sat next to Ms Dell'Olio.

Security, impenetrable at the hotel throughout the tournament, was full of holes now that England were no longer a part of it, and some 200 Japanese fans, nearly all of them young girls, turned the lobby into St Trinians. When Beckham strode in, after the briefest of valedictory press conferences, his appearance provoked high-decibel hysteria, and the fashion icon-cum-footballer had to bolt for the stairs to avoid being mobbed.

Some of the players' wives and families had only joined them in Japan two days earlier, and clothes unpacked on the Thursday were being returned to suitcases less than 48 hours later. This was compelling proof of the view expressed by Rio Ferdinand and others – that the England team genuinely believed that they would beat Brazil and march on to the semi-finals, and beyond. They had been confidence personified after beating Argentina 1–0 and then Denmark 3–0. Now they were in a daze, unable to come to terms with stark reality.

As England left, for the long flight back to Heathrow, the entire staff of the Westin, including chefs in their immaculate whites, turned out to wave them goodbye. Polite and well mannered, they had been genuinely popular guests, and saying 'sayonara' brought lumps to a few throats and tears to many an eye. The plane had barely taken off when the inquests began. Could England have done better?

'We should have done better, and we will always regret that fact,' Eriksson says. 'Personally, I'm very frustrated by it. I really thought we could go all the way, especially after all the shocks there had been, and with Argentina, France and Italy all out. That gave us a great opportunity, but it was a chance we were not good enough to take when we were 11 against 10 playing Brazil.'

He accepted the blame for that. 'Of course I take responsibility for it. I tried to get the message out to the players: "Keep your shape, keep the ball, don't just knock it out anywhere," but it didn't happen. They tried their hardest to get a second goal, but not in the right way.'

Had he learned anything from the World Cup? 'About coaching, maybe not, but definitely about living together as a group, and all the small details that have to be right if you are to get on and work together in harmony for five or six weeks. Mistakes were made which we can't afford to repeat. Also, I learned who is a tournament player and who is not. That's very important.'

This last remark can be interpreted as a veiled criticism of Robbie Fowler, who made little attempt to hide his dissatisfaction with his minimal involvement on the pitch. Fowler left Liverpool because he could not accept playing second fiddle to Michael Owen, and his attitude would appear to be the same at international level. When Owen's groin injury threatened to keep him out of the Brazil game, Fowler spoke of playing Geoff Hurst to Owen's Jimmy Greaves. It was an analogy which did not go down well in the camp, bearing in mind how ill-timed injury at the 1966 World Cup virtually terminated Greaves' international career, and brought him close to self-destruction.

Fowler instantly become the footballing equivalent of cricket's Phil Tufnell – blackballed as a 'bad tourist'. Disaffection in the reserve ranks was not confined to Disgusted of Toxteth, and was the product of Eriksson's off-hand treatment of the back-up players in the squad. Martin Keown and Gareth Southgate were others who felt marginalized, and would have welcomed the occasional solicitous word from the boss. This disregard had not been a problem when the squad was together for a few days for one-off matches, but over a longer period it had started to grate.

On the tactical side, his approach had erred on the side of conservatism and inflexibility.

Gerrard's dynamic drive was missed even more than had been anticipated. 'We never talked about Steven during the tournament, but now we can,' Eriksson said. 'A fit Steven Gerrard would have made a big difference. He is one of the best midfielders in the world today.' Nicky Butt raised his game to a new level in the 'anchor' role, and was singled out for special mention by the coach, but he lacks Gerrard's all-round ability – particularly the Liverpool man's knack of releasing Owen with long, raking passes from 40 yards or more.

Eriksson accepted that he had made mistakes, but was not going to identify, or dwell on them. 'Maybe if I'd lined up the team another way it would have been better, but we'll never know. If you keep regretting what you've done wrong you'll go crazy.'

Elimination from the World Cup brought the inevitable speculation about his future.

Two days after England's exit from the World Cup, I took a boat trip around Kobe harbour in the company of Athole Still, Eriksson's long-time agent.

Still, who was in a position to know, said Eriksson would stay on and attempt to take England to the European Championship, then look to return to club management. He was forever being linked with a return to his old club, Lazio, but said this was a non-starter. 'They are in financial difficulties, and they still owe money to Sven, and to me. There's no way he will be going back there under the present circumstances.' Still could foresee only one situation affecting his client's position in the short term. 'If Sven's private life keeps getting in the papers, he could suddenly say: "That's it. Enough. I'm off."'

With that thought in mind, it was hardly encouraging when England landed at Heathrow on 23 June to be greeted by a story in the News of the World, which read: 'Sven-Goran Eriksson flew back to Britain to the hardest selection decision of his life. He has to make a crucial choice between long-term girlfriend Nancy Dell'Olio and on-off lover Ulrika Jonsson.' The paper went on to say: 'We have a shock for both love rivals. Sven was having secret liaisons with a third beauty. Jayne Connery, a 36DD lapdancer, said: 'For three months we had a very intimate relationship.' 'That's Sven's problem,' Still told me. 'He can't resist a bird.' When the matter came up for discussion with the FA, at the height of the 'Ulrika Crisis', Eriksson couched it in rather more genteel terms, but he did admit that he had a 'weakness for the ladies', and that he had brought the consequent media intrusions upon himself.

CHAPTER TWENTY-SEVEN

THE FINAL RECKONING

'England were one of the biggest disappointments of the tournament. Of all the negative European teams, they were the worst. I was asking myself: "Is this the great, attacking England I used to watch?" Even when they were 2–1 down against Brazil, who were playing with ten men, you didn't see it. It was terrible to see England play like that. I would not have wanted to go out that way. They could not leave with their heads held high.'

GUUS HIDDINK, South Korea coach.

England had exceeded pre-tournament expectations in reaching the quarter-finals, but it was not only their supporters who felt let down at the end. It is never a disgrace to lose to Brazil, but it was the feeble manner in which Eriksson and his team were eliminated that cast their followers into the slough of despond. Not only had they been gormless in their recidivist, long-ball reaction to adversity, they had played without real spirit, which is the minimal requirement, and can usually be taken for granted.

Johann Cruyff, the legendary ringmaster of

Holland's 'Total Football' under Rinus Michels, and a highly successful coach with Barcelona, was among their critics. Of Eriksson's inflexibility, he said: 'You should never, ever keep the same game plan when you have 11 men against 10. Those conditions turn a match into a man-to-man exercise. Every player should identify a player from the undermanned side. If needs be, go round saying: "I'll take the number six, you take the number eight, and so on." In every case you then track your man down, pressure him, don't let him have a moment's peace or a second to think.

'England were losing, they had to commit themselves forward, yet at the moment of truth their superiority in numbers seemed to vanish. They played so poorly you were left feeling Brazil were the ones with the extra man. Brazil had more possession when they were playing with ten men, which was less to do with their capabilities than England's shortcomings. If you give Brazil space and time, they have the technique to pass it around. I counted six consecutive, unchallenged touches by one Brazilian player in midfield. Had England been doing their job, man for man, as they ought to have been, that would never have been possible.'

Cruyff also came up with a familiar cause for England's shortcomings: fatigue caused by playing too much football. 'The organizers of the wider game bear responsibility for this trend,' he says. 'So many big names left the World Cup having given a poor account of themselves because some of them were playing their 80th match of the season. There are too many matches, particularly in countries such as England and Spain, with their 20-club leagues. The ceiling for a top division should be 18 teams – 16 would be ideal. And the way the Champions' League is structured is absurd.'

It is a theme taken up by another of football's true greats, Franz Beckenbauer. 'The Kaiser' saw his beloved Germany get to the World Cup Final yet again, but still professed dissatisfaction with the status quo. 'Billions of people watched the World Cup,' he told me, 'but they were watching tired stars. This is not the future, it is wrong. FIFA has to react to this situation. Look at Patrick Vieira, and his disappointing form for France. How many game had he played – 80? It is impossible to be fresh after 38 league games, 17 Champions' League games and more in the domestic cup competitions. You have to be tired after that, and you could see that players were tired.'

It was Beckenbauer's own club, Bayern Munich, Champions' League winners in 2001, who had proposed that there should be only one group phase in the competition, and the second round should be played on a knockout, rather than round-robin basis. Unarguable common sense, it was an initiative implemented by UEFA during the summer of 2002.

There was more in the same vein from the Arsenal manager, Arsene Wenger, who had tipped England against Brazil. 'The problem was that they were just so tired,' he said. 'I remember Arsenal beating Everton on 11 May, the last day of the season, and 24 hours later the England squad joined up. How are they supposed to be rested and in the right physical shape when that's the case? You could see in the last 25 minutes of every game that they had nothing left to give. Even when they played well against Argentina and Denmark, they still surrendered so much possession in the final stages because they were exhausted.

'The fact that they played badly wasn't down to tactics, or formations. They were just too tired to be able to concentrate properly for the whole game. When your body is so tired, it is unimaginable your mind will not be tired, too. The Brazil game was the worst of all. They were too fatigued to concentrate on the game plan, and when they had to chase a goal, it became impossible. There was a power to England's game, and they were able to dominate even the best sides in the tournament at times. They were superbly organized in defence, they were solid and they counter-attacked clinically and better than any other team. I thought the spirit was very good, too, but when that power went, they became very fragile. It was the same with many European teams. France, Italy and Spain also looked weak in the closing stages of matches. They didn't have the strength to continue dominating, and paid a heavy price.'

Eriksson, who has spoken about the perils of 'over-playing' on numerous occasions, was not about to argue. 'Coming to the World Cup and starting with very tired players is sad,' he said. 'The World Cup is a fantastic party, and it's wrong when the world can't see players at their best. Against

Brazil, we were tired when we started to chase the second goal, and when you are tired in the legs, so is the brain. We didn't score in the second half in any of our games, largely because of tiredness. Whenever David Beckham and Paul Scholes started to tire, we lost our way. We lost our shape and control of the ball, which was very damaging. I don't think it was a coincidence that the fittest player in the squad was Owen Hargreaves, from Bayern Munich, who was the only one who had a winter break. But I'm not just talking about England. France had the same problem, and I've heard complaints from several other managers.' He wanted a break mid-season first of all, to be followed by a reduction in the size of the Premier League, and raised both subjects with his employers at the FA both during, and after the World Cup, with partial success. Arsenal's David Dein, vice-chairman of the FA, immediately championed the cause of the winter break.

Eriksson told me: 'I've come to realize that there's no point pushing for more time with the players, because there are just no free dates to do it. The clubs start playing in the Champions' League and UEFA Cup as early as September, so there's absolutely no chance. The only way is to have fewer teams in the Premier League, but I was told that was not going to happen. I'll keep on to the FA about a winter break and we'll see.'

The strongest non-partisan support for Eriksson came from his nemesis, 'Big Phil' Scolari, Brazil's manager at the World Cup, who subsequently took charge of Portugal. Commenting on events in Japan, he said: 'England proved that they belong in the A-list of football nations. They didn't just show their usual strengths, like passion and commitment. In fact, they surprised me with their tactical sophistication. Against us, Eriksson used no fewer than three different tactical formations at different times in the match, and the players shifted seamlessly between them.

'Eriksson's influence on the team is very obvious. It proves managers are still crucial to getting the best out of a group of players. The England of old, which was all about booting the ball in the air, overpowering their opponents physically and showing no style whatsoever, is finally dead. Going back to the Sixties, England were viewed in Brazil as somewhat unsophisticated – more physical than artistic. Yet I always found it beautiful, in an unusual way. To me, there really was a beauty to their running and to the vigour of their play.

'Eriksson has maintained the old values while adding more dimensions. He had some good players at his disposal, but more importantly he used them correctly on the pitch. I like the way he defended. It was a zonal system, but at the right time it would switch to a man-marking set-up. When they won the ball back, they played it out of defence very effectively, absorbing the pressure and giving both the midfield players and strikers time to make their runs.

'With this nucleus of players, and Eriksson in charge, England may be developing another juggernaut like their great sides of '66 and '70. Most of us in Brazil would have no hesitation in including Michael Owen among the top three players in the world, and David Beckham, when he is fully fit, represents talent in its purest form.

'I know some in Europe see flaws in England's game, or areas where they can improve, but in Brazil we don't view it that way. We look at pure talent and appreciate it. We don't try to find weaknesses at all cost.'

Of Shizuoka, Scolari said: 'We had two detailed plans, and I decided to switch to Plan B at half-time. The players understood perfectly, and did what we had trained for. The right-sided midfielder moved towards the centre, took the ball and immediately punched forward. Cole, their left-back, was completely lost, which was no surprise. Full-backs usually don't know what to do when players come in from the sidelines. It was the only time we changed tactics in the entire tournament, and if it hadn't worked, the story of the World Cup would have had a very different ending.'

CHAPTER TWENTY-EIGHT

THE FA VERDICT

When the Football Association engaged Sven-Goran Eriksson as England coach, for 2001, they had a five-year plan, designed to win the World Cup in 2006. That, not 2002, was Eriksson's brief, and Adam Crozier, the FA's former chief executive, told me in an interview for this book: 'Everything is moving in the right direction. We've got a young team who are on a learning curve, and getting better all the time.' In Japan, Crozier felt, England had played very well at times and poorly at others. 'But overall, I thought the performance was good. The best gauge is always the players themselves, and they really thought they were on the verge of something special.'

'Remember, we had the youngest team at the World Cup. That defeat by Brazil was Sven's first in a competitive fixture, and against teams like Germany, Argentina and also Denmark – people think that was a routine 3–0 win, but they'd just beaten France 2–0 – the players showed, and learned, that when they're on their game, they're capable of defeating anyone.

'Don't forget, attitudes changed while we were out there. We all went out with down-to-earth, realistic expectations. A lot of people didn't think we'd get through a difficult group, but we did that with a terrific win against Argentina. Then we got to the quarter-finals and narrowly lost to Brazil in what was a very tight game. People said we played badly in the second half, but that's for coaches and players to talk about. The disappointment was that having done so well to get to the last eight, the way the tournament had opened up made us all aware that the winner of the match against Brazil had a golden chance. I don't think anyone can say that had we won, we would have won the World Cup, but it is fair to say that whoever won that game had every opportunity.

'I think there was a genuine belief among the players and the coaching staff that we were in with a very good shout for the 2004 European Championship, in Portugal. Quite rightly, in my opinion, they felt they were much further on than they expected to be.'

Crozier was happy to pursue Eriksson's request for a winter break in the Premier League, explaining that the FA were pushing for its introduction in time for the 2003/04 season. He explained: 'While we were out in Japan, Sven and I talked about the subject a lot, and David Richards, the chairman of the Premier League, was there with us. Sven was in favour of a smaller Premier League, as well as a winter break, to ease the workload on his players, and we came to the conclusion that the first thing we should go for was the winter break. We agreed to treat the two issues as separate, and to go for the winter break as the starting point. Talking to football people out there, and back home, most thought the best way to do it was to start the season earlier, finish later and have a maximum break of three weeks in the middle. Any longer than that and the players would have to restart with a form of pre-season training.

'The feeling was that the beginning of January was the best time for a break. David Richards was very positive about that. We agreed to set up a meeting some time in September between the FA, the Premier League and six to eight of the top managers to talk about how we might make it work and its implications. Clearly there's no point creating a break if the clubs then fill it with friendly fixtures, so it would be done on the basis that the FA would not allow any games to be played for that period.

'This is not a club v country argument, which is how some will portray it, it's in everybody's best interests. How often have we seen our players look like world beaters with their clubs in the first stages of European competition, then suffer come March and April, because the other countries' players are fresher? From the England viewpoint, two-thirds of our players are drawn from clubs playing in the Champions' League, so in the run up to the World Cup they were playing all the Premier League games, plus the domestic cup ties, and on top of that you can add up to 17 Champions' League games and ten international matches. They were playing demonstrably more games than anyone else. The very best were getting overworked. Sven said that if we want to win the European club competitions, and do well internationally, it's time to freshen up our players in mid-season. We've had a number of conversations about it. The initial reason the subject came up was that, having tested the players before we left England in May, there was no doubt that the fittest member of the squad was Owen Hargreaves, who had a good rest when Bayern Munich had their winter break.'

The smaller Premier League would have to wait. Crozier told me: 'That's a longer-term issue, but one the clubs have really got to think about. The consensus was that we should park that one for the moment, and concentrate on what could be achieved in the short term.'

The winter break issue would outlast Crozier, and continues to plague his successor, Mark Palios. In early 2004, Eriksson thought he had got his way when, at a meeting with Premier League chairmen, he extracted the promise of a two-year experiment, from January 2005. The agreement was for there to be a fortnight's break after the third round of the FA Cup. Players were to take a holiday, and clubs would not be allowed to use the time for lucrative foreign tours. Sir Alex Ferguson and Arsene Wenger were among those strongly in favour, but FIFA torpedoed the plan by announcing two new international dates. The international calendar takes precedence over domestic fixtures, and so the experiment had to be postponed for a year, until January 2006.

CHAPTER TWENTY-NINE

SUB STANDARD

The interminable media inquest into the second half in Shizuoka lasted through the summer and well into the new season, the consensus being that England could, and should, have done better. The lingering 'if-only' atmosphere was such that the first match after the World Cup, a friendly against Portugal at Villa Park on 7 September, was earmarked for an in-depth debriefing on events in the Far East, only for selfishness on the part of the clubs to devalue the exercise.

Eriksson had prepared individual questionnaires for the players, which were to be answered anonymously, so that any criticisms could be forthright. Written answers were required to 15 questions, about the coach's methods, the input of his assistants, the team's accommodation in Japan, travel arrangements, the work of the medical staff, the desirability of having wives and partners present etc. Eriksson explained later: 'I wanted their honest opinions. If you have any players who aren't happy, you have to try to do something. Coaching is not like being a priest, standing in church and talking down to all those people sitting there silent. It's about exchanging ideas.

'I asked the players to take the questionnaire to their rooms and to write down what we wanted to know, without giving their names. It was my idea. As a manager, it is important to listen. To ask play-ers to stand up in front of the group and tell you what they think about you is unfair. But if they can write down their honest opinions about everything, and give them back without a name, it works.'

The responses showed, among other things, that 90 per cent of the squad were in favour of wives and girlfriends accompanying the players to major tournaments. 'The Germans had their wives and families in Japan for the duration' was a common statement. The replies were wanted to assist in the debriefing, but a good idea was undermined because so many members of the World Cup squad dropped out, and had to send their forms by post.

Gareth Southgate said: 'I handed in mine. It was a good idea and I can understand why it was done. The alternative was the team meeting at which players are invited to air their views, but in my experience they are not that useful. Sometimes people don't want to speak up in public, they tend to get embarrassed or inhibited talking in front of their team-mates. Something like a form, where players can think about things, answer privately and open up, is a much better idea. One of the ques-tions on the form, and something I know had been on the minds of players and coaches alike, was why we were much less effective in the second half of games in Japan. Part of my answer was that we gave the ball away too cheaply. If you do that, you spend most of the time trying to get it back. That takes up valuable energy. If nothing else, we must learn that lesson.'

For his part, Eriksson said he had 'thought many times' about his tactics against the Brazilians, and believed he should have asked his defenders to 'stop attacking', and conserve their energy. When I put it to him that Rio Ferdinand might have done more, not less, to win the numbers game in mid-field, the reply underlined his tendency to err on the side of caution. 'I don't want him to fill-in in midfield.'

Jonathan Woodgate and Lee Bowyer were both available for the game. No longer beyond the pale as far as the FA was concerned, and with the Sarfraz Najeib court case finally behind them, Eriksson chose both, with an eyebrow-raising turn of phrase. 'Now I'm a free man, to pick whoever I want,' he said. 'I wasn't imprisoned before, but I agreed not to pick them because it would have created a lot of confusion around the national team.'

With a new challenge, Euro 2004, two years down the line, it was time to rejuvenate the squad, and Nigel Martyn, Martin Keown and Teddy Sheringham, all 36, were pensioned off. But the new-look team Eriksson had in mind – which would have had Kieron Dyer on the left of midfield – was decimated by the usual welter of withdrawals. Missing for various reasons were Dyer, Gary Neville, Wes Brown, Sol Campbell, John Terry, Steven

Gerrard, Nicky Butt, Paul Scholes, Robbie Fowler and Darius Vassell. And it was to get worse.

That hardiest of perennials, club versus country, reared its ugly head yet again when Sir Alex Ferguson pulled Scholes out of the squad with an injury which was expected to keep him on the sidelines for three weeks, but then played him for Manchester United against Middlesbrough the following day – a match which Eriksson attended. Adding insult to spurious injury, Ferguson withdrew the England captain David Beckham after the game, citing a calf problem. With characteristic bluntness, the United manager said he was not interested in England, his priority was to get both players fit for their next Premiership match against Bolton.

The inevitable furore that followed left the FA's director of communications, Paul Newman, asking journalists to desist in their criticism of Ferguson, and stating, with absurd pomposity: 'We do not need you to fight our battles.' Before Eriksson's eve-of-match press conference, Newman was greeted with howls of derision when he said: 'I think you'll find he won't be answering your ridiculously searching questions this time.'

He was wrong. Eriksson, clearly vexed, said: 'Starting in February, I will use the FIFA rule where every player has to report (to national team headquarters) and stay at least one day before going home if they are injured. I have been a club manager myself, and I hated international friendlies, but I had to accept them. In Italy, if a player has played in his club's last game he has to report to the national team, injured or not.

'I talked to Ferguson on Monday and he said Paul Scholes was injured, so when I saw Scholes in the line-up at Old Trafford on Tuesday of course I was surprised. But if someone should be embarrassed, it isn't me. I got a phone call 15 minutes after the game, when Ferguson said Scholes had got better since Monday. He said he had played him because he needed to gamble for the three points. Ferguson said they had a lack of players available.'

So the half-fit Scholes had started up front, with the fully fit Ole-Gunnar Solskjaer on the bench? Eriksson, smiling, said: 'Get in your car, go to Manchester and ask Ferguson about it.'

Petty club jealousy was also behind England's change of doctors at this time. Dr John Crane and Dr Tim Sonnex also worked for Arsenal, and Eriksson explained: 'Some of the other clubs were thinking there was too much Arsenal in and around the national team.' By way of replacement, he appointed a Swede, Leif Sward, saying: 'We now have an independent doctor, who can't be accused of favouring Arsenal, Liverpool, or whoever.'

The Portugal match, drawn 1–1, was pretty much a non-event, losing any meaningful purpose with Eriksson's seven second-half substitutions, which took his total to 86 in ten friendlies. Michael Owen captained England in Beckham's absence and Alan Smith, on his first start, scored from a Bowyer cross, but Gary Lineker was moved to say: 'If they continue to do that (make so many substitutions), we might as well give in to the clubs and scrap friendlies. If the big players, like Beckham and Scholes, can't insist on playing, then the whole exercise becomes a waste of time. It left a very bad taste in my mouth, and for the life of me I cannot understand why England cannot approach such games properly.'

CHAPTER THIRTY

HUMILIATION

The task of qualifying for Euro 2004 began with back-to-back fixtures against Slovakia and Macedonia. Selection of an England squad is rarely straightforward, and this one was anything but. Rio Ferdinand dropped out ridiculously late to have knee surgery – his condition revealed to the FA by the media, rather than Manchester United, who had not thought to forewarn them. Ferdinand's established partner in central defence, Sol Campbell, also withdrew, with a stomach complaint, and Danny Murphy, another casualty, was replaced by Frank Lampard. Other absentees included Lee Bowyer, Joe Cole and David Dunn, all dropped from the squad after being chosen for the preparatory friendly against Portugal, and David Seaman, whose hopes of extending his international career were fading fast.

So much for football. It was the last we were to hear of it for what seemed like an eternity. On 10 October, the must-read paper on the squad's flight to Bratislava was the *Sun*, with its banner head-line: 'Ulrika Could Blow It For England'. The story beneath read: 'FA bosses are bracing themselves for new revelations by Sven-Goran Eriksson's former lover, Ulrika Jonsson. The Swedish starlet's auto-biography is due out any day now, and there are worries the opening extracts could be revealed this weekend – slap-bang in the middle of England's first two Group Seven clashes.'

When it became known that serialization of Ms Jonsson's book, *Honest*, would begin on the day of the Slovakia match, everybody feared the worst. Paul Hayward, sportswriter of the year and no sensationalist, wrote in the *Daily Telegraph* that it was 'possible to tell oneself that these are the last days of Sven-Goran Eriksson's reign'.

The man himself seemed almost resigned to his fate. 'Fear?' he said. 'What shall I be afraid of? You cannot be afraid of what you don't know. I guess this is my fault, but it's also due to the way things are in the country in which I'm working. The focus here has been much more about things out-side football than I expected.' A trifle naïvely, he added: 'I'm sure that my players are not interested in my private life.'

In the hothouse atmosphere of Bratislava's Forum Hotel, rumour begat rumour, the gossip be-coming more lurid by the hour as reporters from other papers tried to second guess the *Daily Mail* serialization. The late Joe Melling, of the *Mail on Sunday*, an old friend, told me his paper had a 'taster' which hinted at 'some pretty serious stuff'.

Eriksson had told the FA: 'I don't think anything will come out that will worry us', but his employers were fearful that there might have been indiscreet 'pillow talk'. They were not concerned about the extramural activities of two consenting adults, neither of whom was married, but if Eriksson had gossiped about Sir Alex Ferguson, or any of the England players, the potential damage was horrendous.

After so much hype and speculation, the extracts that filled the *Mail* for the next few days came as something of a let down. There was enough material for a new series of *Carry On* films – seduction in the kitchen, built-up heels, suggestions of three-way sex and naughty maids etc – but no careless talk of the sort that costs managerial lives.

To a large extent, events elsewhere took the heat off anyway. The atmosphere in Bratislava had been ominous from the outset, and the night before the match two England fans were shot after a bar-room incident in the city centre. The England players heard the shots, and the wounded men were given first aid in the team hotel before being taken to hospital. A malevolent tone had been set, and it carried over into the game, England coming from a goal down to win 2–1 on a night blighted by racist abuse at one end and rioting at the other. Cold, wet and windy, it was a horrible evening, memorable for the worst of reasons. England's black players had never known baiting like it, and the Slovakian FA was sufficiently embarrassed to apologize afterwards. Emile Heskey said: 'That's the worst I've ever suffered, to have the whole stadium shouting and making gestures was frightening,' and Ashley Cole added: 'Even the stretcher-bearers were making monkey noises.'

Eriksson was appalled. He said: 'I don't think there were 23,000 racists in the ground, but we must do something about it. It's crazy to boo people because they are another colour.'

From the footballing perspective, it was the classic game of two halves, for reasons which were to be of great significance. In the first half, deployed in conventional 4–4–2 formation, England were awful, Scholes lost on the left flank and Gerrard and Beckham outnumbered and ineffective against the Slovakians' five-man midfield. Szilard Nemeth scored after 24 minutes, and looked like a world beater, which must have been a shock to the system for Middlesbrough fans. For the second half, Eriksson switched to a diamond formation and, as he put it: 'From the first minute, it was another music.' Scholes and Gerrard were transformed in the midfield diamond, and Beckham, with a 30-yard free-kick, and Owen, with his 19th goal in 43 internationals, turned deficit into deserved success.

Victory did wonders for Eriksson, and the media's perspective of the embattled coach. The *Sun* reported the game under the headline 'Goodnight Sven – Or So We Thought', Steve Howard writing: 'All around me in the press box, quills were being dipped in vitriol. Ms Jonsson's bedroom revelations, for which she was paid £760,000, proved she is as good at duping newspaper executives as she is gullible, middle-aged football managers. Where were the accusations that, we were told, would make Eriksson's position as England manager untenable? Nowhere to be seen. It seems us tabloid journalists are so far off the pace these days that even the rumours are made up.'

For the second qualifier, against Macedonia at Southampton, Campbell returned after his stomach upset but Dyer, who had got on as a substitute in Bratislava, had to drop out of the squad with back trouble. Eriksson, who had earmarked the Newcastle man for the problem position on the left, confessed his disappointment. 'It is a pity that every time Kieron Dyer is called into the international team he is injured. It is extremely bad luck, because he could do that job.'

Filling the place in question was a recurring problem, and Eriksson said: 'If there was one player in the world I would like in my side, it is Ryan Giggs. I just can't find a left winger like him. There are 30 players on my list of candidates for the left side of midfield, but none are like Giggs.'

The latest attempt to solve the problem saw two left-backs, Ashley Cole and Wayne Bridge, playing in tandem at St Mary's. Perversely, Eriksson discarded the diamond that had served England so well in the second half against Slovakia, and played Bridge on the left of a four-abreast midfield. The result was a first 45 minutes every bit as incoherent as it had been five days earlier.

Macedonia, who had managed only a 1–1 draw with Liechtenstein, took the lead twice. Seaman, restored to the team for what was to be the last of his 75 caps, was badly beaten after 11 minutes by a

driven, inswinging corner from the unheralded
Artim Sakiri. Beckham equalized with a delicious
chip, but Vanco Trajanov punished a mistake by
Campbell, and it took a 20-yard volley from Gerrard
to spare England the embarrassment of defeat at
home to one of the group's makeweights. A bad
night for Eriksson and his team culminated in Alan
Smith's dismissal, late on, for an indisciplined hack
at Aleksandar Mitreski. It was a costly rush of blood
for the Leeds striker, who would not be called upon
by his country again for the best part of two years.

The result, described by the *Daily Mail* as 'one
of the worst in the nation's history', handed the
initiative in the group to Turkey, and fuelled exas-
peration in the England dressing room. The players
preferred the diamond formation Eriksson had
abandoned despite its galvanizing effect in Slovakia,
and were dismayed by the offhand way in which
changes had been made to a winning team. Gareth
Southgate and Nicky Butt, who had played in
Bratislava, were disappointed not to be told personally by the coach that they were being left out five
days later. Both approached Eriksson on the day of
the game, seeking an explanation, and Southgate
said later: 'I was bitterly disappointed not to play.'

Eriksson's coaching assistant and confidante,
Steve McClaren, revealed that events at this time
brought the Swede to the verge of quitting. The
Middlesbrough manager believes Eriksson would
have walked out on England in November 2002,
had he received an approach from any of the top
clubs in Europe.

Another kiss-and-tell story, this time by a 35-year-old blonde by the name of Jayne Connery, caused him new embarrassment at home, while at work he was suddenly deprived of two of his closest allies in the space of 48 hours. On 1 November Adam Crozier lost out in a power struggle at the FA, and resigned as chief executive, and the following day McClaren gave up his coaching role with England, citing the need to devote all his attention to Middlesbrough. Another major problem was the escalating dispute between the FA and the Premier League over control of the England team.

Eriksson says he was 'devastated' by the departure of the man who had employed him, and with whom he enjoyed a close working relationship, and also the coach he had entrusted with much of the preparation of the England team. Of Crozier he says: 'I was shocked and saddened by the news', and of McClaren: 'I was very sorry to be losing him. He is one of the best coaches I know.' Why did Eriksson, employed for his coaching ability, need another coach to work his players? 'I always liked doing the tactical work with my clubs, but when you are not doing it you see much better what is going on by standing off the pitch.'

The Premier League clubs were pushing for a 'Professional Game Board', the blueprint for which indicated that they wanted overall control of the England team. Feeling unsettled and isolated, Eriksson demanded to know who would be his new boss, and at an FA board meeting on 11 November – Armistice Day – a peace deal was brokered. After

David Davies, the executive director, and Nic Coward, the FA's solicitor, had been appointed joint chief executives on a caretaker basis, Eriksson and Tord Grip met David Dein (Arsenal), Peter Ridsdale (Leeds), Robert Coar (Blackburn Rovers) and Dave Richards (Premier League chairman), and the four Premier League representatives assured the coach that he had their full support, and that he would continue to answer only to the chief executive(s). In return Eriksson assured the FA that, despite interest from Barcelona, he would not be the next to leave.

He admits now that it was touch and go. 'If they had wanted to change too many things, then of course I would have asked for my freedom to go. I didn't want three, four or five people above me to report to over every decision. If I want something, I want to be able to go straight to one person who can get it done. I don't want to sit in a committee to discuss whether or not we should play a friendly. I wanted things to go on as they were, and I'm glad to say the Premier League representatives were very supportive of that.

'I needed to know who was going to be my boss, and I was happy that it was David. I very much regret what happened to Adam. He was a very good man who did an excellent job. I asked them (the Premier League representatives) what they wanted to do about friendly games, and they said: "We will do what you want." That was good. I sympathize with the clubs over friendlies, but we must have one prior to an important qualifying game.'

On 19 November 2002, when Eriksson took his players to a reception at Buckingham Palace, his mind drifted from the canapés to the issue of McClaren's replacement. The FA's original plan had been for him to groom McClaren and Peter Taylor as potential successors, but now both had gone. 'If I'm going to take someone working at a club, I don't think I can take a manager again,' he reasoned. 'If it's a coach, it's easier. Adam Crozier wanted one of the coaches to succeed me when he took me on, but then we lost Peter Taylor and Steve for the same reasons.'

A squad get-together, organized instead of a match in November, comprised a two-night stay, with partners, at Champneys Health Farm, in Hertfordshire, and a meal at Eriksson's favourite London restaurant, San Lorenzo. There was much criticism of the expense, at a time when the FA's cashflow problems caused work to be halted on the National Football Centre, at Burton-on-Trent, but the coach was unapologetic. 'Some people disagreed on grounds of cost, but I didn't care', he said. 'It was good for team spirit.'

England's next game was another friendly, against Australia at Upton Park on 9 February 2003. It was to be the nadir of Eriksson's tenure. Having talked the talk about demanding unfettered use of his players from the clubs, he declined to walk the walk, and agreed with the various managers concerned that none of their charges would play for more than 45 minutes. The result was a shambolic embarrassment, with the entire first team substituted at half-time, by which stage England were trailing 2–0.

The preamble had been entirely positive, with widespread excitement about the selection for the first time of the 17-year-old prodigy, Wayne Rooney. At this stage, he had played just 25 games for Everton, and Eriksson had seen him in action for only 25 minutes, but the coach said: 'I have been talking to his manager (David Moyes) and a lot of people who know him better than I do. He has great quality. He is physically very strong, and he makes things happen. It should be one of the biggest days of his career. He is only 17, I know, but so was Pele when he played in the 1958 World Cup and scored twice in the final. I am not saying he will be the next Pele, but Tord Grip has been to see him a lot, and everybody I talk to says he has a special talent. I am picking an under-25 team for the second half, and he has to be there.'

In what was a vain attempt to forestall criticism of wholesale substitutions, Eriksson said: 'I'm going to use up to 11 subs at half-time and in the second half play a team for the future. We are not living in an ideal world. It would be better for the top players to play for 90 minutes, but if you look at the fixtures, I have to think about the clubs who have FA Cup and Champions' League games coming up. It's a problem, but I'm in the same boat as all the other international managers. There's a conflict of interests, and whatever I do, I will be criticized. '

Surely there had to be a better way? 'There is,' Eriksson said. 'It needs FIFA, UEFA and the clubs to sit down together and talk about this. We should try to make the domestic season finish earlier and then play the friendlies. When you are a club manager, fighting to win trophies, it's not good to have an international in the middle of things.'

By making known in advance his intention to give the likes of Rooney, Paul Konchesky (Charlton), Jermaine Jenas (Newcastle), James Beattie (Southampton) and Francis Jeffers (Arsenal) their first caps, Eriksson raised the hackles of his opposite number, Frank Farina, who claimed England were being 'disrespectful' to the Australians. 'The pressure is now on England,' Farina said. 'If it doesn't go their way, there will be hell to pay.' Prophetic words, indeed.

England started with what was, on paper, their strongest team, with Beattie, the Premier League's leading scorer, alongside Michael Owen in attack. The pre-match signals, however, had been all wrong. Given the unmistakable impression that it was a meaningless games of two halves, England played at half-cock, alienating a crowd that had started off in raucous good voice, and trooped off at half-time to hoots of derision deservedly 2–0 down. The second team 'drew' the second half 1–1, Jeffers getting their goal, but the 3–1 defeat, and all the ridiculous comings and goings, infuriated supporters who had paid 'top dollar' to watch Beckham and Owen, not Murphy and Vassell, and it was the young players who suffered the high-decibel outrage at the final whistle.

Beckham was mortified. 'For me,' the captain

said, 'the most disappointing thing was the way the fans booed at the end. We were all disappointed with the result, but it was a bunch of young lads who played in the second half. They deserve better than that.'

The two teams used were:

First half: James, G. Neville, Ferdinand, Campbell, A. Cole, Beckham, Lampard, Scholes, Dyer, Beattie, Owen.

Second half: Robinson, Mills, Brown, King, Konchesky, Murphy, Hargreaves, Jenas, Rooney, Vassell, Jeffers.

England, and Eriksson, had a fearful shellacking in the newspapers. The *Sun* reported the match under the headline 'Kanga Poo', declaiming: 'We used to banish our convicts to Australia. Last night there were another 11 criminals who should have been frogmarched to the boat for a one-way trip Down Under. England's senior team, who played the first half, produced one of the most lamentable displays in our football history.'

Personalizing it, the *Daily Telegraph* went for 'Eriksson's England Are Rightly Ridiculed', with Paul Hayward writing: 'This is what you get when you treat international footballers like precious works of art, borrowed from their owners on the understanding that they are not exposed to harsh light. England go to Liechtenstein for their next qualifying match pursued by anger and ridicule. An ominous statistic of England's bumpy journey since the 5–1 smashing of Germany in Munich almost 18 months ago is that they have won only five of their last 17 matches. Eriksson's refusal to stand his ground in the face of over-protective club managers has come at a real and increasing cost. England have lost the winning mentality.'

The FA, alarmed by the backlash from disgruntled fans, let it be known the next day that they had the power to withdraw the clubs' invitations to UEFA competitions, and could effectively expel Manchester United and Arsenal from Europe unless they started co-operating fully with England. A series of 'summit meetings' was hastily organized to address the club versus country impasse.

David Davies, acting chief executive, said: 'The silver lining to the Australia humiliation was that it brought club v country to a head. People say the FA only want friendlies for revenue, but there are very good footballing reasons for having friendlies. The FA tried to help clubs by saying we wouldn't play so many friendlies, but we have got to get a consensus among clubs that international football has a role to play. You can't suddenly get excited about it in May and expect to win the World Cup or European Championship in June.'

Eriksson, jumping upon what was to become a familiar hobby horse, said: 'I think we have to sit down and talk. I can't make the rules, so it shouldn't just be me and the Premier League managers, it should include administrators from the level above us. We will never have a successful international team unless the players are available.' An old critic,

Jeff Powell of the *Daily Mail*, was having no excuses, and again drew his xenophobic broadsword. 'Is it any wonder that England are going back faster than the French from the front line?', he chuntered. 'Not to me it isn't. Were he not an alien, with all the mystique that goes with it, Eriksson's cover would have been blown some time ago.'

The coach was, by now, inured to such criticism. Much more damaging was the revelation in the press a week later that he had 'shaken hands' on the job when Manchester United offered him the chance to succeed Alex Ferguson more than a year earlier, in January 2002. Peter Kenyon, then still chief executive at Old Trafford, squirmed in the face of questioning on the subject and said: 'We never concluded a deal with Sven,' but, pointedly, he refused to say how far negotiations had progressed. Eriksson said: 'Don Revie (the England manager who decamped to the Arab Emirates mid-contract in 1977) was the most clever of us all. He walked out before they threw him out.'

England's next serious matches were the back-to-back Euro 2004 qualifiers away to little Liectenstein and then home to Turkey. After losing at home to Australia, almost anything seemed possible. In the event of defeat, what would Eriksson do? 'It is easy to take a car from Liechtenstein to Italy,' he said, laughing. Before naming his squad, he admitted that he would like the in-form Alan Shearer in it. 'The way he is playing, he should be in,' Eriksson said, 'but you can't pick a player who doesn't want to play for England, and he won't go back on his international retirement.'

Instead, young Rooney forced his way in at the eleventh hour, on the Sunday the squad was announced, with a goal and an impressive all-round performance for Everton in a 2–1 defeat at Arsenal – a match Eriksson attended. Of the continued contentious selection of Emile Heskey, who had scored four goals in 31 internationals, the coach said: 'He is important to the team, and he has never let us down. On paper, he and Michael Owen should be a good blend. One has pace, the other strength, and they know each other well from playing together twice a week.' Joe Cole was omitted ('he's not had a good season'), but Frank Lampard retained, despite 'not making an impact' against Australia. Sol Campbell dropped out with a sore Achilles, letting in Chelsea's John Terry for the first time.

Billed as a potential banana skin, the match turned out to be a turgid 2–0 win for England, Owen and Beckham scoring the goals. The result was the right one, but a laboured performance against limited, part-time opponents, left a lot to be desired, and at the final whistle Terry Butcher, the former England captain, turned to me and said: 'That was absolute crap. As my wife keeps saying to me: "How much are that lot paid?" There's no excuse for them playing like that, none at all.'

More notable than the result, however, was an outspoken attack by Sepp Blatter, the FIFA president, on Eriksson's attitude to friendly internationals.

Referring back to the Australia game, Blatter insisted England had been 'wrong' to play different teams in each half. 'It's better that you don't play,' he said. 'That was a farce. It is not correct for the opposition, and it is definitely not correct for the public. They paid to watch England's best team, and in the second half they saw another team. People are asking: "What is wrong with the motherland of football?" The FA should not organize such a match between big club fixtures. It will not be allowed in future to play a friendly for 45 minutes with one team and the second 45 with another.'

Eriksson responded by saying: 'Maybe it would be better if we didn't play any international games until the season is finished. Then, from the middle of May, have five weeks for international friendlies. It could be the same all over the world. That would end the problem between club and international football.'

More immediately, one of Eriksson's predecessors as England manager, Bobby Robson, called for Wayne Rooney's promotion to the starting line-up for the qualifier against Turkey at Sunderland's Stadium of Light. Robson said: 'This is a phenomenal talent that must not be denied or restricted. I have watched the boy play on several occasions, and he takes my breath away. He is sensational. He can do things that are way out of reach of our other players, and already he has the confidence to do them.

'Since Japan last summer, our international performances have been lacklustre, and Sven urgently needs to inject a spark, to gain fresh impetus, to lift the mood and raise the optimism. It needs a great player, and Sven seriously considered an England comeback for Alan Shearer, if only for the qualifying games against Liechtenstein and Turkey. He had seen Shearer battle magnificently for Newcastle when we had been reduced to ten men against Arsenal. He saw Shearer rampaging in the San Siro to score twice and dominate Fabio Cannavaro, the brilliant Inter Milan defender. As a former England manager, I could understand the underlying strategy Sven had in mind, but the future had to be Rooney, and Shearer was in the past.'

Eriksson's initial reaction was that Robson was wrong; it was too early to pick the Everton prodigy.

CHAPTER THIRTY-ONE

TURKEY AND THE LAST CHANCE

The mutual antipathy that exists between English and Turkish football fans would suggest to the casual observer that not much has changed since Gallipoli, and the Turks' visit to Sunderland on 2 April was preceded by the usual 'niceties'.

Turkey led the group, with nine points from their first three games; England were second, with seven from three, and the Turks' manager, Senol Gunes, quickly tried to intensify the pressure on Eriksson that was the inevitable consequence of successive poor performances against Australia, Macedonia and Liechtenstein. 'If they lose to us, a decision could be made about his future after the game,' Gunes said. 'I respect Eriksson, but I know the position he is in.' As usual, the *Sun* summed it up succinctly, with the headline 'It's The Chop If You Flop'.

By way of response, Eriksson smiled wanly and said: 'Maybe he (Gunes) wants the job.' Sol Campbell revealed that the coach was worried. 'He is taking charge of the training a lot more, and is voicing his own opinions.' Michael Owen added: 'He has been round a few of us, including me, and spoken to us individually about what is going wrong.'

The first decision taken at England's base camp, in Northumberland, was to release Jermaine Jenas and Francis Jeffers from the senior squad, to reinforce David Platt's Under-21s. Meanwhile, in a poll conducted by the *Sun*, 83 per cent of respondents said they wanted Rooney in the starting line-up, and Eriksson was coming around to the idea. In England's final practice session, Rooney partnered Owen in attack, and the midfield 'diamond' was back, with David Beckham on the right, Steven Gerrard on the left, Paul Scholes just behind the front two and Nicky Butt protecting the back four.

Eriksson said: 'The four of them are the strength of the team. Turkey have Okan, Emre, Tugay and Basturk, who are all excellent footballers, and if we want to beat them, we need to have the petrol in midfield. We have to stand there and be as strong as they are. We must try to be better than them in midfield, and that's not easy.'

At team selection time, the final decision was Rooney or Emile Heskey as the second striker. Still uncertain, Eriksson polled his coaching staff, only for the outcome to be a 2–2 tie. The casting vote was his, and in making up his mind he recalled a moment from training earlier in the day, when Rooney had slalomed around three opponents before drilling the ball into the top corner, to spontaneous applause from all present. Rooney was in, but was not told as much until four hours before kick-off.

The match was a triumph, for England and their embattled coach. Beckham said beforehand: 'I don't like it that our passion is being questioned,' and the captain and his team quickly dispelled the old timers' notion that they didn't care enough about representing their country. The performance was both intense and compelling, Rooney fully justifying Bobby Robson's advocacy and Eriksson's faith with some inspirational touches and runs.

The atmosphere, in the environs of the stadium and inside it, too, bordered on the malevolent, with mounted police working overtime before and after the match to keep some semblance of control. The hostility between the two sets of fans started with verbal clashes, escalated when the home crowd booed the Turkish anthem and spiralled into physical violence outside the ground.

On the pitch, it was red hot, too, with Beckham, in particular, much too pumped up and flying into a series of late challenges that deservedly brought him a yellow card that might subsequently have turned red. Rooney would have scored after 11 minutes but for a last-ditch block by Ergun, and when the ball ran loose, Beckham drove it wastefully wide. A bad miss.

England's midfield diamond successfully negated the Turks' strongest suit, but when Owen limped off after 57 minutes the match was still goalless, and the first signs of frustration were starting to show. The substitution soon banished them. Darius Vassell, on for Owen, broke the stalemate with a quarter of an hour left, and after 89 minutes

Beckham applied the coup de grâce from the penalty spot after another substitute, Kieron Dyer, had tumbled under Ergun's challenge.

England had established a control at the top of the group that they were never to lose, yet all was not sweetness and light. Fans had invaded the pitch to celebrate both goals and Alpay, the Aston Villa defender, kicked out at one after being struck in a mêlée. Outside the ground afterwards there were more fights, and 95 England fans were arrested. An inquiry was inevitable, and in May the Football Association was fined a record £68,000 for the racist chanting and crowd trouble, and was also given a 'final warning'. Mike Lee, UEFA's spokesman, said: 'The fans need to make sure that they do not put the future of the national team in jeopardy with their stupid behaviour. This is a final warning to England, and the FA must realize their track record is deplorable. England came very close to being thrown out of Euro 2000 because of the trouble their supporters caused.'

At least England had regained something like their best form, and Eriksson was relief personified. 'Excellent,' he said. 'We played good football, we deserved the result, and we could have won by even more goals. The new shape (the midfield diamond) was very good. Tactically, the players did exactly what I asked of them, and the effort they put in showed how keen they were to win the game.'

Belatedly, he admitted that he should have kept the diamond formation after Slovakia. The decision to play Rooney had been 'touch and go', but he had got it right. 'I was lucky to go to Arsenal v Everton, where he was absolutely what I was looking for. He showed that he is extremely mature for his age, and that he is ready. Ready for the big games. From the first day we came together for training, he showed that he's not afraid to have a go at Rio Ferdinand and Sol Campbell physically, and to try to beat them as well. That confidence means a lot.'

In terms of his own position, the effect of the result was that 'life changed completely'. Suddenly, he said, 'along came a 17 year old who could be a link between the forwards and the midfield and everybody was happy. Our fate in the group, and my own, was in our own hands again.'

Senol Gunes, never short of an inflammatory quote, said: 'The disrespect to our anthem was wrong, and shows countries said to be advanced culturally are actually behind.' Ominously, there was the away game, in Istanbul, still to come. Gareth Southgate said: 'There was a bit of pushing and shoving and a lot of banter in the tunnel after the match. Their players were shouting: "Wait until you come to Turkey," and even their kit man was drawing his fingers across his throat.'

Eriksson had just 24 hours to savour his success. Then self-interest reared its ugly head yet again when the Everton manager, David Moyes, demanded that Rooney be left out of England's end-of-season trip to South Africa, which was part of their preparation for the resumption of the qualifying campaign, at home to Slovakia on 11 June. Moyes said: 'What's the point in us trying to look after him if he is travelling all over the world for friendlies?'

England were due to leave for Durban on 19 May. On 9 May, Moyes was among a number of Premier League managers who agreed, in writing, that henceforth Eriksson should have carte blanche to select whomsoever he wanted whenever he wanted. Three days later, Everton withdrew Rooney from the squad, saying he had a knee ligament injury. Eriksson, having noted that his exciting newcomer had just played the full 90 minutes for his club, insisted that Rooney must report to headquarters and be examined by England's own medical staff. 'I decided to pick him, have a look at a scan of his knee, and then apply common sense,' the coach explained.

The 'truce' agreement designed to put an end to the age-old club versus country conflict had been violated within days and, privately, Eriksson was furious. 'I talked very straight to Moyes,' he told me. 'I pointed out that Rooney had played all 90 minutes for Everton the previous Sunday, when he was said to have been hurt. There was something the matter with his knee, but it was for the doctors to decide how serious it was.'

On Sunday 18 May, the day before departure day, the row took on a new dimension when Moyes insisted on being present when the FA's doctors examined his player. Only after this examination, which took place at a Heathrow hotel, was it unanimously agreed that Rooney should not travel. Also absent, injured, were Richard Wright, Gary

Neville, Sol Campbell, Jonathan Woodgate, Wes Brown, Danny Murphy and Francis Jeffers, creating openings for Ian Walker, Phil Neville, Gareth Barry, Matthew Upson, Trevor Sinclair and James Beattie. David Seaman was finally pensioned off, after 75 caps. 'He reacted like a great man and a great professional,' Eriksson recalled. 'He accepted that sooner or later it had to happen. It is historic, what he did for England. I'm sure he will always be remembered fondly.'

David Beckham was suspended for the Slovakia match, but decided to go to South Africa anyway – 'because I wanted to meet Nelson Mandela'. And thereby hung a tale. Danny Jordaan, chief executive of South Africa's 2010 World Cup bid, said it was a pre-condition of the television deal underwriting the trip that the England captain had to play. The whole venture was, undoubtedly, a fence-mending PR exercise on the part of the FA, who had smeared South Africa's rival bid for the 2006 World Cup by highlighting 'endemic violence' in the country, which succeeded only in letting in Germany. Eriksson did not approve of the jaunt, which had been the brainchild of David Davies, but the coach had been overruled by his bosses for political reasons.

Most of the players hated the venture, which was more about finance (the FA made £2m in broadcasting revenue) and photo opportunities (notably Beckham and Mandela) than football. The itinerary was the last thing the squad needed at the end of a long, hard season. On 19 May they departed Luton airport at 9.30 pm, arriving at Durban at 10 am the next morning. They trained at 5 pm and on May 21, still jet lagged, they left Durban on the 7.30 am flight, arriving in Johannesburg at 8.40 am for a coach journey to meet Mandela. At 11.30 am they flew back to Durban, landing at 12.40 pm before training again at 5.00. The match against South Africa was at 7.30 pm on 22 May.

In their wisdom, the FA left it to the players to decide whether or not they wanted to go the extra mile to meet Mandela. The result was a PR disaster. Twelve players made the effort, eight (Robinson, Phil Neville, Mills, Southgate, Barry, Gerrard, Joe Cole and Scholes) did not.

Sensitive as ever, the *Sun* headlined the story 'Half Nelson' and spoke of a snub to Mandela, quoting South Africa's captain, Lucas Radebe, as saying: 'I don't know why so many of the England players stayed away, but the entire South African squad was there.' One of the experienced players who stayed behind gave a reason other than fatigue for his absence. 'It was always going to be the Beckham–Mandela show. The rest were only there to make up the numbers, and I couldn't see the point of that.'

The safari was a shambles all round. Shortly before leaving England, two Southampton players, Wayne Bridge and James Beattie, asked for, and received, leave of absence to rest in advance of the Slovakia match. Eriksson, who had reluctantly agreed, was infuriated when they both played in a testimonial match at Aberdeen, the day before England took on South Africa. 'I gave them the opportunity to rest,' he said. 'If they weren't going to do that, they should have been with us.' The FA demanded an explanation from Southampton, and Beattie may care to ponder his lack of international opportunities since.

The match, a 2–1 win for England, saw Southgate score after just 36 seconds. Benni McCarthy equalized before a goalkeeping error allowed Emile Heskey to settle it with a tap-in. More notable than the result, however, was the injury sustained by Beckham, who broke a wrist falling on the hard, bumpy pitch. John Terry and Rio Ferdinand were also hurt, and for the training camp in Spain that followed the squad's return, Jamie Carragher joined up as cover. Better late than never, Rooney had also recovered sufficiently to take his place.

On returning from Durban on 25 May, the whole party flew straight to the La Manga resort for a week's R&R, interspersed with a little light training. Sven and Nancy opted for the privacy of a £3,000-a-week luxury villa, rather than a room along the corridor from the players and their families in the five-star hotel. On the second evening of their stay they hosted a barbecue for ten members of the coaching and support staff. Eriksson picked up the bill – for the villa and the party.

The coach also locked onto the alleged misbehaviour by Rio Ferdinand and John Terry who, after playing pool until 3.30 am, had a disagreement with hotel staff when the table malfunctioned. The players themselves claimed there had been a misunderstanding due to the language barrier. Eriksson conducted an investigation, and found no cause for disciplinary action. He said: 'I talked to the players and the hotel management, and there was nothing. I didn't see a problem. When we left La Manga the players, the wives, the girlfriends and the hotel staff were very happy, and so was I. Whenever we have been together, I have had no complaints about the players' attitude or their behaviour in their spare time. They are no different to players I have worked with in Italy, Portugal or Sweden.'

Of greater concern to the FA was the venue for England's next friendly, against Serbia and Montenegro on 3 June. In the light of the racist behaviour by fans at Sunderland when they played Turkey two months earlier, it suddenly seemed not quite such a good idea to take the England road-show to Leicester, with its large Asian population. Beckham and Eriksson both went on television in the run-up to the game, appealing for calm. The coach said: 'The next time something bad happens, we will be out of Euro 2004, and that will be catastrophic for us. It is important that the players behave on the pitch and supporters behave off it.'

The warning worked. England won 2–1; with goals from Gerrard and Joe Cole, on a prosaic, trouble-free evening, notable chiefly for the lamentable way England played pass the parcel with the captain's armband, debasing the honour. There were four captains on a night when Eriksson made ten second-half substitutions, with David James the only player to stay on for the full 90 minutes.

Bryan Robson, who led England 65 times, was furious. He said: 'Being captain of England should be the greatest honour you can get as a player. That is how I always felt about it, but now the armband was just being handed around all over the place. Caps were being given out right, left and centre, and now it was the same with the captaincy. Almost everyone in the squad was getting a cap. You could end up with ten or 15 and never start a match. Sven was devaluing the whole point of playing for your country.'

Eriksson admitted he was in the wrong. Henceforth, there would always be a vice-captain appointed, ready to take over if needed.

The squad reconvened at the Redworth Hall Hotel, in County Durham, to prepare for Slovakia's visit to Middlesbrough. The focus should have been on the important Euro 2004 qualifier, instead the newspapers were full of David Beckham and his wife, Victoria. Suspended, and therefore unavailable, the iconic captain took advantage of his break to take a self-promotional trip to the United States, where the photogenic couple were pictured mixing with the glitterati at film premieres, parties and the like.

Most of the England players were mildly amused, but one or two were resentful. Eriksson claimed not to have noticed. 'I've never seen any negative impact on the rest of the squad,' he said. 'When David is with us he works very hard, he never asks for special favours, and he sits on the bus with the others. I don't think the rest mind if he has 500 photographs taken and they don't. I have never noticed that they are jealous.'

Beckham just one of the boys? Not exactly. When pressed, Eriksson admitted that had the captain accompanied the squad to La Manga, he would have been 'a special case'. The coach explained: 'He would not have stayed in the hotel, that would have been impossible. We would have put him in a private villa. Normally, we would never consider different arrangements for anybody, but our security people saw problems.'

On the day of the match it was Beckham, rather than England, who was all over the front and back pages. He was not playing, but the news broke that Manchester United had accepted a bid for him from Barcelona.

The captain was not the only absentee at the Riverside. Ferdinand and Campbell were both injured, so Southgate and Matthew Upson formed a new partnership in central defence. Gerrard switched to the right side of midfield to replace Beckham, with Frank Lampard in on the left. Owen, on the occasion of his 50th cap, captained the side, with Southgate vice-captain.

England were poor in the first half, James and Southgate making a hash of combating a free-kick from Vladimir Janocko, which went in from an improbable distance. Mills suffered the indignity of being substituted after 43 minutes, Eriksson's introduction of Owen Hargreaves a tacit statement that the withdrawal of his floundering right-back could not even wait until half-time.

A welcome transformation saw England dominate the second half, Owen scoring twice with only the width of the crossbar denying him a hat-trick. Lampard was also unlucky to have a goal wrongly disallowed for offside. Despite that dodgy start it was a well-merited win.

England needed it. Turkey now led the group with 15 points, although England, with 13, had a game in hand.

CHAPTER THIRTY-TWO

'SVENSKI'

After the Slovakia match, Sven and Nancy holidayed near Rome. While they were away, Real Madrid sacked their coach, Vicente Del Bosque, 24 hours after winning La Liga, provoking speculation that Eriksson was about to succeed him. It was 'a load of old cobblers', according to Athole Still, but what followed certainly wasn't, and gave the FA cause for concern bordering on panic.

Roman Abramovich, the Russian billionaire, had bought out Ken Bates at Chelsea for £140m. It was clear that like a kid given the run of the sweet shop, he wanted to grab anything and anybody that took his fancy. He had immediately decided that Claudio Ranieri was not the man for him, and now he set his cap at Eriksson as the coach likeliest to make optimum use of the galaxy of superstars he was intent on acquiring.

Discreet inquiries (and some that were ~~creet~~) were made, and Eriksson did ~~the approach that resulted. On 3~~ England coach went to Abramovich' home in the company of the 'Mr Fi acquired the prefix 'Super Agent', Pini Zahavi. Abramovich had appointed Zahavi as his recruiter-in-chief, and it was now apparent that his duties extended beyond the acquisition of players. Zahavi had known Eriksson for more than a decade, since they first did business together to take Sergei Yuran, Vasily Kulkov and Alexander Mostovoi from the old Soviet Union to Benfica. They had become friends in the interim, and it was as such that they met Abramovich, just 24 hours after he had completed his takeover at Chelsea.

None of the parties involved is prepared to shed much light on that first meeting, but what is known is that Eriksson replacing Ranieri was mooted, and a salary of £5m a year mentioned. Eriksson was also asked which players he would be interested in, and the names of two old favourites from his Lazio days, Juan Sebastian Veron and Hernan Crespo cropped up, as did those of England's Wayne Bridge, Glenn Johnson, Joe Cole and Owen Hargreaves.

Unfortunately for Eriksson, he and Zahavi had been caught on camera entering Abramovich's West London pile, and the pictures were plastered all over the *Sun* nearly a week later, on 9 July.

Eriksson, embarrassed by the furore that followed, reaffirmed his commitment to England, but at Soho Square, not too many believed that he would be seeing out his contract. Zahavi said: 'It was a very friendly meeting. They talked about football and about players, but there was nothing decided.'

The FA was worried, and understandably so. At first press conference, on 8 August, the new chief executive, Mark Palios, was forced to admit that contingency plans had been made. He thought Eriksson was likely to leave after Euro 2004, probably for Chelsea, and Middlesbrough's Steve McClaren was the preferred candidate to replace him. There had been no apology from the coach. 'Sven and I spoke about the photos, and all he said was that it was unfortunate timing.'

Inevitably, the story rumbled on as Chelsea signed nearly all the players Eriksson had recommended, and before the next international, a friendly against Croatia at Ipswich on 20 August, he said, disingenuously: 'Just because I have a cup of tea with someone doesn't mean I am signing a contract as the next Chelsea manager. I don't feel embarrassed about being seen with Abramovich, though the speculation afterwards was not so good. I want to qualify for Euro 2004, but if we don't, nobody will want me any more. And that is more true than a joke.' He had objected to allegations of disloyalty in the newspapers. 'When you are here, you all seem very nice,' he told the England press corps. 'But sometimes when I read what you write, it is not so nice.'

For the match, which was a warm-up for the qualifier away to Macedonia on 6 September, Campbell and Woodgate were injured, so opportunity knocked once again for Matthew Upson. Phil Neville was preferred at right-back to Danny Mills, who now seemed to be on borrowed time at international level. England won 3–1, with goals from Beckham (penalty), Owen and Lampard, and had now won six on the trot since the Australia debacle. David James was named man of the match, but not far behind him was John Terry, who took over as captain after Beckham's substitution, and of whom Eriksson said: 'He was super – always there with his head or foot, whatever was needed. He is the young player who learned and came on most last season. He just gets better and better.'

There was criticism, however, of Joe Cole's positional indiscipline. 'At 3–1 he left his position and tried to take people on,' Eriksson said. 'At the right time, that's nice to see, but when there are five minutes to play, the important thing is not to give the opposition the opportunity to have a shot. He must learn that in a competitive game, with five minutes to play, we don't need to make it 4–1, and that 3–1 is okay. Joe is a diamond we have to polish, because tactically he is not the best, and you could see that in this game.'

Mindful of the crowd trouble that had occurred in Slovakia, the FA asked England supporters not to travel to Skopje, for the match against Macedonia. Unsurprisingly, the appeal fell on deaf ears.

Rio Ferdinand and Steven Gerrard were both absent, injured, and the game was not going well when Eriksson came up with a timely reminder of the tactical nous some of his critics still claim he lacks. Trailing 1–0 at half-time, to a sloppily conceded goal by Georgi Hristov, England fought back to win 2–1 after changing formation for the second half.

During the interval, Emile Heskey was warming

up on the pitch with the other substitutes when he
was summoned to the dressing room and told that
he would be partnering Michael Owen for the rest
of the match, with Wayne Rooney dropping back to
operate in the so-called 'hole' behind the strikers.
Within eight minutes of his introduction, Heskey
used his height to direct David Beckham's pass on to
Rooney who, at 17 years 317 days, replaced Owen
in the record books as the youngest player ever to
score for England. Beckham, endlessly influential,
won it from the penalty spot, after a foul on John
Terry, but the credit belonged to Eriksson, who said:
'Playing with two strikers and Rooney in behind
was a gamble, but you need to take risks sometimes,
and when it goes well, they say you are a genius.
What do I say? I got lucky. Most teams put an
offensive midfielder, not a striker, in the hole, but
Rooney showed he can do the job brilliantly.

'Becoming the youngest player to score for
England makes headlines not just in England, but
around the world. I hope Rooney can handle it,
because it will not be easy.'

At the final whistle, an exultant Beckham and
his team-mates ran over to salute the supporters
who had defied the FA's plea not to travel. It was a
contentious show of appreciation, but Eriksson was
not about to condemn it. 'It would be wrong for me
to do so, because it came from the heart,' he said.
Not for the first, or last time, the coach was 'off
message' with his employers. He did agree with
them, however, over their refusal to take, and dis-
tribute, any tickets for the match against Turkey in

Istanbul, saying: 'If the security men say there is a problem, you should listen. If you go, you will risk your life – as the Leeds fans did in Turkey (a reference to the two Leeds supporters killed before the UEFA Cup tie against Galatasaray in 2000).'

Before Istanbul, there was the small matter of Liechtenstein at Old Trafford on 10 September – four days after the Skopje game. Beckham and Gerrard, who was fit to resume in midfield, had picked up yellow cards earlier in the competition, which meant that another booking would rule them out of the Turkey trip. To play them or not to play them against little Liechenstein, that was the question.

It was answered not by Eriksson, but by Beckham, fuelling the impression that the captain was now having an inordinately strong say in selection matters. The day before the match, with Eriksson tight-lipped about his intentions, Beckham told the press: 'I think it is a little bit of a risk, but it is my decision to play.' The *Daily Mail*, never reticent about criticizing the Eriksson regime, had a valid point this time when it said: 'Exactly how much power Beckham wields within the England camp has long been a subject for debate, and after the mystery surrounding his late arrival from Madrid last week, yesterday's remarks raised yet more questions. For Beckham to all but announce he would be playing (and so would Steven Gerrard) somewhat undermined the coach's best efforts to keep England's opponents guessing.

'Certain members of Eriksson's squad are growing

tired of Beckham's celebrity and the amount of clout he appears to carry. There was the pre-World Cup party at Beckingham Palace, the plans for a separate villa at La Manga, the circus that surrounded the meeting with Nelson Mandela in South Africa and the revelation that Eriksson had not given the Real Madrid midfielder a specific time when he had to report for England duty in Manchester.'

Confirming that Beckham and Gerrard would both play, Eriksson said: 'If I don't pick them and we lose, I guess you will cut off my head. Liechtenstein are not France, but they deserve our respect.'

Sol Campbell, who was also on one yellow, was not risked and Ferdinand was still unfit, so Terry and Matthew Upson formed a new partnership at centre-back, Lampard was on the left of midfield and James Beattie, who was scoring freely in the Premiership for Southampton, was given his first start, alongside Owen, with Rooney continuing in the 'hole'.

Against stronger opposition, the decision to play Beckham and Gerrard would surely have backfired, for both of them went about their work as if afraid to make a tackle, with the result that Liechtenstein's part-timers did far better than they might have expected in midfield. That said, they were not good enough to cause an upset, and England won comfortably, if unimpressively, with goals from Owen and Rooney.

An undistinguished and unremarkable match was notable only for two significant statistics. With his 24th international goal, Owen had drawn level with

Sir Geoff Hurst, and with their eighth successive win, Eriksson's England had edged Sir Alf Ramsey and company out of the record books.

England were now top of the group, with 19 points to Turkey's 18. A draw in Istanbul would suffice. 'The only thing to worry about now is the fitness of the players,' Eriksson said.

CHAPTER THIRTY-THREE

'ONE OUT, ALL OUT'

The circumstances surrounding England's decisive match in Istanbul were to make it the most eventful 0–0 in their history. Well in advance, the Turks responded with infantile provocation to Eriksson's well-meant suggestion that for English fans to travel was to risk their lives. Inviting them to make the trip, against the wishes of the FA and UEFA, the president of the Turkish FA, Haluk Ulusoy, said: 'I think Mr Eriksson has forgotten Heysel (the stadium in Brussels where 39 spectators died at the 1985 European Cup final, between Liverpool and Juventus). Of course he doesn't want England fans in Turkey to see a defeat. Anyway, he will be sent away from the England job after the Turkey game because he will no longer have any credibility left. He will only be fit to train Patagonia.'

England were not going to be provoked. On 18 September, nearly four weeks before the match, Eriksson proffered an olive branch. He suggested a face-to-face meeting with Turkey's coach, Senol Gunes. What had he had in mind? 'A peace plan,' he told me. 'I wanted to put an end to all the verbal exchanges between the two sides. I proposed a joint press conference with Gunes, for both of us to appeal for calm.'

Turkish football, however, doesn't do calm, and the refusal came within 24 hours. Articulating it, their general manager, Can Gobanoglu, said: 'We would rather not do anything before the game. We are treating it as a normal match. It does have some security risks, but we don't want to talk about hooliganism and segregation, only about football.'

Eriksson now apologized for saying that English fans could be killed. He said: 'The decision not to take tickets was taken by the FA, for security reasons, and it was supported by UEFA. It wasn't my intention to say the words which were reported after the game in Macedonia, and I'm sorry for any upset they caused. In the last few months, England fans have behaved very well, but I still don't think they should travel. Football should be a party, but security must come first.'

England needed further distraction like the proverbial hole in the head, but just 24 hours after Eriksson's apology, high-level sources at Chelsea let it be known that they had offered to double the salary the FA was paying him, to £4.5m, with the added sweetener of a £1m per trophy bonus. They thought they had got their man, but Eriksson wanted to wait until after Euro 2004, while Roman Abramovich wanted him in place to coincide with the arrival of Peter Kenyon, who was to take up his appointment as chief executive in January – in time for the opening of the transfer window. Chelsea proposed a job-share compromise. Eriksson could work for two masters until after Euro 2004. Abramovich's acolytes pointed out that provided England gained the point they needed in Istanbul, they would have no competitive matches for seven months before the European finals.

At one of the off-the-record briefings that were to become notorious under the new regime at Stamford Bridge, journalists were told that the intention was to reach a pre-contract agreement with Eriksson in January, with a view to him taking up his new job in July. Abramovich wanted to head off approaches from other would-be employers by tying Eriksson into a 'gentlemen's agreement'. There was one proviso. The deal would be void if Chelsea won the Premiership, or the Champions' League, under Claudio Ranieri.

In a statement that fuelled, rather than quelled the mounting speculation, Eriksson said: 'One day I will go back into club football, but where I don't know.' By this stage, there was widespread scepticism about his intentions, and the then Liverpool manager, Gerard Houllier, articulated a nation's suspicions when he revealed that he was 'seething' about reports linking Steven Gerrard with Chelsea. Houllier said: 'It was not good timing that Sven went to see Roman Abramovich and then, two days later, there were stories saying Chelsea wanted to sign Gerrard. He (Eriksson) was pictured in the newspapers going in to meet Abramovich, and the next thing is that Chelsea are after Stevie. I was upset about that, and I got on to Sven to let him know. I phoned him and told him the timing was bad. He took the point and accepted what I said. He claimed it was pure coincidence that one event followed the other, but I was not happy about it all.'

Eventually, there was universal belief that nearly all Chelsea's big-money acquisitions were being made on Eriksson's recommendation, not Ranieri's.

On 6 October, five days before the Turkey match, the spotlight shifted from Eriksson to his key defender, Rio Ferdinand, and an unprecedented furore that was to rumble on for weeks, and bring the England squad to the brink of strike action. A fortnight earlier, on 23 September, Ferdinand had failed to take a routine drugs test at Manchester United's Carrington training complex. He did take, and pass, a test two days later, but the initial failure to comply was a breach of FA rule 3.5, which states: 'If a player fails, or refuses to provide a sample, he will be deemed to have committed an offence.'

United's lawyers claimed their £30m man should be given the 'benefit of the doubt' over a 'genuine mistake', but the FA was having none of it, pointing out that its acceptance of the 'I forgot' plea would set a precedent that would fatally undermine their drugs-testing programme.

Mark Palios, the FA's new chief executive, who had taken over in July, was determined to stand up to United and their lawyers in what was the first test of his mettle, and on 6 October he insisted that Ferdinand had to be left out of the team for Istanbul. All hell broke loose. Eriksson had been due to name his squad on the Sunday, at 7 pm, but the announcement was put back until Monday at 2 pm, and then delayed again. Players were told by text message on the Sunday if they were in or not, but Eriksson refused to accept Ferdinand's omission and, as he argued his case doggedly with Palios, the squad announcement was put off, almost on an hourly basis, until the Tuesday.

Eriksson agreed with United, whose stance was that if Ferdinand was allowed to play on for them until his guilt or innocence was established (which he was), then he should be able to play for England.

By the time the squad was finally made public, there was uproar at England's pre-departure hotel, in St Albans. A cadre of senior players – David Beckham, Michael Owen, Gary Neville and David James – expressed the squad's 'strong objections and deep concerns' over Ferdinand's omission to Palios and the FA's head of communications, Paul Barber. And there was the first threat of a withdrawal of labour from Gordon Taylor, chief executive of the PFA, who said: 'The FA have made their minds up not to select him and I find that disgraceful. They have hung him out to dry. He has been named and shamed, and there's been no positive test.

'Manchester United provide many players for the squad, and it was discussed by my members that if the FA were not going to co-operate with United, why should United co-operate with the FA?'

For once, Eriksson's 'Ice Man' mask slipped. He was angrier than anybody had seen him before, and Athole Still said: 'Sven felt ignored and infuriated. He was pissed off. He had barely met Mark Palios, they had no relationship, and Sven was not consulted. There he was, preaching togetherness and unity to the squad because of the hostile nature of the game in Turkey, and here was a prime example of the FA acting without the involvement of the coach. One of his big worries was that there were four other United players in the squad, and this had a divisive, distracting effect on those guys.'

Eriksson convened a team meeting after dinner. He recalled events as follows: 'I could not imagine a worse build-up to a match of such importance. I had to speak to the players to make sure that they were mentally okay. I told them I wanted Rio in Turkey because, as one of the best defenders in the world, we needed him. But I said I had to accept my orders – in this case from Mark Palios. He had made the decision by himself. My opinion was not important.'

With Gary Neville, a member of the PFA executive board, playing the role of shop steward, the players voted unanimously not to travel, and an eight-strong deputation demanded to see Palios, arguing heatedly that Ferdinand should be allowed to represent his country pending the result of any case against him. Palios stood firm. It was 'inappropriate', he said, to select a player who was 'almost certain' to be charged with a drugs-related offence at a hearing which had been scheduled for the following Monday.

It was a stand-off; who would blink first? In the end, public opinion carried the day. The notion of pampered multi-millionaires going on strike and refusing to play for their country was abhorrent to the average fan, and the *Daily Mirror* sided powerfully with the FA, coming out with the front-page headline: 'Who The Hell Do You Think You Are?', beneath which appeared rogues' gallery pictures of all 24 players involved. The editorial thundered: 'The England soccer squad's threat to strike yesterday was a total disgrace, and an insult to every fan in the country. It beggars belief that David Beckham and his team-mates would choose this week to behave like a bunch of petulant, self-serving prima donnas. Consider the facts: Rio Ferdinand "forgets" to have a drugs test, perhaps the most important duty in any professional sportsman's life. He claimed he was preoccupied with moving house that day, but was photographed shopping in Manchester. Mr Ferdinand has been at best an utter fool and at worst a liar. Yet his England team-mates reacted to the FA's perfectly reasonable decision to drop him by throwing their toys out of the pram and threatening not to play in Saturday's crucial game against Turkey.'

There was much more in the same vein in other newspapers, and outside the team hotel fans hung a banner which read: 'Sven: We'll Play If They Won't (And For Free)'. The players had overreached themselves and forfeited public sympathy. They were in a corner and needed a get out, which came in the form of a phone call from Ferdinand, thanking them for their support, but urging them to play the match. Any waverers were brought onside when the FA was warned that failure to fulfil the fixture would see England excluded from Euro 2004, and possibly the 2006 World Cup.

Their brinkmanship having got them nowhere, the squad flew to Istanbul on Thursday 9 October, but the mutinous mood persisted, and as the row rumbled on it went almost unnoticed when Michael Owen was forced to withdraw, with a shin injury. The players issued a statement, claiming that the strike threat had been a bluff, but stressing their support for Ferdinand. It read: 'Rio Ferdinand was entitled to confidentiality and a fair hearing in front of an independent commission. We believe the people responsible for making the decision did not give Rio that due process, and have disrupted and made the team weaker against the wishes of the manager and the players.

'The organization that we represent has not only let down one of our team-mates, but the whole of the England squad and its manager. One of our team-mates was penalized without being given the rights he is entitled to, and without any charges being brought against him. All the players are proud to wear an England shirt, and would never let England, Sven-Goran Eriksson or our magnificent fans down. The events of the past few days have not been easy to deal with when you consider the lack of protection that our team-mate was given once this decision had been made. We apologize to our manager, staff and fans for any concerns that may have arisen over the last few days. In our minds, there has never been any question as to whether we would play this game.'

The captain, David Beckham, added: 'The manager has stayed strong through this, he agreed with what the players thought. He was with us.'

Now it was the FA's turn to be angry. Eriksson had sided with the players against his employers. The subplot, they thought, was that Eriksson was engineering an excuse to walk out on England and join Chelsea. The ubiquitous Ulrika Jonsson said as much, telling reporters at the time: 'I feel this will be the straw that breaks his back. His frustration at not managing a Premiership club with weekly matches, and having to deal with the bureaucratic FA will now have reached fever pitch. He wanted in at Manchester United two years ago, and established a dialogue with Peter Kenyon. This latest incident would give him a good reason to bow out.'

On the day of the match, the Chelsea pot was given a good stir yet again when the *Daily Mirror* reported that Claudio Ranieri had held 'crisis talks' with his bosses over Eriksson's refusal to deny that he had agreed to replace him in the new year. Ranieri's agent, Vicenzo Morabito, said: 'All these rumours . . . Sven should have ended this whole thing out of respect for a colleague.'

Preparations for the game had continued in the most febrile atmosphere anybody could remember. I have been reporting on football at the top level for more than 30 years, and I have never known anything like it. Beckham admitted that the players had been taken aback by the hostility provoked by their strike threat, saying: 'I think we were all surprised by the reaction to the stand we took,' and another statement was issued, as follows: 'While we fully recognize Rio should not have missed the first drugs test, we have gone on record to say that what happened we, as a squad, were unhappy with. The issue is now a matter for the FA, and they have promised to look at their procedures for future cases like this. We do realize we have something to prove, and we will be playing our hearts out for our fans, our country and ourselves.'

CHAPTER THIRTY-FOUR

HEROES AND VILLAINS

England went into the cauldron that is the Sukru Saracoglu stadium without two key players, Rio Ferdinand and Michael Owen. Their places went to Chelsea's John Terry and Liverpool's Emile Heskey, both of whom were to play a full part in a performance which bordered on the heroic.

The match was every bit as explosive as lurid tabloid predictions had indicated it might be, with a brawl in the players' tunnel at half-time, and an ugly clash between Beckham and Alpay which effectively ended the Aston Villa defender's career in the Premiership.

David James, the England goalkeeper, who was to have an exceptional match, said: 'Running out, it was the loudest booing I'd ever heard. I just thought: "Sod it, get on with it." It was a new experience playing in that environment – no fans, everything against us, and knowing we couldn't afford to lose. We were all holding each other during the national anthems, really bonding. Everything in the build-up made us grow as a team. We had meeting after meeting because it was important that we made sure everything was out of the way before-hand. Looking back now, the only thing we did wrong was putting out that statement late on the Wednesday.

'When the time came, we were ready. Sven is not the kind of person to give a 15-minute team talk. He was up there for five minutes, giving a precise outline of what we had to watch out for. He had warned us that Turkey were going to be on edge, so we were prepared for everything. Once we started, we did what we had to do, and we did it well. It was the best defensive performance I have ever played behind, for club or country. I was able to enjoy it. John Terry and Sol Campbell were superb. It was a pleasure to be in goal behind them.'

England lined up in 4–3–1–2 formation, with Paul Scholes, who was playing in the 'hole', behind the strikers, given the added responsibility of deny-ing space to Turkey's playmaker, Tugay. The game plan, largely reliant on defensive discipline, was spot on, piling frustration on opponents whose tem-perament in adversity is notoriously brittle. Hakan Sukur, the Turks' captain and principal striker, had laughed when he heard of Ferdinand's exclusion, and said: 'Without him there, we'll be much more comfortable. I would play with a broken leg.'

It often looked as if he had one, such was Terry's dominance alongside the massively impres-sive Campbell at the heart of the England back four. Good as he is, Ferdinand was never missed. The defenders were well served by Nicky Butt, patrolling just in front of them, and Ashley Cole, at left-back, had good reason to be grateful for Steven Gerrard's assistance when the dangerous Nihat took him on. Heskey and Rooney ran the channels with pace and purpose, and it had been evenly balanced when, with 37 minutes played, Gerrard cut in from his station on the left and was brought down for an obvious penalty. Beckham stepped forward to take the kick, but his left foot slipped as he did so, causing him to send the ball high over the bar in what looked like a textbook rugby conversion.

Cue pandemonium. Alpay stood over the England captain and crowed at his misfortune, Beckham took the bait and reacted with a gesture that inflamed the situation, and the fuse was lit for what was to follow in the tunnel. As the two teams headed for the dressing rooms at half-time, Alpay ran past Beckham, shouted 'Go f*** your mother,' and pushed a finger into his (Beckham's) cheek. Beckham chased him down the tunnel, where others joined in a slanging match that became a free for all. Terry, a tough guy off the field as well as on it, was instantly Beckham's minder, and Heskey lunged menacingly at Hasan Sas, who was not even playing, but still felt the need to spit at Ashley Cole. White shirts piled in from all sides at the first sign of trouble.

Eriksson said afterwards it had been like a scene from the wild west, and fortunately Wyatt Earp was to hand, in the shape of the world's best referee, Pierluigi Collina. A lesser official might have panicked and dished out so many cards that the match would have been abandoned, but the Italian was authority and common sense personified, summoning Beckham and Alpay to his dressing room. 'Calm down,' he said. 'I'm not going to let silly behaviour ruin such an important game. Go now and calm things down.'

The temperature did drop a degree or two in the second half, although boiling point was never far away, and Turkey's goalkeeper, Rustu, was fortunate to escape with a booking when he rushed out of his area and booted Kieron Dyer in the face. The Turks became increasingly desperate, sending on attacking substitutes and throwing themselves to the ground in vain attempts to con the peerless Collina. For England, the clock ticked agonizingly slowly, and Dyer, Vassell and Lampard were thrown into the fray, as much for the substitutions to eat up time as for the fresh legs they provided.

With ten minutes left, Beckham 'scored' with a header, only for the crosser, Dyer, to be ruled offside, and Rooney and Scholes both spurned good chances. Finally, it was all over. England were through to the finals, Turkey condemned to ordeal by play-off for the third tournament in a row. An elated Beckham said: 'The performance was one we can all be proud of. It was tense to the end, but we battled away, and it shows people we really are proud to play for our country. After the week beforehand, this was the biggest test this team has had, and to come through it, with no fans and everything else, was fantastic.'

Of his altercation with Alpay, he said: 'When I missed the penalty, he came up to me and was shouting in my face. The referee did well, and it did go through my head that I had promised everybody I wouldn't get a red card.'

Alpay said: 'Collina made us shake hands and hug each other. Then he told us we were too hot and needed to calm down, making us drink a glass of water before we could leave. Beckham is a good player, and it was a psychological ploy. We wanted to get him to react, but it didn't work. England deserved to win the game.'

Eriksson praised his players, but lost his characteristic cool at the press conference straight after the game, when he came under sustained questioning about his future. Asked if he would still be in charge at Euro 2004, he replied: 'Nothing has changed. As the situation is today, yes.'

What did he mean by 'as the situation is today'?

'Don't you understand me? Is it bad English?' he snapped.

The questioner would not be deterred, and came back with: 'Can you categorically state you will be England boss at Euro 2004?'

With a weary sigh, Eriksson said: 'Yes, I will.'

England, beaten just the once now in 19 competitive matches, were immediately installed as 7–1 fourth favourites for the tournament, behind France, Italy and Portugal. 'This team is very difficult to beat in the games that matter,' Eriksson said. 'We should not be afraid of anyone.'

Gerrard, an England captain in the making, spoke up for the coach, saying: 'There is no one better to be manager of England. He is doing a great job and the criticism he gets is uncalled for. He protected us all week and stuck with us. That is what a manager is supposed to do. Obviously he was in a very awkward situation, and I thought he handled it very well. I don't see why we can't go on and win Euro 2004. We have proved we can mix it with the best.'

There had been rather too much 'mixing it' for UEFA's liking, and planning for the finals had to be put on hold pending the inevitable investigation into the half-time fracas. There was never any danger of England being kicked out of the tournament, but the FA was warned that the suspension of individual players, for violent conduct, was a very real threat. England, after all, had been fined a record £68,000 and warned as to their future conduct after the Turks' visit to Sunderland. With that in mind, eventual exoneration came as a considerable relief.

A good job well done, Eriksson sought time out of the media spotlight by returning home to visit his parents, taking his father to watch Torsby play Rottneros in the Swedish Third Division. Sven senior and junior paid the equivalent of £3 each to join a 'crowd' of 250, but brought their team no luck, Torsby losing 3–1.

Back in London, the rumours linking the England coach with Chelsea would not go away, and were fuelled by Pavel Nedved of Juventus, who had played for him at Lazio, claiming Eriksson had made contact to ask if he would be interested in a move to Stamford Bridge. Clearly something was afoot.

There was another storm brewing, and it would be a big one, but after Turkey its epicentre was still three months away.

It had its roots in what ought to have been a routine friendly against Denmark at Old Trafford in November 2003. It was anything but. After their contretemps with the players in Istanbul, the FA had promised to review their disciplinary procedures as a matter of urgency. But before they could do so, bad was to become worse.

Four days before the match, Darius Vassell had to withdraw from the squad, injured, and Eriksson decided to recall Alan Smith, after a 13-month absence, as his replacement. Smith duly reported to the team hotel – The Lowry, in Salford – the following day, only to be sent home almost as soon as he had arrived when the FA learned that he had been arrested that same morning. His offence was a minor one. Playing for Leeds, in a Carling Cup tie against Manchester United on 28 October, he had thrown a plastic bottle back into the crowd, from where it had come, unintentionally striking a spectator on the head. Unhurt, the woman in question made light of the incident, but Smith was arrested after a complaint from a third party. The case was subsequently dropped.

On the Wednesday night, when Eriksson decided on his replacement for Vassell, the FA knew that Smith had to 'assist police with their inquiries' the following day, but they expected him to be interviewed, not arrested. Cue crisis.

At a press conference to explain Smith's

treatment, Mark Palios was nonplussed when it was pointed out that Nicky Butt had been allowed to play three matches for England while on police bail after his arrest for an alleged assault in June (this case was also dropped). The accusation of double standards had barely died away when somebody reminded Palios that the striker summoned in Smith's place, James Beattie, was serving a 30-month drink-driving ban that also involved 100 hours of community service. The FA's chief executive was dumbfounded. His admission that 'our communication could have been better' was a masterpiece of understatement.

Eriksson was furious, and so were his players – this was Istanbul revisited. The players came up with yet another statement of complaint, which read: 'In the light of recent controversies surrounding team selection for the games against Turkey and now Denmark, we are extremely disappointed at the way the FA have handled the above – in particular the treatment of Rio Ferdinand and Alan Smith, which has undermined the position of the manager and could have seriously affected the morale and the team spirit of the players.

'We feel this has left us with no option but to ask the FA that from this day forward, they make clear the criteria of selection for the England team, so that there is no room for ambiguity and misunderstanding. We have a concern that the FA are reacting to outside pressures, which impacts unfairly on the manager and the players.

'By the FA's actions in withdrawing Rio and Alan

from the squad, in both cases the players have been assumed guilty before the due process has been completed – a right which should be afforded to every individual, not only in football but in society as a whole. Our loyalty to England, as illustrated by our qualification for Euro 2004 unbeaten and top of the group, should be unquestioned. We are merely asking for the same loyalty in return from the same organization that we represent.'

Palios had to admit his embarrassment. 'I spoke to Sven, and clearly he was frustrated by the constant interference', he said. 'For two successive matches he was not able to have the squad he wanted, and I was as "pissed off" as he was. In this day and age, you should be able to find out these things about players, and the circumstances surrounding them. That information should be available.'

Was it FA policy that any player under investigation by the police should not be selected by England? 'We haven't got the policy laid down anywhere, so we're looking for one. We could have picked Smith, but that was not the consensus of opinion among people with far more experience than me.' A policy review was under way.

Palios agreed that the FA's relationship with Eriksson had been damaged, but took a tough, take-it-or-leave-it line, saying: 'He understands our position, he doesn't have to agree. I can't remember what he said, but the gist was that he didn't agree.'

He certainly didn't. Eriksson told me: 'I didn't agree with their (the FA's) actions, and I didn't understand them. I supported the players. My opinion was, and is, that a player should be able to play until he is charged. That's what happens in other countries.'

Back came Palios, with: 'My intention is to make the right decisions, and if the right ones are unpopular, I'll still continue to make them. The relationship between the coach and his players is the key one. My relationship with him is secondary.'

Viewed in the light of a schism now bordering on cold war, England's 3–2 defeat, and the end of a nine-game unbeaten run, was not such a surprise. They were well below full strength, lacking Ferdinand, Campbell, Gerrard, Owen, Scholes, Dyer, Southgate and Vassell, but would have emerged with a creditable draw but for a gaffe by the substitute goalkeeper, Paul Robinson, who gifted Jon-Dahl Tomasson the winner. The England goals were scored by Wayne Rooney and Joe Cole.

CHAPTER THIRTY-FIVE

HERE WE GO AGAIN

When England jetted out from Luton airport on Monday 7 June, their hopes flew higher than the 737 transporting them to Lisbon. The 6–1 annihilation of Iceland in a pre-tournament warm-up had been the perfect send-off and, as the game had shown the best way to accommodate Frank Lampard in a four-abreast midfield, Sven-Goran Eriksson's stock had rarely been higher.

Going into Euro 2004, the squad's opinion of the coach was articulated best by Gary Neville, who said: 'He's the best manager I've known, in terms of handling the England job. Nothing seems to faze him, he stays calm and level-headed. In victory he doesn't get too high, and in defeat he doesn't get too low. You never see him panic, or get angry.

'You get a lot thrown at you when you're England manager. Apart from the Prime Minister, it's the most high-profile job in the country, and Sven is the perfect man for it. I hope people don't take this the wrong way, but he has removed the emotional thing that has gone with England. I don't mean he doesn't care, because he does, and you can see that when he's with us. But he's removed the nonsense that has affected some England managers.'

Neville, first capped by Terry Venables, had also played under Glenn Hoddle, Kevin Keegan and two caretakers, Howard Wilkinson and Peter Taylor. 'Sven is a different sort of man – ice when others are fire,' he explained. 'Top football needs that dispassionate attitude. He puts his full trust in the players, and in return for that we like him because we like to be trusted. We'd like to think we repay him with our performances. We don't want to let this man down.'

Neville's brother, Phil, took up the theme, saying: 'Even though Sven is an international manager, there's more of a club-type relationship with him. We speak regularly with him between England games. If you're injured, he'll phone to check how you are. When my wife had a baby, he rang to congratulate us. In my experience, England managers wouldn't have done that in the past. When we went to Sardinia [for pre-tournament preparation], Sven told us to switch off from football and go and enjoy ourselves with our families.'

Eriksson's demeanour was also popular with his charges. The younger Neville said: 'He doesn't try to impose his will on the players by shouting and screaming, he does it by treating us as adults. He doesn't have many rules, he lets you behave like men. If you want to do something that's part of your normal preparation then, regardless of what the others are doing, he lets you do it. As long as you don't let him down, he'll encourage you to do whatever you think is best. To my knowledge, he has never upset anybody in the squad.'

England began training on Portuguese soil on Tuesday 8 June, when it immediately became apparent that they had a problem. John Terry was unable to take part, working instead with the physiotherapist, Gary Lewin. At this stage, Eriksson was optimistic that the Chelsea centre-half would regain fitness in time to play against France in the opening game, but nothing can ever be taken for granted where hamstrings are concerned, and already eyes were turning to Jamie Carragher and Ledley King as potential understudies.

If Terry's indisposition caused a dip in morale, it was imperceptible, and the loss would have been made good that night, when the Arsenal manager, Arsene Wenger, praised England as 'the up-and-coming team in Europe'. He said: 'They are getting to the stage where they are capable of winning on the big stage. France are the natural favourites, but Wayne Rooney has the audacity to be one of the revelations of the tournament.'

Elsewhere, the French were not so complimentary, Henry criticizing Michael Owen's 'static' style of play, which required that others crafted his scoring opportunities for him, and Patrick Vieira describing England's football as 'one-dimensional' and 'old-fashioned', by which he meant excessively reliant on the long ball.

By Wednesday 9 June, four days before the game, England were sounding a lot less positive about Terry's prospects. Restricted to light jogging, his chances of playing were officially 'in the balance'. Eriksson said: 'The last thing we want to do is risk John when he's not fully fit. There is no point in having him for 45 minutes and then losing him for the rest of the tournament. The decision will be made on Friday.'

The coach was more interested in the psychological aspect of playing the champions, and called a team meeting to remind all concerned that while some of the Frenchmen might be sporting icons, they were also familiar faces encountered in the Premiership week in, week out. 'We shouldn't have a complex about these people,' he said. 'You play against Henry, Pires and Vieira all the time. You shouldn't be in awe of them, we must go into the game believing that we are at their level. They have some fantastic individuals, but so do we, so let's not hype them up more than they deserve. You will fall by the wayside if you are looking across during the national anthem thinking: "I want to be like him."'

Owen, in particular, loved that. He said: 'I think everybody would prefer to pay to watch Thierry Henry ahead of me, but I may have qualities he doesn't possess. I wouldn't like to say what they are. The game is all about results, and his have been better than mine lately. He has scored more goals, and he has won the league, so he is the best in the world at the moment, but I'm going to be trying to change that.

'In my opinion, France are better than Brazil, they are the best team in the world, but I'm very confident in the ability of our players to match up. It would be a travesty if this squad didn't win anything.'

On Thursday, Eriksson was again in upbeat mood after training. 'We're in good shape,' he said, momentarily forgetting Terry, who was not. He preferred to accentuate the positive, such as Gerrard's development into one of the best players in the world. 'Whether he plays for England or for Liverpool, he is the complete midfielder,' the coach enthused. 'He can do everything – he can tackle, he can score goals, he can pass and his engine is incredible. His fitness level today is such that he'll get up and down the pitch for 90 minutes if you want him to do that. Normally a player is better at tackling than passing or the other way around, but Gerrard can do it all. I've had some great midfielders play for me down the years, but I don't remember ever having a player like him.'

Unfortunately Gerrard, like all England's best midfield men, wanted to play in the centre, rather than on the left, where Eriksson had become accustomed to using him. Similarly, David Beckham had moved from the right, where he played for Manchester United, to the middle at Real Madrid, and wanted to do the same at international level. Frank Lampard was only comfortable in the centre, and Paul Scholes was not properly suited to the left, and cut inside all the time. Eriksson maintained there wasn't a problem, but the situation was far from ideal. He revealed: 'On our first day in Sardinia, I took all of them aside and told them:

"Look, I know you prefer to play central, all four of you, but if you can find a system to accommodate all four of you there, then tell me, because I don't have one." The main thing is that all four can play left or right, as well as central. They accept the jobs they are given, and understand the reasons.'

Iron-willed discipline was the key to success against France. Eriksson reasoned: 'If we don't have discipline, we've no chance. We need to keep our shape and organization. If we keep losing the ball, and are badly organized, it will be Christmas Eve for France. We can't be all over the place.' Specifically, he worked on ways to deny Zinedine Zidane and Robert Pires the time and space in which to work their magic just behind the front line. France had an unusual formation, with two midfielders, Vieira and Claude Makelele, 'sitting' in front of the back four, and two more, Pires and Zidane, coming in from the right and left respectively to play in what used to be termed the inside-forward positions. England's problem was how to mark them, or rather who should do it? If Henry came in off the left flank, as was his wont, should Gary Neville follow him, or pick up Zidane when he filled the hole? It was essential, Eriksson told his players, not to give Zidane and Pires time on the ball. If they were allowed to play with their heads up, they would wreak havoc. They had to be put under pressure instantly whenever they gained possession. Vieira was less of a worry; Gerrard could take care of him. 'There will be some good tackles from both of them, and Steven will win his share.'

On the Friday, two days before the game, it finally became apparent that Terry wasn't going to make it. King was chosen as his replacement, ahead of Carragher, because of his greater pace, which was needed to combat Henry's supercharger. 'It was a difficult decision,' Eriksson said. 'Carragher is more experienced, but King is a little bit quicker and a better header of the ball.'

The French were also concerned about their opponents' speed in attack, and left out their ageing captain, Marcel Desailly, preferring to play Lilian Thuram and Mikael Silvestre in central defence.

Clearly intent on raising the stakes psychologically, Patrick Vieira predicted 'a war'. Pointing to the fact that France had not conceded a goal for 11 games, he said: 'I'm not worried because we have the defenders to cope with players like Rooney and Owen.' David Beckham countered with: 'France are a great team, but we are better. I have that much confidence in the players around me. The plan is to go at them and not be fazed by anyone or anything. It's part of our nature to get stuck in and not be frightened, but we also want to play attractive football. It will be physical, played at a high tempo and with a lot of passion, but it will also be a tactical, skilful game.'

Going into the match, Eriksson felt he was 'on trial'. He explained: 'Maybe people will call for my head if it doesn't go well, that's life. People have wanted my head in the past, but it's still on my shoulders. I have a contract for four more years, but lose three games here and who knows?' Not that he was expecting defeat. 'Things look good – on paper,' he said. 'The confidence is big. I don't need to tell the players: "You can beat France if you have a good day," they know that.'

CHAPTER THIRTY-SIX

A CRAZY START

FRANCE 2   ENGLAND 1
Lisbon, 13 June
France: Barthez (Marseille), Gallas (Chelsea), Thuram (Juventus), Lizarazu (Bayern Munich), Silvestre (Manchester United), Vieira (Arsenal), Makelele (Chelsea), Pires (Arsenal), Zidane (Real Madrid), Henry (Arsenal), Trezeguet (Juventus). Substitutes: Wiltord (Arsenal) for Pires 75 minutes, Sagnol (Bayern Munich) for Silvestre 79 minutes, Dacourt (Roma) for Makelele 90 minutes.
England: James (Manchester City), G. Neville (Manchester United), A. Cole (Arsenal), King (Tottenham Hotspur), Campbell (Arsenal), Gerrard (Liverpool), Beckham (Real Madrid), Scholes (Manchester United), Lampard (Chelsea), Rooney (Everton), Owen (Liverpool). Substitutes: Vassell (Aston Villa) for Owen 69 minutes, Hargreaves (Bayern Munich) for Scholes 76 minutes, Heskey (Birmingham City) for Rooney 76 minutes.
Referee: M. Merk (Germany).

The first striking image of an unforgettable night was the Estadio da Luz decked out in red. By hook or by crook, England fans had acquired three-quarters of the tickets and outnumbered their French counterparts three to one. The surroundings may not have been familiar, but in another respect it was like a home game for David Beckham and his team.

During the pre-match kickabout, the attention was drawn, as if by magnet, to Zinedine Zidane and Thierry Henry, who paired off and fine-tuned their touch and control with a series of mesmeric ball-juggling routines. The England players could not fail to notice, and Wayne Rooney, all cheeky chappie, offered to join in.

When the teams lined up for the anthems, Ledley King looked tense. He, too, had witnessed Henry's warm-up routine, and was contemplating the trials and tribulations that lay ahead. The England players, and their supporters, were in good voice, giving a rousing rendition of 'God Save The Queen.' Even Eriksson had learned the words by now, and Nancy Dell'Olio, seated behind the author in the VIP seats in a fetching red and white outfit, mimed dutifully.

France made the better start, dominating possession and passing the ball around nicely, but in front of, rather than behind, the England defence. Ominously, King's first two touches were awful, gifting possession to the French, but the Spurs man quickly overcame his stage fright and came on in leaps and bounds to play a full part in the disciplined performance Eriksson had called for. England had acknowledged that they needed nearly everybody to be at the peak of their game if they were to get the result they needed, and nearly everybody was. The back four were outstanding, both individually and as a unit. The full-backs, Gary Neville and Ashley

Cole, defended assiduously and still found time to supply the attack with width on the overlap, and Sol Campbell was a firefighting colossus when the going got tough. In midfield, Frank Lampard, Steven Gerrard and Paul Scholes all beavered away energetically to combat the craft of Zidane and Robert Pires. Only Beckham was below par. In attack, Rooney scared the daylights out of the French defence with his determined, direct running, but Michael Owen was strangely anonymous.

Eight of the 11 were at their best (nine if you counted David James, who had very little to do), and it seemed to be enough. The French were restricted to optimistic long shots, and then, after 36 minutes, hallelujah! Beckham's free-kick from out on the right arrowed in towards the near post where Lampard, seven yards out, got his head to it first, leaving Fabien Barthez flat-footed and floundering. The impregnable French defence had been breached at last, conceding for the first time in 12 games, or nearly 18 hours of football. England were in front and in control.

The French hit back with increasing urgency, but the line held, and after 73 minutes it should have been 2–0. Rooney, charging at the heart of the French defence at pace, was brought down by Mikael Silvestre for an obvious penalty. Beckham stepped up and struck the kick well, but at the ideal height for a goalkeeper, and Barthez torpedoed to his right to pull off a spectacular save. It was a body-blow for England and a lift for France, but the one goal seemed to be enough.

Eriksson wanted fresh legs. Darius Vassell had taken over from the ineffective Owen after 69 minutes and now, after 76, a double substitution threw on Owen Hargreaves and Emile Heskey for Scholes, who had twisted an ankle, and Rooney. Two of the substitutions were good ones. Hargreaves and Vassell were both livelier than the players they had replaced. The third was little short of a disaster. Rooney had been easily England's most dangerous forward, and the French defenders heaved a collective sigh of relief when he was withdrawn in favour of a blunderbuss striker with five goals in 43 internationals.

Without Rooney, England lost attacking impetus and started giving the ball away. Consequently, they found themselves besieged, defending on the perimeter of their penalty area. Nevertheless, they did it so well that with the stadium clock showing 89 minutes, they were still leading, apparently set for a notable, morale-enhancing victory. Unfortunately, as Brian Clough used to say, it only takes a second to score a goal, and Heskey lost possession and then committed a foul, 20 yards from his own goal, in attempting to regain it. Zidane, who had been kept quiet in open play, stepped forward to take the free-kick and curved it with deft precision into the right-hand corner of James' net.

Oh well, England would probably have settled for 1–1 before the game. But wait. Within a matter of seconds Gerrard misguidedly tried to find James with a back pass which was easily intercepted by Henry. James advanced from his line to meet the danger, couldn't get to the ball in time and brought the Frenchman down for the night's second blatant penalty. Zidane made no mistake with the kick and England's triumph had turned to ashes.

There was stunned disbelief in the stadium – all bar the section where les bleus and their followers were going berserk. The England players headed straight for the tunnel in a daze, until Gary Neville stopped them and reminded them of their duty to acknowledge the fans. When they finally made it back to the dressing room, it was Shizuoka all over again. Everybody sat speechless, heads down, and again it was Neville who stirred them out of their reverie. The shop steward of Istanbul became the Lisbon Lion, standing in the middle of the room and exhorting his team-mates to get their heads up. 'We played well and deserved a result out there,' he said. 'Now let's go and win these next two games and beat that lot, like we should have done, in the final.'

The address concluded with all the players going into the bonding huddle usually performed immediately before kick-off. Eriksson was much impressed. He always said a team had to have four or five leaders and Neville was clearly one. Beckham, however, remained very down. Eriksson said: 'He was alone in the dressing room while all the others were on the bus. I went and talked to him for a while, and told him it was important that the whole team built it up again, mentally and in terms of morale. He had to put the disappointment behind him and give a lead to the rest of the team. He and the other senior players – Gary Neville, Sol Campbell and Michael Owen – were the ones to do it.'

Back at the team hotel, wives and girlfriends were allowed to stay the night (they were based elsewhere in the city) to help repair morale.

The following day (Monday) the media inquest began in earnest. All the newspapers deemed England to have been unlucky, but Eriksson did not escape criticism. The substitution of Rooney was universally condemned as a major mistake. Bobby Robson, the former England manager, told me: 'I just didn't understand that. Their defenders were having kittens every time he ran at them, and you could see their relief when the lad went off.' Eriksson countered that Rooney had been showing signs of fatigue, and in those circumstances he was more likely to lose his discipline and pick up a yellow, or even red, card.

Nobody fell for that one. The response of John Sadler, in the *Sun*, was fairly typical. He wrote: 'Tired? At 18 years old? You don't get tired at that age, in the first game of a major tournament with four days to recover before playing again. And if you do, then serious questions need to be asked about the team's preparation.'

There was more criticism on the way when David James, in a characteristically candid interview, revealed that in all the video footage of the French he had been required to watch in the days leading up to the match, there was not one Zidane free-kick. Better prepared, he felt he would have got to the shot. James also admitted that, with the benefit of hindsight, he should have picked up Gerrard's back pass, rather than going for it with his feet. 'That would have given away a free-kick inside the area, but we could have packed the goal-line, which would have made it more difficult to score from than a penalty.'

The postmortem over, Eriksson was now concerned with preparations for the next game. Nicky Butt had sustained damaged knee ligaments in stretching for the ball in training and was out of the tournament. Attempts to draft Jermain Defoe into the squad were turned down by UEFA, whose rules stipulate that no replacements are allowed after a team's first match, unless in 'exceptional circumstances', such as two goalkeepers being injured.

King had played well against the French, and could count himself unlucky to be omitted in favour of John Terry, who was fit again, as was Scholes, who had recovered from his ankle injury. The team picked itself, but the formation was a different matter. England's habit throughout the tournament was to allow journalists to watch the first 15 minutes of their training sessions, then have them leave while the important work was done. The day before the game, reporters watched the team start to play the reserves with a diamond midfield, and drew the obvious conclusion. The *Daily Mail*'s back-page headline, 'Sven Will Risk The Diamond', was not untypical.

In fact, the session went so badly that Eriksson called a halt after about 20 minutes and started all over again. On the journey back from Coimbra to

England's Lisbon base, the coach thought long and hard about his players' listlessness, but remained determined to use the diamond. Then what was inevitably described in some quarters as 'player power' took a hand. David Beckham and Steven Gerrard took their concerns to the assistant coach, Steve McClaren, who passed them on. Eriksson then called the midfield players together to ask what was wrong, and was told they didn't share his enthusiasm for the system he favoured, and much preferred the orthodox 4–4–2 used against France. The upshot was a vote in which three of the four midfielders were against the diamond, and only Scholes, who wanted to play in the 'hole', behind the strikers, rather than on the left, was for it.

Democracy prevailed, Eriksson changed his game plan. He now says: 'I made the decision on the Wednesday night, after having the four midfield players in my room after dinner. I wanted the meeting, not the players. Before we had it, I felt it would have suited us better to play a diamond against the Swiss, because they use the same formation as Turkey, with one midfielder 'sitting' and one offensive. But the practice session we had didn't look good, so I wasn't sure. As a manager, when you're not sure, you talk to the players and listen to them, you explain and put all your cards on the table.

'I called them in and said: "What's going on? Why didn't we have a good session?" When we started to talk tactics, there was a division. When we came out, we'd decided to do it their way. As a coach, you make the strategy and explain it, to be sure that the players understand it and that they accept it. My job is to make sure the players are happy with what they're doing, and understand it. That's why I had the meeting.

'The first time I had a meeting like it, three years earlier, the players were very surprised. They didn't want to tell me their opinions, but now they do, and I'll always listen. My belief is that we can play two different systems and do it well.' This left him hostage to fortune. If the flat four worked, the 'rebels' would get the credit, if it didn't, the coach would be blamed for irresolute management.

Eriksson was more worried about the temperature, which was 97°F at kick-off time the day before the match. Not that he was making excuses in advance. 'It was worse – more humid – at the World Cup in Japan, and I'm sure we'll handle it,' he said.

The Swiss, who had drawn 0–0 with Croatia in their first game, had reassessed their chances after gaining a point, and come to the conclusion that a similar result would suit them against England, leaving them with all to play for against France.

ENGLAND 3   SWITZERLAND 0
Coimbra, 17 June
England: James (Manchester City), G. Neville (Manchester United), A. Cole (Arsenal), Terry (Chelsea), Campbell (Arsenal), Gerrard (Liverpool), Beckham (Real Madrid), Scholes (Manchester United), Lampard (Chelsea), Rooney (Everton), Owen (Liverpool). Substitutes: Hargreaves (Bayern Munich) for Scholes 70 minutes, Vassell (Aston Villa) for Owen 72 minutes, Dyer (Newcastle United) for Rooney 83 minutes.

Switzerland: Stiel (Borussia Mönchengladbach), Haas (West Bromwich Albion), M. Yakin (Basle), Muller (Lyons), Spycher (Grasshoppers), Huggel (Basle), Celestini (Marseille), Wicky (Hamburg), Chapuisat (Young Boys), Frei (Rennes), H. Yakin (Stuttgart). Substitutes: Gygax (Zurich) for Chapuisat (half-time), Cabanas (Grasshoppers) for Celestini after 53 minutes, Volanthen (PSV Eindhoven) for H. Yakin after 83 minutes.

Referee: V. Ivanov (Russia).

Eriksson had two concerns before the match – one was that his team could not afford to lose, the other that the quaint university town of Coimbra had been pinpointed as the likeliest venue for hooliganism ever since the draw had been made, in December. Trouble on the Algarve had already raised the dreaded prospect of England getting thrown out of the competition because of their followers' misbehaviour. But he need not have worried on either account.

The conduct of the England fans, who outnumbered the Swiss four to one, drew praise from the hosts and, after facing Zidane and company, the match was a walk in the park. The temperature was again in the high thirties, but Switzerland are hardly hot weather specialists, so England were not at a disadvantage. There was an ominous start, when Rooney was booked after only 18 minutes for a studs-raised challenge on Jorg Stiel, the Swiss goalkeeper, leaving the young Evertonian walking a disciplinary tightrope. Another yellow card in the third game, against Croatia, would see him suspended for the quarter-finals. Five minutes later,

Rooney made a much more welcome contribution, heading in from five yards after an attractive passing move was launched from deep by Gerrard. Rooney was the youngest player to score in the European finals; England were up and running.

At half-time, with only one goal in it, any result was possible, but after an hour the balance changed, numerically and territorially, when Bernt Haas, the Swiss defender, was sent off for the second of two yellow cards. Rooney, scenting blood against ten men, went into rampaging mode, and drove in his second after 75 minutes, via the back of Stiel's head. Gerrard made it 3-0 and Vassell should have added a fourth just before the end. It was the good, restorative win England needed, and suddenly Rooney, just 18, was the talk of the tournament.

Before the match, writing in the *Daily Mail*, Tony Adams had advocated dropping the teenager, on the basis that he was not a good foil for Michael Owen. Now, suddenly, it was 'Wayne's World', with Chelsea and Manchester United among those prepared to pay a king's ransom to prise him away from Goodison Park. 'Rooneymania' was the front-page headline in the *Sun*, where it was reported that 'England went Rooney-mad yesterday.' He was the new 'Gazza', according to another tabloid. One hopes not.

Quizzed time and again about his overnight sensation, Eriksson embarrassed his employers by saying that if he was a club manager, he would have been beating a path to the door of Rooney's agent. His Football Association minders winced at that.

Managers 'tapping up' players via their agents may go on all the time, but it is against FA rules, and there are pretences to be maintained. The coach was on safer ground when he said: 'I can't say I know Wayne very well because he doesn't talk much, but then he doesn't need to. He just goes out there and does it. He's like a boy out on the school pitch, saying: "Give me the ball and let me enjoy myself." I had Roberto Baggio and Rui Costa at a similar age, they were good but Rooney is special. Players of 18 normally need to be talked to in training, and coached through games. They make mistakes and need to be protected from the media. But Rooney needs no protection. He has no nerves and already acts like a senior player. Everyone loves the way he is.'

After the celebrations, in the cold light of day, there were still causes for concern. Beckham and Scholes were not playing well, and Rooney's success contrasted sharply with Owen's strangely subdued form. The senior partner of the two was not looking like scoring, and was doing nothing to disguise the fact that he disliked being substituted and having the limelight focus elsewhere. 'Michael started slowly, which shows that in football there are no certainties,' Eriksson said later. 'It's not like programming a computer, when you know what will happen. Some players start a tournament slowly, others right at the top. I always knew Michael would score in the end.'

One newspaper, the *Mail on Sunday*, went as far as to speculate, inaccurately, that Owen was 'facing the axe'. In reality, Scholes, who had not scored for England for more than three years, was much closer to losing his place, to Owen Hargreaves, and Beckham, whose physical condition was increasingly suspect, should have been in as much jeopardy as anyone.

Between games, it now became apparent that Rooney was not the only England player in demand at home. Team-mates inevitably talk about such matters during tournaments, and after a conversation with Frank Lampard, who revealed what was on offer, Steven Gerrard became intent on moving from Liverpool to Chelsea, who were prepared to double his wages, to £125,000 a week. On his own admission, Gerrard had his head turned by the prospect, and particularly by the presence in Lisbon harbour of the Chelsea hierarchy, on a yacht owned by the club's billionaire backer, Roman Abramovich. Fearing such distractions, Eriksson had banned players' agents from the England hotel, and also the English newspapers, being purveyors of unsettling transfer speculation. What he could not ban, however, were the mobile phones and personal computers which the FA had provided to each player, thereby given them access to all the internet tittle-tattle imaginable.

The same evening that England beat the Swiss, the French could draw only 2–2 with Croatia, so now the group was wide open. Switzerland, with one point from two matches, were out of contention, but any two of the other three teams could qualify. England needed only a draw against the

Croats to be sure of doing so, but if they lost, they would be going home. Eriksson warned his players that nothing could be taken for granted, and that playing for the draw was too fraught with potential mishap to warrant serious consideration. Croatia were technically accomplished, but could also be ruggedly provocative. Rooney would need to keep his temperament in check.

CROATIA 2   ENGLAND 4
Lisbon, 21 June

Croatia: Butina (Bruges), Simic (Milan), R. Kovac (Bayern Munich), Simunic (Hertha Berlin), Zivkovic (Stuttgart), Rosso (Maccabi Haifa), Tudor (Juventus), N. Kovac (Hertha Berlin), Rapajic (Ancona), Prso (Monaco), Sokota (Benfica). Subsitutes: Mornar (Portsmouth) for R. Kovac half-time, Srna (Shakhtar Donetsk) 67 minutes.

England: James (Manchester City), G. Neville (Manchester United), A. Cole (Arsenal), Terry (Chelsea), Campbell (Arsenal), Gerrard (Liverpool), Beckham (Real Madrid), Scholes (Manchester United), Rooney (Everton), Owen (Liverpool), Lampard (Chelsea). Substitutes: King (Tottenham Hotspur) for Scholes 70 minutes, Vassell (Aston Villa) for Rooney 71 minutes, P. Neville (Manchester United) for Lampard 84 minutes.

Referee: P. Collina (Italy).

England fans were everywhere in the Estadio da Luz; just how they came by so many tickets was a constant puzzle. This time they outnumbered the Croats five to one, making it a home game for Beckham and company, who signalled their appreciation before the kick-off. Sympathetic environment or not, England were immediately on the back foot, Croatia ahead in under five minutes when David James saved, but failed to hold, a shot following a free-kick, and the unsung Niko Kovac, of Hertha Berlin, forced in the loose ball. Scholes should have equalized, but shot too close to the goalkeeper from 12 yards, and then Tomo Sokota and Dado Prso both had James in action again, and the English legions fell into an apprehensive silence.

All was well again after 40 minutes, when Scholes headed in at close range from a clever assist by Rooney, and on the stroke of half-time the Everton prodigy was back in his primary role, shooting sweetly into the goalkeeper's right-hand corner. The interval found France and the Swiss drawing, so England, temporarily at least, led the group.

Early in the second half, Rooney put Owen through, one on one with the goalkeeper – the sort of situation when normally you would stake your mortgage on him scoring. As if to demonstrate that things weren't normal, England's master striker dithered, then tried a maladroit chip which ended up on the roof of the net. Fortunately, when the roles were reversed, Rooney showed his senior partner how such things should be done, and England were 3–1 up.

Eriksson now revealed the defensive instincts that at a later stage were to be his team's undoing. Two goals to the good, he withdrew an attacking player, Scholes, in favour of a defender, Ledley King, who went on to play in the centre of midfield. Within three minutes the rationale was undermined when Igor Tudor headed in from a set piece to throw the game back into the balance at 3–2, and there was a dodgy moment or two before Lampard's left-footed screamer from the edge of the penalty area put the issue beyond doubt. Even then it took a notable save from James to deny Prso. France, meanwhile, had gone on to beat Switzerland 3–1 in Coimbra, and therefore topped the group, with seven points from their three games. England were runners-up with six from three. They would play Portugal, the hosts, in the quarter-finals.

With two more goals, Rooney was the leading scorer in the tournament on four. Rooneymania knew no bounds. 'England Rocking To Rooney Rhythm' was one headline, 'The Boy King' another. The *Daily Mirror*, with 'Rooski', had Chelsea bidding £80m for Rooney AND Gerrard. Even Eriksson, hardly known for hyperbole, got carried away, likening his precocious 18 year old to the best player of all time. 'I was ten years old in 1958, when I watched Pele in the World Cup final against Sweden,' he said. 'I remember it well, because we did not all have televisions in Sweden then, and it was something new for me to watch a game that way. It was the first time I'd seen football on tele-vision. It was the summer, and I was staying with a friend in the countryside. I remember one of the goals Pele scored in that game (Brazil won 5–2), when he knocked the ball over a defender's shoulder and volleyed it in.

'I'm reluctant to compare Wayne to Pele, because of the pressure it will put on him, but when you have someone who scores four goals in three games at a major international tournament, you can't avoid it. It's there in front of you, in the way he plays. I hope he will go on to be one of the greats. You never know, but the way he has started has been incredible.'

After qualifying for the quarter-finals, England were greeted as heroes when they returned to their hotel. Staff applauded them off the team coach and into the reception area, which was festooned with red and white balloons. The players were joined for an overnight stay by their families and partners, Eriksson explaining that a dose of 'normality' was in order. The 'normality' lasted all of 12 hours. 'The families came on the Monday night and stayed until midday Tuesday, when they returned to their own hotel,' Eriksson said. 'When you are away from home, in these big tournaments, boredom is one of the big enemies. You need to live as normally as possible, and a normal life means seeing your wife and children. I have nothing against that, it seems to help the players relax.'

CHAPTER THIRTY-SEVEN

DÉJÀ VU

Some big teams had fallen by the wayside, strengthening England's belief that they could go all the way. The day after they had secured their place in the last eight, much-fancied Italy were eliminated in agonizing fashion, beating Bulgaria with a last-minute winner, but going out because Denmark and Sweden achieved the one result that would see them both through at the Italians' expense, a 2–2 draw. Twenty-four hours later, the Germans, too, were packing their bags, after losing 2–1 to the Czech Republic. Now if England could only beat Portugal . . .

Inevitably, the match was billed as Eriksson's chance to avenge himself on Luis Felipe Scolari who, as Brazil manager, had knocked England out of the World Cup at the same stage two years earlier, before he took charge of the Portuguese. Eriksson took heart from the fact that his team would be at full strength this time, unlike in Shizuoka, where Gary Neville and Steven Gerrard had been missing and David Beckham and Michael Owen were hampered by injury. This would be the 'real' England, he said.

His only concern was the lack of recovery time after the Croatia game. 'We had only two days before we played again,' he explained. 'It meant we didn't even have one real training session before taking on Portugal. The day after Croatia, the players stayed in the hotel, did some stretching, had ice baths and relaxed in the pool. There was a bit of work on exercise bikes, and a little running, but basically it was a rest day. I was confident because we had no real trouble with injuries or suspensions.'

Despite individual evidence to the contrary, Eriksson insisted the team, as a whole, was at a 'high level of fitness'. He said: 'We were able to run and work for 90 minutes, which we didn't do in Japan. That was an improvement. It seemed like we were getting better and better. The players certainly believed in themselves.'

Typically, he played down the personal rivalry with Scolari. 'I don't think the fact that he was on the bench altered anything. I like Scolari very much. As a human being, he's always been very nice, and he's obviously very good at his job. People say I'm not as emotional as him, and that's true. I come from Sweden, he comes from Brazil, where the mentality, as well as the climate, is very different. It would be difficult to change at my age, and anyway, I don't want to. I may seem calm on the outside, but inside I get very excited and a little bit nervous. My body needs that adrenalin rush.'

Portugal had also been nervous in their opening game, when they lost 2–1 to Greece, but their confidence had been restored by subsequent results against Russia and Spain, and Eriksson knew what to expect. 'I worked in Portugal for five years, and always said that they were the one side in Europe that really compared with the Brazilians, technically speaking. I also know the Portuguese mentality. Their confidence goes from rock bottom to right up high, and when it's up there, as it was when we played them, they are very dangerous. They play good, attacking football, using two wingers, and if you're not organized against them you have to chase the ball a lot, which is always hard.'

Despite their coach's confidence, England were not without their problems going into the quarter-finals. Beckham was nowhere near the top of his game, Scholes was struggling on the left side of midfield and Owen was a pale shadow of the predator of old. England's principal striker had scored just once in nine internationals, and admitted his barren run was getting him down. 'Of course not scoring bothers me,' he said. 'There's always something missing when we win a game and I've not scored. I didn't score against Croatia, and while half of me was ecstatic that we were through, it was in my mind that I hadn't scored again. I like the responsibility for scoring England's goals. In my position, you've got to do that. It was great to see Wayne Rooney getting the goals, and I suppose it took the pressure off me in a way, but I need to be scoring as well.'

Portugal's match-winning wingers, Cristiano Ronaldo and Luis Figo, were England's pre-occupation in the run-up to the match. Gary Neville and Ashley Cole would need to be at their very best to contain them. Eriksson told his team: 'We have to stay compact and keep our shape. If you give Ronaldo and Figo space, they will murder you. They drift all over the pitch, and if you lose concentration for one moment you won't be sure where they are. If they are allowed to attack you one on one, they can beat anybody with their quick feet. Stay compact and stay in your zone as much as possible when we are defending.'

Graham Taylor, with a prescience he did not always show during his ill-starred reign as England manager, forecast that it would go to penalties and, 'just in case', Eriksson had his players practise them in the stadium the day before the match. David Beckham had missed his last two, against Turkey and France, but said he was 'up for it' again and Frank Lampard promised that he would be one of the first to volunteer. 'If you approach it with real confidence, you have every chance of scoring,' he said. 'I'd like to think I could handle it if it came down to penalties.'

Beckham announced that England, whose team would be unchanged, were full of confidence. 'When the players talk, it's: "We're going to beat them" and "We're going to go out and win this game." We really believe we can do it. I've never sensed a belief like this, never. There's no negativity in our hotel at all, no nervousness. In the past, it wasn't always like that. In Japan, some of the players would express concern about the opposition. This time, I've not heard anything like that. The manager is very relaxed around the place, and that affects the whole team.' Four years earlier, Kevin Keegan's England had played Portugal in their first match at Euro 2000, and threw away a two-goal lead to lose 3–2. Beckham had an angry exchange with supporters that night, and now said: 'We don't want a repeat of that feeling, walking off the pitch, and I wouldn't want to experience the fans' reaction again.'

The last word of preamble belonged to that most quotable of managers, Scolari, who said: 'If things don't work out right, I'll hang myself. When I took the job, I said that anything less than making the semi-finals would be a failure, and I stand by that.'

The FA arranged a post-match party for the England players and their wives, partners and children, even installing a bouncy castle in the grounds of the team's hotel. On a more sombre note, it was decided that black armbands would be worn, in remembrance of a fan named Stephen Smith, who had been stabbed to death in Lisbon.

PORTUGAL 2   ENGLAND 2
(after extra time), Portugal won 5–4 on penalties.
Lisbon, 24 June
Portugal: Ricardo (Sporting Lisbon), Miguel (Benfica), Jorge Andrade (Deportivo La Coruna), Carvalho (Porto), Nuno Valente (Porto), Maniche (Porto), Costinha (Porto), Deco (Porto), Figo (Real Madrid), Nuno Gomes (Benfica), Ronaldo (Manchester United). Substitutes: Simao (Benfica) for Costinha 63 minutes, Postiga (Tottenham Hotspur) for Figo 75 minutes, Rui Costa (Milan) for Miguel 79 minutes.

England: James (Manchester City), G. Neville (Manchester United), A. Cole (Arsenal), Terry (Chelsea), Campbell (Arsenal), Gerrard (Liverpool), Beckham (Real Madrid), Scholes (Manchester United), Lampard (Chelsea), Rooney (Everton), Owen (Liverpool). Substitutes: Vassell (Aston Villa) for Rooney 27 minutes, P. Neville (Manchester United) for Scholes 57 minutes, Hargreaves (Bayern Munich) for Gerrard 81 minutes.

Referee: U. Meier (Switzerland).

Playing the hosts is normally a major handicap, but in this instance home advantage was all but negated by England's huge following, who had bought so many tickets from Portuguese fans, at up to 1,000 Euros (£640) a time, that the country's best-selling sports paper, *A Bola*, carried the front-page headline: 'Portugal Play Away'. Certainly, England supporters were in a comfortable majority in the capacity crowd of 65,000, and some were still taking their seats when their team took the lead. Owen had been well below his best in the first three games, but now he came good, opening the scoring after just 2 minutes 28 seconds with a dextrous, instinctive volley after a long punt from James had elicited a poor header by Costinha. It was the start of which English dreams were made.

Figo and Ronaldo swapped wings, as was their custom, but neither of them could make real progress against the assiduous attentions of Neville and Cole, and when Ronaldo did worm his way into a shooting position, Campbell imperiously snuffed out the threat with a blocking intervention. Maniche, one of the stars of the tournament in the

Portuguese midfield, demanded a reaching save from James, but England were giving as good as they got, and Owen and Campbell both went desperately close to improving their lead.

The complexion of the game changed midway through the first half, with a hammer blow from which England never really recovered. Rooney, who had become their talisman, as well as goalscorer extraordinaire, emerged from a challenge by Jorge Andrade with a boot off and a metatarsal bone fractured. He tried to carry on, but it was hopeless, and after 27 minutes he limped off for good, to be replaced by Vassell. Portugal could hardly believe their good fortune. The most dangerous striker in the tournament had been removed from the equation. Their confidence headed skywards as England's sagged. Owen lifted his team-mates' spirits with a bristling shot that brought a top-notch save from Ricardo, but Portugal had the initiative now, and Neville and Gerrard were both booked trying to stem the tide before England reached the sanctuary of half-time with their slender lead still intact.

It was all hands to the pumps again in the second half, the loss of Rooney ruining the shape and balance of a team which, without him, had become compartmentalized. The young Evertonian was not just a goalscorer, he was unusually adept at dropping deep to provide a link between the midfield and attack. Without that conduit, England players in possession in their own half were looking for somebody to pass to, only to see the backs of Owen and Vassell vanishing over the horizon.

The logical change was to move Scholes from the left to the support striker's role, instead of Vassell, and to bring on Hargreaves. Instead, stuck in what-we-have-we-hold mode, Eriksson introduced Phil Neville in place of Scholes, to stiffen the midfield. It was a timid move that didn't deserve to work, and England's third and final substitution was even worse. Beckham, in dressing-room parlance, was breathing through his backside, patently exhausted, but when moves were made from the bench to bring him off he waved his arms in a clear gesture of dissent, insisting on playing on. Not for the first time, Eriksson let him have his way, to the detriment of the team. Instead, he withdrew Gerrard, on the dubious pretext that he was suffering from cramp. Beckham played on – or rather stayed on. His incapacity was such that England, in effect, were down to ten men.

For a long time it seemed Eriksson might get away with it. Portugal made all the running, but Cole was having the game of his life, taking the ball off Ronaldo like a cat toying with a mouse, and Neville ran Figo down so many blind alleys that he was withdrawn, to his obvious disgust, with a quarter of an hour of normal time remaining. Scolari, plainly, was not as complaisant as his opposite number. The Portuguese captain's replacement was Helder Postiga, a striker who had come from a terrible season with Tottenham, for whom he had scored just once in the Premiership (after the tournament they offloaded him, back to Porto). No worries there, surely?

Wrong. Sod's law came into play after 83 minutes, the white elephant of White Hart Lane suddenly becoming the Lisbon Lion, and rising powerfully, à la Alan Shearer, to head home a cross delivered from the left – an area where the heavy-legged Beckham was repeatedly AWOL. Extra-time beckoned, but wait. With the stadium clock on 89 minutes, England had the chance to settle it. Beckham stepped up to take one last free-kick, and the colossus called Campbell headed against the crossbar, then forced home the rebound at close range. Cue pandemonium. The England players and fans exploded in relief, only to have their celebrations curtailed when the referee disallowed the goal. Unlike his assistant, who had run towards the halfway line, Switzerland's Urs Meier had seen a foul on the goalkeeper by John Terry. The contact was minimal, the decision questionable, at best, and poor Campbell, in particular, couldn't believe it. Exactly the same thing had happened to him at the 1998 World Cup, against Argentina.

And so to extra-time. Amid can't-look tension that escalated towards the unbearable, there was no 'silver goal' (it was the last tournament at which such a tie-breaker would be used) in the first added period, but with 110 minutes played Rui Costa, on as a late substitute, broke the stalemate with a high-velocity shot from 18 yards that ripped in via James' crossbar. Brave to the last, England weren't finished, and within five minutes they were level again, Lampard driving home from six yards after Terry had supplied him from Beckham's corner.

Two-all after two hours, and so history repeated itself. For the fifth time in 14 years, it was ordeal by penalty again. At the 1990 and 1998 World Cups and twice at Euro 96 England had been involved in these nerve-shredding tie-breakers, failing three times out of four. Surely it had to be their turn this time? The supporters did their bit, with a lusty rendition of 'God Save The Queen', followed by 'There's Only One David Beckham' as the captain stepped forward to take the first kick. He had made a mess of his last two, but now all was about to be forgiven. Or not. The ball sailed high over the bar, just as it had done in Istanbul, and no amount of glaring at an allegedly 'loose' penalty spot could redress the fact that England were at a disadvantage straight away.

Deco scored for Portugal, Owen did likewise. 1–1. It was Sabrosa Simao's turn, and he was fortunate to get away with a piece of gamesmanship that is not, strictly speaking, within the rules, pausing momentarily during his run-up and waiting for James to commit himself before taking his shot. Lampard, as he had promised, belted home the sort of kick that brooks no argument, and it was 2–2. England still needed a break, and had one now, when Rui Costa fired over. Terry did his duty, shooting straight and true, and England were ahead for the first time, 3–2. Ronaldo, Hargreaves, Maniche and Cole were all successful, cranking up the excitement, before Postiga added insult to earlier injury with a slow chip that bordered on mickey-taking. 5–5. Time for some kidology from the Portuguese goalkeeper,

Ricardo, who made Vassell wait while he removed his gloves. The ploy had the desired effect, Vassell losing his composure and striking a poor shot, easily kept out. If Portugal scored now, it was all over. Ricardo, on a high after his crucial save, seized the ball and drove it low, into James' right-hand corner. Devastated, England players sank slowly to their knees. They were out.

Vassell was distraught. Alone at first as the Portuguese players cavorted all around him (England's were prostrate on the halfway line), he was grateful for the prompt reaction of Gary Neville, who ran towards him, pausing only to call Beckham forward to help console their young team-mate. Eriksson embraced Rui Costa, who had played under him at Benfica, shepherded his own players away to show their appreciation for the excellent support they had enjoyed throughout the tournament, then joined them in a catatonic dressing room, where the scene was Shizuoka revisited. The players were in a 'state of shock', Eriksson said, and he decided it was the wrong time for speeches or analysis. That could wait.

Back at the team's hotel, the celebration party that had been planned turned into a wake. Rooney walked in first, his right foot in plaster. His declaration that he was 'absolutely gutted' set the tone. Eriksson and Nancy Dell'Olio stayed only briefly before retiring to their room. Beckham was virtually speechless. When one of the players' wives said: 'You must feel terrible,' he replied: 'I do.'

The following morning, the coach called the

squad together and sought to raise their sub-
terranean spirits by talking of the fine line that
divided success from failure. 'We were that close,'
he said. 'In three-and-a-half years we have lost
three competitive games, and the way we lost all of
them shows the difference between winning and
losing is next to nothing. That gives me the confidence that we can beat anyone, and do better
in 2006.'

It was a vain effort. The team coach was like a
morgue en route to Lisbon airport, England running the gauntlet of jeering Portuguese fans before
flying back to Luton, where they dodged supporters
waiting to greet them. Shortly before landing,
Beckham went around the cabin, shaking the hands
of everybody aboard. The faces were ashen, tears
not far away.

Eriksson flew back for the semi-finals, but
couldn't face the final, preferring to seek solace in
his Swedish haven, in the arms of his lover Faria
Alam. Cue trouble.

INDEX